ENDORSEMENTS

Again Prophet Rob Sanchez releases potential within us to excel and succeed. This book will inspire you and will speak growth to your souls. You will want to buy two, one for you and one for someone else! Enjoy!

- **Joey Zamora**
  Founder and Senior Pastor, World Life Christian Center, Pasco, WA

Prophet Rob Sanchez is a powerful and effective voice for the move of God in our generation, and Rob has done something groundbreaking in this new devotional. He did something needed for this new generation. Rob has taken the power of the prophetic utterance and combined it with daily devotion. Rob has written with significant and relevant truths that will help you walk deeper in the things of God daily. As he reveals truth though prophetic insight, it will cause you to have the courage to face whatever you may have to face on that particular day. Let those who have an ear to hear, listen intently at the level of significance that this daily devotion offers.

- **Rudy Sanchez**
  Senior Pastor, Sound Life International Ministries, Merced, CA

The Life is Very Good Devotional - Seasons of Hope is a timely word to a people that are still holding on and pressing in when all things are looking contrary. Rob and Juanita have given birth to this book with prophetic words with such practicality in the perfect era for such a time as this. The words in this devotional will come alive and breathe life to your soul. The authors of this devotional are a blessing and are voices to the local assembly and the nations with clarity and passion with the message of Love. We are always honored when they come to minister to us and encourage us that Life is Very Good!

- **Arthur "A.J." & Claudia Nunez**
  Senior Pastors, New Covenant International Ministries, Fresno, CA

LIFE IS VERY GOOD

SEASONS OF HOPE

BY
ROBERT SANCHEZ

Firstprints Publishing

LIFE IS VERY GOOD

Published by:
Firstfruits Publishing
P.O. Box 3726
Merced, CA 95344
www.prophetrobsanchez.com/firstfruitspublishing

In Partnership with:
A Book's Mind
PO Box 272847
Fort Collins, CO 80527
www.abooksmind.com

ISBN: 978-1-939828-58-3

THIS DEVOTIONAL IS DEDICATED TO:

My family: Juanita, Zoe, Hannah and Carly. I am so appreciative of all the support, encouragement, and help you have always given, not only with this devotional, but with everything I pursue. I love you all very much.

Extra thanks to Michelle Black and Susan Fanciulli, for sowing time, energy and effort into this project. It's people such as yourselves that help the Kingdom of God expand by pouring yourselves out and sharing the gifts God gave you with the world.

And a special dedication goes out to all those who have faced hard times, fought the good fight, and continued on in their journey. May this devotional bring encouragement and strength to you each and every day. In all things, never forget that this is your season - your season of hope. Continue to believe, desire and trust, knowing that God will bring you through.

And let us not grow weary while doing good,
for in *due season* we shall reap if we do not lose heart.
Galatians 6:9 NKJV

"Blessed is the man who trusts in the Lord,
And whose *hope* is the Lord.
For he shall be like a tree planted by the waters,
Which spreads out its roots by the river,
And will not fear when heat comes;
But its leaf will be green,
And will not be anxious in the year of drought,
Nor will cease from yielding fruit."
Jeremiah 17:7-8 NKJV

JANUARY 1
THE SHADOW OF HIS PRESENCE

PETER'S SHADOW THAT HEALED MANY WAS THE TANGIBLE PRESENCE OF GOD THAT OVERSHADOWED THEM. YOU ARE THE TABERNACLE OF THE LORD, AND WHEREVER YOU GO, YOU CARRY AND RELEASE THE POWER OF GOD. YOU ARE HIS GLORIOUS ATMOSPHERE.

LIFE IS VERY GOOD!

You must understand the significance of a shadow in order to understand the revelation of its power. For a shadow to occur there must be light. And, sunlight produces some of the greatest shadows. Therefore, you can see how the Son of God, the light of the world, was instrumental in creating Peter's shadow. The closer the light is to the object, the larger the shadow. Likewise, the farther away the source of light is, the smaller the shadow. You see, it wasn't Peter that healed people with his shadow (Acts 5:15-16). Rather, it was his source of light: Jesus. When you are so full of Jesus inside, you will exude the light of His Goodness. It will touch all those around you and impact your world just as Peter did during his time. I don't know about you, but I want to shine with light. How about you? Let's do it!

The Lord Says...

Seek me and I shall be found. I will be your light in the darkest of places. The more you know Me, the more light will shine upon you and your shadow will be great in this world. Be encouraged and seek the light for I Am the light.

If you believe it, say, "Oh yeah!"

JANUARY 2
LOVE PORTRAITS

IF YOUR RELATIONSHIP IS BEING TESTED, REMEMBER THIS: WHEN WE CHOOSE TO WALK AND DEMONSTRATE HIS LOVE, IT WILL BUILD PATIENCE AND MANIFEST KINDNESS. LOVE IS A DEVELOPER, RESTORING HIS GREATER IMAGE IN THE ONE WE CARE FOR. LOVE CREATES A BEAUTIFUL PORTRAIT.

LIFE IS VERY GOOD!

Look at the portraits of Love the Bible displays: God's love for humanity as He created a helper for Adam. God loved Adam so much that He cared about his needs. Consider Isaac who worked for years (and then some) to have Rachel as his bride. We see Mary, the betrothed of Joseph, who loved and dared to believe even in the face of public shame and ridicule. The woman who washed Jesus' feet with her perfume…Oh, what love! And, above all, the greatest portrait of love was when Jesus willingly died for you but rose again on the third day. That, my friends, is love. How are you creating portraits of love in your life?

The Lord Says…

I have created you and you are good. You are my portrait of love to the world. You are My ambassador. Be a man, woman or child of Galatians 5:22-23 and you will find that love will always lead the way. Be the love you yearn to receive from others.

If you believe it, say, "Oh yeah!"

JANUARY 3
JOY IN GOD IS LOVE

REMEMBER THIS: TRUE LOVE CAN MAKE YOU DIZZY AND OFTEN FEELS LIKE A ROLLER COASTER WITH ITS EXTREME UPS AND DOWNS. BUT, LOVE IS NEITHER A MERRY-GO-ROUND NOR A ROLLER COASTER. THE JOURNEY SHOULD BE, HOWEVER, FILLED WITH JOY. YES, MUCH JOY FOR HIS LOVE NEVER FAILS.

LIFE IS VERY GOOD!

Here's the thing about happiness and joy: Happiness is temporal, brought on by circumstances and things. Joy, on the other hand, resides within. Joy is a permanent outlook on life that, when rooted in God, may be challenged but not easily broken. Romans 15:13 says, "May the God of hope fill you with all joy and peace as you trust in him, so that you may overflow with hope by the power of the Holy Spirit". Joy…it does the body, mind and spirit good. God is love. Receive His joy!

The Lord Says…

I Am the joy of the world. Find Me and receive joy. Joy, My child, is My gift to you. Don't worry about tomorrow, be joyful right now. If you seek joy, you shall find it in this and every moment. Even your trials shall you count as joy. It's available. Will you choose it? Seek joy today!

If you believe it, say, "Oh yeah!"

JANUARY 4
COUNT ON ME

THERE ARE TIMES LOVE CAN OVERWHELM YOU LIKE THE OCEAN'S WAVES. THERE ARE OTHER TIMES LOVE CAN COMFORT YOU LIKE A GENTLE STREAM THAT FLOWS DEEP IN A VALLEY. HIS LOVE WILL CARRY YOU, ACCEPT YOU, SUSTAIN YOU AND FILL YOU WITH HOPE. YOU CAN ALWAYS COUNT ON HIS LOVE.

LIFE IS VERY GOOD!

1 John 4:16 says, "And so we know and rely on the love God has for us. God is love. Whoever lives in love lives in God and God in them". Just meditate on the power of love for a moment. When you live in love, you are living in Christ and He abides in you. This is because the scripture declares, "God is love." When you are so deep in the valley and the mountain seems too hard to climb, just remember His love is all you need. When you feel like you are drowning in the ocean as the waves of life and all its circumstances overtake you, be still and in your quiet moment, know that HE is God; let His love overtake every worry, fear, and concern. He is able and He will sustain you.

The Lord Says…

My love will see you through the worst of times and the greatest of times. You are a Kingdom child, and all you have need of resides within Me. I Am love and love guides, directs, comforts, cares, is kind and gentle and stern yet true. Love will lead the way. Won't you embrace it?

If you believe it, say, "Oh yeah!"

JANUARY5
IT'S A CHALLENGE

THE TRUTH ABOUT LOVE IS THIS: LOVE REQUIRES GREAT EFFORT. IT CHALLENGES YOU TO LOVE YOUR ENEMIES AND BLESS THOSE WHO SPEAK AGAINST YOU. AT THE SAME TIME, LOVE ENABLES THE CIRCUMSTANCES TO DEVELOP HIS CHARACTER IN YOU. LOVE IS WORKING TOGETHER AT ALL TIMES AND THROUGH ALL THINGS. WE ARE BETTER TOGETHER.

LIFE IS VERY GOOD!

Throughout the Bible, God seems to often speak in two's. Here we see that love does two things: Love challenges you to love your enemies and bless them as well. The Bible tells us not only about the first Adam who sinned but about Jesus, the second Adam, who saved us from ourselves. God created Eve for Adam because it was better for man not to be alone. Moses had Joshua and, in the book of Joshua, two spies were sent into the land. Because the number two is the first number used to conduct division, it often gets categorized as meaning "divided". However, God sought to use it for good. In fact, Matthew 18:19-20 says, "Again, truly I tell you that if two of you on earth agree about anything they ask for, it will be done for them by my Father in heaven. For where two or three gather in my name, there am I with them". Now that's power. Sometimes love doesn't feel like love when your character is being tested, but know this, He is always with you and the two of you together can conquer anything! Do you believe it?

The Lord Says...

Son and daughter, I Am with you always. Even when in the natural you are alone, you are never truly alone. Love is not always easy to express or convey, whether ally or enemy. But, practice, practice, practice and love will flow from you because, when you are in me, I Am in you. Be encouraged! Together, all things are possible.

If you believe it, say, "Oh yeah!"

JANUARY 6
HIS POWERFUL LOVE

THE POWER OF LOVE IS NOT SELFISH OR CAUTIOUS. THE POWER OF LOVE IS GENEROUS TO THE POINT OF EXTRAVAGANCE. REAL LOVE IS NOT LOOKING TO GET SOMETHING BUT DESIRES TO GIVE SOMETHING. JESUS GAVE ALL OF HIMSELF AT THE CROSS SO THOSE WHO WOULD BELIEVE IN HIM COULD HAVE A WHOLE AND LASTING LIFE! THAT'S EXTRAVAGANT LOVE!

LIFE IS VERY GOOD!

Luke 6:38 says, "Give, and it will be given to you. A good measure, pressed down, shaken together and running over, will be poured into your lap. For with the measure you use, it will be measured to you". This is God's bottom line on giving and receiving. When you give, you get back more. So give love the same way. If you can give love to the unlovable, mean spirited and selfish, you will see them as Jesus sees them. I challenge you to try it. Maybe it's your boss, a family member, co-worker or spouse. Begin to see them through the eyes of Jesus. Looking through His eyes of love, you will be amazed at what you see. And, that love just might change a life. Jesus gave it all and He was all in. Are you all in?

The Lord Says...

I Am all in for you; won't you be all in for others? I give you strength, wisdom and clarity. Walk in Me and you cannot fail. Walk in My love today. Be the love your world needs and ask yourself, "What can I do?" Then, do it!

If you believe it, say, "Oh yeah!"

JANUARY 7
WE ARE COMMANDED

REMEMBER ALWAYS...TO LOVE SOMEONE IS NOT AN OPTION, IT'S A COMMAND. WE ARE TO LOVE ONE ANOTHER AS CHRIST LOVES US. TRUE LOVE IS UNSELFISH. TRUE LOVE IS A WILLINGNESS TO LAY DOWN YOUR LIFE FOR A FRIEND. GO AHEAD, EXPRESS HIS LOVE TODAY.

LIFE IS VERY GOOD!

Let's ponder this idea of love for a moment. One, it's a command, so we have to do it if we are Christ's disciples. Two, in order to love like Christ, we must love with reckless abandon, forgetting about the past, mistakes, hang-ups or concerns. God's our daddy. He doesn't want any excuses, He just wants it done and for love to be your way of life. Have you ever been assigned a chore by your parents and had ample time to finish but failed to do so? I have. Then your mom or dad comes in to inquire on your chore status only to hear you roll off every excuse as to why you couldn't get it done. Then your mom or dad responds and it sounds something like this, "I don't care how long it takes or how many breaks you have, you can get it done now or be here all day." God never said it would be easy. I will tell you from experience that it's not. When your family member, best friend or boss hurts you to the core, it's much easier to retaliate in anger than to respond in love. But, to have the love of Christ takes hard work and diligent discipline. When you respond in love, it may never change the receiver, but it just might change you. Are you up for the challenge, to love like you never have before?

The Lord Says...

I Am love and I will help you to love like Me. I will enlarge the capacity of your heart if you will only say YES. Say Yes to love and No to anger and strife. Together, you and I can show the world how to love!

If you believe it, say, "Oh yeah!"

JANUARY 8
LOVE IS A VERB

LOVE IS NOT JUST A WORD WE SAY, LOVE IS AN ACTION THAT WE DEMONSTRATE. AS BELIEVERS, WE ARE TO WALK IN LOVE, SO LOVE CAN HEAL, RESTORE AND TRANSFORM OUR LIVES AND THE LIVES OF OTHERS. HIS LOVE IS AMAZING SO SHARE IT WITH SOMEONE TODAY!

LIFE IS VERY GOOD!

I think some people view love as just an embrace but that is simply not true. Women are great barometers of love. It's the simple things such as remembering your neighbor's birthday and getting them a card or thinking of your boss' favorite color when you get that Christmas gift. It's showing honor where honor is due. Love is earmarking your offering for random acts of kindness like unexpectedly paying for the gas, groceries, or drive thru order of the individual behind you. Love is taking your pastor to lunch, donating Dollar Store coloring books to your local hospital's pediatric wing or visiting the children's hospital. Love is holding a book drive for a teacher, school or organization, or simply holding the door open for others. Indeed, love is action. We know this because John 3:16 says, "For God so loved the world that he gave his one and only Son, that whoever believes in him shall not perish but have eternal life". God is always giving love just as He gave His only son. And Jesus willingly gave his life. Love is contagious. What will you give to show your love today?

The Lord Says...

Love is a powerful action. Love changes hearts, which changes lives. I need you on this earth to be My conduit of love to a hurting, confused and dying world. One drop of joy can save a sorrowful heart. One smile or a single gesture of love will show the world that I Am alive. I Am alive in you!

If you believe it, say, "Oh yeah!"

JANUARY 9
WHAT'S IN YOUR HOUSE?

HAVE FINANCIAL BURDENS WEIGHED YOU DOWN AND TAKEN YOUR JOY? REMEMBER THIS... THERE'S POWER IN THE PROMISE. IN 2 KINGS 4:1-7, THE WIDOW AND HER SONS SHUT THE DOOR BEHIND THEM AFTER COLLECTING EMPTY VESSELS. THEY ANTICIPATED THE MIRACLE BASED ON THE PROPHETIC PROMISE GIVEN TO THEM BY ELISHA. INCREASE CAME BECAUSE THEY ACTED IN FAITH AND POURED OUT. HOLD ONTO HIS PROMISES – ESPECIALLY IN THE TIME OF LACK - FOR HE IS ALWAYS FAITHFUL.

LIFE IS VERY GOOD!

Psalm 115:14-15 says, "May the Lord cause you to flourish, both you and your children. May you be blessed by the Lord, the Maker of heaven and earth". It is God's desire that you increase both financially and in your faith. The story of the widow is found in 2 Kings 4:1-7. The woman was in Elisha's inner circle. Her husband had died and her sons were going to be taken into slavery to pay their debts. BUT, in her great time of need, God intervened and sent Elisha. Elisha asked the widow the same thing God is asking you. God is at the door of your heart asking, "How can I help you?" And, "What do you have in your house? Do you have a gift, talent, or treasure in your house?" Once the prophet finds out what the widow had, he activated her to take charge of her situation, go forth and increase. God is telling you the same thing. He is telling you to hold onto the promise for He is faithful. God is telling you He has already activated you to go forth with what's in your house and increase. This command not only benefited the widow but it saved her sons from slavery and added increase and strengthened the faith of her whole house. What can you do with what's inside of you and in your house today?

The Lord Says...

I Am the giver of increase. When you step out in faith and believe I Am with you, together we can do great and mighty things. Look at life as one big opportunity and seize the moment, for you were made for such a time as this.

If you believe it, say, "Oh yeah!"

JANUARY 10
LAUGHING AT LIMITATIONS

YOUR PHYSICAL CIRCUMSTANCES CANNOT STOP GOD'S PROMISE FROM BEING YOUR REALITY. ABRAHAM WAS CONSIDERED TOO OLD AND SARAH WAS CALLED BARREN YET THEY DID NOT WAIVER IN THEIR FAITH. AT THE APPOINTED TIME, ISAAC WAS BORN. IT'S TIME TO 'LAUGH' AT YOUR CIRCUMSTANCES.

LIFE IS VERY GOOD!

Proverbs 17:22 says, "A cheerful heart is good medicine, but a crushed spirit dries up the bones". I have learned that, in order to live a Kingdom life, one must think like a Kingdom child. This means that your thinking must contain an essence of expectancy. For example, Jesus is the King of Kings and your Heavenly Father. As a child of the One True King, you must have an expectancy built into your thought and speaking processes. If the Bible tells you in Matthew 6:25-34 not to worry about what you will eat or the clothes you have need of, then you should understand that a King's child is covered. Start speaking it today that your needs are met even to abundance and see what God will do. Today, will you speak like a King's child, expecting nothing but the best from God? Do it! Watch and see what He will do.

The Lord Says…

Know that what you speak today will become your reality tomorrow. Speak life and expect greatness from yourself, for I see greatness within all My children. My promises are true so go through your circumstances with a merry heart and your circumstances do not define you. It is the heart that speaks.

If you believe it, say, "Oh yeah!"

JANUARY 11
PROSPERITY IN FAMINE

SOMETIMES GOD WILL HAVE US DWELL IN UNLIKELY PLACES BUT IT IS IN THOSE UNLIKELY PLACES WHERE HIS PROMISE IS MOST FRUITFUL. WHEN ISAAC DWELT IN A LAND OF FAMINE, GOD REMINDED HIM OF HIS PROMISE TO HIS FATHER ABRAHAM. ISAAC SOWED IN THAT LAND AND, DURING THAT TIME OF GREAT FAMINE, BEGAN TO PROSPER. ISAAC CONTINUED TO PROSPER UNTIL HE BECAME VERY PROSPEROUS. IT'S TIME TO LAUGH AT FAMINE BECAUSE PROSPERITY IS ON ITS WAY.

LIFE IS VERY GOOD!

Isaiah 43:19 says, "See, I am doing a new thing! Now it springs up; do you not perceive it? I am making a way in the wilderness and streams in the wasteland". You see, no matter where you are located geographically, God is there. When you walk with God you can prosper anywhere because prosperity is all about your mindset. If a king moves his home to a new castle, will he still have the same authority and prosper as he did in the old location? Will he face trials? Most certainly. Life just comes with those. Trials help you grow and become stronger. So look up and dare to believe that His Word is true and that He will never leave or forsake you. Will you dare to believe Him and laugh at famine or drought if it comes your way?

The Lord Says…

I Am the Lord your God, and My words do not fall to the ground. I Am the same yesterday, today and forever. I Am the keeper of your promises. And, even in famine or drought, I Am able to do above what you could ever think or imagine. I Am yours and you are Mine, My beloved!

If you believe it, say, "Oh yeah!"

JANUARY 12
THE PROMISE OF THE RAINBOW

WHEN THE FLOODS OF LIFE SEEM TO OVERTAKE YOU, THINK ABOUT GOD'S COVENANT WITH
NOAH. GOD PLACED A RAINBOW IN THE SKY AS A SIGN OF HIS PROMISE TO NEVER DESTROY
THE EARTH BY WATER EVER AGAIN. GOD SAID HE WOULD LOOK ON IT AND REMEMBER WHAT
HE ESTABLISHED BETWEEN HIMSELF AND HIS CHILDREN. REJOICE, THE RAIN HAS STOPPED
AND THE SUN IS SHINING. GOD WILL NEVER FORGET HIS PROMISES.

LIFE IS VERY GOOD!

It's in Genesis 9 that the story of the rainbow is told. God is a covenant keeper and He always keeps His Word. There are seven rays of light in a rainbow: red, yellow, orange, green, blue, indigo and violet. Seven in the Bible often reflects the number of perfection. The world was created in seven days, Jesus performed seven miracles and taught seven different parables in the New Testament. God means business with the number seven. However, it's not just the number seven that's wrapped up in the promise in the rainbow. It's the fact that when God speaks, He means it. So, no matter how high the water gets in your life (you could even be neck high and treading water), God's promise are always "yes and amen". And remember, even when you cannot see the sun shining, it is still shining, so look through the clouds and focus your eyes towards heaven. Jesus stands at the door. Will you knock?

The Lord Says…

My child, trust in Me, for I will never leave you nor forsake you and nothing is impossible. Dare to believe. Look not at the circumstances that surround you but focus on My word. It is My word that will sustain you through the chaos of life. Remember, if you seek Me, I will be found.

If you believe it, say, "Oh yeah!"

JANUARY 13
RELEASE IT

REMEMBER THIS: GOD DOESN'T WANT HEALING TO ONLY MANIFEST IN A CERTAIN PLACE. HE WANTS IT TO MANIFEST IN EVERY PLACE. NOT JUST WHEN THE WATER IS STIRRED, BUT WHEREVER HE IS. AND, SINCE HE DWELLS WITHIN US, THE POSSIBILITIES ARE ENDLESS. RELEASE THE MIRACULOUS TODAY.

LIFE IS VERY GOOD!

Let's think about the miraculous here for a moment. An act of a miracle is something extraordinary. Birth in itself is a miracle of divine nature. Do you recognize that you are a miraculous creation? You were uniquely and wonderfully made. You were created in His image. You look like your daddy God, and where you are, there He is also. He has called you to be whole in body, mind and spirit. So do it! Release your healing, your gifts, your talents, your abilities, your prayers, your finances. All He has endowed you with and all He has called you to be. Release it and you will become all He has planned for you to become. What miracles will you release today?

The Lord Says…

I have called you to be a whole, strong, abundant and courageous individual who walks in love. Who do you say that I Am? I have released the power of the miraculous in your life. Begin to expect the unexpected favor of your daddy, King Jesus, your God.

If you believe it, say, "Oh yeah!"

JANUARY 14
FROM JUST A SEED

REMEMBER THIS WHEN YOU NEED A BREAKTHROUGH: IN LUKE 21:1-4, WHEN THE WIDOW GAVE HER FINAL TWO MITES INTO THE TREASURY, MANY SAID SHE HAD NOTHING LEFT BUT HER GIFT RELEASED THE MIRACULOUS. HER SEED CAPTURED THE HEART OF JESUS AND HER GIFT IS STILL SPOKEN ABOUT 2000 YEARS LATER. YOUR SOWN SEED HAS A VOICE!

LIFE IS VERY GOOD!

The example of a seed is used in many times throughout scripture but, what it all boils down to is this…A seed is anything that, once planted, will multiply or increase to be harvested. A man delivers his seed. The woman becomes pregnant and a child is born. A plant grows from a seed and produces increase. Corn is a beautiful example. A seed kernel is planted and a whole stock of multiple pieces of corn grows to be harvested on the stock. We sow the gospel into the hearts of the world and they reap the harvest of salvation. Jesus was and is the Master Gardener. Jeremiah 29:11 tells us that God wants an abundant harvest in our lives. What seeds will you sow in the lives of your family, your colleagues, at your church and to strangers in the city?

The Lord Says…

Go! Be planters of the fields and fishers of men. The harvest is truly ripe but the laborers are often few. Will you please plant and harvest? Make the investment in a life today for somewhere, and at one time, someone invested in you. Sow seeds of prayer, finances, love and joy. Then watch what I will cultivate for an amazing harvest. Be a blessing to your world.

If you believe it, say, "Oh yeah!"

JANUARY 15
WHO'S YOUR BFF?

WHEN THE PROBLEMS OF LIFE HAVE YOU PARALYZED, IT PAYS TO HAVE TRUE FRIENDS. WHEN OTHERS RUN, TRUE FRIENDS WILL RISE AND TEAR THE ROOF OFF FOR YOU. THEY'LL ALWAYS GET YOU TO WHERE YOU NEED TO BE. NEVER UNDERESTIMATE THE POWER OF FRIENDSHIP.

LIFE IS VERY GOOD!

There is nothing like a BFF (best friend forever), or just that person you know will have your back no matter what time; day or night. Those people who are not afraid to shoot straight with you because they love you and you respect them for that. The type of person who knows when to listen and when to speak, who lifts you up instead of tearing you down. Proverbs 18:24 says, "One who has unreliable friends soon comes to ruin, but there is a friend who sticks closer than a brother". And John 15:13 says, "Greater love has no one than this: to lay down one's life for one's friends". Truly, to have a close friend is a gift and God understands because Adam was once His very best friend. Now, however, God wants YOU to be His BFF. Being God's BFF requires spending quality time with Him. Will you rise to the occasion? Will you be Jesus' BFF?

The Lord Says...

Child of mine, I long to be with you. I wait for you near the river's edge in the cool of the day. I paint sunsets on the earth and make the birds sing My praise to get your attention. I created the sound of ocean waves and droplets of rain to quench the earth and soothe your soul. I gave you My Son that we might meet again. My love for you is endless and boundless. I love you when you're happy, angry, sad and joyful. I Am with you in triumph and heartache. I Am yours. I love you.

If you believe it, say, "Oh yeah!"

JANUARY 16
FAITH + FAVOR

WHEN THINGS IN LIFE SEEM TO RUN DRY, A MOTHER'S FAITH IN HER SON CAN BRING CHANGE. AT THE WEDDING FEAST, THE REPORT WAS THAT THERE WAS NO WINE. WHEN THE WATER POTS WERE FILLED & WATER DRAWN OUT, IT WAS TRANSFORMED INTO THE BEST WINE. FAITH MIXED WITH FAVOR CAUSED THE IMPOSSIBLE TO BE POSSIBLE! COME TO THE FEAST, THE NEW WINE IS SERVED.

LIFE IS VERY GOOD!

Optimism is one thing but, when someone believes in you, it creates an atmosphere ripe for transformation. The story of turning water into wine is found in John 2. Jesus, His mother and the disciples had been invited to a wedding in Canaan. Mary (Jesus' mother) took notice that the wine was running out and mentioned it to Jesus because she believed He was capable of transforming the situation. Jesus, on the other hand, wasn't too thrilled to be bothered with the issue. Imagine it; our response today may have been something like, "So what, it's not my wedding." Jesus didn't want to get involved. He didn't want to step out. He didn't want to be what He was called to be that day. We all have had those days. But someone believed in Him: His mother. She believed so much that He could make a difference that, in verse 5, Mary tells the servants to do exactly as Jesus says. Jesus' mother had faith in Him even when He may not have. Likewise, God believes in you, even when you do not believe in yourself. Look at Gideon. In Judges 6 when Gideon finally stepped out of his doubt and fear, the impossible became possible. God believes in you and so do we. Step up and step out. It only takes a moment of faith to change the atmosphere. Are you ready for some new wine? Then make it happen, friend! Get your faith on and become who you were called to be. Not tomorrow, but today!

The Lord Says…

I Am the light unto your path. I Am the fresh air you long to breath when the storms of life come crashing down. I Am more than enough. Trust and see that I Am good, yesterday, today, and for all your tomorrows. I walk with you now and forever.

If you believe it, say, "Oh yeah!"

JANUARY 17
CLIMB INTO THE TREE

WHEN YOU NEED SOMETHING TO SHIFT, DO WHAT ZACCHAEUS DID AND RUN TO THE TREE. HE SAT IN THE MERCY OF GOD AND ALLOWED THE POWER OF THE MOMENT TO CHANGE HIS MIND. WHEN HE CAME DOWN, HIS LIFE SHIFTED FROM BEING A TAKER TO BEING A GIVER. TAKE A STAND IN VICTORY AND LET THE FAVOR OF GOD RAISE YOU UP.

LIFE IS VERY GOOD!

I hear you saying it; that's great for Zacchaeus, but sitting in a tree isn't going to solve anything for me. Look a little deeper. The tree represents Christ, who was nailed to a tree for your transgressions. When you are in Him and He is in you, it changes everything. It changes how you think. It changes how you speak. It changes the pep in your step. It changes the position you hold your head from down to up. It changes your heart. It changes your outcome and you cannot help but want to give it away. Christ makes you want to become a giver because it is His innate nature to give to and for you. His character becomes contagious once you get a hold of Him and never let go. Change is never easy, but it is necessary. So let God raise you up. Seek Him so He may be found. Keep a prayer journal, study the scriptures deeper than you ever have before. Inquire of His will and His ways. Then watch and see how His favor raises you up in this life. Are you ready to snuggle with daddy God, to get to know Him intimately so that when you come down like Zacchaeus, you are changed? He waits with open arms.

The Lord Says…

Oh, child of mine. I long to spend the mornings with you and the evenings at sunset; to ride home with you on your commute to and from work and to be a part of your triumphs and your tragedies. My arms are open wide to hug and to hold you through all the burdens that life requires you to carry. Spend time with Me and I will lift these burdens from you. My love will overtake you and make you smile. My concern for you is great. To know Me is to love the life you live and embrace intimacy in my arms. I wait for you. You are loved.

If you believe it, say, "Oh yeah!"

JANUARY 18
SPEAK UP

DON'T LET THE PROBLEMS YOU FACE IN LIFE HAVE A GREATER VOICE THAN WHAT GOD HAS SPOKEN TO YOU, FOR OUR AFFLICTION IS BUT FOR A MOMENT. REMEMBER, GOD'S PROMISE IS WORKING OUT FOR US A FAR MORE EXCEEDING ETERNAL WEIGHT OF GLORY. LET THE POWER OF HIS SPOKEN WORD REIGN OVER YOUR LIFE.

LIFE IS VERY GOOD!

Here's the thing. If you stood around all day being pessimistic because of whom you are or once were in this carnal life, you'd find yourself disappointed. I mean, look at the leaders of antiquity. David was an adulterer and a murderer, Moses a murderer, Rahab was a prostitute, Jacob was a liar and Mary, the mother of Jesus, was seen as unclean in her world because who could comprehend a pregnancy by God? In our world, you'd think she was nuts. Yet God's covenant redeemed them all and it still redeems you even today. He loves you enough to see who you really are in Christ. From the beginning, God said in Genesis that His creation was very good. This means you. You are His creation, created in His image, therefore, you are very good. No matter what you go through or who the world says you are, God says, "You, my friend, are very good". There is power in His Words. From His Words you were created and from His Words you are deemed very good. In Proverbs 3:5-6, your daddy God is asking you to trust Him; to trust Him in a way that you won't always understand with your own understanding, but rather to acknowledge that He's your dad and has been around a little bit longer than you. He cares deeply about what happens to you in this life. In doing so, you begin to trust His spoken word in your life and you will live by it. Will you trust Him today, that He has your best interests at heart? Let it go and let God.

The Lord Says…

I Am the way, the truth and the life. I will tell you like it is and I always have your journey in mind. Trust Me with your heart, your career, your family, your finances and all that you have. Watch and see what I will do. When you trust and believe then you will receive.

If you believe it, say, "Oh yeah!"

JANUARY 19
BECAUSE IT'S THERE

IT'S BEEN SAID THAT GREAT THINGS HAPPEN WHEN MEN AND MOUNTAINS MEET. WHEN JESUS MET HIS MOUNTAIN, HE RELEASED VICTORY TO THOSE WHO WOULD BELIEVE IN HIM. WE CAN STAND IN GOD'S BLESSINGS BECAUSE OF WHAT HE DECLARED ON THE MOUNTAIN, "IT IS FINISHED!"

LIFE IS VERY GOOD!

There was a man named George Mallory who, in the 1920's, participated in 3 expeditions to climb Mount Everest. He wanted to be the first to reach the top. Sadly, in June of 1924, he and Andrew Irvine died in what was their last attempt. It's not known whether or not they reached the summit before their death. In 1924, when Mallory was asked by a New York Times reporter why he was trying to climb Everest, he answered, "Because it's there." In the eyes of many, George Mallory may not have attained his goal, but for Mallory, the victory was in taking the challenge.

There are hundreds of people who take on challenges each and every day of their lives. It could be running a race such as a 5K or a half-marathon. It could be learning a new language or losing a certain amount of weight. For others, the challenge may be a lot more personal, such as surviving a sickness or just making it through each day. When you stand before your mountain, you have to believe you can overcome it. The apostle Paul wrote to the Roman church that they were "more than conquerors through him" (Romans 8:37). Realize that you can because He already did. Jesus spoke 3 memorable words just as George Mallory did, but the words Jesus spoke bring not only an assurance, it also brings peace to any and all storms. Jesus walked to the mountain, climbed the mountain, was crucified on the mountain and declared His victory from the mountain. Stand in what Jesus did and know His 3 words have all power to help you conquer any mountain that you face.

The Lord Says...

I believe in who you are because you are My child. I have given you My Spirit and all that you have need of is in Me. I will always help you walk through your circumstances and trials. Whatever is before you, know that I stand with you. Nothing is impossible when the God of heaven, your Father, fights on your behalf.

If you believe it, say, "Oh yeah!"

JANUARY 20
HIS VOICE IS OVER ALL

WHEN YOUR HOUSE SEEMS TO GET FLOODED WITH THE STORMS OF LIFE, REMEMBER THIS: THE VOICE OF THE LORD RULES OVER THE WATERS WITH POWER AND MAJESTY. HEAR HIS VOICE THUNDER & CLEAR THE SKIES AS IT RELEASES HIS STRENGTH AND PEACE OVER YOU.

LIFE IS VERY GOOD!

Sometimes you create storms in your own life. Whether it be a lack of patience (like Abraham who wanted the son God promised but couldn't wait and had Ishmael) or your own disobedience. It happens. There are storms that others bring on but you are the one on the boat, just like Jonah in Jonah 1. Everyone on the boat that day was negatively affected by Jonah's decision to try to run from God. There are also storms that come from nowhere. You didn't ask for it or to be a part of it. You just wish you could get out of it. This is how I imagine the disciples felt in Mark 4 when they were in the boat and Jesus was peacefully sleeping. One minute they were fine and the next minute they were in a panic in a fierce storm. But, in all these situations, God spoke. His voice became the answer. In Abraham's case, God said that HE would give Abraham a son. Abraham's lack of trust caused him and Sarah to try to accomplish what God had promised and only He could do. In Jonah's case, God had already spoken, telling him to go to Nineveh, yet Jonah refused and ended up in a great storm and then in the belly of a great fish. On the disciple's boat, Jesus just spoke to the storm and told it to be still...and it was. Christ is in you and you are in Him, so release His Words over your situation and begin to declare the outcome of your situation and watch as the gray clouds move past. Your strength, trust and faith will increase and circumstances will begin to change. Are you ready for a shift in your circumstances? Speak life.

The Lord Says...

Speak and declare the positive spoken word over your life. Declare the scriptures out loud, in song, in prayer and meditation. Know that I Am with you always, but even though I have faith in you, you alone must activate your faith by speaking, "I call my family to know you Lord, my marriage or body healed, my strength or finances restored." Call it out. Together we are a force to be reckoned with. What do you have need of from Me today?

If you believe it, say, "Oh yeah!"

JANUARY 21
THERE'S SUNSHINE IN THE FORECAST

WHEN LIFE SEEMS TO RAIN DOWN TRIALS AND FRUSTRATIONS, ALL YOU NEED TO DO IS LOOK TO THE HEAVENS. GOD'S RAINBOW WILL ALWAYS APPEAR IN A CLOUD TO BRIGHTEN YOUR DAY. HEAR HIS VOICE AS IT DECLARES HIS GREATER PROMISES.

LIFE IS VERY GOOD!

I like the beginning lyrics to the Temptations' song, "My Girl." They say, "I've got sunshine on a cloudy day/When it's cold outside, I got the month of May." In other words, it may look one way in life but something better is just around the corner. When it's pouring rain in your life, remember that it only lasts for a moment or, in some cases, a season. President Abraham Lincoln once took a phrase from Persian poetry that said, "And this too, shall pass away." It's so true. So many things we worry about are temporal. Just knowing that even on a cloudy day, the sun will show itself again, the rain will stop and, in the midst of chaos, you will find favor. That should brighten your day. I challenge you to find the good in anything that could be construed as negative in your life. Are you up for the challenge? Your rainbow awaits. His voice is clear and His promises are yes and amen.

The Lord Says...

Indeed child, My promises are yes and amen. There is always reason for gratefulness. Look up and consider that I smile upon you, even in your darkest or most joyous of times. Find the good when others cannot and opportunity awaits you. Keep on smiling.

If you believe it, say, "Oh yeah!"

JANUARY 22
HEART HEALTH

REMEMBER THIS: THE CONDITION OF YOUR HEART WILL AFFECT OTHER'S HEALTH. YOUR HEART CAN BE FILLED WITH HIS JOY & BE MEDICINE TO A PERSON'S SOUL OR YOUR HEART CAN BE CLOUDED WITH GLOOM & LEAVE PEOPLE TIRED TO THEIR BONES. GOD'S JOY HEALS; A BLEAK ATTITUDE STEALS. SHARE HIS LOVE TODAY.

LIFE IS VERY GOOD!

I recently heard this phrase: Today's decisions will become tomorrow's reality. I love that because it's so true. If your heart is filled with doom and gloom, then you will plant seeds of doom and gloom and reap the harvest thereof. Galatians 6:7 tells you that whatever you sow, you will reap. So if you sow joy into your life and the lives of others, you will reap it just the same. You have a choice today.

Ask yourself where the seeds you are planting have come from. If they are from God, then you will sow goodness into your life and the lives of others, for God is love. Know where your seeds are coming from. Are you ready to make a choice? Plant smart, garden well and reap a beautiful harvest.

The Lord Says...

I Am the Master Gardener and, if you will follow My will and My ways, you and your garden will harvest great fruit. The world will know you by the fruit you produce. Condition your heart towards love, preset the frequency of your life to speak positively and you will overcome.

If you believe it, say, "Oh yeah!"

JANUARY 23
IT'S ALL IN THE PREPARATION

WHEN DARKNESS SURROUNDS YOUR LIFE AND THERE SEEMS TO BE NO ANSWER TO YOUR PRAYERS, REMEMBER THIS: THE LORD IS ALWAYS WITH YOU. GOD SHOWED JOSEPH MERCY AND GAVE HIM FAVOR IN THE JAILHOUSE. YOU MIGHT FEEL LIKE YOU ARE IN THE DUNGEON BUT YOU ARE CLOSER TO THE PALACE FLOOR THAN YOU THINK! HIS MERCY AND FAVOR ARE WITH YOU. IT'S YOUR TIME TO RULE!

LIFE IS VERY GOOD!

They say that preparation is 90% of the process. That doesn't mean we like it. Sourdough bread provides a great example. The best of sourdough bread is first made with a starter, consisting of water, flour and bacteria. This simple concoction must be kept in a stable environment and diligently cared for, for up to several days, before it will be ready to use. It is a preparation process that makes sourdough bread even possible. Preparation takes a lot of work. The seasons seem very long and often times there are potholes in the road you aren't expecting. It's all shaping and molding you into who it is you are to become. Joseph's preparation for ruling and reigning allowed him to understand the value of patience, the art of forgiveness and empathy for others. You might think of it this way. In the Jewish faith, you are only Jewish if your mother is Jewish. In the end, God knew of Joseph's journey before it even began.

Technically, because Joseph married an Egyptian woman, his children Ephraim and Manasseh were not considered Jewish and, therefore, would not have been able to partake in the blessing of Isaac's family. It is for this reason that Isaac blesses both children into the Jewish family and it is the first instance we see in the Bible of a gentile conversion. God might have prepared Joseph by using the pit, the prison and the palace just to bring his family together and his descendants into the kingdom. Think about it. This is why God says to trust Him in Proverbs 3:5-6, but not with your own understanding. Your own understanding will only get you so far. At some point you have to let go and let God. Are you ready to rule and reign over the circumstances in your life? Then trust God to be your light in the pit, while in shackles and in your victories. He is able to do above what you could ever think or imagine.

The Lord Says...

I Am able. Are you willing? The journey can be adventurous. The road can be bumpy. But, the view when you arrive will knock your socks off. You already rule and reign. Seeing is not always believing. Believing is seeing. Thomas was an illustration, but you already know what I Am capable of and I have already endued you with power from the very throne room of My Father. Your authority in Me will shift the atmosphere and things will begin to change. Believe it. Preparation is always meant for purpose.

If you believe it, say, "Oh yeah!"

JANUARY 24
PUSH THROUGH

DIFFICULT TIMES ARE NOT SEASONS TO SULK, POUT OR COMPLAIN. DIFFICULT TIMES STIMULATE YOU TO HOLD ONTO THE DREAMS GOD GAVE YOU BECAUSE THEY ARE MANIFESTING GOD'S PURPOSE IN YOUR LIFE. YOUR DREAMS ARE READY TO BECOME A REALITY. OH YEAH!

LIFE IS VERY GOOD!

I remember hearing the phrases, "you are what you eat from your head down to your feet" and "what you think you will become." I don't know who said these but they do have merit. Science has found that if you feast on junk food filled with sugars and starches every day, you will become obese. Likewise, most successful people will tell you that they imagined who they were as a success before they ever became a success. Dreams are first born within. Most dreams of substance (I'm not talking the dream to own a 1956 Porsche 356A 1500 GS Carrera) are founded out of your passion, which is found in the purpose God gave you at birth. If you are always looking towards the prize, you will not be deterred by sulking, pouting or complaining. We are all human, so you will have those moments, but it's just a pit stop so don't let a moment become your mantra. Fuel up on God's praise and get back on the road to make your dreams a reality. Ask yourself what your dream requires in order to be fulfilled. Then, set a course to make it happen. Are you ready to get started and put your dream plan in place? God's just waiting for you to say, "Let's do this!" He will help you set the course.

The Lord Says...

All I have planted inside of you is ready to come forth. You were born for this moment. Buckle up, prepare your road map and I will be your guide. It may be dark, scary and lonely. You may feel tired, tried and tested, but the reward is sweet. It's called the accomplishment and fulfillment of purpose. We got this, so let's go. Transformation...ignited.

If you believe it, say, "Oh yeah!"

JANUARY 25
IT'S TIME TO ASK

WHEN NOTHING IS GOING YOUR WAY AND EVERY DOOR YOU OPEN SEEMS TO LEAD TO A DEAD END, REMEMBER THIS: THE WAY OUT IS TO A.S.K. ASK AND YOU WILL RECEIVE, SEEK AND YOU WILL FIND, KNOCK AND IT WILL BE OPENED. CHRIST IS THE ANSWER THAT LEADS TO OUR DESTINY. A.S.K. HIM AND HE'LL LEAD YOU IN THE RIGHT DIRECTION.

LIFE IS VERY GOOD!

Remember when you were a kid and asked your parents how to do something? They would give you one way to do it. I don't know about you, but it always seemed like parents did know best in the end. You decide to try things your way, and it doesn't work out as you planned. Then, you circle back around to Mom and Dad's way, never letting on that you took a detour at all. Sometimes we go around in circles because we either refuse to ASK or we ASK and we do not like what we hear. It's important to remember that you're not supposed to bring God with you on the journey; you are supposed to go with God on the journey. There is a vast difference. In one instance you are subjecting God to follow along with your will and your ways, and in the other you are following God in His will and His ways for your life. When the Bible says in Hosea 4:6 that "people perish for lack of knowledge", this is exactly what it means. If you don't A.S.K., then you will never know the answer to your destiny or anything else along the way because you will be like the blind leading the blind without God's direction and guidance. It's okay to ASK and A.S.K. of the Lord. He awaits your arrival. He stands at the door. Ask yourself if your destiny is worth a moment of activation? By Asking, Seeking and Knocking, you are stepping out in faith that whatever answer the Lord provides is the one for you.

The Lord Says...

I know you better than you know yourself, for not even you know the number of hairs on your head. Ask Me and I will answer. Seek Me and I will listen. Knock at the door of My heart and I will open doors no man can shut. You are worth it. You are loved indeed.

If you believe it, say, "Oh yeah!"

JANUARY 26
THINK BEFORE YOU ASK

WHEN YOU ASK FOR THE RIGHT THING FROM THE LORD, MORE WILL BE GIVEN TO YOU. SOLOMON COULD HAVE ASKED FOR ANYTHING BUT INSTEAD HE CHOSE TO ASK FOR WISDOM. IN RETURN, GOD BLESSED HIM WITH FAR MORE RICHES, WEALTH AND HONOR THAN HE COULD HAVE OBTAINED ON HIS OWN IN MANY LIFETIMES. IT PAYS TO ASK FOR THE RIGHT THINGS.

LIFE IS VERY GOOD!

Be strategic with your prayers. Humbleness is a key ingredient in prayer. In II Chronicles 34:27, King Josiah, through humbleness, repents and God takes notice. Be humble and be sincere. How do you approach God? Through prayer with reverence, respect and honor. Prayer is your way of talking to and spending time with God. He is the King, so treat Him with reverence. He is your Father, so come to Him with honor. He is your Counselor and Friend, so come to Him with respect.

The Lord Says…

I Am here for you, My child. You have not because you do not ask. My goodness is available to all. Ask and you shall receive. Believe and believe again.

If you believe it, say, "Oh yeah!"

JANUARY 27
HE'LL DO IT

HAS FEAR CREPT IN OR UNBELIEF TROUBLED YOUR HEART? THE WAY OUT OF TROUBLE IS BY CALLING OUT TO HIM. REMEMBER CHRIST'S PROMISE TO YOU; WHATEVER YOU ASK IN HIS NAME, HE'LL DO IT, THAT THE FATHER WOULD BE GLORIFIED. YOUR DELIVERANCE IS ONLY ONE QUESTION AWAY. LET YOUR REQUEST BE HEARD.

LIFE IS VERY GOOD!

The Lord does know what you have need of, yet relationships are a two-way street. Since time began, God has been relational. He communed with Adam in the garden and started the first family in Eden because He enjoyed the company. He wants to be included in your life. So ask Him. Call out to Him and He will be there for you, no matter the time or the hour.

The Lord Says…

Believe without fear or reservation that My promises are true and still relevant for you. My covenant did not end with Abraham; it merely began with him, and continues in you and future generations. How can I help you today? What can you do for others? Ask the question, then expect and receive.

If you believe it, say, "Oh yeah!"

JANUARY 28
ASK BIG

WHEN YOU DESIRE SOMETHING BAD ENOUGH, YOU NEVER A.S.K. SMALL. ELISHA ASKED FOR A DOUBLE PORTION AND, THOUGH WHAT HE ASKED FOR WAS CONSIDERED A HARD THING, HE RECEIVED IT! LOOK UP! WHAT YOU ASKED FOR IS COMING DOWN. IT'S NOW YOUR SEASON TO RECEIVE.

LIFE IS VERY GOOD!

Each season comes with a purpose. When that purpose is fulfilled, it passes the baton onto the next season. Does it snow in the summer? Not in most places. But, my friend who grew up in the state of Montana remembers when it snowed in June. God loves to do the extraordinary in your life. He's your daddy and He loves it when you smile. Stop thinking that you don't deserve big dreams and purposes to be fulfilled. You are more than a conqueror and, because you are the KING'S child, you are capable of conquering any valley, mountain, lion or bear that stands in the way of your destiny. It's time to get real with God, leave behind the mundane dreams and begin to dream big again. Ask Him for the tough stuff. Do you think you're worth it? I hope you said yes, because nothing is impossible with God and He thinks you are the apple of His eye, a diamond being shaped by the Master Craftsman. Who do you say you are and what will you ask of Him?

The Lord Says…

May you be filled with purpose and destiny in every season of your life. In the season of rest (winter), new life (spring), activation (summer) and harvest (fall). If you ask and believe, then all things are possible. It surely is your season to shine! Receive the mantel and run with this race with purpose. Watch as opportunity meets destiny in your life.

If you believe it, say, "Oh yeah!"

JANUARY 29
UP TO HALF MY KINGDOM

WHEN THERE IS AN ASSIGNMENT ON YOUR LIFE, GOD'S FAVOR WILL POSITION YOU FOR YOUR REQUEST TO BE MADE KNOWN. THE KING SAID, "ESTHER, WHAT DO YOU DESIRE? I'LL GIVE YOU UP TO HALF MY KINGDOM." THE KING IS READY TO RELEASE. REMEMBER, WHAT YOU A.S.K. FOR CAN DELIVER A NATION.

LIFE IS VERY GOOD!

The story of Esther is so significant in Judaism that the event is celebrated as Purim. Purim is the day Jews remember how they were saved from being murdered. Those of the Jewish faith celebrate with food and party festivities, but the most important part of Purim is the reading of the book of Esther. So be encouraged. When you abide in God, He abides in you. When you combine that knowing with your purpose, destiny and God's timing, you cannot fail. It is you that must believe in it. Stop second-guessing yourself and be a modern-day Esther. Don't be afraid to step out into the deep waters. Have you been saving and planting seeds to open that business, make that deal, adopt a child or even change careers? God has called you for such a time as this!

The Lord Says...

There are two places people make mistakes. One, they are double minded and say they believe but do not believe whole heartedly. Two, they may be in the right purpose and destiny but the wrong timing. I hope that you garner wisdom on your walk and the knowledge to understand when I speak so that you may walk in purpose and destiny within the right time. Then all blessings will come. Philippians 2:13 says, "for it is God who works in you to will and to act in order to fulfill his good purpose". You see, I Am vested. I Am vested in YOU.

If you believe it, say, "Oh yeah!"

JANUARY 30
WHO YOU ARE IS ENOUGH

To overcome your giant, you have to remove what isn't tested and grab hold of the gifts that God has given you. David had a staff and a sling and chose 5 stones from a brook instead of a suit of armor. One stone, together with the knowledge of who you are in Him, will deliver you every time.

Life is very good!

Ask yourself this question: What do I have that is not common and could possibly make a difference in me and the lives of others? You may not think of yourself as a great speaker or preacher and that's okay, but you still have been through some stuff that not everyone has gone through. You have something to share, something to teach and something that might change your world. Think about it for a minute. David didn't trust in the stones for they themselves would have failed him. He didn't trust the sling or staff. He did, however, trust that God had raised him up for such a time as this. He trusted that God had given him the ability to make a change and that, if he took the first step, would signify that he put his full trust in God. It worked for David and it will work for you too. Do you believe you have what it takes and do you trust God enough to go for it?

The Lord Says...

You can do <u>all things</u> through Me for I Am the One who strengthens you (Philippians. 4:13). Declare it within your spirit: I can do all things through Christ who strengthens me. Then believe it, for I have settled it in the heavens and it is done on the earth.

If you believe it, say, "Oh yeah!"

JANUARY 31
IT'S ALL IN YOUR HANDS

WHATEVER SITUATION YOU FACE, YOU HAVE THE RIGHT TO TRANSFORM IT. ELISHA STOOD BEFORE BITTER WATER IN A BARREN LAND. WITH A NEW BOWL IN HIS HAND AND A WORD IN HIS MOUTH, HE WENT TO THE SOURCE OF THE PROBLEM AND CAST IN THE SALT. THE WATER WENT FROM BITTER TO SWEET, FROM BARREN TO FRUITFUL, FROM DEATH TO LIFE. THE POWER TO CHANGE YOUR CIRCUMSTANCE IS IN YOUR HANDS.

LIFE IS VERY GOOD!

Check it out, Luke 1:37 says, "For no word from God will ever fail". That is as powerful as it gets, folks. This literally means that you can change the circumstances of your life and situation. You may be asking this question, "How do I do that?" I am glad you asked. When you agree with God and His Words, the results are as noted in Luke 1:37. Let's break it down. "For no word from God..." The Bible is His Word so, whatever it says, you have access to. Whatever it says you are, you are. Whatever it says God will do for you, He will do. It "will never fail". As the remainder of the scripture shows, His Word will never fail. That is amazing! So ask yourself if you are asking God to tag along with your agenda or are you chasing after His agenda or destiny that He had planned for you all along?

The Lord Says…

Do not be afraid to change your circumstances. Choose not to reinvent the wheel, it wastes precious time. I have called you. You have been chosen. You are forgiven. You are successful. I have given you a brilliant mind and body to facilitate the work I have called you to since birth. You are My child. You are loved, special, significant, worthy and good. Now go and believe that what I proclaim is "yes and amen". Believe it and receive. In My Kingdom, you cannot fail. There are only lessons learned.

If you believe it, say, "Oh yeah!"

FEBRUARY 1
GOD HAS YOU

WHEN THE ODDS ARE STACKED AGAINST YOU, REMEMBER ELISHA'S WORDS TO HIS SERVANT, "FEAR NOT, THERE ARE MORE FOR US THAN THOSE WHO ARE AGAINST US." ELISHA PRAYED THAT HIS SERVANT'S EYES WOULD BE OPENED TO SEE WHAT ELISHA KNEW TO BE TRUE…THAT THE GREAT ARMY WAS NO MATCH FOR THE HOST OF HEAVEN THAT WAS WITH THEM. GOD'S GOT YOUR BACK.

LIFE IS VERY GOOD!

Joshua 1:9 says, "Have I not commanded you? Be strong and courageous. Do not be afraid; do not be discouraged, for the Lord your God will be with you wherever you go". God is reminding you with a question; not only to remember that you are strong and courageous but not to be afraid or get discouraged because He is with you wherever you go; that is in spirit, soul and body. He is there. Are you in a pit? He is there with you; the lamp unto your feet in your present darkness. Is your spirit grieved? He is with you and will comfort you and bring you up to high places. Are you stuck in the valley and it seems like this particular season will never end? Keep your eyes on Him because every season passes onto another and winter always seems more dreary and longer than the rest. Keep imagining summer. Is your body physically ill, tired or drained from the stresses of this world? Fear not, for He is the God that heals you. He is your Provider, your Doctor, your Advocate, your Counselor, Daddy and Friend. He knew your name before you were born and cares so much for you that He knows the number of hairs on your head. I bet you thought you knew yourself real well, right? Well, God knows you better, because even you don't know the number of hairs on your head. That alone is intimate and incredible. The enemy of this world is indeed no match for the God of Abraham Isaac and Jacob; your God and your King.

The Lord Says…

I Am and always will be in your corner. I Am the great I Am. You are never alone in this life, so let fear be gone from you. Walk in My abundant peace and harmony, knowing that I Am for you. For the Word says in Romans 8:31, "What, then, shall we say in response to these things? If God is for us, who can be against us?". Let it be so, yes and amen!

If you believe it, say, "Oh yeah!"

FEBRUARY 2
HE WILL DELIVER

WHEN LIFE'S TROUBLES SURROUND YOU, JUST REMEMBER THAT GOD IS WITH YOU AND WILL PROTECT YOU. LIFT UP YOUR VOICE TO THE LORD LIKE KING ASA DID. GOD HEARD ASA'S CRY AND DELIVERED HIM FROM AN ARMY TWICE THE SIZE OF HIS. GOD CAN WORK THROUGH MANY OR BY FEW. NOTHING IS IMPOSSIBLE FOR GOD.

LIFE IS VERY GOOD!

Psalm 34:17 says, "The righteous cry out, and the Lord hears them; he delivers them from all their troubles". This is just like God; you do one thing and He does so much more. All you have to do is cry out to God. Then, He says two things: one, that He hears you, and two, that He delivers you from ALL your troubles. Come on somebody, shout right there! It does not say some troubles, only financial troubles or just troubles with your spouse or kids. Thank you Jesus, it says **ALL** your troubles. In other words, He will help you with every single trouble you have in your life. That is glorious news. If you were down and out then this should make you stand up and rejoice. God is great indeed. Life is very good!

The Lord Says…

On this day and every day, learn to rejoice for things that are not always what they seem. Speak things that aren't, believing that they will be as you speak life into your tomorrows. Don't sit down on your tomorrows. Stand with your hands raised and your face looking up toward the heavens. I Am here to listen and meet you at every crossroad.

If you believe it, say, "Oh yeah!"

FEBRUARY 3
LAUGH AT THE IMPOSSIBLE

AGAINST ALL ODDS, GOD FULFILLED THIS PROMISE HE GAVE TO ABRAHAM; THAT ABRAHAM AND HIS WIFE WOULD HAVE A SEED FROM HIS LOINS. JUST THINK…A MAN PAST HIS PRIME AND A WOMB CONSIDERED TOO OLD, GAVE BIRTH TO THE SON GOD PROMISED. GOD "LAUGHS" AT WHAT WE THINK IS IMPOSSIBLE.

LIFE IS VERY GOOD!

You see, if God could just get you to see what He sees, all doubt and insecurity would be far from you. Low self-esteem, self-harm and the search for meaning in your life would be far from you because God sees you like a diamond in the rough. You may not be perfect, but you are His child and He thinks you are incredible, amazing, beautiful, smart and knows that you can do all things you set your heart and mind to. He believes that goodness resides in you. Genesis 1:31 says, "God saw all that he had made, and it was very good. And there was evening, and there was morning—the sixth day". In other words, everything that God created includes you, and you are very good. So laugh with God at the sight of the impossible for God is still in the miracle working business.

The Lord Says…

My dear child, laugh with Me at the impossible and worship your way through because tomorrow is a new day. The odds are better when you and I walk together. Expect the impossible to become possible.

If you believe it, say, "Oh yeah!"

FEBRUARY 4
DEATH TO LIFE

IF LIFE HAS HIT A DEAD END AND IT SEEMS LIKE THERE'S NO WAY OUT, REMEMBER GOD CAN OPEN UP A DOOR THAT NO MAN CAN SHUT. LAZARUS WAS DEAD 4 DAYS BEFORE JESUS SHOWED UP AT THE TOMB AND, WITH ONE PRAYER, HE CALLED A DEAD MAN TO LIFE. YOUR SEASON HAS CHANGED FOR HE IS THE RESURRECTION AND THE LIFE.

LIFE IS VERY GOOD!

I am not sure you can really grasp a picture of Lazarus' miracle without truly digging deep into what it means to be dead for four days. To go into Lazarus' tomb to pray for him took more than willingness. It took a faith that was not distracted by the present world. Why? Because after four days, Lazarus' body was already putrefying and the gases coming from his body would have produced a stench that not many people would be willing to endure. In addition, Lazarus' body would likely have started to change color as the blood in his body began to settle. It's possible his eyes would begin to sink into his skull and his body would begin to bloat as a result of the gases. Come on somebody, Jesus was more concentrated on Lazarus' living than his dying. The normal person would have thought He was crazy to go in there because Lazarus was dead. If God can resurrect Lazarus, He can bring resurrection to your marriage, your health, your finances, you job/career and to your heart. Do you believe in miracles today?

The Lord Says...

Today I Am bringing resurrection life into your journey, your heart and your life. Believe, no matter what it looks like. Seasons come and seasons go but I Am the same yesterday, today and forever.

If you believe it, say, "Oh yeah!"

FEBRUARY 5
IT WAS AT THE CROSS

IN LIFE, IF YOU ARE STRUGGLING TO SEE CLEARLY, LOOK TO CALVARY. GOD SAID TO ABRAM, "LIFT YOUR EYES NOW AND LOOK FROM THE PLACE WHERE YOU ARE (YOUR TRIAL), NORTH, SOUTH, EAST AND WEST (THE CROSS). ALL THE LAND THAT YOU SEE I GIVE YOU AND YOUR DESCENDANTS FOREVER." IN THE MIDST OF STRUGGLE, THE CROSS STILL SHINES THROUGH.

LIFE IS VERY GOOD!

The refrain lyrics of the old hymn "At the Cross," reads:

"At the cross, at the cross where I first saw the light,

And the burden of my heart rolled away,

It was there by faith I received my sight,

And now I am happy all the day!"

What I love about this refrain is how it tells you that it all comes back to the Cross. Repeating the word "cross" twice in the first sentence signifies its importance that you understand that the cross is the place where you first saw the light, the place where you found faith and your eyes were opened like a new born babe. Powerful stuff. If you're struggling today, just get on your knees, sit in a chair or stand and raise your hands. However you can, come to the cross and tell Him how much you need Him. Guess what? He needs you too. Come and pray..."Jesus, I come to you today. My burdens are heavy and my journey has been through many a pothole in the road. I have struggled, but yet I believe. Take these burdens from me, Lord, as I lift my heart and my hands to You and believe for a better tomorrow. You said all things are possible Lord, so let it be so." Do you believe it? Now receive His goodness.

The Lord Says...

Oh child, you are My beloved. Every moment you spend with Me, I treasure. It brings music to My heart. My word says in Psalm 91:11, "For [I] will command [My] angels concerning you to guard you in all your ways". Angels are round about you, so rest in Me.

If you believe it, say, "Oh yeah!"

FEBRUARY 6
PEACE BE WITH YOU

HAVE YOU EVER GONE TO SLEEP AND WOKE UP THE NEXT MORNING ONLY TO FIND TROUBLE AT YOUR DOORSTEP? IF SO, REMEMBER THE SERVANT OF ELISHA. HE ROSE EARLY AND WENT OUTSIDE ONLY TO SEE A GREAT ARMY SURROUNDING THEM. AS HE RETURNED, ELISHA SAID, "DO NOT FEAR, THERE ARE MORE WITH US THAN THOSE WITH THEM", AND PRAYED TO THE LORD TO OPEN HIS SERVANT'S EYES. AS QUICKLY AS THE TROUBLE AROSE, GOD PUT IT TO REST. DWELL IN HIS PEACE TODAY.

LIFE IS VERY GOOD!

2 Thessalonians 3:16 says, "Now may the Lord of peace himself give you peace at all times and in every way. The Lord be with all of you". There is something about peace that God wants His people to understand. It's more than just the opposite of conflict. Peace also means being at peace in your life and in your own heart. When you have peace in your life, you rest well, you trust God wholeheartedly (like a Kingdom child should), knowing that He would never ever let you down. You may have the peace of no conflict in your life and that is terrific, but you may not be at peace in your marriage or relationships. You may not have peace about your job or the direction your finances or your children are going. Lack of conflict can be just a different kind of conflict but God wants you to have the peace that allows you to rest for in this world, even when the odds will always seem like they are stacked against you. God, however, is a big, suddenly God and when you surrender your conflict and burdens to your daddy God and internalize peace, watch and see what He will do!

The Lord Says...

I Am the Prince of Peace. Peace I leave unto you, for indeed I Am with you and you will never face a conflict alone in this life. Be still and know that I Am God and we shall dwell together.

If you believe it, say, "Oh yeah!"

FEBRUARY 7
PLAY BALL!

ARE YOU TIRED OF HEARING BUT NOT SEEING THE PROMISES GOD HAS GIVEN YOU? REMEMBER JONATHAN AND HIS ARMOR BEARER? THEY BECAME CATALYSTS TO STIR A NATION TO SEE WHAT GOD WAS DOING. TWO MEN CAUSED A NATION TO REMOVE THEIR ENEMIES AND DISCOVER HIS VICTORY. COME OFF THE BENCH! HE'S CALLED YOU TO BE A PART OF HIS KINGDOM PURPOSE.

LIFE IS VERY GOOD!

Proverbs 16:9 says, "In their hearts humans plan their course, but the Lord establishes their steps". Sometimes the promises of God may not be coming forth in your life because your plans are not in sync with God's plans and/or you may be out of sync with His timing. Seek Him so He may be found by you. When you come off the bench in baseball, you don't just run out onto the field. You wait for the coach to call you out. God is calling you into your purpose. The question is, are you allowing Him to establish your steps or are you establishing them? Stop for a moment and listen. What is your Father, your life coach, telling you to do in this season? Get your purpose on people! Your pastors cannot do everything alone. God has called you to the marketplace. Bring your A-game ~ it's time to play ball!

The Lord Says...

To work in your purpose means to walk in My steps and in My timing. Many people know their purpose but they fail to walk in My timing. Rome was not built in a day and I build season upon season in your life. Enjoy the season of fruitfulness and also the season of rest, for the season of planting and activation will surely follow. If life was always filled with harvesting and activation, when would the planting and rest begin? In life there must be balance; that balance is the fragrance of My peace.

If you believe it, say, "Oh yeah!"

FEBRUARY 8
SEEING IN THE SPIRIT

SOMETIMES WHAT YOU SEE WITH YOUR PHYSICAL EYES IS DIFFERENT FROM WHAT IS TRULY IN THE SPIRIT. NICODEMUS AND JOSEPH OF ARIMATHEA PLEADED FOR THE BODY OF JESUS BECAUSE OF WHAT THEY SAW: LIFE WITHIN A DEAD BODY. DECLARE TO YOUR CIRCUMSTANCES WHAT THE EYES OF YOUR SPIRIT SEES, NOT YOUR PHYSICAL EYES, AND YOU WILL EXPERIENCE A RESURRECTION TO YOUR DREAMS. SEE HIS LIFE IN ALL THINGS.

LIFE IS VERY GOOD!

If you can train yourself to do this one thing, see the supernatural instead of the natural, you are one step in the right direction as a Kingdom child. The king and his court were usually privy to what others could not see. They had spies, armies and people who could report on the conditions of conflict. But, a king must look forward, farther into the remedy and the solution, thereby becoming a strategist. God wants you to know that when you can see things that aren't as though they were, you can begin to speak life into the things that you are believing for and, with nothing more than your speech, you are changing your mindset. This means you are beginning to see things as God sees them. He does not understand the limitations of impossible that you speak of, for He is good and He is possibility; all things are possible through Him. I challenge you to begin decreeing with your words, not what you physically see but what you want to see, and what you believe in the spirit. If God has called you to business, an example of your decree would be, "I declare that I am profitable in business because God has called me to the marketplace of business and God alone establishes my steps. Together we are establishing a good work that is profitable, blesses others with work and glorifies the Kingdom." You may only have a business idea or name. Get it going by speaking it forth. That's kingdom, folks!

The Lord Says...

Colossians 3:17 says, "And whatever you do, whether in word or deed, do it all in the name of the Lord Jesus, giving thanks to God the Father through him.". When you work, when you play, when you believe, when you teach others and when you are yourself, do your best in all things as if I were your guest. And, never forget to be grateful for even the tiniest of things. See it in your spirit and begin to thank Me for it.

If you believe it, say, "Oh yeah!"

FEBRUARY 9
JUST ONE TOUCH

WHEN YOU ARE DESPERATE FOR CHANGE, REMEMBER THE WOMAN WITH THE ISSUE OF BLOOD. SHE FOUGHT THROUGH A CROWD OF PEOPLE JUST TO TOUCH THE HEM OF JESUS' GARMENT. HER TOUCH OF FAITH CAUSED HIS VIRTUE (SUPERNATURAL HEALING POWER) TO FLOW OUT FROM HIM. WHAT WAS IMPOSSIBLE IN HER EYES WAS POSSIBLE FOR JESUS. NEVER LET THE CROWD KEEP YOU FROM YOUR BREAKTHROUGH.

LIFE IS VERY GOOD!

The story of the woman with the issue of blood is found in Mark 5:25-31. The cultural significance of this story is something taken for granted in our society because we often do not consider the social context of antiquity when we read the scriptures. The scriptures say that this woman had been bleeding continuously for twelve years and no doctor had been able to help her. In the Mosaic law, women were not allowed to touch anyone when they were bleeding. This woman was so desperate for change that she decided to forget about political correctness and go after her miracle herself. She may have had an illness and lost all she had but, the one thing this woman did not lose was her faith. As a result, she was healed when she touched just a piece of cloth on Jesus' garment hem. Some of you have been in the same place. Maybe you've had an illness but you haven't lost your faith. Well, my friend, hold on for just a little bit longer and keep reaching to touch Him. He is available to you. Change is in the wind. Let His Spirit blow upon you.

The Lord Says...

The winds of change have come to you. Your season of suffering is coming to an end. There is indeed much to be joyful over. So rejoice, this is your season and you cannot fail for I Am your victory!

If you believe it, say, "Oh yeah!"

FEBRUARY 10
STRONG COVENANT

SOMETIMES YOU CAN BE DOING WHAT IS GOOD AND ADVERSITY WILL FIND YOU. ONE OF THE SONS OF THE PROPHET ELISHA LOST THE AXE-HEAD HE HAD BORROWED. THE POWER OF RELATIONSHIP CAUSED WHAT WAS HIDDEN BENEATH THE SURFACE TO RISE. COVENANT PEOPLE WILL ALWAYS HELP SPEAK LIFE INTO YOUR DREAMS.

LIFE IS VERY GOOD!

Deuteronomy 19:4-6 recounts the law of Moses concerning an accidental death (i.e., manslaughter). In the story, a man travels to the woods with his neighbor. They are cutting down trees and, as the man swings, his axe head comes off and hits his neighbor and kills him. In the Orthodox Jewish Bible, the man whose axe head fell off and killed his neighbor is referred to as the "slayer" (OJB).

The story of the axe head and the son of the prophet Elisha is found in 2 Kings 6:1-7. Here, however, the story is redemptive. Elisha didn't really want to go on this trip. He told his spiritual sons to go, but that he was not going. If you study out the scripture, you come to understand there was conflict between Elisha and his sons as to whether or not this trip to the Jordan should have been made. One son came to Elisha, begging him to come with them and Elisha conceded. It was this very same son who broke the axe head. However, it wasn't just any axe head, for it was borrowed, and the son had a moral obligation to make sure he returned it to its owner in the same condition he borrowed it. So, losing the axe head basically cost him his job and he had no means to repay the debt he had now incurred.

The son called out to Elisha and what did Elisha do? He threw a stick in the water. This stick, representing Christ, made its way into the water and the water became the source by which the moral responsibility for the loss of the axe head was reversed, relieving the bearer of his burden and debt. Elisha and his prophetic sons may not have always agreed on everything, but one thing was for sure; they were covenant people. Notice that Elisha did not say, "what in God's name did you do? I told you I didn't want to come here. Now look what you've done!" No, Elisha punished no one. He only gave positive reinforcements and, when mistakes were made, he acted as a true father and helped bring his son out to free him from his burdens. That's what powerful covenant looks like, friends.

The Lord Says…

I Am with you always. Even when you walk into dark and gloomy places, you only need to call My Name. As I give grace unto you, so must you give grace unto others. So speak life, even in the midst of mistakes and unwise choices, for life rebuilds from the inside out and creates an atmosphere of lessons learned.

If you believe it, say, "Oh yeah!"

FEBRUARY 11
HE IS THE LIGHT

IF YOU'RE FEELING DOWN TODAY, REMEMBER THIS; THE LOVE OF CHRIST IS A FORCE THAT NO SCIENTIST CAN EVER EXPLAIN. JESUS SAID, "IF I BE LIFTED UP, I DRAW ALL NATIONS TO MYSELF." I CAN FEEL HEAVEN PULLING US HIGHER. IT'S TIME TO DWELL IN THE HIGH PLACES.

LIFE IS VERY GOOD!

When you think of heaven, what is a prominent feature that comes to mind? I think of the illumination of light and life. Heaven is light. Its streets are paved with gold and even Psalm 50:2 says, "From Zion, perfect in beauty, God shines forth". When you live in a darkened world and life has left you no hope, Jesus draws you and people of all nations unto Himself (the light). You see, in John 12:20-47, where Jesus said, "If I be lifted up, I will draw all nations to myself," Jesus was teaching the people about the light. He told them that He was the light and to believe in the light because, as He said in verse 35, "whoever walks in the dark does not know where they are going." If you have ever walked into a pitch black room without light, you understand what Jesus was saying here. Has the lamp that lights your way become a little dim? Do you need more light in an area of your life? Then look no further but up and God will draw you unto Himself. Dwell with Him and He will refuel the oil in your lamp and light the way.

The Lord Says…

I Am the Light of the World, even unto you. I Am the oil that keeps your lamps burning and lights the way for you to walk with wisdom and understanding. Walk with Me all your days. Dark days may come but darkness is only the absence of light. Always keep reaching for My illuminated light. It is found in your prayer closet, in your worship, in your study, in your speech, in your giving and when your hands are lifted high. Shout because I Am able to do exceeding above what you could ever think or imagine.

If you believe it, say, "Oh yeah!"

FEBRUARY 12
IN THE MIDNIGHT HOUR

WHEN TIME SEEMS TO BE RUNNING OUT ON A MATTER, REMEMBER THAT GOD CAN RENEW THE TIME. HEZEKIAH SAW A MIRACLE WHEN GOD CAUSED THE DIAL ON THE CLOCK TO GO BACK 15 DEGREES. WHEN ORDER IS IN THE HOUSE, TIME IS NOT LOST, IT'S GAINED.

LIFE IS VERY GOOD!

You know, God is in the midnight hour business. I'm sure you know people whose breakthroughs came just in the nick of time (i.e., the midnight hour) or maybe you've been there yourself. In Psalm 31:14-15, David called upon the Lord saying, "But I trust in you, Lord; I say, 'You are my God. My times are in your hands; deliver me from the hands of my enemies, from those who pursue me'". He called out unto God not just because it was the natural thing to do, but because David understood that God is all about results. God had seen David through many trials but David's footsteps were still ordered by God through all of his mistakes. Go to God with David's prayer and decree it to be so. Then, expect God to move on your behalf. He is good, indeed.

The Lord Says...

I Am no respecter of time. I Am your shelter and the hand that opens and closes doors on your behalf. You are My child, the apple of My eye, and the highly favored. Though trials will be with you and storms may come and go, know this; seasons are limited in their time, their scope and their capacity. Be courageous! Get your house in order, one step at a time, and watch as peace returns and time slows down for you.

If you believe it, say, "Oh yeah!"

FEBRUARY 13
STEPPING IN TIME

HAVE YOU EVER FELT OUT OF STEP WITH GOD'S TIMING? IF SO, REMEMBER IN THOSE TIMES THAT GOD PLANTED A TREE, IN A SPECIFIC PLACE AND FOR A PERFECT MOMENT IN TIME, SO ZACCHAEUS COULD CLIMB IT FOR HIS PERSONAL CLOSE ENCOUNTER OF THE CHRIST KIND. DON'T BE AFRAID TO ANTICIPATE WHERE CHRIST WILL MEET WITH YOU. ONE MOMENT WITH HIM WILL CHANGE EVERYTHING.

LIFE IS VERY GOOD!

Sometimes God puts you in geographic regions or circumstances you may not fully understand in that moment. Jeremiah 29:11 is a well-known scripture that says, "For I know the plans I have for you," declares the Lord, "plans to prosper you and not to harm you, plans to give you hope and a future". Many times we may read this scripture but fail to read the next three verses. Verses 12-14 say, "Then you will call on me and come and pray to me, and I will listen to you. You will seek me and find me when you seek me with all your heart. I will be found by you," declares the Lord, "and will bring you back from captivity. I will gather you from all the nations and places where I have banished you," declares the Lord, "and will bring you back to the place from which I carried you into exile".

In other words, God knows the plans He has for you and He lays out those plans in Jeremiah 29:11. In verses 12-14, God tells you that as a result, you will call on Him, pray to Him and He will listen to you. When you seek Him, He will be found by you. As a result of this relationship, in this time and in this place, God will bring you out from captivity. So, don't sweat the small stuff for God has you covered. Seek Him, and all His wisdom, and the understanding will be revealed to you. Who knew that a single tree could be planted for the purpose of bringing one man (Zacchaeus) into relationship with the Lord, his God? The same is true for you. God has set you in this place for such a time as this. Do you trust Him? If you do, then seek Him and He promises that He will be found.

The Lord Says...

Oh, how I love you, how I love you, indeed. Seek Me with your whole heart, not part of your heart, for I long for My time with you. You are special, My child. Do not worry for tomorrow for I have seen it and it is good. You are loved.

If you believe it, say, "Oh yeah!"

FEBRUARY 14
BECAUSE HE LOVED US

TODAY IS A DAY THAT PEOPLE CELEBRATE LOVE AND DEVOTION FOR ONE ANOTHER. BUT WE MUST REMEMBER THIS; THAT HIS LOVE WAS FIRST GIVEN TO US, THAT'S WHY WE CAN LOVE OTHERS. BE A VALENTINE TO SOMEONE AND EXPRESS HIS LOVE TODAY, AND EVERY DAY.

LIFE IS VERY GOOD!

1 John 4:8 says, "Whoever does not love does not know God, because God is love". So, the best way to show who God is, is to live a life of love in your heart, in your speech and all that you do. Love one another. A smile, a card, expressions of thoughtfulness and appreciation, they all go a long way in this life to make someone's day a little bit brighter. Remember, you might be the one person who makes a difference in a someone's life, just because you expressed the love of God and more importantly, you expressed God Himself. God's love can heal, it can forgive, it can redeem, it can transform, it can bring joy. God's love is all you need, and then some. You are able to love others because of the love He gave to you. Don't hold back; express the image of Christ by His love today and every day.

The Lord Says...

Love is all you need. It covers a multitude of sins. It allows forgiveness the freedom to flow. It makes the heart smile, creates peace and harmony and is where I dwell. Choose to express My love today.

If you believe it, say, "Oh yeah!"

FEBRUARY 15
TIMING IS EVERYTHING

IT IS SAID THAT GOD IS NEVER LATE, NEVER EARLY BUT ALWAYS RIGHT ON TIME. HAVE YOU EVER FELT GOD NEEDS A NEW WATCH? A WATCH THAT SYNCHRONIZES WITH OUR WANTS AND NEEDS (YEAH, RIGHT!)? WE HAVE TO REALIZE THAT GOD'S TIMING MAY NOT MANIFEST ITSELF WHEN WE WANT, BUT IT'S ALWAYS PERFECT. ALL THINGS ARE BEAUTIFUL IN HIS TIME.

LIFE IS VERY GOOD!

Think about it, not only does God's watch not manifest itself the way we want, but it also doesn't manifest in the way we expect. In fact, this very thing happened in II Kings 3:16-17, "and he said, "This is what the Lord says: I will fill this valley with pools of water. For this is what the Lord says: You will see neither wind nor rain, yet this valley will be filled with water, and you, your cattle and your other animals will drink". Now, if you heard that, you'd probably be scratching your head asking yourself how the ditches would be filled, especially in the desert (of all places!). In fact, King Joram did nothing but complain until Elisha delivered the Word of the Lord you just read. It's human nature to think inside of the box but God wants you to think outside of the box. When God says jump, you should say "how high?" That is exactly what the Israelites did after the Word was spoken; they began to dig ditches. Miraculously, the next day God came through. So, are you questioning what God's telling you to do? Don't! He knows your needs far better than you do.

The Lord Says...

I Am your Father, and I know you better than you know yourself. Therefore, do you not think that I will always want the best for you? When a parent sees their child struggling, they naturally try to do everything within their power to meet their child's needs, to the best of their ability, and in a way that guides and teaches. I Am calling you to step outside the box because you cannot expect the unexpected if your mind only operates within a certain framework. Dare to believe in Me and what I can do instead of believing in only what you can do.

If you believe it, say, "Oh yeah!"

FEBRUARY 16
ONE STEP AT A TIME

IT IS SAID THAT, TO FIND SUCCESS, YOU MUST PUT YOUR BEST FOOT FORWARD AND DON'T LOOK BACK. DON'T LOOK TO YOUR PROBLEMS, ONLY LOOK TO THE ANSWER: THE CROSS. LOOKING TO CALVARY WILL HELP YOU MOVE FORWARD INTO HIS PROMISES. THIS IS YOUR MOMENT! TAKE A LEAP OF FAITH.

LIFE IS VERY GOOD!

Ahhh, remember the story of Lot's wife turning into a pillar of salt? The story is found in Genesis 19:26. Lot's wife is a prime example of someone who looked back, not only at the problem left behind them, but what use to be. It's as if Lot's wife thought what she left behind was the best for her life. The familiar tends to have that hold on people, but God has so much more for you. This is why God wants every step you take to be looking right at the cross and moving forward into your destiny. Gomorrah was not God's destiny for Lot and his family. Gomorrah was just a hitching post along the way, a mere detour until the timing was right to move on. If you have to look back, then look back at Calvary because when you do, you are really looking forward. The season has come. Are you willing to take this leap of faith? The family of Abram and Lot were blessed because they took the same leap of faith you're about to embark upon. Come on, somebody! Give God the chance to set you up and bring you out!

The Lord Says…

Let it be known to all men that My plans for you encompass many roads, potholes, switchbacks, detours, destinations and enjoyments along the way. Destiny is a "work in progress" and, even when you arrive at the right place in the right time, your destiny is always moving forward. Don't be afraid to take the leap of faith for I Am with you. Give Me a chance to bring you forward, even over the potholes. Together we will maneuver the switchbacks, navigate the detours and rejoice in the destination.

If you believe it, say, "Oh yeah!"

FEBRUARY 17
DON'T SETTLE FOR LESS

BEFORE YOUR GREATEST MOMENT OF BREAKTHROUGH HAPPENS, IT SEEMS LIKE YOU MUST STARE DOWN ADVERSITY. FOUR MEN SAW A CROWDED HOUSE BEFORE THEM AND MADE THE DECISION TO TEAR THE ROOF OFF. THIS BREAKTHROUGH WASN'T FOR THEM; IT WAS FOR THE FRIEND THEY LOVED. LET NOTHING STAND IN THE WAY OF YOUR MOMENT.

LIFE IS VERY GOOD!

This story is found in Mark 2:4. What I love about this particular story is not necessarily the story's main focus (the healing of the paralytic man). What stands out the most to me is how his friends and the people on the roof began to tear down and tear off the roof. When you are going through desperate times and your season of winter is lingering a little too long, people will do one of two things: settle and accept their plight or fight like mad to get to Jesus because they know there must be something better. God wants you to not be afraid to tear the roof off your prayers, tear the roof off to get to your destiny or tear the roof off your speech and make a change. When the room is filled, the doorways are blocked and people are standing around every entrance, ask yourself if you would have just stood outside or torn the roof off to get to Jesus?

The Lord Says...

No matter where you are geographically or on the journey in your life, one thing remains the same. When you seek Me, I will always be found. Meet Me there, wherever I Am. Just get there. I Am able and I Am willing. Your needs tug at My heart. I Am with you always.

If you believe it, say, "Oh yeah!"

FEBRUARY 18
STORMS OF ADVERSITY

IN LIFE, YOU MAY FEEL LIKE YOUR BOAT IS SLOWLY TAKING IN WATER AND SINKING. BUT, IN THE TIME OF ADVERSITY, ONE SPOKEN WORD CAN CHANGE EVERYTHING. DECLARE HIS PEACE OVER YOUR LIFE AND WATCH THE STORM BE STILL. IT'S TIME TO STEP OUT OF THE BOAT AND ONTO THE SHORELINE OF DESTINY.

LIFE IS VERY GOOD!

In Mark 4:35-41, Jesus told the disciples to take the boat to the other side. Jesus was tired from a full day of teaching and touching the lives of others so He went down into the boat to sleep. He had a faith that all was well. This story paints a great picture of the natural and of the supernatural. Sometimes it seems like every time you make a new move, you become uncomfortable until you find yourself within the familiar. That night on the boat, the wind began to create an uneasiness and the disciples became afraid. Jesus addressed their faith and then did the most logical thing someone who walks in the supernatural would do… Jesus spoke to the storm and said, "Peace be still!" At least Peter had the guts in Matthew 14:22-33 to have supersonic faith until his natural surroundings got the better of him. Jesus addressed Peter's faith as well. So, what will you do? Will you speak destiny over your life and walk out onto the water? If you have your eyes on the cross, you can do anything!

The Lord Says…

Speak to your storm the Word I have given you and have faith that the storm shall subside. Then, ask yourself why this storm came upon your life to begin with. When you can rest during a storm, you will know that you can truly trust Me and believe I Am taking care of you. Be like a sailboat and sail right on through the storm. I Am always at the helm and I will always steer you in the right direction.

If you believe it, say, "Oh yeah!"

FEBRUARY 19
PERFECTLY REDEEMED

REMEMBER THIS: OUT OF THE DARKEST OF PLACES, A CHOSEN SEED WAS BORN. JESUS' LINEAGE WAS NOT PERFECT; IT WAS REDEEMED. FOUR WOMEN (TAMAR, RAHAB, RUTH AND MARY) THAT WOULD BE REJECTED BY RELIGION OVERCAME IMPERFECTIONS AND PRODUCED THE GENEALOGY THAT CHRIST CAME FROM. NO MATTER HOW BAD YOUR FAMILY MAY SEEM, GREATNESS WILL COME FORTH.

LIFE IS VERY GOOD!

During your greatest struggles, it may be easy to say that Jesus just doesn't understand what it is you are going through. But, in reality, He gets it more than you know. Just look at the time He was born into. Herod had just given orders that every male child under the age of 2 years old was to be executed. Herod's decree was an effort to kill the newborn King (according to Matthew 2:16) and identifies the social volatility of that time. The fact that Matthew lists Tamar, Rahab, Ruth and Mary in the genealogy of Jesus would have been scandalous during this time. Women had little rights outside of being the matriarch of the family. If your mother was not Jewish, you were not considered Jewish. But God knew that Jesus would be able to identify with you because both men and women in His family were sinners; sinners who had been redeemed. Tamar, whose first and second husbands die (Judah's sons), was not given to Judah's youngest son to marry when he became of age (which was customary). Out of desperation, the widow Tamar concocted a plan to represent herself as a prostitute and slept with her father-in-law, Judah. She used deception, but bore twin boys, one of which (Perez) became part of the kingly line of Jesus. Rahab, a prostitute and mother of Boaz, secured Joshua and Caleb when they spied out the land. Ruth, a Moabite who converted to Judaism, was not accepted as a real Jew in social circles. The society of that time likely thought Mary was mentally ill and was really having an illegitimate child. After all, how crazy would she sound telling you that God made her pregnant? So, do you still think Jesus doesn't understand your circumstances or dysfunctional family? He completely understands.

The Lord Says...

When your family seems to let you down, don't fret. Look up, for your greater family in heaven is cheering you on. I Am with you always and through your trials it will be made known that redemption and victory are just around the bend. Don't stop now. Keep moving forward.

If you believe it, say, "Oh yeah!"

FEBRUARY 20
NO GOING HALFWAY

When God delivers you, He doesn't do it part way. He does it all the way. The children of Israel had to be pursued by Pharaoh all the way to the Red Sea or it would have been easy for them to turn back. The time is now, move forward into your Promised Land.

Life is very good!

I believe Jesus wants us to be people who seize the moment. Matthew 9:29 says, "Then he touched their eyes and said, "According to your faith let it be done to you". In this one chapter, Jesus healed a paralytic man, called a man everyone hated (Matthew the tax collector) into the ministry, taught his disciples about fasting, healed a woman who had been bleeding for years, raised a girl the world said was dead, healed a blind man and a demon possessed man who could not speak and closed out the chapter by teaching his disciples about the harvesting of souls. Jesus was clearly a man who seized the moment. The greatest rewards come from the things you work so hard for. Go for it! Seize the day. This is your moment. What would happen if you grabbed hold of each season's destiny in your life and you ran with it? Each season prospers in its purpose. Will you?

The Lord Says...

Prosperity is more than the money you have earned. It is having good health and quality relationships that challenge you to become all I have meant for you to pursue. Prosperity is living the dream by fulfilling your passion and pursuing the purpose ordained just for you. Prosperity is having the ability to trust Me in all things with a childlike faith. Prosperity is finding happiness every day because you live a life of joy. And, prosperity is when you walk with Me, not ahead of Me or behind Me. I know the plans I have for you, and they are very good. Believe it and enter in.

If you believe it, say, "Oh yeah!"

FEBRUARY 21
A COMPLETE MOVE

Just because you change your location doesn't mean the attitude of your heart has changed. Remember, Israel was delivered from Egypt but Egypt still needed to be delivered out of them. Quit looking back at what was and look forward to what can be. Let your heart shift; there's a promise waiting for you.

Life is very good!

Sometimes it seems like life's circumstances move you geographically, whether you lose your job, get transferred, have an ill family member to care for or for whatever reason. But remember, God knew you would move before you even got there, so take comfort in knowing that He is two steps ahead of you all the time. It's the human race that plays catch-up with God. Sometimes God allows you to be in a place for a reason. Do you need character building? Maybe it's time to trust God instead of only trusting yourself. Maybe you need to pray for your enemies, thereby learning to release anger and frustration. Maybe God knows there will be a medical need. Or, perhaps He wants you to conquer in an area someone else or yourself previously couldn't. Whatever the case, don't even look back. What was is never as good as what will be. With God, you go from glory to glory. In fact, 2 Corinthians 3:16-18 says, "But whenever anyone turns to the Lord, the veil is taken away. Now the Lord is the Spirit, and where the Spirit of the Lord is, there is freedom. And we all, who with unveiled faces contemplate the Lord's glory, are being transformed into his image with ever-increasing glory, which comes from the Lord, who is the Spirit". I challenge you to not look back at what was or what might have been because the future is only going to be better. I know it is hard to imagine anything better than what you had, but it's out there. This was the lesson God had to so harshly teach Abram and Lot when Lot's wife turned back and died. The stress of always thinking about what you used to have will cut short your life. I challenge you to fret not, but rejoice, for tomorrow your portion shall come.

The Lord Says...

If you know Me, you know that I Am forward thinking; a "big picture" God. Your journey in life will travel down gravel roads full of potholes and will not be as comfortable as driving on the smooth asphalt. That is quite okay, for no matter where the road may take you, I will give you a greater peace that is useful yesterday, today and forever.

If you believe it, say, "Oh yeah!"

FEBRUARY 22
DIAMOND IN THE ROUGH

As you deal with difficult times, remember this: adversity is not a limitation but an invitation to greater promises. It's your gateway to God's blessing. If you allow your opposition to limit you, you'll never see what God has on the other side. Let nothing stop you from overcoming. Rise up to the occasion!

Life is very good!

Most people would never recognize a gemstone in its natural rock form. First it must be discovered, then polished to uncover its beauty, examined to analyze its worth and cut to become part of a beautiful adornment we know as jewelry. You are just like a precious gem. Life may look like a rock, nothing spectacular. But, in reality, you are destined for greatness just like the precious gem. Once the gem is polished, it shows what it really is. Sometimes you have to go through some polishing before you really find your purpose and destiny. Don't let the process of preparation sideline your dreams. It is necessary in the pursuit of purpose. Are you up for the challenge? Take the lid off adversity and make it an opportunity for growth and greatness.

The Lord Says...

I have made you for such a time as this. Preparation has its pitfalls but they are filled with purpose. I will help you walk through and make it to the other side. I saved Jesus from Herod, Moses in a basket, David from Goliath and so will I take you through adversity to conquer in sweet victory.

If you believe it, say, "Oh yeah!"

FEBRUARY 23
JUST BELIEVE

FOR GOD TO MOVE ON YOUR CIRCUMSTANCE, ALL IT TAKES IS FAITH, WHETHER IT'S GREAT FAITH OR ONLY A LITTLE FAITH. THE CENTURION HAD GREAT FAITH WHILE THE DISCIPLES WERE REBUKED FOR HAVING LITTLE FAITH BUT, IN THE END, THE CENTURION'S SERVANT WAS HEALED AND THE STORMS WERE CALMED. GREAT OR SMALL, FAITH IN HIM CAN STILL MOVE MOUNTAINS. ALL YOU NEED TO DO IS BELIEVE.

LIFE IS VERY GOOD!

Matthew 17:20 says, "He replied, "Because you have so little faith. Truly I tell you, if you have faith as small as a mustard seed, you can say to this mountain, 'Move from here to there,' and it will move. Nothing will be impossible for you". One single mustard seed is only about 1 millimeter in size. To give you a visual, it takes approximately 25 millimeters to make one inch. Now compare that to the tallest mountain in your area. You only need enough faith to comprise one millimeter, equal to one mustard seed. What are you worried about that's too big for God, anyhow? I challenge you to refrain from worry and let God be your source.

The Lord Says...

I Am your source, your more than enough, your all in all and everything you need. Let your faith ground you in trusting Me, that I love you enough; enough to calm your storm, to see you through, to touch your body. Believe that I Am who I say that I Am.

If you believe it, say, "Oh yeah!"

FEBRUARY 24
FACE IT

REMEMBER THIS WHILE YOU FACE ADVERSITY: OVERCOMING YOUR PRESENT SEASON OF DIFFICULTY PREPARES YOU FOR THE SEASON YOU WILL MOVE INTO. DAVID COULDN'T RUN AWAY FROM THE GIANT LIKE THE ISRAELITES DID. BY FACING AND SLAYING GOLIATH, DAVID BECAME THE MAN GOD HAD DESTINED HIM TO BE: A KING, ONE WHO NEVER BACKED DOWN FROM A BATTLE. LET YOUR ADVERSITY PUSH YOU FORWARD INTO GOD'S VICTORY.

LIFE IS VERY GOOD!

You were born for this moment. Remember that God knew where you would be in life before you even got there. When you run with God long enough, you begin to build your confidence in Him. In his own nature, David would never have been capable of slaying a giant. But, he ran with God and he saw firsthand how God, and only God, had seen him through. In 1 Samuel 17:32-51, you can recount the story. But here's the thing…you must go through the little battles before God will allow you to slay the giants in your life. Take on the challenge. Adversity means you have the opportunity to conquer. You already have the victory and each season comes with change.

The Lord Says…

When you first learned to walk it started with baby steps. First you crawled and then your parents challenged you to stand and take steps holding onto furniture, pushing toys and holding their own two hands. Sometimes I must push you through adversity because, even though you may not think you can make it, I Am your daddy God and I know what you are capable of accomplishing. Trust Me and know that this season shall pass. As you walk with Me daily, there will be no doubt that I will see you through the next season that comes your way.

If you believe it, say, "Oh yeah!"

FEBRUARY 25
NO MOUNTAIN TOO HIGH

REMEMBER: THE DESOLATE, PARCHED AND DRY PLACE, WHICH LOOKS LIKE A MOUNTAIN OF ADVERSITY BEFORE YOU, IS A MOUNTAIN THAT BELONGS TO GOD. DAVID SAID EVEN IF HE MADE HIS BED IN HELL, GOD WAS THERE. HIS HAND HOLDS US IN OUR HIGHEST OF HIGHS AND DEEPEST OF DEPTHS. THERE IS NOTHING YOU CAN FACE THAT HIS SON DIDN'T ALREADY CONQUER.

LIFE IS VERY GOOD!

If you could learn one thing about what it means to be a Kingdom child, it's this: God, as King and Father, never leaves a child behind. If He said He would take the mountain in your life, He will take it. He also meets you in the valley. So many people focus on the mountain because it's so grand, comparing the greatest battles of their lives to a mountain that needs to be conquered. However, the valley experience is necessary in order to reach the mountain in the first place. You might as well sit back, use wisdom and follow God while you are there. The valley is a place of prosperity where many crops grow well. Yet it is also the place where flooding occurs and where thieves are known to prey upon the people. Remember, not only the mountain but the valley also belongs to God. Let wisdom be your guide as God directs your path through the valley and on to the mountaintop.

The Lord Says…

No valley is too low and no mountain is too high for Me. I will be the hands that hold you, the light that guides you and the stream you need in the desert places. Be not dismayed. Trust and walk in the light.

If you believe it, say, "Oh yeah!"

FEBRUARY 26
IT DOESN'T FEEL GOOD

DURING YOUR SEASON OF CRUSHING, IT NEVER FEELS GOOD. YOU CRY OUT BUT IT SEEMS LIKE GOD ISN'T THERE. WHY? BECAUSE IN THE MIDST OF A TEST, THE TEACHER IS ALWAYS SILENT ALTHOUGH THEIR PRESENCE IS SEEN. KNOW THAT GOD IS AN EVER PRESENT HELP IN A TIME OF NEED. YOUR VICTORY IS ON THE HORIZON.

LIFE IS VERY GOOD!

Crushing grapes is absolutely necessary when making wine because the skin must be punctured for the grapes to provide the maximum juice necessary to make the wine. In addition, the crushing also rids the grapes of their stems which enables the grapes to produce a much desired flavor when processed into wine. Life, both spiritually and naturally, is much the same. Crushing is a necessary part of the process for you to become the new wine God has called you to be. It is never comfortable but, as the winemaker, trust that He knows what He is doing in your life. Trust that you will become the new wine and walk into your destiny as He desires for you to do.

The Lord Says...

In all the crushing know this: I have not forgotten you. I Am here and you are becoming all that I have called you to become. Change is not easy, but every season produces its best and poses different challenges. I will never give you more than you can handle and, when it hurts, just cry out and worship and watch peace become your portion. Say to yourself, "I can and God is able." Then believe it.

If you believe it, say, "Oh yeah!"

FEBRUARY 27
WINNING WORDS

VICTORY IS MORE THAN A WORD, IT'S A LIFESTYLE. WHEN YOU SPEAK IT, BELIEVE IT AND WHEN YOU FACE WHAT SEEMS TO BE IMPOSSIBLE, LIVE IT OUT! DAVID'S LANGUAGE AND LIFESTYLE DEMONSTRATED THIS WHEN HE TALKED TO KING SAUL, "YOUR SERVANT KILLED A LION AND BEAR AND THIS PHILISTINE SHALL BE LIKE ONE OF THEM." VICTORY STARTS WITH YOUR LANGUAGE AND IS OBTAINED BY ACTIONS IN TIMES OF ADVERSITY. IT'S TIME TO SLAY YOUR GIANT.

LIFE IS VERY GOOD!

Your words are so powerful. Like a mother who says that you are what you eat, you are what you speak. When you speak something, you believe it. Luke 6:45 says, "A good man brings good things out of the good stored up in his heart, and an evil man brings evil things out of the evil stored up in his heart. For the mouth speaks what the heart is full of". In other words, what's in your heart comes forth. I challenge you to change your speech and see what will happen. Expect great things.

The Lord Says...

Have I not been with you today, yesterday and am I not with you forever? Yes, yes I Am. When the impossible comes your way, speak My Word and the shutters to the windows of heaven will swing open wide and the rivers will begin to flow. Victory starts with you. What will your heart speak? Even if you think you can't, speak that you can for I have given you the words. Even if you feel like a failure, speak who you will become for I have already placed destiny within you. For if you could see what I see, you would surely speak differently. In the beginning, I said that you were very good and so you shall be.

If you believe it, say, "Oh, yeah!"

FEBRUARY 28
JUST HOLD ON

VICTORY IN LIFE OCCURS WHEN YOU ARE ABLE TO SHAKE OFF ADVERSITY AND HOLD ONTO THE PROMISE SPOKEN TO YOU. PAUL SHOOK OFF THE VIPER AND STOOD ON GOD'S WORD THAT NO LIFE WOULD BE LOST. YOU CAN TRUST THAT HIS WORD WILL NOT RETURN VOID. GOD'S PROMISES ARE "YES AND AMEN." JUST SHAKE IT OFF! YOUR VICTORY IS ON ITS WAY.

LIFE IS VERY GOOD!

As I minister around the world, I meet many people. Sometimes it seems like people come to church on Sunday and just treat the Bible like another historical book they have on the shelf. The Bible is filled with history, archeology, law, ethics, art, romance, mystery, wisdom and power. It's time you learn its promises and read its words with a new revelation. My prayer for you is this: the next time you read God's Word, it won't just be a book you are reading or the same scripture you have read a thousand times. This time, the scripture will breathe life into your bones, minister to your soul and you will experience a new revelation of something that you may have read many times before. The Word is alive and that is so powerful. If you need a word of knowledge, you don't have to wait for a prophet to come to town. Jesus was the greatest prophet to live on the face of the earth and His Words in the Bible will absolutely not return void in your life according to Isaiah 55:11, "So is my word that goes out from my mouth: It will not return to me empty, but will accomplish what I desire and achieve the purpose for which I sent it ". Shake it off! You are standing on Holy Ground and He will see you through to victory.

The Lord Says...

I Am the banner of love that covers you. I Am the words that speak life into your heart. I Am the light that guides you through Egypt. I Am the grace that saves you. I Am the comfort that holds you, the power that strengthens you, the healing that restores you and the builder of your house. I Am that I Am. Who do you say that I Am? My promises are true yesterday, today and for always.

If you believe it, say, "Oh yeah!"

MARCH 1
JUST KEEP MOVING

NEVER STOP IN THE SEASON OF TROUBLE. THOUGH THE VALLEY IS DEEP AND THE MOUNTAIN HIGH, TO OVERCOME DISAPPOINTMENT, YOU HAVE TO KEEP MOVING. REMEMBER, WHEN YOU STOP YOU ALLOW TROUBLE TO GAIN MOMENTUM. VICTORY COMES ONE STEP AT A TIME.

LIFE IS VERY GOOD!

Isaiah 43:2 says, "When you pass through the waters, I will be with you; and when you pass through the rivers, they will not sweep over you. When you walk through the fire, you will not be burned; the flames will not set you ablaze". I think the Word speaks for itself. He is with you wherever your foot may tread. The seasons are consistent; they know when to begin and when to transition to where the next season begins. One step at a time and you will walk it through. Sometimes life is meant to be an adventure. Keep moving forward in God's wake.

The Lord Says...

Sometimes when you are swimming in a wake it can seem overwhelming. However, if you keep your head above the water and find joy in the moment, the wake will become an adventure you enjoy. Joy will see you through any circumstance because it lightens the burden. Find My joy, for laughter is always good medicine.

If you believe it, say, "Oh yeah!"

MARCH 2
JOY FOR THE JOURNEY

REMEMBER, IF YOU ARE LOOKING FOR HAPPINESS IN YOUR LIFE, IT'S NEVER A DESTINATION. HAPPINESS IS ONLY TEMPORARY, DEPENDENT ON THE THINGS AROUND YOU. JOY IS FOUND ALL ALONG THE JOURNEY BECAUSE IT'S A LIFESTYLE, A PERSON LIVING WITHIN YOU. RECEIVE HIS JOY TODAY, IT MAKES THE JOURNEY WORTHWHILE.

LIFE IS VERY GOOD!

1 Thessalonians 5:16-18 says, "Rejoice always, pray continually, give thanks in all circumstances; for this is God's will for you in Christ Jesus" (NIV). When you can rejoice all the time, pray all the time and give thanks all the time, your mind and your mouth do not have a chance to stop and walk through pessimism.

The valley and the mountain both seem equal and the challenges you face become the Lord's.

The Lord Says...

You are never alone on your journey or in the midst of the battles you face on this earth. I see, I know and I hear you. Life is a journey and when I live within you, your joy will be fulfilled.

If you believe it, say, "Oh yeah!"

MARCH 3
SHAKE IT OFF

WHEN YOU COME OUT FROM BEHIND THE VEIL OF LIMITATION AND BEGIN TO DEMONSTRATE HOW BIG GOD IS INSIDE OF YOU, THE IMPOSSIBLE BECOMES POSSIBLE. IT'S OUR HOUR TO SHAKE OFF ALL THAT HAS OPPRESSED US AND LET HIS GLORY BE REVEALED. DEMONSTRATE HIS GREATNESS.

LIFE IS VERY GOOD!

What would happen if you woke up every morning and said, "Okay God, I'm running with you today"? Who will we touch? What doors will you open? And, you talked to Him like he was not just your boss, but your father and your friend. He takes off your limitations and when you embark on your journey every morning saying, "Let's go, God! Let's go to work", you certainly are including Him in your everyday life and your limitations begin to come off. For with Him all things are possible and you cannot fail. He has already set you up for success. Walk in it.

The Lord Says...

Ah, how I long to walk with you everyday; in the valley, up the mountain, at your work, in the gym, at your board meeting, when you have lunch, everyday and all day. Smile, for I Am indeed present and today you will demonstrate My goodness in all you do.

If you believe it, say, "Oh yeah!"

MARCH 4
SHINE BRIGHT

DIAMONDS ARE FOUND IN COAL MINES DEEP IN THE MOUNTAINS; PEARLS ARE FOUND IN THE SHUT MOUTHS OF OYSTERS DEEP IN THE OCEAN. BUT AS ONE IS MINED AND THE OTHER IS HARVESTED, THESE DARK PLACES PRODUCE THE MOST VALUABLE GEMS. GOD WILL USE THE DARK SEASONS IN YOUR LIFE TO BRING MATURITY AND PRODUCE HIS BEST. GOD'S WORK IN YOU HAS MADE YOU PRICELESS.

LIFE IS VERY GOOD!

Philippians 1:6 says, "being confident of this, that he who began a good work in you will carry it on to completion until the day of Christ Jesus". Revelation 21 describes what heaven looks like. Verses 17-21 say, "The wall was built of jasper, while the city was pure gold, like clear glass. The foundations of the wall of the city were adorned with every kind of jewel. The first was jasper, the second sapphire, the third agate, the fourth emerald, the fifth onyx, the sixth carnelian, the seventh chrysolite, the eighth beryl, the ninth topaz, the tenth chrysoprase, the eleventh jacinth, the twelfth amethyst. And the twelve gates were twelve pearls, each of the gates made of a single pearl and the street of the city was pure gold, like transparent glass". I say all this so you realize how valuable you really are. He is not finished with you yet. And, do you think He created streets of pure gold because HE, God, likes to look at it? No. He did it all for you. You deserve the best because you are Kingdom, a prince and a princess, His heir, saved by grace. It has always been about you. From the garden to the cross. You indeed are priceless. If you can believe it, you will look at your image differently; how He sees you instead of what you see in the natural. Look beyond the mirror.

The Lord Says...

I always look beyond the mirror. I have prepared a place for you that man cannot describe. Colors you have never seen and wonders too beautiful for words. You are worth all I do for you because I love you to the moon and back. When darkness comes your way, just know I Am the light that shows you the way as you plow through this journey called life. You are valuable my child.

If you believe it, say, "Oh yeah!"

MARCH 5
BEING UNIQUELY YOU

THE POWER OF GOD'S CREATION IS AWESOME. GOD CREATED THE BUMBLEBEE, WHO DEFIES THE LAWS OF PHYSICS BY FLYING AN OVERSIZED BODY WITH UNDERSIZED WINGS. HE CREATED THE HUMMINGBIRD, WHICH IS ABLE TO MAKE A COMPLETE STOP WHILE FLYING IN MID-AIR. BUT NEITHER OF THOSE COMPARE WITH THE PRICELESS WORK OF ART HE CREATED IN YOU. YOU'RE HIS GREATEST CREATION.

LIFE IS VERY GOOD!

Psalm 139:13-14 says, "For you created my inmost being; you knit me together in my mother's womb. I praise you because I am fearfully and wonderfully made; your works are wonderful, I know that full well". Think about this. The bumblebee, the hummingbird and you have something in common; you are unique. There is no one like you, no one. And the scripture says that you were fearfully and wonderfully made. The world is filled with over 7 billion people, all His creation, all different, all unique and special in their own way.

The Lord Says...

I have known you before you were knit into your mother's womb. You have been made in My image and are filled with goodness. When life seems like a bummer, just remember that My power resides inside of you and, because of that, you can change the atmosphere in which you abide. When you abide in me, I abide in you. I love you!

If you believe it, say, "Oh yeah!"

MARCH 6
YOUR PIVOTAL MOMENT

LIFE'S JOURNEY HAS A WAY OF LEADING YOU TO A MOMENT WHERE EVERYTHING AROUND YOU CHANGES. REMEMBER, TO CROSS THIS BRIDGE, YOU MUST EMBRACE THE CHANGE NO MATTER HOW DIFFICULT IT MAY SEEM AT THE MOMENT. THE OTHER SIDE IS FULL OF HIS PROMISES. TO SUCCEED, JUST KEEP MOVING FORWARD. A GREATER SEASON AWAITS YOU.

LIFE IS VERY GOOD!

I love to see the faces of people as the seasons change. From summer to autumn, the kids are sad but the parents are excited; the kids are going back to school. From autumn to winter, joy comes over the faces of boys and girls as they anticipate the annual tradition of gift giving during Christmas. When the flowers begin to bloom and the rain takes place of snow, smiles grace the faces of many that the long dark days of winter are almost over. And, when the sunshine warms your face and gets you outside into the great outdoors, you begin to long for summer sunshine, warm lakes, rivers, oceans, vacation, no school and plain old relaxing. There is something great about every season we experience. The same is true in your spiritual and physical life. Cross the bridge and do not be afraid to embrace the next season. Ecclesiastes 3:1 says, "There is a time for everything and a season for every activity under the heavens:". Get ready because it's time for your cup to run over with His goodness and abundance in your life. This is your season of opportunity.

The Lord Says...

This is your season of opportunity. When the seasons change in your life, it is never easy. When you walk with Me and embrace the change, pursue your passion and your purpose, get ready, because in every season you will find joy, no matter what you face on your journey. I Am with you always, in every season.

If you believe it, say, "Oh yeah!"

MARCH 7
STRENGTH IN WEAKNESS

THERE ARE TIMES IN LIFE WHEN STRUGGLES COME AND THE PAIN LEAVES US EMOTIONALLY PARALYZED. BUT IT'S DURING THESE MOMENTS THAT WE FIND A GREATER STRENGTH WITHIN. DWELL IN HIS PRESENCE AND LET HIS VICTORY AT CALVARY MOVE YOU FORWARD. YOUR WEAKNESS IS MADE PERFECT IN HIM.

LIFE IS VERY GOOD!

Philippians 4:13 says, "I can do all this through Him who gives me strength". Take courage in knowing that, when you are so broken that your heart and emotions feel paralyzed, God alone will be your strength. He will lift up your arms so you can worship and, as you pray in the spirit, His strength will begin to take root inside of you. Through him you can do all things and sometimes you need to come to the end of yourself so you can recognize it is in HIM that you live and move.

The Lord Says...

I understand your pain for I put My son on a cross for you; a place where stakes went through His flesh and bone. I was disappointed when Adam and Eve chose to ignore the one thing I asked of them. I gave them the whole garden and coveted My time with them, but they chose to separate themselves from Me. Yet in this, have courage. Your pain will be replaced by gladness for this is only a season. One day Jesus was in pain and then He resurrected. I Am still in the resurrection business. I resurrect marriages, families, lives, businesses, ideas, deals and so much more. If you are in need of resurrection from your brokenness, just call out My Name and I will be there.

If you believe it, say, "Oh yeah!"

MARCH 8
THERE'S MORE TO LIFE THAN WORK

THE REALITY OF LIFE IS THAT, ONCE YOU'RE BORN AND START GROWING, YOU'RE ONE STEP CLOSER TO DYING. OUR NATURAL LIFE LEADS TO DEATH, BUT THE WAY OF THE KINGDOM LEADS TO ETERNAL LIFE. MAKE SURE YOUR NAME IS WRITTEN IN THE LAMB'S BOOK OF LIFE AND LIVE LIFE TO THE FULLEST EVERYDAY. TO BE ABSENT OF THE BODY IS TO BE EVER PRESENT WITH THE LORD.

LIFE IS VERY GOOD!

Ecclesiastes 5:18 says, "This is what I have observed to be good: that it is appropriate for a person to eat, to drink and to find satisfaction in their toilsome labor under the sun during the few days of life God has given them—for this is their lot". I know some of you, and you work too hard and do not enjoy your life. God didn't put you on this earth to work yourself to the bone just to provide food, clothing and shelter. He says that it is appropriate for you to eat, drink and find satisfaction in your labor, relaxing under the sun and this is what you're supposed to do. I get a lot of people that say that I have traveled a lot this year. They see my wife and I going out of town and my family going on vacation. Family is number one and God wants you to enjoy what you have. My wife is worth the time to get away and, if you have kids, you know that they grow up way too fast. So turn it around. Begin to enjoy your life. Get out and hike, if you have a boat, gas it up, BBQ with friends in the summer or take a weekend getaway with your family. I love to see my kids smile every time we go to Disneyland. Nothing can take the place of that feeling. Stop living to work and just begin living. Do what you love and love what you do.

The Lord Says...

I have created this earth, not for Me to look at from the heavens, but for you to enjoy. How will you explore it, thank Me for it, love it and treasure it? There is so much to see just outside your backyard. Be ready, in season and out of season and become the gospel to the world. They are ready, are you?

If you believe it, say, "Oh yeah!"

MARCH 9
UNCLUTTERED CLARITY

WHEN ISSUES IN LIFE HAVE YOU OVERWHELMED, YOUR MIND BECOMES CLUTTERED. WHEN THIS HAPPENS, YOUR HEART BECOMES CONFUSED AND YOUR PATHWAYS SEEM UNCERTAIN. THE JOURNEY OF CLARITY BEGINS BY ALLOWING HIS PRAISE TO RENEW YOUR MIND, STANDING ON THE WORD AND ALLOWING HIS TRUTH TO FORGE A NEW PATHWAY. REMEMBER, HIS PRESENCE MAKES ALL THINGS NEW.

LIFE IS VERY GOOD!

It's human nature to sometimes feel like everything is crashing in around you and you can't find a way out. But when you feel this way, do not allow yourself to wallow in the confusion. Jacob many times ran away to 'clear his head' and God always found him where he was. In Genesis 28, Jacob was on his way to Haran when he stopped for the night. He pulled up a rock as a pillow and that night he had a dream. "Then he dreamed, and behold, a ladder was set up on the earth, and its top reached to heaven; and there the angels of God were ascending and descending on it" (Genesis 28:12). God assured Jacob that He was always with him and once again gave him a promise of his future. "Then Jacob rose early in the morning, and took the stone that he had put at his head, set it up as a pillar, and poured oil on top of it" (verse 18). Jacob worshiped the Lord, even in the midst of confusion, because he knew that it would open up his spirit to see what the Lord had for him. When everything seemed uncertain, when he was running away from his brother or his father-in-law, or when he was fighting to realize who he truly was, Jacob would always worship and find all the answers to the questions he had. Are you ready to have the clutter removed? Lift your voice in praise and allow God to blow away the confusion so you can see clearly.

The Lord Says...

I, your Father, have cleared the pathway for you to walk on but it starts with your worship. When you worship and praise, you're not seeing with physical eyes, you see with your spirit. Praise renews your heart and mind, and gives you perspective on the future I have for you. I don't want to see you confused for I've given you a sound mind. I don't want to see you fearful for I've given you bold-ness. My truth will show you the way in the wilderness and My love will always make you new.

If you believe it, say, "Oh yeah!"

MARCH 10
WALKING IN FREEDOM'S SONG

LIFE'S JOURNEY MAY BE FULL OF UPS AND DOWNS BUT, WHEN A BLOW KNOCKS YOU OFF YOUR FEET, IT DOESN'T MEAN YOU'RE OUT. STAND UP IN HIS IDENTITY, STEADY YOURSELF IN PRAYER AND FINISH THE GOOD FIGHT OF FAITH. THIS BATTLE ENDS WITH YOUR HANDS RAISED IN HIS VICTORY.

LIFE IS VERY GOOD!

When Moses lost his status as a prince and the only family he had ever grown up knowing wanted to now kill him, what did he do? He went away. He was forced out. And in this new place he found the Lord and His direction. When he came back to face Pharaoh, he no longer stood only as Moses but stood rather as the called, the chosen and the redeemed man who walked with God on God's mission to set a people free. This just happened to be Moses' destiny. When you stand in God's image and you go where He goes, you cannot fail. It may seem like it takes forever but He will see you through, just like He did for Moses.

The Lord Says...

I Am the way, the truth and the life. All who come to Me will walk in My grace, and those who listen to My words will walk where I walk. There you will find freedom's song.

If you believe it, say, "Oh yeah!"

MARCH 11
TOGETHER WE SHALL SEIZE THE DAY

HAVE YOU EVER FELT INSIGNIFICANT, FEELING LIKE YOU'RE JUST WANDERING THROUGH LIFE? REMEMBER, YOU ARE NOT AN ACCIDENT OR A MISTAKE. YOU HAVE BEEN PURPOSED BY GOD FOR THIS MOMENT AND FOR THIS TIME TO DO SOMETHING GREAT IN HIS KINGDOM. RISE UP AND SEIZE YOUR DAY.

LIFE IS VERY GOOD!

John 15:16 says, "You did not choose me, but I chose you and appointed you so that you might go and bear fruit—fruit that will last—and so that whatever you ask in my name the Father will give you". How amazing is it to know that you have been adopted, grafted into the vine of Christ. Really, I mean take hold of that. He, the Lord God, chose YOU! You are not only chosen but He has appointed you as well. He has commissioned you to the task of bearing fruit, but not just any fruit, the fruit that will last. And, on top of that, He leaves you with the idea that, if you ask in His name, whatever it is, He will give it to you. Wow, what more can you ask for? You must know by now that God's purpose has always had you in mind. Rise up in His name and know that you are meant for such a time as this.

The Lord Says...

You should know that I do not make mistakes and, for every moment, there is a purpose. Even when you find your emotions down, you are not out, only shaken. I Am here to hold your hand. Meet Me where you are and together we shall seize the day, even if it is only minutes or hours at a time. You can do this. Keep smiling. I Am able, even when you are not.

If you believe it, say, "Oh yeah!"

MARCH 12
THE "SWEET TIME" SEASON

IN LIFE, SOMETIMES TRIALS COME AND TEST OUR FAITH, BUT A TRIAL'S PURPOSE IS TO PRODUCE PATIENCE. WHEN WE HOLD STEADFAST TO WHAT WE BELIEVE WITHOUT COMPLAINT, PATIENCE WILL PRODUCE ENDURANCE. ENDURANCE, IN THE MIDST OF ADVERSITY, WILL PRODUCE VICTORY. KEEP HOLDING ON AND KNOW THAT HIS LOVE HAS DELIVERED YOU.

LIFE IS VERY GOOD!

Isaiah 40:31 says, "but those who hope in the Lord will renew their strength. They will soar on wings like eagles; they will run and not grow weary, they will walk and not be faint". You know what's so great about being a Kingdom child? You don't have to worry; you just live your life knowing that God has your back no matter what. In the world it seems like the phrase, "there's an app for that", is supposed to solve all your issues. God's like that, you know. Whatever circumstance you are going through, He's got an answer for that. He is the way, the truth and the life. No matter how hard it gets, Isaiah tells you that all you have to do is put your hope in the Lord and He will recharge you with strength. Not only will He give you a renewed sense of strength; He will make you soar through life like eagles do, all while you run doing it. An added benefit is that you will not get weary or faint doing so. That covers a lot of ground right there and, I know, it can sometimes seem like God is taking His sweet time. Maybe He is. In the meantime, you are growing with patience, filling up with courage, exercising your strength, internalizing your faith and this, my friend, gives you the endurance to face the world in ANY circumstance.

The Lord Says...

Ah, taste and see that I Am good, for I do an exceptionally good work in you that you may become who you were destined to be. My love for you is deep and very wide. Complaining only costs you. Look at Moses; he was never able to physically walk into the promised land. Speak life, even if you cannot see it. If you do it long enough, you will believe it.

If you believe it, say, "Oh yeah!"

MARCH 13
A CURVEBALL HOME RUN

IN THIS LIFE, WE ARE ALWAYS MET WITH CHALLENGES. IT'S GOD'S WAY OF SEEING WHAT IS TRULY INSIDE OF US. AFTER WALKING THROUGH SEASONS OF FAVOR, TIME AFTER TIME, JOSEPH WAS STRIPPED OF HIS GARMENTS. HE COULD HAVE GIVEN UP BUT HE CHOSE TO HOLD ONTO HIS DREAMS. JOSEPH KNEW GOD HAD SOMETHING BIGGER FOR HIM THAN WHAT HE COULD EVEN SEE. FACE YOUR CHALLENGES HEAD ON. HE'S LIFTING YOU UP TO REIGN IN DOMINION.

LIFE IS VERY GOOD!

James 1:2-3 says, "Consider it pure joy, my brothers and sisters, whenever you face trials of many kinds, because you know that the testing of your faith produces perseverance". Now, when life throws you that curveball, you have this scripture to hold onto; the promise that you should consider it joy when you face trials. Why? Because from it all, you will gain perseverance. That is awesome. Like Joseph, this scripture will see you through. Hold onto it with all you've got and do not let it go. What God has for you is bigger than anything that would try to keep you from it. Keep plowing through and victory will be revealed.

The Lord Says...

You may be broke, your marriage looks destroyed, your boss seems unhappy, you're up to your neck in debt, your kids aren't living as they should, your blood pressure is through the roof, or maybe you have major medical issues, but, am I still not greater, bigger and stronger in your life than all of those things? Is not the dream of passion's purpose still resident inside of you? If I can see Joseph through betrayal and the dehumanization of being sold as a slave, to the prison house to betrayal again where his character was on the line, will I not do the same for you? Yes, the answer is yes, yes, yes!

If you believe it, say, "Oh yeah!"

MARCH 14
DON'T REINVENT THE WHEEL

SOMETIMES IN LIFE, GOD LAYS OUT A PATH BEFORE YOU THAT MAY SEEM IMPOSSIBLE TO WALK. IF YOU CHOOSE TO RUN AWAY, REMEMBER JONAH; HE WENT DOWN TO TARSHISH, DOWN TO THE BOTTOM OF A SHIP AND THEN FOUND HIMSELF DOWN IN THE BELLY OF A FISH, ONLY TO END UP IN EXACTLY THE PLACE GOD DESIRED. REMEMBER, HIS PURPOSE IS GREATER THAN OUR UNDERSTANDING. WALK IN OBEDIENCE TODAY.

LIFE IS VERY GOOD!

Sometimes running away seems a whole lot easier than facing real life situations. However, it seems that, whenever someone runs away, they always come back full circle to the place they left to begin with. I have a close friend who ran away when she was sixteen. It was winter and she ran to the neighbor's house. They gave her some hot chocolate, listened to her plight and sent her home. That is a literal running away. Though that type of running away still occurs in our modern age, there is a whole other kind of running away. Men, you don't want to deal with your wife when you get home, so you run away to the gym, fishing, using your toys or just plain old working late in an effort to not deal with the issues you are facing. Women, on the other hand, you often run to whomever will listen to your plight, or you find solace in running away to your favorite department store. Some people (men and women) run away to food, alcohol and other destructive behaviors, unhealthy for their lives and relationships. Kids run away with their earbuds and their music, their video games and their friendship culture. God wants you to run to Him.

Matthew 11:28-29 says, "Come to me, all you who are weary and burdened and I will give you rest. Take my yoke upon you and learn from me, for I Am gentle and humble in heart and you will find rest for your souls". Listen, if you aren't obeying God, then you are carrying a heavy burden in life. Jonah felt the burden and told his shipmates to throw him overboard. He couldn't take it anymore but he wasn't quite willing to obey. Obedience surely would have been better than the sacrifice of a whale belly experience, wouldn't you agree? Stop trying to reinvent the wheel. Learn from the mistakes of others, including your biblical forefathers of the faith. You know what is best for your kids, right? God knows what is best for you just the same.

The Lord Says...

Oh child, I Am your Father and I wish only good for you. Sometimes, though, you choose to not hear My voice or listen when I speak, or you do not consult my wisdom for your life. If only you would hear, listen and choose wisdom, the understanding would come to you in due time. You are My greatest treasure. Walk in the light.

If you believe it, say, "Oh yeah!"

MARCH 15
UNDERDOG TO VICTORIOUS WARRIOR

IN LIFE, THERE ARE TIMES WHEN YOU FEEL LIKE YOU'RE THE UNDERDOG. BUT IF YOU HAVE A LANGUAGE OF VICTORY, YOU CAN OVERCOME ANY OBSTACLE. DAVID TOLD GOLIATH THAT HE WAS ALREADY DEFEATED AND NOTHING COULD CHANGE DAVID'S MIND. DECLARE HIS WORD OVER YOUR CIRCUMSTANCES AND WATCH IT FALL BEFORE YOU.

LIFE IS VERY GOOD!

1 Samuel 17:45-47 says, "David said to the Philistine, "You come against me with sword and spear and javelin, but I come against you in the name of the Lord Almighty, the God of the armies of Israel, whom you have defied. This day the Lord will deliver you into my hands and I'll strike you down and cut off your head. This very day I will give the carcasses of the Philistine army to the birds and the wild animals and the whole world will know that there is a God in Israel. All those gathered here will know that it is not by sword or spear that the Lord saves; for the battle is the Lord's and he will give all of you into our hands".

Most people do not realize that David was declared to be a bastard's son and this is why he became a shepherd. It was not a job of honor. David's father, Jesse, came from a Moabite lineage. He married a Jewish woman. Years later when Jesse was old, he began to feel that his marriage was inappropriate so he shunned his wife of close to 30 years. Like Tamar, Jesse's wife pretended to be a prostitute, laid with Jesse and David was conceived. When Jesse finally came to this knowledge, he had to live with the idea that David was then considered a bastard son (Weisberg, Chana).

So you see, you look at David as a victorious warrior but he fought many battles from birth until death. In every battle, he knew who his God was and that all things were possible with God. His speech on the battlefield that day was not out of conceit but it was the strength and courage of God because he had already been down this type of road before; a road when he needed God to come through. God had never failed David and He will never fail you. David spoke truth. You must speak truth and it will set you free. Remember that the Word is your truth.

The Lord Says...

Speak My truth and it will always set you free. I Am the Word and the Word is in Me. Put the Word inside of you and begin to speak it. Watch and see how your situation will change. When you believe, all things are possible.

If you believe it, say, "Oh yeah!"

MARCH 16
DEMONSTRATE THE LAW OF MULTIPLICATION

JINGLES OR SLOGANS HAVE "EVANGELIZED" THE WORLD THROUGH MARKETING TECHNIQUES AND THE POWER OF SUGGESTION. JESUS, WITHOUT ANY MULTI-MEDIA OR ADVERTISEMENTS, INFLUENCED THE WHOLE WORLD THROUGH A LIFESTYLE THAT SAID, "FOLLOW ME", AND DEMONSTRATIONS OF HEALING THE SICK AND THE BROKEN-HEARTED FOLLOWED. HIS LIFE SHOWED THAT ONE MAN'S LIFE CAN MAKE A BIG DIFFERENCE. SO CAN YOURS.

LIFE IS VERY GOOD!

Jesus was the greatest businessman of all time, a network marketer genius. Whoever says word of mouth is an ineffective strategy is crazy. Jesus took twelve men. He challenged them to learn, lead and teach the same principles of the gospel to others. Here we are, thousands of years later, still preaching the same messages as they were taught in the days of antiquity. A simple, "Follow me." The disciples didn't even ask, "What's in it for me?" They knew and understood the power of His demonstration and the law of multiplication made sense. You make a difference everyday. When you send your offering to ministries like ours, other faith based organizations, the Red Cross during times of disaster, or when you give your time, talent and money for a good cause, you are spreading the love of Jesus through you and making a difference in the world. When you reach out to your neighbors who are struggling, your family who is ill, or your co-worker who has just enough money to put gas in the car without anything left to go out to lunch with everyone else, you are making a difference in the world. Ask yourself these questions: Am I available? What can I do today? Be the change in the world. Mark 16:15-16 says, "And he said unto them, Go ye into all the world and preach the gospel to every creature. He that believeth and is baptized shall be saved; but he that believeth not shall be damned" (KJV). You don't have to be a preacher, just be a carrier of love.

The Lord Says...

Go! Go and touch the world. It is as simple as that. I need you to make a difference.

If you believe it, say, "Oh yeah!"

MARCH 17
GROW BIGGER SHOULDERS

IN LIFE'S JOURNEY, WE ALWAYS ASK GOD TO TAKE AWAY WHAT IS HARD OR TO REMOVE WHAT WE DON'T LIKE SO OUR LIFE IS MADE EASIER. WOULDN'T IT BE GREATER TO ASK GOD FOR BIGGER SHOULDERS VERSES A LIGHTER BURDEN? HE'LL NEVER GIVE YOU MORE THAN YOU CAN HANDLE. HE CARRIED HIS CROSS, YOU CAN CARRY YOURS, TOO.

LIFE IS VERY GOOD!

Sometimes, this is just something you don't want to hear, but listen, we all travel down our own road in life. The seasons can wreak havoc on a road. If you have ever been in a place that has four seasons, you know and understand. Many roads get potholes from all the moisture and the expansion and contraction wet and sunny weather brings. Some roads you travel aren't paved at all; they are just less traveled country roads. When you travel the roads in life, you must learn to navigate those roads. The same can be said about life and the burdens you carry. First of all, if you employ Proverbs 3:5-6 and lean not unto your own understanding, then you are letting God be God in your life. So, let Him be who He is in your life and walk it through. You will be the stronger for it.

The Lord Says...

Trust Me with all your heart. Your human nature will not always make sense nor will the path(s) I lead you on. But, when you trust Me, all will be revealed and your journey understood. Stand in courage and trust. Endurance shall be your reward.

If you believe it, say, "Oh yeah!"

MARCH 18
JESUS' SHADOW

IN LIFE, SUCCESS ISN'T MADE BY WHAT YOU KNOW; IT'S BUILT ON WHAT YOU DO IN TIMES OF DIFFICULTY. JOSEPH REMAINED FAITHFUL, EVEN WHILE IN PRISON AND THE LORD PROSPERED ALL THAT WAS IN HIS HANDS. YOUR FAITHFULNESS WILL PROPEL YOU FORWARD AND BREED SUCCESS. DON'T WORRY, THE LORD IS WITH YOU AND HIS FAVOR IS UPON YOU.

LIFE IS VERY GOOD!

Psalm 84:11 says, "For the Lord God is a sun and shield; the Lord bestows favor and honor. No good thing does he withhold from those who walk uprightly". Favor comes with one pre-qualification: walking uprightly. Joseph prospered not because of his heritage, the color of his skin or his skills, per say. He was favored because he was faithful; he walked uprightly before God. In times of trouble, David also never faltered in his love for God. This was why, after all his mistakes, David was so loved by God. Above all, David loved God and because of that, he was able to recognize his mistakes and come back to God. God is with you day or night. Imagine for one day that, wherever you walked, a shadow would follow you and experience everything you did. Now imagine that shadow is Jesus. Would you live differently? Would you still be faithful and proclaim His Good News even in the midst of pain and trial like Job? God believes in you more than you believe in yourself. If you could just see what He sees in you, you would declare His love for you during both tragedy and triumph.

The Lord Says...

It is well when you are weary. It is well when you are weak. It is well when tragedy brings you to My feet. It is well not just when the sun shines. It is well, my child, all the time. You may not see it and that's okay. The sun (Son) is always shining, even on the cloudiest of days.

If you believe it, say, "Oh yeah!"

MARCH 19
THRIVE, DON'T CRUMBLE

THERE ARE PEOPLE WHO THRIVE DURING ADVERSITY AND OTHERS WHO CRUMBLE UNDER
PRESSURE. THE MENTALITY OF A CONQUEROR HAS AN ATTITUDE THAT SAYS, "I WAS BORN FOR
THIS". HE SEES SETBACKS AS OPPORTUNITIES FOR GREAT COMEBACKS. IT'S TIME TO OVERCOME
AND RISE UP IN HIS VICTORY. WE WEREN'T MADE FOR DEFEAT.

LIFE IS VERY GOOD!

Think of it like this. You cannot have a comeback without a setback. You cannot have a mountain experience without first having a taste of the valley. You cannot be a victor if you have not fought a battle. You cannot have a testimony without a test. For every action, there is a reaction. This is why praise is so necessary. The Bible says to "put on the full armor of God, so that when the day of evil comes, you may be able to stand your ground and after you have done everything, to stand" (Ephesians 6:13). The best way to stand, when you have done all you can do, is to praise. Praise strengthens the spirit within you and turns your focus to God instead of the circumstances at hand. Will you rise up in worship so you can be a victor, have a comeback, reach the mountaintop and have a testimony of His goodness in your life?

The Lord Says...

Together we are on an adventure. You may fall, but together we shall rise. You, indeed, were born for this moment. The opportunity is before you; see it for what it will be, not what it looks like, then believe with all you have inside, never doubting Me. Watch and see that it is good. I Am in the delivery business and My blessings will always come at the right time.

If you believe it, say, "Oh yeah!"

MARCH 20
BE A PERCEPTION SLAYER

WHEN YOU ARE OVERWHELMED BY A SITUATION, FEAR COMES TO TRY AND PARALYZE YOUR PERCEPTION. IT'S TIME TO TAKE EVERY THOUGHT CAPTIVE AND REMEMBER THAT GOD HASN'T GIVEN YOU A SPIRIT OF FEAR, BUT OF LOVE, POWER AND A SOUND MIND. LET HIS FAITH ARISE IN YOU AND YOUR ENEMIES WILL BE SCATTERED.

LIFE IS VERY GOOD!

Have you ever noticed that one man's perception is not always the same as another's? Perception is the perceived notion of a situation. Perception is your natural man's viewpoint. Perception is the opposite of faith because it is not based on anything but what is seen. Slay your perception. Romans 4:17 says, "As it is written: 'I have made you a father of many nations.' He is our father in the sight of God, in whom he believed—the God who gives life to the dead and **calls into being things that were not**". In other words, you will not always have the Thomas opportunity where seeing is believing. Faith will require the blind believing, which comes by seeing not what is perceived, but what shall be.

The Lord Says...

I Am the Lord your God; the light, the Father of the unseen, of all things good and what shall be. I Am the creative force behind all creation, the breath you breathe and My hand is in the sun, moon and stars. What more can I create for you when you believe the impossible? I love the challenge of the impossible. Won't you dream big and bigger and answer the call of your destiny? It is bigger than you could ever imagine. It is time. I stand at the door and knock. Are you home?

If you believe it, say, "Oh yeah!"

MARCH 21
FAVOR IS NOT A FAIR-WEATHERED FRIEND

IT'S A MISCONCEPTION TO THINK THAT FAVOR COMES ONLY TO THOSE DOING WELL. THE TRUTH IS, FAVOR CAN VISIT YOU EVEN IN THE TIME OF ADVERSITY TO SHOW THAT GOD HAS NEVER LEFT YOU. IN EVERY STRUGGLE JOSEPH FACED, GOD'S FAVOR WAS WITH HIM AND CAUSED EVERYTHING IN HIS HANDS TO PROSPER. FAVOR COMES THROUGH FAITHFULNESS, REGARDLESS OF THE SEASON YOU'RE IN. THE FAVOR OF THE LORD IS WITH YOU.

LIFE IS VERY GOOD!

Every season has its beauty, its wrath and its purpose. In winter, the deep freeze can paralyze your life, down power lines and make roads too icy to travel on. Yet winter is necessary for plants to rest and regroup and for animals that hibernate to receive rest. The picturesque views of trees and mountaintops covered by snow is a beauty to behold. Springtime brings the beauty and fragrance of new life, which serves its purpose. Yet melting snow and ice can cause disastrous flooding during spring. In each season you travel through, favor can be found. It may not look the same, but it's there. It may not seem like it's coming your way, but it is. God is never late; He is always right on time.

The Lord Says...

Favor is yours, says the Lord, but there are some who do not believe they are good enough to receive it. You have not because you ask not. You do not seek, so you have yet to find it. The difference between the mountaintop and the valley is this: the view. The mountaintop view allows you to see what you couldn't see from the valley because it changes your angle of perspective. Change your view and your opinion about yourself. You are My child and you're worthy of all I have for you.

If you believe it, say, "Oh yeah!"

MARCH 22
UNCOVER YOUR BURIED TALENTS

MANY TIMES, WE LIMIT OURSELVES BECAUSE WE FEEL LIKE WE'RE ONLY GOOD AT ONE PARTIC- ULAR THING. BUT, WHEN SOMETHING IN OUR ENVIRONMENT CHANGES, WITH A LITTLE DEDI- CATION AND HARD WORK WE CAN BE GREAT AT OTHER THINGS. JAMES AND JOHN WERE MORE THAN FISHERMAN, THEY WERE MIGHTY APOSTLES. AMOS WAS MORE THAN A SHEEP-BREEDER, HE WAS A PROPHET. YOU'RE MORE THAN WHAT YOU SEE WITH YOUR OWN EYES. GOD SEES UNLIMITED POTENTIAL IN YOU.

LIFE IS VERY GOOD!

The widow, who tried to save her sons from having to pay the family debt by becoming slaves, didn't find out she was more than a mother until she fell on hard times. The prophet told her to find every vessel she could and fill them with oil. It looked impossible. She didn't have much oil to begin with. She quickly found that not only did God call her to be a mother, but He called her to be a woman of business as well (2 Kings 4:1-7). You are more than you think you are. God made you unique, with gifts and talents that you need to take stock in. There are things you are good at that I would not be good at; this is because it is your gift. Find those gifts and talents. Cultivate them and nurture them to grow so God can use you in ever-increasing ways. Mothers, you were not destined to just be barefoot and pregnant. God is calling you out to be all that He has called you to be. Hus- bands, you were not called to work yourself to the bone. When you uncover your gifts and talents and begin move in them, your potential is limitless. Purpose will have been found.

The Lord Says...

Be all that I have called you to be and purpose will be revealed. Your passion lies within your gifts and talents; the things you love and nurture. Crave My will and My ways and follow Me all your days. You were destined for greatness; in the city and out of the city. My hand is upon you.

If you believe it, say, "Oh yeah!"

MARCH 23
SPEAK TO THE PHARAOH IN YOUR LIFE

WHEN YOU WANT SOMETHING TO CHANGE IN YOUR LIFE, REMEMBER THIS: JESUS NEVER SPEAKS TO THE THINGS HE WANTS, BUT SPEAKS TO WHAT'S HOLDING IT. WHEN MOSES WANTED THE CHILDREN OF ISRAEL OUT OF EGYPT, HE SPOKE TO PHARAOH. WHEN JESUS WANTED FISH, HE SPOKE TO THE WATER. WHEN GOD WANTED MAN, HE SPOKE TO HIMSELF, "LET US MAKE MAN IN OUR IMAGE." SPEAK TO YOUR PHARAOH TODAY AND WATCH YOUR CIRCUMSTANCES CHANGE.

LIFE IS VERY GOOD!

This is powerful. When your mind grabs ahold of this kingdom concept, your life will begin to change. It is not easy to change your speech, but it is one of the most effective ways to change your circumstances. What would happen to marriages if husbands loved their wives so much that they never spoke anything negative over them, to them or about them (even if they really wanted to)? But instead, built them up with praise, love and affection. The wife would feel loved unconditionally and she would begin to prosper in all she was called to do. When your wife prospers, husbands, you prosper. Wives, what would happen if you ceased from complaining about all you think your husband needs to do but doesn't and all he should be but isn't and instead, built him up with praise, thanks and encouragement? Husbands would feel loved, honored and appreciated. Speak to separation and divorce to receive restoration. Speak to anger and strife to receive joy. Speak to loneliness to receive fulfillment. Speak to addiction to receive freedom. Speak to illness and pain to receive healing. Speak to abandonment to receive acceptance. Speak to self-harm to receive deliverance. Speak to finances to receive wealth. You get the idea. Speak to these things and them to let go. Mark 11:23 says, "Truly I tell you, if anyone says to this mountain, 'Go, throw yourself into the sea,' and does not doubt in their heart but believes that what they say will happen, it will be done for them". The key here...do not doubt, just speak it and say it is so. God said if you don't doubt but speak to the mountain it will be removed. Don't be afraid, it's just the way it is…it's protocol. If you want things removed in your life, then you have to use your authority and tell them where to go.

The Lord Says...

When I speak, the world responds. When you speak, the atmosphere responds in like manner. The same authority that lies within Me now lies within you. That which Jesus did, so are you equipped to do: cast out demons, pray for the sick, believe and receive. No pharaoh is too big for us. We walk together, remember?

If you believe it, say, "Oh yeah!"

MARCH 24
THE MANY FACETS OF REST

WHEN YOU HEAR THE WORD "REST", YOUR FIRST THOUGHT IS A PLACE OF RELAXATION AND PEACE. BUT IT ALSO MEANS "A PORTION YOU DIDN'T KNOW GOD HAD STORED UP FOR YOU". ELISHA COMMANDED THE WIDOW TO SELL ALL THE OIL SHE AND HER SONS HAD COLLECTED TO PAY OFF HER DEBT AND THEN LIVE ON THE REST. THE "REST" SUPPLIED HER NEEDS AND OVERFLOWED IN ABUNDANCE. KNOW THAT GOD HAS HIS REST STORED UP FOR YOU IN THIS SEASON. HE WON'T FAIL YOU.

LIFE IS VERY GOOD!

Wouldn't you love to have so much that you had to ask the question, "What should I do with the rest?" The problem is that most people do not have rest (sleep and relaxation) and they do not have rest (peace) because they do not have the rest (portion left over). The widow listened and obeyed the prophet. Her obedience resulted in her ability to have the three types of rest because the scripture says she paid off her debt and lived off the rest of the oil. Her obedience set her up and her cup ran over. Now, that's Kingdom living.

The Lord Says...

My abundance is for more than just you. When you give, it comes back to you so much that you cannot contain it. My people operated the first social services programs. Why is the state responsible for the homeless, the widows, the orphans, the veterans and the single parents? My heart is that you would be the light. You be the source that rebuilds cities when anger burns them to the ground. You be the source when a mother has no place to place her head. You be the source when food is scarce for your neighbor. You be the source because I Am the source for you.

If you believe it, say, "Oh yeah!"

MARCH 25
THE POWER OF THE RIDICULOUS

FOR THE LORD TO BRING VICTORY TO A REGION, HE DIDN'T NEED 32,000 PEOPLE TO GET THE JOB DONE. ALL HE NEEDED WAS A UNIFIED 300. GIDEON, WITH ONLY 300 MEN, DID WHAT AN ARMY OF 32,000 COULD NOT: DEFEAT THE MIDIANITES. WHEN PEOPLE UNIFY IN OBEDIENCE TO HIS WORD, ALL THINGS ARE POSSIBLE. LIFT UP A SHOUT AND TAKE YOUR LAND!

LIFE IS VERY GOOD!

Sometimes God will ask you to do something that seems so ridiculous to the natural man but makes very good sense to Him. Even before Gideon fought with only 300 men, God asked him to do something that put his very life on the line. You can read about it in Judges 6:25-32. In order to understand what was happening in this scripture, here is some context. The Midianites were conducting raids on Israel, stealing their produce and anything else they could get their hands on. Israel was not living for God because the present generation had no recollection of the past miracles and wondrous things God had done for their people. In response, God turned Israel over to the Midianites. Even Gideon's own family members were worshiping Baal. Gideon was the only one found to be righteous.

God asked Gideon to do the ridiculous: to break apart the altar of Baal in his father's house. He was also to take two bulls, make a sacrifice with the 7 year old bull and destroy the Asherah tree. Gideon knew he would likely be killed for such an action but obeyed God anyway. And, for the 4th time, God said He would protect him. God was testing Gideon to see if he had everyday faith in HIM, not the miraculous. Gideon never really had a whole lot of faith in God at all. God had a mission for him and He was not letting go. Imagine the conversation when God told Gideon to release the majority of the army. God was trying to teach Gideon that his faith could not be in man, but in Him alone. Gideon's influence in the city and his history may have been different had he obeyed God from the beginning. In the end, he learned a hard lesson that all things are possible with God and God alone. Where is your faith grounded? In God? In man? In yourself? Put your life in order and watch it prosper.

The Lord Says...

My ways are narrow but they are good. Refuse to take the roundabout; it is only a distraction. Distractions equal delays and get you off the path I have for you.

If you believe it, say, "Oh yeah!"

MARCH 26
FALL FORWARD TO SUCCESS

BECAUSE YOU ARE IN A SEASON WHERE YOU CAN'T FAIL, REALIZE THERE ARE MORE IN THE HEAVENS STANDING WITH YOU THAN THOSE ON THE EARTH STANDING AGAINST YOU. THERE ARE MORE WANTING TO SEE YOU SUCCEED THAN THOSE WHO ARE HOPING YOU FAIL. DON'T QUIT NOW! YOUR MOVEMENT FORWARD CAUSES THE HEAVENS TO REJOICE.

LIFE IS VERY GOOD!

Psalm 103:21 says, "Praise the Lord, all his heavenly hosts, you his servants who do his will". In other words, God has His folks in heaven (angels and the like) doing His will for Him. There has never been, since the beginning of time, a moment or a thought that you would not succeed. There is nothing negative about God because God IS Love. So quitting, rejection, abandonment and failure, they are all real and yes, in the natural they do happen in life, but those qualities do not determine who you are, how you move forward or whether you will succeed in life. God says that, despite those things, you cannot fail. You first must believe it. Do you believe it?

The Lord Says...

Failure is only a stepping stone to success. Failure is not whom I say that you are. Abandonment is someone else's loss, for you are My child, whom I carry in My heart and in My arms. You are more than enough for Me. Those who reject you only reject Me. So, My child, love without limits, even when you think you can't. Determine to step one foot in front of another, listen for wisdom, get understanding and obey in My time. I love you, My child, you are more than enough.

If you believe it, say, "Oh yeah!"

MARCH 27

BE THE MIRACLE

IN LIFE, WE ARE ALWAYS LOOKING FOR GOD TO "SUDDENLY" APPEAR IN OUR SITUATIONS. WE NEED TO STOP WAITING FOR THE UNEXPECTED; WE MUST BECOME THE UNEXPECTED HAPPENINGS OF GOD. EVERY ENVIRONMENT YOU'RE IN, GOD HAS PLACED YOU THERE FOR THAT MOMENT TO BECOME HIS EXPRESSION OF CHANGE. THIS IS YOUR NOW SEASON TO BE A WORLD CHANGER.

LIFE IS VERY GOOD!

I believe that attitude is everything. It shapes your mindset, will bring you up, bring you down and determines the attitude in your life. Philippians 2:5 says, "In your relationships with one another, have the same mindset as Christ Jesus". In other words, you were made in the image of Christ, so I encourage you to act like it. What does this mean? It doesn't mean being so heavenly minded that you are no earthly good. It means to stop worrying about every little detail in your life and let God handle it. Make yourself more concerned with the lives of others than that of your own life. What can you do for your neighbor? Can you be the miracle they need? Did you know that, in the Jewish faith, there are two types of tzedakah (or charity)? There is the first tzedakah, which is charity, and the second tzedakah, which is called the ma'aser kasifim (the 10% commanded by God). The highest form of tzedakah is to help someone before they become destitute; assisting them in finding a job, helping them secure a loan or start a business, all so they do not become dependent on anyone else for their livelihood. Imagine if someone came to your door. They had a family of four and had lost their livelihood. We have it all wrong in the world. Wealth was never meant for us alone; wealth was meant to spread the love of Jesus. If this form of tzedakah is required by Jews, imagine, they have to have some money to spread the love around. Could you help that couple that came to your door to find work, secure a loan or start a self-supporting business? The majority of people could not, but one should strive to. It is the church that should feed the church. Will you be what your neighbors need? Will you be the miracle from heaven that delivers gas, groceries, pays the bills or rent for a year? Will you be the one who buys all the prescription drugs or pays for doctor co-pays? What would happen if you paid off all your bills and were debt-free then, once debt-free, used that money to do the same for someone else or help sustain a life? Maybe your neighbor needs a suit for an interview or something as simple as a haircut. You can become the expression of change in your neighborhood, community, church, state and nation. It starts with just one. Will you go?

The Lord Says...

I need you, the moms who cook, to deliver meals to those who cannot. I need you, the teachers who teach, to tutor those who can't pay. You, the mechanics, to fix cars for those who don't have the means. I need your communities to build one another's homes and to show My love by families loving other families. I need the different, the rejected and ashamed and know that I love them by you loving them. Will you be the one? All you have to do is believe in Me. Miracles occur everyday and sometimes, that miracle takes YOU!

If you believe it, say, "Oh yeah!"

MARCH 28
CHANGE GEARS

To shift your situation of despair, you need to overcome the words of limitation that have confined you. You overcome them when you grow tired of the words of restriction holding you hostage. Be like Mary Magdalene, who broke open her flask and poured her offering over Christ, not allowing the Pharisees' words to confine her. It's time to break the chains and allow His freedom to transform your situation.

Life is very good!

Colossians 4:6 says, "Let your conversation be always full of grace, seasoned with salt, so that you may know how to answer everyone". This includes answering yourself. What does your self-dialogue tell you everyday? Never let the words of others hold you hostage, but, equally important, don't let your own tongue hold you hostage. When the world says you can't, replace it with the scripture that says you "can do all things through Christ" (Philippians 4:13). Pour out to God with your tongue, a sweetness like honey and transform yourself and others through the power of the Word.

The Lord Says...

Yes, both life and death are in the power of your tongue. Restrict not, but flourish much. Become who you were meant to be and let your tongue know Who reigns in you and through you. Do not be limited by the words of others but move forward by what I, your Father, have spoken over you.

If you believe it, say, "Oh yeah!"

MARCH 29
ENOUGH IS ENOUGH

TO OVERCOME YOUR ADVERSITY, IT STARTS WITH A CHOICE. THE FOUR LEPROUS MEN COULD
HAVE CHOSEN TO SIT AND DIE IN THEIR STRUGGLE, BUT MADE A CHOICE TO MOVE FORWARD.
THEIR DECISION ALLOWED GOD TO MOVE ON THEIR BEHALF. WHEN YOU RISE UP AND TAKE A
STEP OF FAITH, GOD WILL MAKE YOU A MIGHTY SOUND THAT CHASES AWAY YOUR ADVERSITY.
GO AHEAD, RISE UP TODAY.

LIFE IS VERY GOOD!

Take a lesson from these leprous men. Being diagnosed as a leper meant more than a skin condition. Leprosy is a contagious disease that attacks the nerves. It is evident by lesions on the body and can disfigure people. In antiquity, a leper represented someone with an incurable disease who was filled with sin. Leviticus 13:4 calls the leper "unclean." During this time, the King of Syria had conquered the city and famine was rampant in the land. The lepers could not enter the city; they stayed outside the city gates. They were dying of hunger. In II Kings 7:4, they were contemplating their life. They determined that, whether they went into the city or not, they were going to die. Yet, in verse 3, the lepers convinced themselves that they couldn't just sit there outside the city and die. They decided "enough was enough" and reasoned to move in the night. They went into the abandoned Syrian tents and ate, drank and retrieved riches. The key was this: The lepers rose up and took a leap of faith because, after all, what did they have to lose? I challenge you today…what do you have to lose? Give it up. Give it all to Jesus, be renewed and refreshed. He's got your back.

The Lord Says...

I Am the God of more than enough and I have great plans for you. You may feel defeated, but you are not forsaken. You may feel abandoned, but you are not alone. You may feel rejected, but My love is enough. I Am all that you will ever need.

If you believe it, say, "Oh yeah!"

MARCH 30
VICTORIOUS EVEN BEFORE THE BATTLE

THE POWER OF DECLARATION MAKES EVIDENT THE THINGS HIDDEN IN DARKNESS. IT SHINES
GOD'S LIGHT UPON IT AND CAUSES THE DARKNESS TO BE TRANSFORMED. SPEAK TO THE
MOUNTAIN AND IT WILL BE REMOVED. SPEAK TO THE FISH AND LOAVES AND THEY WILL BE
MULTIPLIED. SPEAK TO THE INFIRMITY AND HEALING WILL COME. SPEAK HIS VICTORY TODAY!

LIFE IS VERY GOOD!

Joshua 1:8 says, "Keep this Book of the Law always on your lips; meditate on it day and night, so that you may be careful to do everything written in it. Then you will be prosperous and successful". When you are meditating on the Word day and night, you cannot help but be successful. Those mountains cannot help but move and multiplication becomes your portion. Why? Because the attitude of expectancy and faith as a King's child reigns true not only on your lips, but your actions and your attitude. A King knows he has the victory before the battle has ever been fought. You cannot be double minded in your ways and expect the earth to move on your behalf; only faith has this privilege. Believe and speak it. Believe it and see it. Believe it and know it is done.

The Lord Says...

I Am the first and the last, the same today as yesterday and all your tomorrows. I Am the way, the truth and the life. Every battle you try to fight tires you because the battles are Mine and the victories are ours. Believe it, see it, speak it and walk it out, for it is done.

If you believe it, say, "Oh yeah!"

MARCH 31
PATIENCE = PROGRESS

WHEN WE'RE IN THE SEASON OF CHANGE, WE WANT TO SEE A FULL TRANSFORMATION OVERNIGHT. IN DOING SO, WE OFTEN OVERLOOK THE EMERGING GROWTH AND CHANGE TAKING PLACE. WE NEED TO REALIZE THAT, AS A PERSON BLOSSOMS, IT'S A SIGN THAT IMMATURITY IS FADING AND MATURITY IS STARTING TO FLOURISH. BE PATIENT, MORE IS BEING ACCOMPLISHED THAN WHAT YOUR EYES CAN SEE.

LIFE IS VERY GOOD!

Psalm 24:1 says, "The earth is the Lord's and everything in it, the world and all who live in it". This passage tells us that all belongs to God and, as you were created in His image, that includes you. Let this season of change allow you to emerge into all He created you to become. When you look into the mirror, begin to discover who it is that God sees. Be patient, He is not finished with you yet. You are always a work in progress.

The Lord Says...

I Am my beloved's and you are mine. I have much love for you and there is much work to be done. Have patience, dreams do not come to pass overnight. They take goals, planning and walking it through. Dreams require dedication, determination and perseverance...no matter the cost. This brings forth much growth and change that are necessary for your days ahead. Trust me. I know the plans I have for you and I can see much farther down the road than you can ever imagine.

If you believe it, say, "Oh yeah!"

APRIL 1
THE REALITY OF YOUR DREAM

IN DIFFICULT SEASONS, WE ARE QUICK TO DECLARE WHAT WE CAN'T HANDLE, BUT IF WE LOOK AT THE APOSTLE PAUL, HE WAS SHIPWRECKED, BITTEN BY A VIPER, STONED AND WHIPPED 5 DIFFERENT TIMES TO THE BRINK OF DEATH, BUT YET, HE ENDURED. THE WORD SAYS THAT PEOPLE WITHOUT VISION PERISH, SO THE TRUTH IS, PEOPLE WITH VISION LIVE, THEY OVERCOME AND CONQUER ALL. GOD'S VISION WILL KEEP GIVING YOU LIFE!

LIFE IS VERY GOOD!

Here's the thing: a vision represents your destination and/or your goal. When you have a vision, you will stop at nothing to get there. And, when you use wisdom along the way, you will avoid as many potholes as possible. Reading Psalm 29:18, it says, "Where there is no revelation, people cast off restraint; but blessed is the one who heeds wisdom's instruction". Walk in it. Sometimes potholes and detours are out of your control. You might lose your job, get in an accident and it eats your funds or something just comes up; that happens. But, when you have Jesus, you need never lose hope. Keep the dream alive. Life is worth every moment. Resurrect your vision. If you want a great marriage then set some goals and make a plan do what it takes to achieve that vision. If you strive to be a successful entrepreneur, set goals so you can reach your destination. Maybe you need a career change to get where you're going or lessons to sharpen your craft. It's time to shine and let God arise in the vision He has placed inside of you. He's the reality of your dream.

The Lord Says...

Speak it, believe it, plan for it, walk in My ways and it shall be so. With you and I together, all things are possible. Pray, believing for the promise. Believe without an ounce of doubt and even mustard seed faith will see that you conquer the giants before you. Seek Me and I shall be found. Knock and the door will be opened to you. I Am here, just a breath away.

If you believe it, say, "Oh yeah!"

APRIL 2
BE GOD-FOCUSED

IN A WORLD FULL OF DISTRACTIONS, THE KEY TO APPREHENDING WHAT YOU DESIRE IS MAINTAINING YOUR FOCUS. ELISHA WAS ABLE TO KEEP HIS EYES ON ELIJAH THROUGH THE CHARIOT AND HORSES OF FIRE AND THE WHIRLWIND. WHEN YOU DESIRE THE GREATER TO MANIFEST IN YOUR LIFE, DISTRACTIONS WILL COME TO DETER YOU, BUT NEVER TAKE YOUR EYES OFF WHAT YOU'RE CHASING. FOCUS ON IT UNTIL YOU RECEIVE IT.

LIFE IS VERY GOOD!

Colossians 3:2 says, "Set your minds on things above, not on earthly things". Be wise. Keeping your eyes on the vision is important, but keeping your eyes on the vision without God can be disastrous. Look what happened to Abraham. He was so focused on the son God promised him that he orchestrated the vision to come forth without considering God's ways. Abraham's focus became a distraction. When God's vision for Abraham's life came to pass, God had to make sure Abraham was focused on HIM, not his son. So what did God do? He tested Abraham to see if he would sacrifice the very vision HE alone gave him. Keep your focus on Jesus in the midst of finding your way towards the vision that He gave you for your life. Take your eyes off yourself, but not off of HIM!

The Lord Says...

I Am the way, the truth and the life. By Me and through Me, your vision shall come to pass in the time to which its purpose must be fulfilled. Be patient and endure.

If you believe it, say, "Oh yeah!"

APRIL 3
JESUS IS THE ANSWER

NO MATTER HOW DIFFICULT OR TRYING THE SITUATION YOU FACE IS, REMEMBER THIS: WHAT YOU ARE GOING THROUGH, HE ALREADY WENT THROUGH. YOU CAN DO IT BECAUSE HE'S ALREADY DONE IT. YOU ARE VICTORIOUS BECAUSE HE IS VICTORIOUS!

LIFE IS VERY GOOD!

Hebrews 4:15 says, "For we do not have a high priest who is unable to empathize with our weaknesses, but we have one who has been tempted in every way, just as we are—yet he did not sin". Come on, somebody! This is great news! In other words, Jesus, our high priest, has been through some serious stuff. He knows pain, heartache, betrayal, temptation, illness and sacrifice. He is able to carry your burden. He walks with you when you feel alone. He carries you when your strength is all but gone. He lifts your hands when you are too weak to praise on your own. He comforts you, guides you, strengthens you, hides you, builds you up, is your light and whatever you have need of. He is the answer. Do you have need of Him? Because, in this life, the difficulty compounds when you try to do it alone. You really do need Him.

The Lord Says...

You need Me, My child and I have need of you. Together we can make the world a place of love, joy and peace. You are victorious. Walk in your victory today.

If you believe it, say, "Oh yeah!"

APRIL 4
YOU ARE NEVER ALONE

THERE MAY BE TIMES WHERE YOU FEEL LIKE YOU'RE WALKING IN THE DARK, BUT KNOW IN THIS JOURNEY THAT YOU ARE NEVER ALONE. THERE IS NO PLACE YOU CAN GO WHERE HE IS NOT PRESENT. FROM THE HEIGHTS OF HEAVEN TO THE DEPTHS OF HELL, HE IS THERE. HE IS THE LIGHT THAT ALWAYS SHINES IN THE MIDST OF DARKNESS.

LIFE IS VERY GOOD!

Science tells us that the sun is always shining. When it's night in your area, it's day somewhere else. When it's day in your area, it is night somewhere else. Even when the clouds cover the sky or when darkness falls, the sun is always shining. 1 Corinthians 15:46 says, "The spiritual did not come first, but the natural and after that the spiritual". In the natural, the sun is always shining. In the spiritual, the Son is also always shining in your life. Even in your darkest hour, the Son will light your way. He did it for everyone in the bible and He will do it for you. In every season, He is with you.

The Lord Says...

I Am with you, even until the ends of the earth. I Am the light in a darkened world for there is only darkness in the absence of light, but true light is always shining. I Am the light of the world. Come unto Me this day. Rest in Me and I will light the way for you. I Am the candelabra to guide your steps and the lighthouse light to guide your ways. I Am here and, because I Am, it is well.

If you believe it, say, "Oh yeah!"

APRIL 5
UNLOCK THE FUTURE

THE POWER OF YOUR WORDS CAN UNLOCK OR CONFINE THE FUTURE FOR SOMEONE ELSE. BE WISE IN HOW YOU SPEAK. SPEAKING AN ENCOURAGING WORD WILL NUDGE SOMEONE FORWARD AND HELP TO UNFOLD THEIR DESTINY. BUT, GIVING A NEGATIVE COMMENT IS LIKE SLAMMING THE DOOR IN SOMEONE'S FACE. USE THIS DAY TO UPLIFT THOSE AROUND YOU. RELEASE HIS GOOD NEWS!

LIFE IS VERY GOOD!

Ephesians 4:29 says, "Do not let any unwholesome talk come out of your mouths, but only what is helpful for building others up according to their needs, that it may benefit those who listen". Taking care to build up and not tear down other people in life is essential to spiritual maturity. It isn't easy but it is necessary. When you think about it, you have the power to change someone's life; for better or worse. If you smile and give an encouraging word, how much more will that person do than if you were to tear them down with a discouraging word? It's easy to lash out in response to your emotions. However, the cleanup isn't always great. I challenge you to hold your tongue. Pray in the spirit. Pray and cover that person with love from your tongue even when you feel like doing something else. The people around you need Jesus as much as you do.

The Lord Says...

I Am the Master Builder. I know what you need and where it needs to go. When you go rogue in this life without Me, do I speak badly of you? No, even My chastisement comes with a dose of love. Be the love you seek to receive. Be the words you long to hear. Give them and they will come back to you again.

If you believe it, say, "Oh yeah!"

APRIL 6
SEEDS OF HOPE

HAVE YOU EVER NOTICED THAT IT'S EASY TO DO THE MEANINGLESS THINGS IN LIFE BUT, ON THE OTHER HAND, TO DO THE THINGS MARKED FOR GREAT PURPOSE IS OFTEN DIFFICULT? REMEMBER THAT THE PATHWAY OF THE MEANINGLESS LEADS TO A DEAD END WHILE THE ROAD OF PURPOSE IS AN OPEN HIGHWAY OF OPPORTUNITY. PUT YOUR HEART INTO THE THINGS THAT HAVE ETERNAL MEANING. I GUARANTEE THAT IT PAYS OFF IN THE END.

LIFE IS VERY GOOD!

Have you ever known a person that seems to have everything, at least everything that you could ever want? They may have a really nice house, cool cars, a great education for their children or a few weekend toys. They may frequent decent eating establishments or wear expensive clothing. They seem to have it all, but they tell you they feel empty. This is because material things will never satisfy you. Material things are temporal; meaningless in the scope of life. When you have Jesus, it's the little things that matter; asking someone if they need prayer, baptizing a friend who came to know Jesus, discipling a new brother or sister in the Lord or being the light of Jesus to your world. Those things have meaning. They are deeper than the surface and they are life changing. Be HIS image in all that you do and you will find more meaning in life than you could ever imagine. Galatians 5:13-14 says, "You, my brothers and sisters, were called to be free. But do not use your freedom to indulge the flesh; rather, serve one another humbly in love. For the entire law is fulfilled in keeping this one command: 'Love your neighbor as yourself'". Serve in love and find more meaning.

The Lord Says...

I was first a servant. I created for you. I cared for you. I sent My Son for you. I do all for the love of you. You, too, must first serve others and here you will find more meaning than you will know what to do with. You will touch more lives than you could ever imagine. You will plant seeds of hope. You will see faith bloom. You will witness the harvest of meaning in the lives of others as the chain continues. Be the seed and faith will grow.

If you believe it, say, "Oh yeah!"

APRIL 7
LEAVE YOUR TROUBLES BEHIND

FOR CHANGE TO HAPPEN, THE HARDEST STEP TO TAKE IS THE FIRST ONE. DON'T LET THE THOUGHT OF FAILURE KEEP YOU PARALYZED FROM MOVING FORWARD INTO YOUR DESTINY. YESTERDAY AND ITS TROUBLE ARE BEHIND YOU. TODAY AND HIS PROMISE ARE BEFORE YOU. TAKE THAT STEP OF TRANSFORMATION. YOU'RE IN A NO FAIL SEASON.

LIFE IS VERY GOOD!

You may not think fear is holding you back but, when you begin to analyze where you are and where you want to go, you will often find that the reason you haven't reached your destination is because of fear.

I know a woman who was never great at math. In the midst of high school she had already reasoned that she couldn't go to college for two reasons: one, she was poor and two, she was not good at math. She knew even if she could go to college that she wouldn't be able to pass the math. So, she graduated from high school and got the courage to attend a local community college. She proved herself right by earning a "D" in a math economics class. She worked three jobs to pay the rent and decided that she couldn't do it. Fast forward twenty-seven years into the future and she finally comprehended that, in order to reach her destiny, she would need an education in her craft.

Applying for college was easy. The hardest step was that first math class and reasoning in her mind that she was Kingdom and she could do it. She attended every math tutoring session possible and learned that, while math may not have been her gift, she could conquer it. She never earned less than a B! Pretty good for someone who never went to college because of math to begin with, right? She left her trouble behind her and graduated cum laude from a prestigious university in the Pacific Northwest. She became the first in her family to graduate from college with a Bachelor's degree and, all at 45 years old. Now, her gift is making room for her. Transformation may take time but opportunity is waiting. This is your time and this is your hour. Step into your season.

The Lord Says...

You see, My child, with Me you cannot fail. For I Am with you always. Every road may not be perfect for this is an imperfect world. But, you can conquer just the same. When you reach for the stars, you'll land somewhere in the stars but if you never reach, there is nowhere to land. Nothing plus nothing will always equal nothing. To change and transform your life, you must do something different today than you did yesterday because the same thing you're doing in life will not transform your life into something different than it already is. Change is never easy, but it can be great for you.

If you believe it, say, "Oh yeah!"

APRIL 8
GRACE FOR MISTAKES

IN LIFE, MAN LOOKS AT WHAT HE'S DONE WRONG AND CALLS THAT FAILURE. GOD SEES OUR "FAILURE" AS STEPPING STONES AND CALLS THEM "OPPORTUNITIES TO LEARN." DON'T TEAR YOURSELF DOWN. LET HIS WORD BUILD YOU UP ONE STEP AT A TIME. KEEP MOVING FORWARD.

LIFE IS VERY GOOD!

Pain is meant to alert you that something is off, wrong or out of order. Mistakes are meant to teach you right versus wrong, what works and what doesn't. This is why kids should be given grace to make mistakes, especially at home. Home is their training ground for life, the place where they learn what works and what doesn't. By being disciplined to make their beds everyday, maybe they'll keep their office desk clean. By making mistakes, they will learn what it takes to solve their problems with workable resolutions. We all make mistakes. In the book of John, Jesus acknowledged the mistakes of the adulterous woman, but He also told her to live her life and to not make the same mistake anymore. God wants you to learn from your mistakes, forgive yourself and keep moving forward. There is little time to waste. He is coming back soon. So listen to the direction of His Word and do not let mistakes keep you from your tomorrows. Every season has its journey, its weather and its attitude. Embrace your time within it.

The Lord Says...

To everything there is a season under the sun. Every mistake is covered by My grace. My love covers and My grace rescues. Mistakes only become lessons learned. Embrace them, but do not repeat them for time is too short to dwell on what has passed. I will always be there for you.

If you believe it, say, "Oh yeah!"

APRIL 9
WAIT ON GOD

In life, when you come to a crossroads, don't see it as a difficult choice. Perceive it as an intersection where each pathway can lead to blessings and opportunity. Remember, the steps of the righteous are ordered by the Lord. He is the perfect pathway that leads you to victory.

Life is very good!

The crossroads. It sounds so daunting, doesn't it? It can be if you are not living a life of prayer, reading the word and listening to God. This is why I Thessalonians 5:17 says, "pray continually". When you're in consistent prayer and you come to a crossroads, the "if" questions will be answered as you wait on God. You will know in your "knower" (your spirit) the direction God wants you to go. Remember, He will never lead you astray. If you put Him first and seek Him, He promises that He will answer you with awesome deeds of righteousness (Psalm 65:5). Give God a try. He's yet to let anyone down. Sometimes His answer may not be the answer you want. At those times when His answer doesn't agree with what you wanted, what you really wanted was for God to come along with you on your journey instead of you traveling with Him on His journey planned especially with you in mind. God just doesn't work that way. Stay on the straight and narrow, for He is there.

The Lord Says...

I Am on the path. Will you take My hand and walk with Me? Will you talk with Me? Will you be My first love? Will you embrace Me, My will and My ways? Will you listen when I speak? Will you run to Me each day to come and see Me? Will you sit by the river and enjoy My company? Will you pray, for even a moment? I Am the way, the truth and the life and, to come to the Father, you must first embrace ME.

If you believe it, say, "Oh yeah!"

APRIL 10
DESIGNED FOR VICTORY

GOD HAS DESIGNED YOU TO OVERCOME EVERY PROBLEM AND SITUATION YOU FACE IN LIFE. THERE IS NOTHING THAT YOU CAN'T SOLVE, NO MOUNTAIN YOU CAN'T CLIMB AND NO BURDEN THAT YOU CANNOT CARRY! GO AHEAD AND OVERCOME. YOU CANNOT FAIL!

LIFE IS VERY GOOD!

Victory first starts in the mind. God thought about His creation in His imagination, and then He spoke it into existence. The same is true for you. You will never have the victory if you cannot see it first. A king never entertains defeat. He is always thinking of victory. It's time to train your brain for victory. See victory, even through the whirlwinds of life. Speak victory, even if you need a walking stick to make it up the mountain. Walk with your head up high like you are victorious. And, most of all, keep your eyes on Jesus. When you come to the river's edge, Jesus is already on the other side with His hand stretched out…waiting for you. Sometimes, though, too many people stop at the river's edge and look at the raging current instead of Jesus. Jesus wants you to be like a child who hasn't seen their military parent in nine months. Nothing gets in the way of that child hugging their parent. So when you get to the river's edge, don't see the water, just see Jesus. Don't let the water of renewal become the barrier that keeps you from your victory. You cannot fail when your eyes are on Jesus alone for, when you begin to think, speak and walk like Him, you become victorious like He is victorious. Philippians 4:13 says, "I can do all this through him who gives me strength". Do you believe it? Let it be your yes and amen.

The Lord Says...

I wait at the river's edge for you and together we will continue the journey on the trail I have set before you. You can cross the river if you only believe. Look into My eyes and do not let go. Reach out your hand and feel My hand upon yours, My arm around your shoulder and My smile of encouragement that will bring you through. It is only you that keeps you from victory, for the victory has already been won.

If you believe it, say, "Oh yeah!"

APRIL 11
THE UPTAKE ADVANTAGE

WHEN A MESSAGE OF VICTORY IS DEPOSITED INTO AN UNDERDOG, HIS MINDSET SHIFTS AND HE REALIZES HE HAS NOTHING TO LOSE. HE IS FREE TO GO FOR IT. TODAY, KNOW THAT YOU'RE ALREADY VICTORIOUS BECAUSE HE IS. FULFILL YOUR DREAMS. YOU HAVE EVERYTHING TO GAIN.

LIFE IS VERY GOOD!

The underdog syndrome has an advantage called uptake. The underdog has a greater chance of taking his/her game up and having a greater streak of victory simply because of the ground they must cover to obtain victory. In other words, when you're at the bottom, you can only go up and the victory of an underdog is much sweeter because no one expects the underdog to win. Sometimes, not even the underdog expects a win. To win as an underdog requires the uptake of skill, determination, passion, fire and abandoning all other voices for victory's sake. You may feel like the underdog, but don't count yourself out just yet because God is in the underdog business. He thrives on taking the underdog and resurrecting them for His goodness. Endurance is the prize an underdog receives that makes his/her victory even sweeter. 1 Corinthians 9:24 says, "Do you not know that in a race all the runners run, but only one receives the prize? So run that you may obtain it". You be the one, the underdog, who puts in the time and wins the race.

The Lord Says...

Practice, practice, practice! Practice what you preach. Practice where you want to go. Visualize it in your heart. Declare it as so. You can do anything if you only believe in Me. So run, I say. Run strong. Run long. Run to the music. Run in the wind. Run and watch what I will do in your life. I will meet you in your endurance and I will give you strength. I will meet you at the finish line and I will give you peace. So run the race and run it well, My child. Run and run again. I wait for you.

If you believe it, say, "Oh yeah!"

APRIL 12
THE STONES OF DESTINY

DO YOU WANT TO KNOW A WAY TO GET THE ENEMY REALLY UPSET? PURSUE YOUR GOD-GIVEN ASSIGNMENT. CHASING AFTER YOUR DESTINY INVOLVES COMPLETELY TRUSTING SOMEONE OTHER THAN YOURSELF AND LAYING DOWN YOUR OWN LIFE TO TOTALLY WORSHIP THE ONE WHO LAID HIS LIFE DOWN FOR US. AN ADDED BENEFIT OF UPSETTING THE ENEMY, THERE'S A JOY THAT COMES FROM KNOWING THAT ONE MORE PERSON IS PART OF THE KINGDOM. GO AFTER HIS ASSIGNMENT FOR YOUR LIFE!!

LIFE IS VERY GOOD!

Sometimes I wonder if David really even knew his God-given assignment. His father put him in the fields as a shepherd and he became good at it. Quite possibly, he didn't even realize that he was good at leading because he could lead sheep. But God saw a greater vision for his life. David, however, just walked in what he knew. He pursued the skills used by a sheepherder in general life. In other words, if he could kill a lion and a bear with just a sling shot and God's help, then he could do the same in other realms of life. God used what David was good at to give him access to the King's court, so David could begin to learn and taste what it would mean to be King one day. David's brothers weren't happy about David's presence on the battle field. By stepping up, David's courage made his brothers feel inadequate. Saul wasn't happy with David, either. David's integrity and courage intimidated Saul. So, walking in your destiny is never easy, but David had a heart of worship and reconciliation towards God and God loved him. Don't be afraid. Pick up the stones and take a shot at your destiny in life. What are you good at? What ignites your fire? Your assignment is closer than you think.

The Lord Says...

You are My ambassador; the voice of heaven in the earth. In you I have placed many gifts and talents. Gifts and talents that speak to your fulfillment and bring you great joy. Worship Me and allow Me to use your hands for My glory. May the fire of My Spirit ignite the flames of destiny inside your heart.

If you believe it, say, "Oh yeah!"

APRIL 13
THE PROCESS OF THE PROMISE

WHEN GOD GIVES YOU A DREAM, THE DREAM SPEAKS OF A PROMISE, BUT NOT THE PROCESS.
IF WE KNEW THE COST OF THE JOURNEY, IT WOULD BE EASY TO SAY NO. WHEN WE SEE THE
PROMISE, IT GIVES US A PASSION TO MOVE FORWARD. DON'T LET YOUR SEASONS DISCOURAGE
YOU. HIS PROMISE IS WORTH LIVING FOR.

LIFE IS VERY GOOD!

Walking in your life's passion and purpose is 99% process and 1% opportunity. You cannot have opportunity without process. If God gave you the opportunity
without the process, you would never appreciate the opportunity when it presented
itself to you. Even in the process, your purpose will go through transformations
in due seasons. Perhaps you purpose to be a teacher. You obtain your teaching
credential and you receive a job offer. Your passion and purpose are now fulfilled,
so now what? The season will change. You will begin to grow and prosper in that
purpose; maybe expanding to a specialty within that purpose or go higher than you
thought you would in an effort to produce growth and change. Joshua 1:9 says,
"Have I not commanded you? Be strong and courageous. Do not be afraid; do not
be discouraged, for the Lord your God will be with you wherever you go". I love
that. Throughout the process, you are never alone. He is truly able to meet your
needs, so be strong and courageous, unafraid and encouraged and know that GOD
is with you always.

The Lord Says...

My child, I Am with you always. Be encouraged not discouraged, for I will
make you strong. Do not be afraid, for you never walk alone. Let process make the
way for opportunity in your life.

If you believe it, say, "Oh yeah!"

APRIL 14
REDEEM THE TIME

To be instant in season or out of season has nothing to do with being ready for something; it means being consistent in all things. God is watching how you handle your weary season, so don't faint, because in due time you will receive your reward. The greater promises are looking for you.

Life is very good!

This scripture is found in 2 Timothy 4:2, which reads, "Preach the word; be instant in season, out of season; reprove, rebuke, exhort with all long suffering and doctrine". In other words, redeem the time, in your weariness and in your strength. Do not let distractions or potholes in the road derail you from your purpose. Be thoughtfully consistent in all that you do. Your life becomes a living testimony of Christ's image on the earth. What will your life say? Be the gospel and the ambassador of Christ to your world. It's not up to the pastor of your church to win your community, it's up to you. He said first to "preach the Word", so don't be afraid to deposit in others what Christ has first deposited within you.

The Lord Says...

If you are in Me and I Am in you, then where I go you go and what I speak you speak. The disciples were not just the twelve. You, My child, are My disciple, so raise up your neighbor with My image expressed through your voice, your actions and your life. Be kind one to another and love for I Am love. This is the Word come to life in the world and they will know Who I Am. The One who loves. The One who cares. The One who heals. The One who gives. The One who sets in order. I Am that I Am. Who do you say that I Am today?

If you believe it, say, "Oh yeah!"

APRIL 15
NO FAIL SEASON

THE WORD PROCLAIMS, "DECLARE A THING AND IT WILL BE ESTABLISHED." WHEN YOU ESTABLISH SOMETHING, IT'S MADE FIRM AND STABLE IN YOUR LIFE. NOW THAT IT'S FIRMLY ROOTED, LET'S MAKE IT OUR ANTHEM. OUR "NO FAIL SEASON" IS MORE THAN JUST VOCABULARY, IT'S OUR LIFESTYLE.

LIFE IS VERY GOOD!

It may sound crazy to walk around proclaiming your healing, your new job or your relationships restored when, in the natural, they seem far from healed. Believing is first seeing, not the other way around. Seeing not with the natural eyes, however, but seeing with the spiritual eyes. If you can see your healing, then you can believe with that child-like faith that it has already been done and you receive it. If you can speak and declare that job you see yourself in, you will become that in which you speak. Begin speaking God's Word into your life because it establishes who you are, your authority, the strength of your faith and plays a hand in how far your endurance will take you. Endurance is a necessary skill. Anyone can run a race. How long you last in that race is based on your endurance training. Cultivating endurance in your life must start with the declaration of the word in your life. Once the word is established and comes to pass in your life and you believe it, you can begin to believe for other things.

The Lord Says...

Be encouraged to speak what I speak, hear what I say, listen to My words of encouragement and discipline, walk where I walk and then, your endurance will be tried and tested. Strength belongs to those who rise with Me and take joy in who I Am in their life.

If you believe it, say, "Oh yeah!"

APRIL 16
SEEDS OF TALENT

PHYSICAL STORMS ARE NOT AN ACT OF GOD'S JUDGMENT OVER A REGION; THEY ARE JUST A PART OF LIFE. WHAT IS AN ACT OF GOD, HOWEVER, IS HOW WE, THE BODY OF CHRIST, COME TOGETHER WITH COMPASSION TO RESTORE WHAT MAY HAVE BEEN LEFT IN RUINS. BE A HAND THAT HELPS REBUILD, A HEART THAT SHOWS MERCY AND A VOICE THAT SPEAKS LIFE.

LIFE IS VERY GOOD!

I was recently moved by an Act of Kindness that displayed who the church is meant to be on this earth. In the spring of 2015, there was a violent unrest in the city of Baltimore. A senior center, which was being built largely by a local church to provide housing, employment assistance and a variety of programs to the Baltimore community, became a target of the unrest and was burned to the ground. On a local news channel, the pastor of this local church was being interviewed by the evening news anchors. To his surprise, a businessman in the Midwest (who ran a highly sought after architectural firm) heard the pastor's story. This businessman called into the news program and offered to rebuild the church. He promised to submit architectural plans better than what the senior center previously had acquired. I thought this story was amazing.

So many people talk bad about the church for having money, but during the storms of life, it is the church who is supposed to support the welfare systems of the community. How great would it be if wealthy Christians were able to build churches, businesses, support unwed mothers' homes, community centers, after school programs or just pay off someone's debt? Imagine how great it would feel to build up, plant into and support your community in such a way. Together, we are making a difference. Every time you support your local church, our ministry and others, you are taking part in restoration of people in regions all around the world. Ask yourself this question, "What can my hands do?" When you find that answer, plug in, go into all your world and become the gospel your world seeks. Your pastor is but an arm in this journey. You are the feet.

The Lord Says...

That which the world seeks lies within your hands: compassion, love, kindness, mercy, goodness, gentleness, self-control, meekness and all the fruit of the Spirit. This fruit bears fruit. When you plant one apple seed, do I not give you more than one apple? You are forever receiving multiplications of apples and seeds from just one seed. I have given you seeds of talent and giftedness, seeds of purpose meant to be fulfilled, not for your purpose alone, but for the life of others, that they too may benefit, be moved, shaken and changed for My glory. Amen.

If you believe it, say, "Oh yeah!"

APRIL 17
STAND STRONG

WHEN YOU FACE A SEASON FILLED WITH ADVERSITY, REMEMBER, STAND FIRM IN YOUR FAITH OR YOU WILL NOT STAND AT ALL. YOU WILL EITHER BE LIKE A DEEPLY ROOTED TREE PLANTED BY THE RIVERS OF LIVING WATER OR LIKE A TUMBLEWEED BEING BLOWN BY EVERY GUST OF WIND. DON'T STOP CONTENDING! KEEP BELIEVING AND GOD WILL ANSWER.

LIFE IS VERY GOOD!

Have you ever seen a tumbleweed? They are dry, brittle and, though they may be small, they seem to grow and grow by attaching themselves to other tumbleweeds. A herd of tumbleweeds blowing in the dry wind is a force to be reckoned with; they don't stop for anyone. They keep on rolling in the wind without direction and certainly will not provide you with any needed shelter. In contrast, let's look at the great oak tree. It provides amazing shelter. Its trunk and branches, though aged, are strong and sturdy. Even during a storm, the oak tree will continue to stand. Jesus doesn't want you to be a tumbleweed in life. Be like the oak; stay planted by the river and let the living water soak into your roots. Deuteronomy 31:6 says, "Be strong and of good courage, do not fear nor be afraid of them; for the Lord your God, He is the One who goes with you. He will not leave you nor forsake you". Now, that's something you can stand on. No matter how hard you get hit by the storms of life, your strength and courage lies in Christ alone so there is no reason for fear to be near you. He is with you always. That's a gift.

The Lord Says...

Be courageous. I did not create you to be like a tumbleweed, being blown by the winds that try to come against you. Stand like a tree, planted and strong, knowing in Whom you have your identity. Be a contender of the faith. I Am with you always.

If you believe it, say, "Oh yeah!"

APRIL 18
MORE THAN A CONQUEROR

WHEN DIFFICULT THINGS SEEM TO MANIFEST IN YOUR LIFE, REMEMBER, IT'S NOT AS IT SEEMS. EZEKIEL SAW A VALLEY OF DRY BONES, BUT GOD SAW AN EXCEEDINGLY GREAT ARMY. GIDEON CALLED HIMSELF THE LEAST IN HIS FATHER'S HOUSE, BUT GOD SAW HIM AS A MIGHTY MAN OF VALOR. MOSES SAW HIMSELF AS A MAN WHO COULDN'T SPEAK BUT GOD SAW HIM AS A DELIVERER OF HIS PEOPLE. IT DOESN'T MATTER HOW YOU VIEW THE CIRCUMSTANCE, ALL THAT MATTERS IS HOW GOD SEES IT AND HE SEES YOU VICTORIOUS!

LIFE IS VERY GOOD!

2 Kings 6:17 says, "And Elisha prayed, 'Open his eyes, Lord, so that he may see.' Then the Lord opened the servant's eyes and he looked and saw the hills full of horses and chariots of fire all around Elisha". If you ask God to open your eyes, He will. If you could see what God sees when He looks at you, instead of the image in the mirror, you would walk victoriously everyday. You are HIS workmanship, a temple of the Holy Spirit. You more than a conqueror, fearfully and wonderfully made, a citizen of heaven, a prince/princess of God's kingdom - His child, the redeemed, blessed with every spiritual blessing and forgiven - that's just the start of who you are. So when you look in the mirror and all you see are the past and present mistakes, failures and a lack of strength, look again. One more time, look again and begin to see Jesus that resides in you. He is the risen King, the healer, the One who can bring the dry bones of your life and relationships to life once again. He is the One who can raise you up to pray for the restoration of your marriage and family. He is the One who can deliver you from your oppression. He is indeed the same today as He was then. He is able. Are you willing to put in the work?

The Lord Says...

I Am God in all of your situations and I change not. I Am the same God of Abraham and the One you serve today. I Am able to do above and beyond what you could ever think or imagine. You are My inspiration and for you the world was created - for you and My glory.

If you believe it, say, "Oh yeah!"

APRIL 19
A SURE FOUNDATION

WHEN THE STORMS OF LIFE COME UPON YOU, IT'S EASY TO BECOME DISCOURAGED AND ALLOW OTHER'S FEELINGS TO AFFECT YOU. THE WAY TO OVERCOME IS TO MAKE A FIRM DECISION AND NOT BE TROUBLED. BE LIKE DAVID, WHO ENCOURAGED HIMSELF IN THE LORD EVEN WHEN HIS MEN SPOKE OF STONING HIM. BE LIKE SHAMGAR WHO, USING AN OX GOAD, REMOVED 600 PHILISTINES AND DELIVERED ISRAEL. BE LIKE SHAMMAH WHO DEFENDED HIS FIELD EVEN WHEN EVERYONE ELSE RAN AWAY. YOUR DECISION TO STAND OPENS THE DOOR FOR GOD TO INTERVENE. MAKE UP YOUR MIND AND WATCH GOD MOVE.

LIFE IS VERY GOOD!

James 5:11 says, "As you know, we count as blessed those who have persevered. You have heard of Job's perseverance and have seen what the Lord finally brought about. The Lord is full of compassion and mercy". Endurance allows you not to be troubled when a tornado comes ripping through your house. Your natural man may be affected by the present circumstances, but it is your firm foundation in Christ that keeps you grounded. Praise the name of the Lord no matter what; that's what endurance looks like. When you can be beat up from head to toe by this world but can still say, "yet will I praise Him", you have chosen to stand and let God move.

The Lord Says...

Be like the wise man who built his house upon Me, the Rock of Ages, and not the sand. For in a storm, is it better to be grounded on a sure foundation and not on a surface that so easily shifts. Be encouraged and watch as I open doors for you in due season.

If you believe it, say, "Oh yeah!"

APRIL 20
DO NOT WORRY

WHEN GOD IS CALLING US TO GREATER THINGS, THERE IS ALWAYS A MOVEMENT THAT NEEDS TO TAKE PLACE. HE IS LEADING US TO GOOD THINGS BUT IT TAKES EFFORT FOR OUR FAITH TO LINE UP WITH HIS THOUGHTS. EMBRACE THE ADVENTURE THIS NEW LEADING BRINGS AND ENJOY THE TREASURES IT HOLDS FOR YOU.

LIFE IS VERY GOOD!

Acts 17:28 says, "For in him we live and move and have our being. As some of your own poets have said, 'We are his offspring'". How cool is that? You are alive because of God and you live, you move and you have your being because of Him. Instead of reading the Bible just as words on a page or books within a book, actually take it in. Let His Words breathe upon you so that you may walk in the image you were meant to walk in - His image. For example, perhaps funds are super low to non-existent this month. Stand on Matthew 6:25, which tells you not to worry about the food you will eat, the clothes you need to wear or to worry about your life. God knows what you have need of. Stand on that scripture, continue to give of your time, your talent and your tithe/offering. Then watch as doors that never existed begin to open for you. Trust HIM, He knows what you have need of and the adventure with Jesus is far better than trekking it alone.

The Lord Says...

Whatever you have need of, I Am here. Take My Hand and have no fear. Whatever it is, I Am able to deliver. Enjoy the journey with Me and trust that I have My best in store for you. Will you believe?

If you believe it, say, "Oh yeah!"

APRIL 21
FOR THE LOVE OF YOU

WHEN IT COMES TO GIVING, LOVE IS AN ESSENTIAL PART. REMEMBER, GIVING WITHOUT LOVE IS POSSIBLE BUT LOVING WITHOUT GIVING IS IMPOSSIBLE. JESUS CHRIST CAME TO EARTH BECAUSE HE LOVED AND, BECAUSE HE LOVED, HE GAVE EVERYTHING OF HIMSELF FOR US. TO BE TRULY LIKE HIM, WE NEED TO DO THE SAME.

LIFE IS VERY GOOD!

Love...to Jesus it's a simple choice. The human nature, however, contemplates the condition to which one loves, which was never Jesus' intention. John 13:34 tells you that to love is not something God is asking you politely to do. It is something God is commanding you to do. What does that mean? Like a parent, He is telling you that you MUST do it. It is required. And, to let you know how serious He is about it, Matthew 5:43-48 requires one to love not just the lovable, but the unlovable; your enemies. Not only does God require you to love them, but He requires you to pray for them, too. When you're at odds with someone, that is a tall order. When someone doesn't believe like you, that's a tall order. But, the more you do it, the more you love and pray for everyone (including your enemies and those who persecute you), the more filled with love and compassion you will become. After all, John 3:16 says that God loved you so much that He gave the only Son He had to come down on earth, face ridicule, humiliation, beatings and torture, just to die for you. Wow! I think you can stretch your heart and love beyond yourself. Be HIS image and love to the limits.

The Lord Says...

I Am love. My breath, My touch, My comfort, My forgiveness, My redemption, My sacrifice and My kindness. All I have to give, it is all for the love of you. Without love, what have you on this earth? I Am the living hope found in love. When you find love in Me, you find hope and realize you are never alone.

If you believe it, say, "Oh yeah!"

APRIL 22
HARVEST YOUR DESTINY

TO SEE LIFE CLEARLY, YOU NEED TO HAVE THE RIGHT PERSPECTIVE. A PERSON CAN COUNT HOW MANY SEEDS ARE IN AN APPLE BUT THE SAME PERSON CAN'T TELL HOW MANY APPLES ARE IN A SEED. REMOVE THE VEIL OF LIMITATION UNTIL YOU SEE WHAT HE SEES. A SEED HAS ENDLESS POSSIBILITIES AND SO DO YOU. DREAM BIG.

LIFE IS VERY GOOD!

A seed seizes the opportunity presented. When the seed is planted in the ground, the soil, moisture and light are the maintenance and all work together, in tandem, allowing the seed to fulfill its destiny. You can plant a seed for your dream but, without a plan that works in tandem, you create the limitations to which your dream can grow. Like a seed planted in the ground, a dream needs a good foundation (soil). What are you doing for that foundation? Are you saving funds to start your business as a corporation, trademark your name, copyright your music or, perhaps, you need an education? What about watering the dream (moisture)? Did you create a good soil but fail to write a business plan or put yourself in an environment where you dream might flourish? Your dream must be watered with wisdom, planning and marketing. If you've done those two things, then your business or your dream should be close to operational. Now, it's time for maintenance. Get out there, live it, and don't neglect it. Manage your dream and give to others. A seed will grow…it just needs the opportunity to flourish. Provide yourself with that same opportunity.

The Lord Says...

Go into all the world. Get out of the church walls and into the city, the marketplace, the homes of family and friends, the community and organizations. Be the light where your dream is built and maintained. I Am in you, not the four walls of the church. Therefore if I Am in you, then I Am wherever you are and I meet the needs of the world to which you are engaged. Seek Me and I will be found. After all, your dream is within My plan.

If you believe it, say, "Oh yeah!"

APRIL 23
BE A WISE LEADER

YOUR ATTITUDE IN DIFFICULT SITUATIONS REFLECTS WHO YOU FOLLOW. AN IMMATURE LEADER
WILL PRODUCE CHILDISH ACTIONS IN HIS FOLLOWERS. BUT, A FATHER OR MATURE LEADER
WILL DEPOSIT IN YOU A FRUITFUL NATURE TO MAKE WISE CHOICES. FOLLOW HIM, FOR HE HAS
THE BEST IN STORE FOR YOU AND WILL NEVER LEAD YOU ASTRAY.

LIFE IS VERY GOOD!

Exodus 18:21 shows the type of person to look for in a leader and what makes good leadership. It reads, "But select capable men from all the people—men who fear God, trustworthy men who hate dishonest gain—and appoint them as officials over thousands, hundreds, fifties and tens". Leaders are capable, God-fearing, trustworthy and without selfish gain. A father-type leader is not intimidated by the next generation. In fact, he/she takes pride in the idea that those they lead may become equally as good, if not better, because of their mentorship. This should be a compliment to leaders so I encourage you to pour into people who value your gifts and your talents. Look forward to God raising you up, not by those who want use of your gifts and talents for their own gain. Be wise; always put your eyes on Jesus, not the works of any man or woman. Jesus will guide you down the straight and narrow every time. The rewards will be great.

The Lord Says...

Let patience do a work in you. Be wise with your choices of leadership and the attitude of your heart. The circle that surrounds you should propel you into your purpose, not create a stench of stagnation in your life. Go therefore and be all I have ordained you to be. Pursue, overtake and recover all; not some, but ALL.

If you believe it, say, "Oh yeah!"

APRIL 24
GRANTOR OF MULTIPLE CHANCES

THE FORECAST OF YOUR LIFE MAY HAVE LOOKED DARK AND GLOOMY BECAUSE OF YOUR PAST FAULTS, BUT THEY ARE ALL BEHIND YOU. GOD IS THE AUTHOR OF NEW BEGINNINGS AND THE GRANTOR OF SECOND, THIRD AND FOURTH CHANCES. DON'T GIVE UP ON YOURSELF BECAUSE GOD WON'T GIVE UP ON YOU.

LIFE IS VERY GOOD!

This is a prime example why it is necessary to renew your mind daily. The enemy loves to remind you of your past. He does that so he can inhibit the growth of your future. What would happen if you forgave yourself, never looked back and purposed never to repeat the same mistakes in your life? Jesus has already done that for you. When you asked for forgiveness, He forgot; threw it into the sea of forgetfulness. He looks forward to your tomorrows and gives you a clean slate. Too many people think the devil inhibits their future when they inhibit their own growth by allowing yesterday to dictate today and tomorrow. Unbelievably, due to a lack of creativity, in his younger years, Walt Disney was fired from his job at a local newspaper. What would have happened if Walt Disney would have allowed this impactful event in his life to dictate what he could accomplish in his future? Mickey Mouse and Disneyland may not exist today. Years later, through the acquisition of the ABC network, Walt Disney ended up owning the very newspaper that fired him. Now, millions of people flock to Disneyland properties worldwide to pursue fun and entertainment; all from a dream that did not die. Have you given up on a dream because the road's been too tough? Dig it up! It's resurrection time.

The Lord Says...

There is a purpose for everything under the sun and failure is only but a stepping stone to a greater glory in your life. Without pain, you won't know what to fix. Therefore, the pain of failure is a tool in the footprints of success. Every success first had a failure. Believe again. Walk in victory for I have already overcome.

If you believe it, say, "Oh yeah!"

APRIL 25
REST IS A GOOD THING

THERE ARE TIMES WHEN WE GET SO OVERWHELMED WITH THE CARES OF THIS WORLD THAT OUR MINDS GET SCATTERED. WE BECOME LIKE SHEEP THAT WANDER OFF ON A DARK AND CLOUDY DAY. BUT, THE LORD WILL SEEK US OUT AND LEAD US TO A PLACE OF REST AND PROVISION. LET HIS LIGHT SHINE ON YOU TODAY. HE MAKES ALL THINGS NEW.

LIFE IS VERY GOOD!

Rest is a misunderstood subject. There are two types of rest, but we rarely focus on both; "rest" as in sleep, calming or relaxation and "rest" meaning a form of peace or resolve. Allies form a peaceful agreement and they have resolve. When you go on vacation, you go for rest and relaxation. When you sleep at night, it is to get rest. You really need more of both. Stress is literally killing people with heart attacks and high blood pressure because it raises the cortisol levels to a consistent fight-or-flight level. Your body was never intended to live in a flight-or-fight mode. You are working just to live and strapped from pay-check to pay-check. You don't go on vacation, you can't sit still and you never take time off for yourself or with your family.

People often ask me how many vacations we go on because we get out a lot. I finally decided that I need Rest and Rest. To keep peace in your marriage, you have to wine and dine your wife for life. I enjoy rest and relaxation with my wife and with my family. So, we get away, we go on vacations and we try to lay low and have fun as much as possible. Start living! Even if you only have enough funds for a cup of coffee with a friend or your spouse, get out and do it. Move more; walk with friends at the park. When Abraham stepped out, he didn't know where he was going, but he went for it and God came through. Are you resting? Do you have peace in your life? If your life is in chaos and you're always tired, then you need to re-evaluate the stress vs. rest/peace in your life. If God said He rested then it must be a good thing.

The Lord Says...

Rest, rest, rest! Rest in Me. Live in peace a life without regrets. Recharge and rejuvenate your body, mind and spirit. I have given you this earth as your playground; the water, the land and sky. Love it and live.

If you believe it, say, "Oh yeah!"

APRIL 26
BREATHE LIFE

WHEN UNEXPECTED DRAMA COMES INTO YOUR LIFE, IT CAN CHANGE YOUR SEASON INTO
A DIFFICULT ONE, FILLED WITH FRUSTRATION AND DISAPPOINTMENT. BUT, IN THE TIME OF
DESPAIR, BEGIN TO SPEAK HOPE. IN THE MIDST OF TRIBULATIONS, BELIEVE HIS GOOD NEWS.
TURN THE SEASON AROUND AND WATCH YOUR LIFE CHANGE.

LIFE IS VERY GOOD!

Psalm 43:5 says, "Why, my soul, are you downcast? Why so disturbed within me? Put your hope in God, for I will yet praise him, my Savior and my God". You may be facing that difficult time in life, but praise Him even more. When you praise and speak His Word into your life's circumstances and that of others, you are literally breathing and speaking life into them. When you speak life and His Good News into your life and others, you will begin to see how God is more than able to move mountains on your behalf. Speak life even when you feel like you can't. Just the act of faith can produce miracles. Look at what happened when Moses spoke life to Pharaoh and told him to let his people go. Moses was doing exactly what God told him to do and, eventually, it turned their season around and changed their lives.

The Lord Says...

Don't be afraid. The world needs more Esthers, Gideons, Joshuas, Calebs and Moseses who are not afraid to stand and speak life amidst their circumstances. You can set a miracle in motion. I Am a miracle working God and I will work on your behalf. Stand strong and in My might.

If you believe it, say, "Oh yeah!"

APRIL 27
THE BEAUTY OF CHANGE

YOUR LIFE IS BETTER DEFINED BY WHERE YOU'RE GOING RATHER THAN WHERE YOU'RE CUR-
RENTLY STANDING. THE STRUGGLES OF TODAY ARE OLD NEWS TOMORROW. WHAT WAS CAN
NO LONGER BE, BECAUSE CHANGE HAS COME. THE PAST IS GONE AND YOU ARE WALKING INTO
YOUR NO FAIL SEASON. IT'S A NEW DAY IN HIM.

LIFE IS VERY GOOD!

Really contemplate the idea of change for a minute. Change occurs every second in your life. What happened one second ago is in the past in this moment. What happened ten minutes ago is the past already. How cool is that? God is in the starting over business, but change is a constant in life. You have to be willing to roll with the punches. Jeremiah 29:11 says that God "knows the plans [he has] for you." So, yeah, you may get off the path but just dust yourself off, stand up and pull your life back into order and start running again. When you begin to understand that you cannot fail, you will begin to live it everyday. For in Him is life and life more abundantly. The day has only just begun.

The Lord Says...

I Am for you, therefore who can be against you? I Am with you to guide and to keep you. What more do you have need of? Your yesterdays - gone. Your tomorrows - filled with possibilities. Make a decision today, to live for tomorrow, not yesterday or only today. Become a big picture people.

If you believe it, say, "Oh yeah!"

APRIL 28
INFECTIOUS ATTITUDES

IN LIFE, YOUR ATTITUDE IS CONTAGIOUS. A GOOD ATTITUDE IS WORTH CATCHING WHILE A BAD ATTITUDE IS LIKE A PLAGUE, INFECTING THE ENVIRONMENT AROUND YOU. SAUL'S DAUGHTER DESPISED DAVID WHILE HE DANCED AND HER MENTALITY LEFT HER BARREN. DON'T LET NEGATIVITY OR MISUNDERSTANDING CAUSE GOD'S PROMISE TO BE UNFRUITFUL IN YOUR LIFE. LET YOUR ATTITUDE BE CHANGED BY HIS LOVE.

LIFE IS VERY GOOD!

You've probably heard it said that your attitude will determine your altitude. It's so true. Put a pessimist and an optimist in the same room. Give them a challenge and the optimist will fight till they find an answer and the pessimist will try a few things and find it's just not possible. Jesus is the greatest example of attitude. We sometimes forget, though He was 100% God, He was also 100% man. Jesus had the attitude of giving and, because He always thought of others, His attitude created an atmosphere of prosperity. Prosperity isn't just financial. He prospered in relationships (friendships), business, ministry, leadership and health just to name a few. People wanted to be around Him so what He had could be multiplied and rubbed off onto them. It's too easy to get caught in "me and mine." For example, maybe you have donated a ton of time to an organization or a ministry and begin to wonder why they haven't mentioned your contribution to anyone… after all the work you did for them? Instead, isn't it better just to know that you donated your time to a good cause that will benefit others? Doing so has made you into the image of Christ to your world. That's the giving attitude that Jesus had. Do you have the giving attitude? When my friend's mom saw that she and her sibling were having a bad attitude, the mom would say, "attitude check" and the kids were supposed to respond with "Praise the Lord." From time to time, everyone needs to check in their attitude with a little "Praise the Lord." Hallelujah!

The Lord Says...

Praise Me in the morning and when the sun goes down. Praise Me when the moon shines bright and the stars twinkle at night. Praise tears down the "you" and lifts Me up and will change your attitude. Give and it will be given, more than you could ever contain.

If you believe it, say, "Oh yeah!"

APRIL 29
REVIVAL BEGINS FROM WITHIN

RELIGION PREACHES A MESSAGE, EXCITING US FOR A MOMENT, BUT NEVER CHALLENGING US TO GROW. THE MESSAGE OF THE KINGDOM CAUSES US TO LAY DOWN OUR CURRENT SUCCESS TO DO EVEN GREATER THINGS THAN WHAT JESUS DID. THE DISCIPLES LEFT BEHIND ALL THEY HAD BECAUSE THEY KNEW THERE WAS SOMETHING MORE THEY COULD ATTAIN. RISE UP TODAY AND GO AFTER IT!

LIFE IS VERY GOOD!

Revival begins within. The root of the word revival is "revive." Kingdom messages provoke revival within the hearts of man, prompting people to fulfill their destiny. Religion, on the other hand, often preaches at you, telling you what to do and what not to do. I don't know about you, but being preached at gets old. I'd much rather be equipped to become than preached at to become. Jesus didn't preach religion to the disciples; he challenged and taught them to become the message. In like manner, Jesus is challenging you to step outside your box and become in a greater capacity. John 5:8 says, "This is to my Father's glory, that you bear much fruit, showing yourselves to be my disciples". With Jesus, multiplication always follows and the disciples understood this concept.

The Lord Says...

Give and it shall be given. It is a simple and profound principle. Choose to live a Kingdom life, unbound by religion. I will teach you what you need to know in order to mature and grow into what I have called you to do. I designed you to flourish. I have given you life so you can revive others from their sleep. Ignite someone today.

If you believe it, say, "Oh yeah!"

APRIL 30
FAITH AGAINST ALL ODDS

WHEN FEAR MANIFESTS IN YOUR LIFE, IT PARALYZES YOU AND KEEPS YOU FROM DOING WHAT GOD HAS CALLED YOU TO DO. WHEN FAITH MANIFESTS, IT MOBILIZES YOU TO DO WHAT IS SEEMINGLY IMPOSSIBLE. NOAH BUILT AN ARK FOR THE DELIVERANCE OF HIS FAMILY. SARAH HAD HER PROMISED CHILD EVEN WHEN SHE WAS PAST CHILDBEARING AGE. AGAINST ALL ODDS, STAND IN FAITH AND RECEIVE YOUR PROMISE. YOU'RE IN YOUR NO FAIL SEASON.

LIFE IS VERY GOOD!

I Corinthians 2:5 says, "So that your faith might not rest on human wisdom, but on God's power". When fear manifests in your life, it's because you allowed it to seep in and take root. That's the "human wisdom" this scripture is talking about because fear is not an attribute of God. God can only manifest faith in your life. It is for this reason that the scripture tells you to lean on God and His power instead of your own. You cannot fail when faith and trust in God is the fuel for your life.

The Lord Says...

Trust that I love you and know you better than you know yourself. Trust that I will deliver you. Trust with all the faith you have that it may saturate fear and mobilize destiny in your life. Amen.

If you believe it, say, "Oh yeah!"

MAY 1
SEASONS OF STRENGTHENING

WHAT YOU HAVE EXPERIENCED IN LIFE, GOOD OR BAD, CAN BE USED FOR GOD'S PURPOSE. HE CAN TAKE YOUR MESS, PUT AGE ON IT AND MAKE IT YOUR MESSAGE. HE CAN DELIVER YOU FROM A TESTING AND GIVE YOU A TESTIMONY. YOUR SEASON, WHICH SEEMED TOO DIFFICULT TO HANDLE, HAS ACTUALLY SEASONED YOU FOR THE GREATEST BREAKTHROUGH. HE DID IT FOR JOB, APOSTLE PAUL AND I KNOW HE IS DOING IT FOR YOU!

LIFE IS VERY GOOD!

I Peter 3:15 says, "But in your hearts revere Christ as Lord. Always be prepared to give an answer to everyone who asks you to give the reason for the hope that you have. But do this with gentleness and respect". Your message and your testimony allow you to become the salt of the earth. And, in so doing, the world will know that Jesus is King in your life. He brought you out, pulled you through and prepared you for your greatest breakthrough. He is your hope today and forever. He is no respecter of persons. Therefore, what he did in the days of antiquity, he can and will do for you. He will do miracles, signs, wonders, deliverance and bringing into order lives filled with chaos. He did it for Job and the Apostle Paul, do you believe he will do it for you too? He will.

The Lord Says...

Believe and then receive. All the goodness I Am is poured out for you. Your process becomes an opportunity and your chaos, an architectural blueprint for reconstructive change. I Am your construction crew and your contractor. I get results, just take My hand and trust me through your process. Amen.

If you believe it, say, "Oh yeah!"

MAY 2
GOD IS A VISIONARY

IN LIFE HAVE YOU EVER FELT LIKE YOU'VE COME UP SHORT, OR DOES THE PAST SEEM TO HAUNT YOU? REMEMBER, GOD HAS A WAY OF TAKING WHAT YOU WERE, AND TRANSFORMING IT INTO WHO YOU ARE. HE SEES THE GREATER YOU. THERE IS NO MISTAKE; WE'VE BEEN MADE GREATER BECAUSE OF WHAT HE DID ON THE CROSS. IN CHRIST, ALL PATHWAYS LEAD TO VICTORY.

LIFE IS VERY GOOD!

One thing that I love about God is that He's all about the big picture; He is a visionary. In our flawed human nature, it's so easy to get stuck in the moment; the chaos happening in your present. It then becomes difficult to see the greater picture of your life. Take a look at Joseph's life. God had the big picture in mind for Joseph, but he probably did not see it through his pain and chaos. Can you imagine a Joseph story happening today? It almost seems unimaginable. I work with young people all the time and I cannot even imagine a youth being sold in our day and age. But put yourself in Joseph's shoes for just one moment. How would you feel if someone sold you? You may feel like God left you to die, or had forgotten about you. You certainly wouldn't be thinking of how great the future would be. But God...God does see the greater picture. He knew Joseph had to go through some stuff in an effort for Joseph to become all that God had planned for his destiny. You're going to go through some stuff, but allow God to transform your heart, your mind and your soul. Jesus paved the way for your success and just because you go through some stuff in the process doesn't mean you will come out defeated on the other side. Take up the sword, your word, and declare your victory through the process. Then watch as God turns your midnight hour around. Keep your eyes on him alone.

The Lord Says...

No matter what Joseph went through, he never forsook Me. He always loved Me and cried out for Me in his midnight hour and I met him; in the pit, in the jail cell, in Potiphar's, during a famine and when his family returned. I thought of everything and I was with him on the whole journey, just as I Am with you on your journey too. You are blessed for I hold your big picture in My hand and the earth is My footstool.

If you believe it, say, "Oh yeah!"

MAY 3
LIFE LESSONS FROM THE CARPENTER'S SON

MANY TIMES WE DEAL WITH INSECURITIES IN OUR LIVES THAT CAUSE OUR FOUNDATIONS TO FEEL UNSTABLE. BUT WHEN WE REALIZE OUR LIFE IS BUILT ON THE ROCK, NOTHING CAN SHAKE US. PETER STOOD STRONG AFTER JESUS AFFIRMED HIM SAYING, "FEED MY SHEEP." THOMAS HAD NO REASON TO DOUBT AFTER HE TOUCHED JESUS' HANDS AND HIS SIDE. WHEN YOU FIND SECURITY IN HIM, YOU CANNOT FAIL.

LIFE IS VERY GOOD!

In Matthew 7:24-27, Jesus exhorts that everyone who hears His voice should heed His wisdom and build their house upon the rock. Building upon the rock will help your house stand firm and grounded as opposed to being built upon the sand where the house will be tossed in the wind and/or destroyed by the first storm it encounters. Jesus grew up a carpenter's son, so He's giving a life lesson. If you are building a home, you build it on a solid foundation. Today's foundations are usually built of concrete. They are necessary for the home to stand properly and hold up the home, like your legs and feet hold up your body. Jesus is telling people that if they build their life on HIM as a foundation, when the storms of life pass by, they will not be shaken, they will stand strong and secure in that Jesus has never and will never fail. In California, they retrofit many buildings for earthquakes. Quite often when there is an earthquake, buildings will sway for a couple minutes after the earthquake is finished. Now when the storms of life come your way, you may feel shaken, but that's okay because you'll still be standing with your firm foundation. God is strong, even in the midst of the storms.

The Lord Says...

I Am your sure foundation and I Am with you through the storm. Stand strong in faith, hope and love. You may feel an impact but don't fret, I Am at your side and will keep you secured under the shadow of My wings.

If you believe it, say, "Oh yeah!"

MAY 4
STAND UP AND MOVE FORWARD

THE WRONG THING TO DO IN A SEASON OF TROUBLE IS TO LIE DOWN AND HOPE IT JUST PASSES BY. IT'S TIME TO RISE UP AND DECLARE HIS WORD AND LET HIS PEACE REIGN. REMEMBER, YOUR DIFFICULT SEASON HAS PREPARED YOU FOR YOUR GREATEST BREAKTHROUGH. YOU'VE COME TOO FAR TO QUIT NOW!

LIFE IS VERY GOOD!

Have you ever played with one of those Rubik's cubes and tried to match all the colors on every side? It's easy to give up because you feel like you're just spinning your wheels and you're never going to solve the puzzle. But, I know people who have taken the time to learn the algorithms of this puzzle and can solve the Rubik's cube in a flash. Sometimes, instead of lying down and giving up, find another avenue, a different route, a new method, or a better path; that's what Thomas Edison did when inventing the light bulb. When one avenue didn't work, it just became a sign of what not to do. Did his breakthrough come? Absolutely. But, if he would have destroyed his laboratory after the first road block, he may never have found victory. Keep one foot in front of the other and refuse to keep spinning a wheel that doesn't work anymore.

The Lord Says...

I Am the answer, the way, the truth and the life. When trouble comes your way, lift it up, hand it over and I will take it from you and replace it with peace. Your miracles are birthed at the crossroads of adversity and opportunity; keep watch for them.

If you believe it, say, "Oh yeah!"

MAY 5
CHANGE YOUR PERSPECTIVE

DO YOU FEEL SURROUNDED OR EVEN BEATEN BY YOUR TROUBLES? REMEMBER, IT'S ALL ABOUT PERSPECTIVE. THE WAY YOU VIEW A MATTER CAN CAUSE YOU TO OVERCOME A CIRCUMSTANCE OR BE OVERCOME BY IT. ELISHA'S SERVANT WAS OVERWHELMED BY WHAT SURROUNDED THEM, BUT WHEN HIS EYES WERE OPENED AND HE LOOKED UP, HIS PERSPECTIVE CHANGED. DON'T WORRY; THERE ARE MORE WITH YOU THAN THOSE CAUSING YOU TROUBLE. WHEN YOU SEE WHAT HEAVEN SEES, YOU CAN'T FAIL.

LIFE IS VERY GOOD!

The story of Elisha's servant can be found in II Kings 6:16-17. Elisha's servant had no vision and in an effort to change his perspective, Elisha asked God to open his eyes; to give his servant a glimpse, some vision of what Elisha himself saw. When the servant saw the angelic hosts fighting on their behalf, he walked in confidence and peace. There is a great video on godtube.com that has made its rounds on social media sites. It's called "Jesus is Always with You." The video depicts Jesus washing a car with a man, watching some kids skateboard from the top of a skate ramp, at a birth of a child, in the kitchen with a mom cooking, sitting with the kids while they play video games, hugging a woman when she hears of a family member's death in the hospital. It is a powerful 4 minute video, but depicts what we do not see and what Elisha's servant could not see. Jesus is always with us and His angelic hosts are constantly fighting on our behalf. I know it's hard because you are wired with human nature. But with the faith of child, hand over your trouble and your worries to Him. If you could see what heaven sees, you wouldn't stress about the little things in life so much. Jesus has your back and then some. You can't fail, even if you tried. Now that excites me, how about you? Make this the best season of your life, and a worry free one.

The Lord Says...

Worry lacks positive attributes. Therefore, worry is far from Me. I Am a God of peace and order. You have not because you ask not, so seek Me out and turn over your worry. In its place I will give you peace, understanding and a vision of the larger picture in your life. Life is about connecting the dots, learning from your mistakes and moving forward without ever looking back. You got this, because I'm with you.

If you believe it, say, "Oh yeah!"

MAY 6
LEAVING BEHIND THE LOST THINGS

GOD SAID TO DAVID, "YOU SHALL PURSUE. YOU SHALL OVERTAKE AND WITHOUT FAIL, RE-
COVER ALL." WE FOCUS ON THE WORDS "RECOVER ALL", BUT IN THIS JOURNEY, WE'VE LOST
SOME THINGS THAT DON'T NEED TO BE RECOVERED. THEY NEED TO REMAIN IN THE PAST. WE
NEED TO FOCUS ON THE OTHER 2 WORDS: WITHOUT FAIL. WHAT WOULD YOU DO IF YOU KNEW
YOU WOULDN'T FAIL? SEE WHAT GOD SEES FOR YOU.

LIFE IS VERY GOOD!

The story of David's inquiry can be read in I Samuel 30. David became troubled at the sight of an Amalekite invasion. The Amalekites not only destroyed and
plundered their property, but took the women and children. In verses 7-8, David
asked the priest for the ephod and then inquired of the Lord. I find it interesting
though that David basically had two questions: Should I pursue the Amalekites for
what they have done and should I overtake them? God not only replied with direction, but He gave David a vision of victory. As a warrior who was troubled, David
needed to be reminded that he could not fail because God stood with him. So God
not only told David to pursue the troops and to overtake them, but He also told
David to do it without fail. It is without fail that would allow him to recover. All
things are possible if you believe, so what is in your hand? What will you do? You
can't fail, so what is the dream or what is the plan or goal to pursue and overtake so
you might recover its fulfillment? Stop waiting for tens of thousands of dollars to
find their place on your kitchen table before you ever jump in and begin pursuing
the destiny that resides within you. It is much closer than you think.

The Lord Says...

If you could only see what I see for you. But you can because I Am opening
your eyes to the bigger picture and the vision I have for your life. Pursue your
passion and overtake it, doing so without fail. Never stop. Never quit or sit down
on the job. You are a warrior and you have access to the Kingdom. Destiny awaits
you.

If you believe it, say, "Oh yeah!"

MAY 7
BACK IN "THE DAY"

WHAT HINDERS PEOPLE FROM MOVING FORWARD IS RELISHING IN THE PAST, THOSE "GOOD OLD DAYS." CHRIST CAME TO WIPE AWAY OUR PAST BY GIVING US A FUTURE AND A HOPE. IT'S TIME TO UNDERSTAND THAT THE MERCIES OF THE LORD ARE NEW EVERY MORNING. TODAY IS GOING TO BE GREATER THAN YESTERDAY. IT'S TIME TO MOVE FORWARD.

LIFE IS VERY GOOD!

In Jewish culture, the state of moving forward for travelers is dependent upon Jewish hospitality. During the days of antiquity, Jews were required by law to offer hospitality to strangers and/or the poor. It is said that when Lot invited the men who were really angels into his home, he asked his wife to go door to door to obtain salt; salt and bread expressed the Jewish hospitality. But rabbis say that being a native Sodomite, Lot's wife did not agree with this custom or the taking in of strangers. So she did as Lot asked, went door to door to obtain salt, but she also told everyone that her husband was taking in a stranger. In other words, Lot cared about the moving forward of other people, because as a Jew he knew what it was like for his people to be strangers in a land as they were trying to forget their past and move forward. When Lot and his family left the city of Sodom and Gomorrah, God gave them one rule to obey: do not look back at your past because He was giving them a greater future that would be greater than yesterday. Lot's wife relished the "good old days," and her complaint, mixed with her disobedience became her downfall: salt. So don't be afraid to move forward, especially if God is giving you clear direction. What better guide could you have than Jesus? There isn't one. And has He ever let you down yet? No, I don't think so. Run when He tells you to move and know that His mercies are new every morning.

The Lord Says...

I know the plans I have for you; they are great, purposeful and prosperous. Do not be afraid of what tomorrow brings, stepping out into the dark and giving up what yesterday held for you because tomorrow will always be greater than today. Life is meant to be experienced. There is pain and there is sorrow. There is disappointment and there is loss. But the greater always remains: peace, joy, love and thanksgiving; for everyday with Me is sweeter than the day before.

If you believe it, say, "Oh yeah!"

MAY 8
YOU VS. THE GIANT SITUATION

IN TIMES OF CRISIS, WE OFTEN THINK WE STAND ALONE IN OUR FAITH; IT'S US AGAINST A GI-
ANT SITUATION. BUT THE TRUTH IS THAT THERE ARE MANY STANDING AND BELIEVING FOR THE
SAME MIRACLE YOU ARE. ELIJAH THOUGHT HE WAS THE ONLY MAN WHO HAD NOT WORSHIPED
BAAL, BUT THE LORD REVEALED THERE WERE 7000 THAT WERE HUNGRY FOR MORE OF GOD!
AFFIRM THOSE AROUND YOU THAT THEY'RE NOT ALONE.

LIFE IS VERY GOOD!

Acts 20:35 says it all, "In everything I did, I showed you that by this kind of hard work we must help the weak, remembering the words the Lord Jesus himself said: 'It is more blessed to give than to receive' ". One thing is for certain, giving just makes you feel good inside. When you give, you are not only blessing someone else, but your own heart begins to expand. You no longer are completely focused on your issues, but you care more deeply about someone else. This is the nature of Jesus; caring for others first. It is in these moments of sharing and caring that you find out that other people are really dealing with similar circumstances as you are. Then, you are able to minister one to another, praying for one another, lifting them up and sending encouraging words. I challenge you to affirm those around you this week and see how it changes you inside. I expect you will be smiling because it just feels great to make someone's day. I know you're up to it. Remember, give and then it shall be given back to you.

The Lord Says...

Yes, give out of little and give out of much. Give of your time, your talent, and your treasure. What do you have in your hand? What can you do with it? The object of climbing the mountains in life isn't just to reach the top. The object is to reach the top, then go back down and bring someone else up to the top because you're already familiar with the trail. Your strength is stronger when there are two or more, but with three, you can be unstoppable. I will always be the third in your midst. I will always be for you.

If you believe it, say, "Oh yeah!"

MAY 9
IT'S A DOUBLE-DOG-DARE

THINK ABOUT IT. IF YOU KEEP LISTENING TO THE WRONG VOICES, YOU'LL START REPEATING WHAT THEY SAY; SHORTLY YOU'LL BEGIN DOING WHAT THEY DO. DON'T LET OTHER VOICES AND ACTIONS PERSUADE YOU FROM YOUR TRUE IDENTITY. HIS SHEEP KNOW HIS VOICE AND WILL NOT FOLLOW THE VOICE OF STRANGERS. LET HIS VOICE LEAD YOU INTO A SEASON WITHOUT FAIL!

LIFE IS VERY GOOD!

Have you ever been around a child that repeats things their parents say? Or perhaps you have heard an adult use foul language and then in a similar circumstance, around his/her peers, the child does the same thing? When they are young we think it's cute, until it becomes a part of the daily vocabulary. A sheep that knows God's voice can discern His voice amongst all the others because they know that in which He speaks. If you are not a man or woman of the Word, how can you know what He speaks? It is when you do not know or understand the word that you can be swayed by all forms of doctrine. So let His voice lead you. Dig into the word and find out who He is. There are sixty-six books in the Bible. I double-dog-dare you to read them, one at a time. Pull out their lessons, their objectives and learn His ways. For when you do, you will not fail because His voice will become the only voice you know as truth.

The Lord Says...

To know the truth is to love the truth and only then can the truth set you free. I Am the truth and I can set you free from any chain that has you bound. Know Me and what I have already spoken about you so you can stand against any lie the enemy tries to throw at you. My voice will always lead you in the right direction.

If you believe it, say, "Oh yeah!"

MAY 10
THE TREE THAT CHANGED A LIFE

THINK ABOUT THIS. LIFE IS FULL IS CHOICES BUT FAILURE SHOULD NEVER BE ONE OF THEM. A DIFFICULT SITUATION IS YOUR OPPORTUNITY TO RISE TO A NEW LEVEL. ZACCHAEUS ROSE OVER PUBLIC OPINION THAT HE WAS A SINNER AND TOOK A STAND FOR HIS NEW FOUND SALVATION. HIS CHOICE TO REMAIN STRONG CAUSED JESUS TO DECLARE HIM A SON OF ABRAHAM. STAND FIRM IN YOUR FAITH AND OTHERS WILL TAKE NOTICE.

LIFE IS VERY GOOD!

The story of Zacchaeus can be found in Luke 19:1-10. Here is some frame of reference for this story. Zacchaeus was a Jew, but he worked for the Romans as a tax collector. The people did not trust the tax collectors because they were known to be shady and defraud the people of their money. Anything over what the Romans collected in taxes, the tax collectors kept. To a Jew, tax collectors were as bad as prostitutes and robbers. But Zacchaeus made a choice to change his perspective and the perspective of those around him. He climbed a sycamore tree in order to see Jesus. According to Martha Modzelevich at www.flowersinisrael. com: "In ancient Israel, sycamore [its fruit] was mostly eaten by the poor who could not afford the more expensive fruits". Additionally, Modzelevich states that the sycamore tree's name means to "restore, regenerate and reestablish (Modzelevich 2015). In other words Zacchaeus, knowing who his former self was, ran to the tree of the poor and climbed it to get a change of perspective as his eyes became focused on Jesus. As Jesus ministered to Zacchaeus, his life was reestablished in Christ, his sight was regenerated and Jesus restored more than anyone would have ever expected him too. You are a son and daughter of Abraham. Stand firm on the cross and Jesus will take notice, just as He did with Zacchaeus.

The Lord Says...

I notice when people do extraordinary things that take them outside their comfort zone, not just for their sake, but for the sake of others. Zacchaeus was one of those people. He came to the tree of the poor, admitted his mistakes, searched for a change in life and I was there to greet him despite the naysayers. I was there to bring life to him with kindness and My words. He looked for me and I was found. You too can search for Me and change your perspective. I have been with you all along; every season and everyday.

If you believe it, say, "Oh yeah!"

MAY 11
FROM THE SHIPWRECK TO THE DESTINY

YOU KNOW GOD HAS PLACED A CALL ON YOUR LIFE WHEN YOU FACE A PROBLEM THAT'S BIG-GER THAN YOU. BUT THE SITUATION IS NEVER BIGGER THAN GOD WHO LIVES INSIDE OF YOU. DAVID FACED GOLIATH. ELIJAH FACED 450 PROPHETS OF BAAL. PAUL FACED A STORM AND A SHIPWRECK. FACE YOUR OBSTACLE TODAY AND KNOW THAT YOU ARE VICTORIOUS.

LIFE IS VERY GOOD!

Matthew 18:2-4 says, "He called a little child to him and placed the child among them. And he said: 'Truly I tell you, unless you change and become like little children, you will never enter the kingdom of heaven. Therefore, whoever takes the lowly position of this child is the greatest in the kingdom of heaven'". What God is intending to teach you here is this: As an adult you are easily dependent on yourself; your skills and abilities create income and success in your life. Children however, are dependent on, trust and love their parents. Have you ever seen one of those parent/child military reunions on video? Sometimes it happens that a mom or dad who has been serving in the military overseas is able to surprise his/her kids with their return. When the children see their parent, they drop everything and run to them with open arms. This is what Jesus is looking for. When your circumstances seem larger than life, just be God's child. Run to your Father, depend on Him, trust Him completely and love Him enough knowing that He will never, ever let you down. He is the epitome of a world class father. He never fails and He will never disappoint you. You will face storms and it may seem like you've lived through a shipwreck or two. Obstacles will challenge your faith but in the end, no matter what you face, you have Daddy God by your side. He is enough.

The Lord Says...

I will never leave you nor forsake you. Through the greatest of storms, floods and muddy waters, grief and sorrow, I Am here with open arms. You can trust that I love you and depend on My words for they never fall void to the ground. My heart breaks when yours breaks, so much so that I bottle your every tear. I know the number of hairs on your head and give you sunshine to make you smile. Together, every day may not be easy, but something about it will be good.

If you believe it, say, "Oh yeah!"

MAY 12
CAST THY CARE

SOMETIMES IN THE JOURNEY OF LIFE, WE GET TIRED OF THE STRUGGLES AND TRIALS AND FEEL LIKE GIVING UP. DON'T GIVE UP, JUST GIVE IT TO JESUS! CAST YOUR CARES ON HIM BECAUSE HE CARES FOR YOU. REMEMBER, YOU ARE VICTORIOUS BECAUSE HE IS. IT'S YOUR NO FAIL SEASON.

LIFE IS VERY GOOD!

There is an old hymn in the public domain that was originally published anonymously in 1783 and re-written by George Rawson in 1853 called "Cast Thy Burden on The Lord." The first few verses of the lyrics say:

Cast thy burden on the Lord,
Only lean upon His Word;
Thou wilt soon have cause to bless
His eternal faithfulness.

Ever in the raging storm
Thou shalt see His cheering form,
Hear His pledge of coming aid:
"It is I, be not afraid."
(George Rawson, Public Domain)

Can you picture it? In fact I Peter 5:7 says, "Casting all your care upon Him, for He cares for you". When you cast your burden on the Lord, lean on His Word only, you are telling God that you trust Him completely to sail with you through the storm, chanting like a coach, encouraging you to not be afraid because He is with you. Jesus is your constant companion, coach, father, friend and savior. When your burden is heavy, He makes it light.

The Lord Says...

Did I not bare the cross for your sake? The blood, the sweat, the lashes, the spikes, the thorns, the ridicule and the tears? I care for you deeply child. Your burdens are My burdens. Your cares are My cares. My hands are stretched out towards you. Take My hand and I will take the heavy weight you carry upon Myself. I will carry it for you. Trust me and know that My Word is good. I Am able to do above and beyond what you could ever think or imagine. Giving up your burdens is not failure, it is indeed success - a relinquishing and a transfer as any parent would do for a child. You are loved and you are worthy.

If you believe it, say, "Oh yeah!"

MAY 13
HE WILL TURN IT AROUND

WHEN FEAR OVERWHELMS A PERSON, IT CAUSES THEM TO CHOOSE THE LESSER RATHER THAN THE GREATER. LOT CHOSE A CAVE IN THE MOUNTAINS RATHER THAN THE CITY WHERE THE ANGEL SPOKE OF. THE END RESULT: HE FATHERED NATIONS THAT BECAME ISRAEL'S ENEMY. WHEN WE SETTLE IN DARKNESS, WE BIRTH THE WRONG THINGS. LET GOD'S LIGHT SHINE ON YOUR SITUATION AND ALLOW HIS PROMISES TO BE BIRTHED THROUGH YOU.

LIFE IS VERY GOOD!

Ephesians 6:12 says, "For our struggle is not against flesh and blood, but against the rulers, against the authorities, against the powers of this dark world and against the spiritual forces of evil in the heavenly realms". When you fully grasp that the dark places are ruled by powers other than God, you can begin to let go and let God. For the scripture says that you wrestle not against human flesh, but against other powers that would love for you to settle there. But the Bible also tells us in Isaiah 40:31, "But those who hope in the Lord will renew their strength. They will soar on wings like eagles; they will run and not grow weary, they will walk and not be faint." For every action there is a reaction. Isaiah tells you that if you wait upon Him, He will give you strength to soar and you will not be weary or feel faint. That is good news. No matter what darkness comes your way, let Him shine in your life and He will turn it all around.

The Lord Says...

Darkness only exists in the absence of light. Let My light be in your life and darkness will be far from you. When it does try to come your way, My strength will cause you to soar like the eagles and you will have the vision of discernment to see that for what it really is.

If you believe it, say, "Oh yeah!"

MAY 14
BE A DREAM CHASER

TO CHASE A DREAM AND COME UP SHORT IS NOT FAILURE. IT'S ONLY A DELAY, NOT DEFEAT; IT'S A BUMP IN THE ROAD, NOT A DEAD END. IT'S TIME TO RISE UP AND USE YOUR ADVERSITY TO FUEL YOUR DREAM AND MAKE IT INTO REALITY. CONTINUE TO PURSUE, OVERTAKE AND RECOVER ALL. THERE ARE MORE WHO BELIEVE IN YOU THAN YOU REALIZE.

LIFE IS VERY GOOD!

I bet when you read your kids a Dr. Seuss book, you don't call Dr. Seuss a failure right? Why? Because it's irrelevant. He is one of the bestselling children's book authors of all time. But did you know that Dr. Seuss' first book was rejected by 27 publishers? He didn't let the rejection of his dream stop him. He pushed forward. As a high schooler, Michael Jordan was cut from the basketball team. He was crushed, but that didn't stop him. Later in life he became a 6-time NBA Champion. What failures are stopping you from your future? Let this be a season of growth and change, one where you realize your dream is not far out of reach. Put a plan in place to achieve it. You can do it!

The Lord Says...

Through Me, all things are possible. Work hard and believe. Then, you will receive. Declare it and it will come forth. When I Am on your side, there is nothing you cannot achieve, there is nothing that can stop you, there is nothing you cannot do.

If you believe it, say, "Oh yeah!"

MAY 15
A LITTLE DETOUR IS NOT SUCH A BAD THING

FAILURE CAN BE LOOKED AT AS A TEMPORARY CHANGE OF DIRECTION. DON'T LET A SETBACK CHANGE THE COURSE OF YOUR DESTINY. RISE UP AND RESET THE COURSE TO ITS ORIGINAL DESTINATION. FAILURE IS NOT AN OPTION. HE'LL LEAD YOU TO THE FINISH.

LIFE IS VERY GOOD!

Have you ever traveled down a road during the summer months and ran into construction? Many times the construction crew places signs on the road that say 'detour' and you have to go around the construction on your way to your destination. That's all failure is: a detour in your life. If you stay focused on the road you are traveling on, you will still make it to your destination. It may take a little extra time, but you'll get there. Don't be deterred by the 'detour' signs in life. They'd love to throw you off-course but you are smarter than that.

The Lord Says...

A little detour never hurt anyone. The goal is to stay focused. I Am never late, but always on time. When you listen to My voice and follow where I lead, you will never go astray. But even if you veer off the path for a while, don't think I have lost sight of you. Wherever you are, My eyes are on you and My promises are still 'yes and amen' for your life. My hand will always lead you back.

If you believe it, say, "Oh yeah!"

MAY 16
EVERY STEP YOU TAKE

SMALL STEPS LEAD TO GIANT REWARDS. REMEMBER, IT'S NOT HOW FAST YOU MOVE THROUGH
LIFE BUT HOW WILLING YOU ARE TO MOVE FORWARD AND FACE IT. TAKING SMALL STEPS IS THE
FAITH-WALK OF AN OVERCOMER. THE MORE STEPS YOU TAKE, THE MORE YOU WILL ACCOM-
PLISH.

LIFE IS VERY GOOD!

I've never been in a car accident where it hindered my ability to walk but I have prayed for many people who have been. Rehabilitation is never an easy thing. The legs have to be re-trained all over again and the person is just like an infant, taking slow steps every day. Muscles have stiffened and strength must be regained. The process can prove to be very frustrating and long. But in the midst of the disillusion, God has still called you an overcomer. It's not how fast you complete the race, but just the fact that you take part in it. For when you are too tired to continue, Christ is there to pick you up and carry you forward. You are a winner. Don't see yourself as anything less. Hebrews 12:1-3 says, "And let us run with perseverance the race marked out for us, fixing our eyes on Jesus, the pioneer and perfecter of faith...so that you will not grow weary and lose heart." Jesus ran his race all the way to the cross and overcame. Whatever situation you are going through, don't think you need to run, just take it one step at a time. Jesus is walking right beside you.

The Lord Says...

Running a race is never easy but I Am with you and will never leave your side. When you are weary, I will give you strength. When you feel like you can't take another step, I will hold you up. My joy will fill you up and cause you to move forward in every area of your life. Strive for the promises I have for your life. Face your mountains and overcome them for I Am holding the victor's crown in My hand and it's ready for you.

If you believe it, say, "Oh yeah!"

MAY 17
A FRESH PERSPECTIVE

WHEN NEW YEAR'S DAY CAME AROUND IT WAS LIKE EVERYTHING CHANGED BUT NOTHING WAS DIFFERENT. MOST PEOPLE RETURNED TO LIFE AS THEY KNEW IT, WITH PROMISES AND RESOLUTIONS FRESH ON THEIR MINDS, BUT STILL FACING THE SAME REALITY. IT'S SEVERAL MONTHS INTO THE YEAR AND THE REALITY IS THIS: THE NEW YEAR DOESN'T GIVE YOU A NEW START AS MUCH AS IT GIVES YOU AN OPPORTUNITY FOR A FRESH PERSPECTIVE. USE THIS OUTLOOK TO PUT TO REST YOUR DAY OF TROUBLE AND SEE THE REMAINING NEW YEAR AS A "YEAR FOR BREAKTHROUGH", DECLARING THAT YOU ARE DOUBLY FRUITFUL.

LIFE IS VERY GOOD!

Perspective is everything. It is the barometer by which you measure your life and choices. Jesus wants you to see life from His perspective. Philippians 3:10-14 says, "I want to know Christ—yes, to know the power of his resurrection and participation in his sufferings, becoming like him in his death and so, somehow, attaining to the resurrection from the dead. Not that I have already obtained all this, or have already arrived at my goal, but I press on to take hold of that for which Christ Jesus took hold of me. Brothers and sisters, I do not consider myself yet to have taken hold of it. But one thing I do: Forgetting what is behind and straining toward what is ahead, I press on toward the goal to win the prize for which God has called me heavenward in Christ Jesus". This scripture in Philippians gives you greater insight into God's perspective. Let fresh revelation of His Word from your mouth declare a thing in your life and expect to be fruitful and see multiplication come forth. One great thing about God is that He is all about do-overs. Every minute of your life and everyday is an opportunity for a do-over. How cool is that?

The Lord Says...

I Am the God of mercy, the God of do-overs. I have a relationship with the sea of forgetfulness that benefits you every moment of the day. Nothing is too good for you. You are more than enough. Remember who you are in this life; an ambassador of heaven, My daughters and My sons.

If you believe it, say, "Oh yeah!"

MAY 18
THE COST OF FREEDOM

IN THE MIDST OF OUR TRIALS, WE SEARCH FOR GOD'S SALVATION, WAITING FOR HIM TO RESCUE US. WE NEED TO REALIZE THAT SOMETIMES GOD DELIVERS US FROM OUR STRUGGLES AND SOMETIMES HE DELIVERS US THROUGH OUR STRUGGLES. YET NO MATTER HOW YOU GET DELIVERED, THE END RESULT IS HIS FREEDOM. HE IS ALWAYS OUR LIFELINE.

LIFE IS VERY GOOD!

God delivered Paul and Silas from their prison struggle and He delivered them through their struggle via praise. God may have delivered you from a broken relationship and now He will deliver you through the heartbreak. Freedom is never free; it does come with a price. There is no easy way out, but pure trust and faith in the living God that He will be your manna from heaven; all that you need.

The Lord Says...

If I was there for David, for Abraham, for Paul and Silas, for Zacchaeus and all those in the days of old, have I not been there for your ancestors and for you as well? I Am no respecter of persons, only just a God of My word; and thus I have said that I Am with you always, whether through your struggles or in your struggles.

If you believe it, say, "Oh yeah!"

MAY 19
PERSEVERING CREATES STRENGTH

MANY TIMES IN LIFE WE SEARCH TO FIND ANSWERS ON A MATTER TO OVERCOME VARIOUS TRIALS WE MAY FACE. THE TRUTH IS, NOT ALL ANSWERS ARE FOUND THROUGH WISDOM. SOMETIMES ANSWERS ARE FOUND THROUGH PERSEVERING. THE EXPERIENCES WE GO THROUGH NOT ONLY GIVE US STRENGTH, BUT CAN ALSO TEACH US. DON'T GIVE UP, YOU'LL FIND WHAT YOU'RE LOOKING FOR.

LIFE IS VERY GOOD!

Perseverance is relevant to your trials because it creates endurance. Athletes can be strong, conditioned and talented at their sport, but without endurance they cannot sustain their A-game. When you endure through perseverance, you will find out who you are and experience God's steadfast faithfulness that will see you through any trial you face. If David had not persevered through trials with a bear and a lion, he may never have had the answer when facing Goliath. Hebrews 10:36

says, "You need to persevere so that when you have done the will of God, you will receive what he has promised".

The Lord Says...

Those who renew their strength in Me will mount up with wings like eagles without being weary in well doing. Find your strength in Me and you shall soar to heights unknown to you.

If you believe it, say, "Oh yeah!"

MAY 20
THE CONSISTENCY OF CHANGE

IN LIFE THERE IS ONE CONSTANT REALITY: CHANGE. WHAT WASN'T HERE TODAY CAN SUDDENLY APPEAR AND WHAT WAS HERE TODAY CAN BE GONE TOMORROW. LEARN TO APPRECIATE AND CHERISH WHATEVER LIFE GIVES YOU. JUST BECAUSE THE JOURNEY HAS TWISTS AND TURNS, DON'T SEE IT AS A BAD THING, SEE IT AS A GOD THING. ENJOY THE UNEXPECTED.

LIFE IS VERY GOOD!

Ecclesiastes 3:1 says, "There is a time for everything and a season for every activity under the heavens". Time is something you cannot exchange with currency. It is not transferable. If you set out on a day hike in a mountainous area, you are bound to approach a variety of terrains. Climbers who trek up Mt. Kilimanjaro traverse through five different ecosystems, each one affecting their body in different ways. Inasmuch, life is the same way. You are bound to face a rocky trail, one with smooth dirt and one with deep crevices. Pick up a walking stick, your WORD, and let it help you up the mountain of life. God wants you to be worry free about the task ahead and to enjoy the journey. Learn something new, grow and change your mind and your heart. Be the change in your world and the unexpected will feel refreshing and delightful. Enjoy the change.

The Lord Says...

I change not because you need Me as I Am. When you change, you are refreshed. You grow. You even grow up. When you make it up the mountain, come back down and give someone else the strength and encouragement to make the same journey as you have done.

If you believe it, say, "Oh yeah!"

MAY 21
PUT GOD FIRST

WHY IS IT THAT WHEN THINGS ARE GOING GOOD, IT GATHERS A CROWD? BUT WHEN THINGS LOOK BAD, EVERYONE WANTS TO LEAVE! CONSISTENCY MEANS "WITHOUT VARIATION OR CONTRADICTION." DON'T LET YOUR EMOTIONS ON HOW THINGS APPEAR DETOUR YOU FROM GOD'S PROMISE. BE STEADFAST, KNOWING HE WILL SEE YOU THROUGH. THIS IS YOUR DUE SEASON.

LIFE IS VERY GOOD!

Matthew 6:24 says, "No one can serve two masters. Either you will hate the one and love the other, or you will be devoted to the one and despise the other. You cannot serve both God and money". In other words, you cannot serve up consistency and inconsistency in your life, it only detours your journey. When you know the master you serve, you hear his voice and his ways will take priority in your life. Therefore if you trust yourself, your career and the money it brings in more than God, then you will put work before God. But if you put God before those things, then you truly trust Him. God wants you all-in for HIM and all those things will be added unto you. Stand tall and steadfast in Jesus.

The Lord Says...

I Am the way, the truth and the life. My will and My ways are greater than the world will offer you. The journey together can be great. Be strong and of good courage. I Am by your side.

If you believe it, say, "Oh yeah!"

MAY 22
THE ROAD TO FULFILLMENT

EXCUSES ARE THE EASY WAY OUT OF SOMETHING LEFT UNDONE. THEY ARE WORDS USED TO TRY AND COVER REGRETS THAT PAVED THE WAY TO DISAPPOINTMENT. BUT, FULFILLMENT IS TO ACHIEVE OR ACCOMPLISH A SET GOAL, WHICH IS A ROAD THAT LEADS TO VICTORY. DON'T LET EXCUSES ROB YOU OF YOUR SUCCESS. HE HAS STARTED A GOOD WORK IN YOU AND IS FAITHFUL TO FINISH IT.

LIFE IS VERY GOOD!

I Thessalonians 5:24 says, "The one who calls you is faithful and he will do it". God is faithful to do His part. It's now time you get your dream and your passion in life off the ground. A potter must have clay to work with. What do you have in your hand that God can work with? He is already trying to mold your heart and shape your mind. Exchange your excuses for the goals that will see your vision forward to fulfillment. You can do it! Believe in yourself. We believe in you and more importantly, God believes in you. He has given you a hope and a future!

The Lord Says...

I Am faithful to complete the work I have started in you. I Am with you every step of the way, in every bump in the road and in every season. Don't allow excuses to hold you back from what I Am trying to do in your life. You are meant to succeed. And I Am with you always.

If you believe it, say, "Oh yeah!"

MAY 23
OTHER PEOPLE'S OPINIONS

WHY DO OTHERS USE SOMEONE'S PAST TO DEFINE WHO THEY PRESENTLY ARE? THE MEN SAID OF MARY THE HARLOT, THAT IF JESUS KNEW WHO SHE REALLY WAS, HE WOULD NOT LET HER ANOINT HIM. BUT JESUS FORGAVE HER. DON'T LET OTHER PEOPLE'S OPINIONS STUNT WHO GOD HAS CALLED YOU TO BE. WHAT MAN THINKS OF YOU DOESN'T MATTER COMPARED TO WHAT GOD SEES IN YOU.

LIFE IS VERY GOOD!

Matthew 7:3-5 says, "Why do you look at the speck of sawdust in your brother's eye and pay no attention to the plank in your own eye? How can you say to your brother, 'Let me take the speck out of your eye,' when all the time there is a plank in your own eye? You hypocrite, first take the plank out of your own eye and then you will see clearly to remove the speck from your brother's eye". The scripture spells it out quite simply; don't be so quick to point out the sins of others when you have sins of your own. Let God do the judging and you do the loving. Just know this: people will have opinions about you, but those opinions do not define who you are. Jesus says you are more than people say you are. He thinks you are fearfully and wonderfully made!

The Lord Says...

Love, it is the only thing that heals hearts, changes lives and renews the hearts of people. I never saw people as they were because people aren't perfect. I saw them and continue to see them through the blood that I shed on Calvary. Become a man and woman of love and watch a transformation in your community occur.

If you believe it, say, "Oh yeah!"

MAY 24
PROVISION FOR THE BREAKTHROUGH

WHEN FACING A CRISIS IN LIFE, IT'S LIKE WALKING WITH BLINDERS ON. IT CAUSES A PERSON TO FOCUS SO INTENSELY ON THE PROBLEM THAT THEY CAN'T SEE THE ANSWER. CRISIS GIVES YOU TUNNEL VISION, WHEREAS CHRIST GIVES YOU PROVISION. LOOK UP, HIS BREAKTHROUGH IS NEAR.

LIFE IS VERY GOOD!

Here's the thing: in order for you to see the provision while in the midst of a tunnel vision crisis, you must transform your mind in Christ. Romans 12:2 says, "Do not conform to the pattern of the world, but be transformed by the renewing of your mind. Then you will be able to test and approve what God's will is - his good, pleasing and perfect will". The prophet Elijah had to come to the widow in the midst of the famine to open up her vision and show her that God wanted to provide for her and her household (1 Kings 17:8-16). She only saw what she had: a little bit of flour and oil. She planned to make a small cake for herself and her son and then wait to die. In his word to her, Elijah caused the widow to transform the way she viewed her situation. By giving to the prophet first, the widow, her son and their household was sustained until God brought rain to the land. That was 3 1/2 years! If you're focused on the crisis, you will never see the provision. Take the blinders off and allow God to adjust your view.

The Lord Says...

Let the words I speak, the scriptures you have access to bring life to your situation and vision as your provision. When you renew your mind daily in Me and declare My words for your life, you will most assuredly hear My voice. Don't allow your crisis to blind your vision. Open up your eyes and see what I have in store for you.

If you believe it, say, "Oh yeah!"

MAY 25
CHOOSE A CHARACTER OF EXCELLENCE

A MAN'S REPUTATION IS AN ESTIMATION OF WHO HE IS OR WHAT OTHERS THINK OF HIM, BUT CHARACTER IS A TRAIT OF MORAL EXCELLENCE OR TRUTH. JESUS MADE HIMSELF OF NO REPUTATION BY COMING TO THIS WORLD AS A SERVANT AND THROUGH TRIBULATIONS HE PERSEVERED, DEVELOPING CHARACTER AND HOPE. STAND STRONG; YOUR TRIALS IN LIFE HAVE PRODUCED CHARACTER AND NO MATTER WHAT PEOPLE THINK OF YOU, GOD IS NOT DISAPPOINTED IN YOU. HE ONLY THINKS THE BEST.

LIFE IS VERY GOOD!

Proverbs 22:1 says, "A good name is more desirable than great riches; to be esteemed is better than silver or gold. Rich and poor have this in common: The Lord is the Maker of them all". Though reputation matters, this proverb goes on to say that the generous will be blessed because of their generosity, one who loves a pure heart will have the king for a friend. In other words, character matters. Character is like a caption written on the cape on a superhero. If you're honest, have integrity, are kind or generous, your superhero cape will speak it for everyone to hear. Everyone wears their character. Take your character and your reputation seriously. What does your superhero cape say to the world? Your life is a testimony of Christ. Let it shine as the light it should. When you make mistakes, God is there and He is not disappointed. His grace and mercy will bring you through. Your best today may not have been your best yesterday, but thankfully, everyday God allows for do-overs.

The Lord Says...

I Am the same yesterday, today and forever. You were created in My image so take My character, the traits of your father and your spiritual DNA and wear them so you can become the light of the world and the salt of the earth. The world needs to know that everyone makes mistakes but I Am the God of redemption, character and chances restored, lives redeemed and the author of life and all its abundance. Reach the hurting and ashamed with your testimony of mistakes and failures. Allow them to minister to the hearts that feel too far gone because of their character and reputation. I will love them through you and restore them just the same. Two can touch the world greater than one.

If you believe it, say, "Oh yeah!"

MAY 26
GOOD CHARACTER SPEAKS LOUDLY

THE GIFT OF GOD IN YOUR LIFE WILL OPEN DOORS AND MAKE ROOM FOR YOU, BUT GODLY CHARACTER AND INTEGRITY WILL KEEP THE DOORS OPEN AND CAUSE YOU TO COME INTO A FRUITFUL PLACE. LET THIS BE THE SEASON WHERE YOUR GIFTING AND INTEGRITY COME TO-GETHER SO GOD CAN LEAD YOU WHERE HE DESIRES. IT'S TIME TO LET HIM SHINE.

LIFE IS VERY GOOD!

Hebrews 4:12 says, "For the word of God is alive and active. Sharper than any double-edged sword, it penetrates even to dividing soul and spirit, joints and marrow; it judges the thoughts and attitudes of the heart". I would challenge you to become not just hearers of the Word, but doers and speakers of the Word. When you really begin to speak God's Word and apply its wisdom in your life daily, your character and integrity will become as the mind of Christ. You will use wisdom when you speak instead of just speaking or responding. The scripture says that the Word is alive and it's active; meaning it breathes and it moves. Anything that is alive must have breath and, if it's moving, then it can breathe and move in your life as well. As believers (or Christians), it is even more important to be men and women of character. I have heard many business people say things like, "dealing with Christians is the worst." That should not be the case. You should be the businessman or woman the world seeks out because your excellence is as unto the Lord, you are true to your word, which gives you a great reputation in your field of expertise and your character speaks for itself. Don't you want to be the hairdresser every woman wants to recommend? "Oh, sister Tabitha does my hair. She's been in the business a long time, does excellent work, gives to the community and her reputation speaks for herself." Now, that's an opportunity to get someone in the chair and tell them of God's goodness and get to love on them a little. Come on, be of excellent character and let the Word breath and move in your life.

The Lord Says...

Every time your character speaks for itself, it shines for Me. When you become a man or woman of good reputation, I will open the doors not only for you but for the Gospel to reach into the nooks and crannies of the hearts I place within your reach. As you begin to build relationships with clients and community members, they will not be able to deny My light that resides within you. Today is a good day. Go forth in Me.

If you believe it, say, "Oh yeah!"

MAY 27
WHEN REJECTION BECOME SWEET

HAVE YOU EVER BEEN REJECTED WHILE TRYING TO HELP SOMEONE? MOSES TRIED TO STOP BRETHREN FROM FIGHTING ONLY TO HAVE THEM BECOME ANGRY, SAYING WORDS LIKE, 'WHO MADE YOU RULER AND JUDGE'? LET THOSE WORDS OF REJECTION SERVE AS A PROPHETIC PROMISE FOR YOUR LIFE. NOT ONLY DID MOSES DELIVER A NATION, HE WAS USED BY GOD TO RULE IT AS WELL. THE VOICE OF REJECTION DOESN'T HAVE TO BE BITTER BECAUSE, WHEN GOD TOUCHES IT, IT WILL BE SWEET WORDS OF TRUTH. TRUTH ALWAYS PREVAILS.

LIFE IS VERY GOOD!

Know this: Psalm 118:22 says, "The stone the builders rejected has become the cornerstone". This scripture may be small but it packs a powerful punch. If a mason or builder rejects a stone, then they do not believe the stone to be worthy enough to build a stable structure. But, what God is saying is this: the builders didn't really know the quality of the stone too well because the stone they rejected actually was the best stone and that is why it became the cornerstone. In other words, Christ knows and understands what it's like to be rejected in life but He is your cornerstone, the rock that will not fail you and your sure foundation. When built on this cornerstone, you will stand the test of time. So just remember, when the world rejects you, you must see yourself as Jesus sees you; fearfully and wonderfully made. Search the scriptures and find out who HE says you are and what it means. You are grafted into the vine, the apple of His eye, His beloved, heirs to the throne, blessed and unique; and that's just a start. Replace what the world says with who God says you are and repeat it daily. It will transform your life.

The Lord Says...

When you speak My Word daily, it will transform your life because My Word does not return void. You are who I say you are and I Am the One Who matters. Believe Me above all others and watch as your gift makes room for you.

If you believe it, say, "Oh yeah!"

MAY 28
BE ACCESSIBLE

MANY PEOPLE TELL GOD, "HAVE YOUR WAY IN MY LIFE." THEY LET GOD KNOW THEY ARE AVAILABLE BUT ONLY ON THEIR TERMS. WHAT WE NEED TO BE IS ACCESSIBLE; NOT RESTRICTING OURSELVES TO A TIME FRAME BUT BEING COMPLETELY OPEN TO GOD'S INFLUENCE BY HAVING A WILLING HEART TO SERVE. ALLOW HIS NATURE TO BE REVEALED THROUGH YOU AND WATCH YOUR SEASON CHANGE. BE ACCESSIBLE, NOT JUST AVAILABLE.

LIFE IS VERY GOOD!

This is a huge dilemma in the church. Many are available but when was the last time you made yourself accessible to the Word? "Sunday-go-to-meetin'" Christianity doesn't cut it anymore. God is a relational person. We can tell this because He created the world in seven days for Adam to enjoy. In addition, creating family was all about how God viewed Adam and relationships. God wants your time and not just in doing a work. He wants you to become a person who walks and lives the Word daily because so much of it resides in your spirit. Service by works is good, but service with works and Word is so much richer. Consider challenging yourself with scripture memory. Choose a theme: healing, mental health, love, marriage, parenting, or honesty and dig in deep. Know that you know that you know what the Bible speaks in relation to that topic. Then, watch how it fills you.

The Lord Says...

My Words are life and out of them come overflowing abundance and prosperity for all things in life. I have always said that if you seek Me, I will be found. I Am available to you whenever you need Me. All you need to do is call My Name. But I Am also accessible; easy to approach and talk to. It was true then and it is true now.

If you believe it, say, "Oh yeah!"

MAY 29
PRUNING STIMULATES GROWTH

FOR THERE TO BE GROWTH IN OUR LIVES, SOMETIMES WE NEED TO BE PRUNED. BUT DON'T
THINK OF IT AS A BAD THING. TO BE PRUNED IS TO BE CLEANED AND MADE PURE, TO CUT OFF
WHAT ISN'T PRODUCING TO STIMULATE A GREATER INCREASE IN GROWTH. DON'T FIGHT THE
PROCESS BUT ATTACH YOURSELF TO THE TRUE VINE AND WATCH YOUR LIFE FLOURISH. THIS IS
YOUR DOUBLY FRUITFUL SEASON.

LIFE IS VERY GOOD!

John 15:2 says, "He cuts off every branch in me that bears no fruit, while every branch that does bear fruit he prunes so that it will be even more fruitful". Pruning is a popular practice in horticultural fields. Bonsai plants are pruned to control their growth, shape, while other plants are pruned of their dead parts and to make them healthier. It is also a common practice to prune plants for regrowth or what's known as "transplanting". Kids love to see the pruned hedge trees in the shaped into animals or other characters. That type of pruning reminds me of the movie "Edward Scissorhands." Oftentimes you may think the devil is keeping you from something in life but honestly God may just be pruning your branches, shaping you and transforming you to go a different direction or transplanting you in a place He knows you will flourish. So no matter how painful pruning may seem, seek out God so you know what season you are in. And if you're in a pruning season, get ready for the harvest will surely come. Trust Him according to Proverbs 3:5-6.

The Lord Says...

I Am the vine, you are the branches. Branches receive a pruning when I, the gardener of your life find it necessary to shape, change, enhance growth and cause you to flourish. I Am the way, the truth and the life and would never do anything to hurt you. Trust Me, pruning is not always easy, but the change is always beneficial.

If you believe it, say, "Oh yeah!"

MAY 30
WILL YOU GIVE UP OR GIVE IN?

THERE IS A DIFFERENCE BETWEEN GIVING UP AND GIVING INTO A SITUATION. TO GIVE UP MEANS TO QUIT, SURRENDER OR RELINQUISH; WHILE GIVING IN MEANS A WILLINGNESS TO YIELD TO A SUPERIOR POWER OR FORCE. IT'S TIME TO GIVE UP OUR FRUSTRATIONS AND DISAPPOINTMENT AND GIVE IN TO HIS PURPOSE AND PROMISE. THIS TYPE OF GIVING LEADS TO HIS VICTORY.

LIFE IS VERY GOOD!

In our human nature, giving up and giving in are two of the most challenging positions to play in this game of life. The reason it is so difficult is because people often do not follow the word. One, they don't trust themselves, but they lean on themselves more than God and that is contrary to Proverbs 3:5-6. Secondly, Matthew 6:33-34 spells it all out: "But seek first his kingdom and his righteousness and all these things will be given to you as well. Therefore do not worry about tomorrow, for tomorrow will worry about itself. Each day has enough trouble of its own". God knows how you think, particularly as it relates to worry, so He tells you what to do first, then why. He says, "give it up and seek Me." What does that mean? It doesn't mean just an everyday prayer, "Oh God, what do you want me to do?" He's told you what to do; you have to seek it out. What does the word say about your situation? What scripture will you declare as your victory? That's seeking Him, finding Him in the words He has breathed life and action into. What is the result if you seek Him? All those things will be added to you, so don't even worry about it. Life will give you plenty to worry about so refuse to worry. Give it up and give in to God and see what He will do. You are His child! That is not something He will ever forget. Let your spirit lead your life, not your five physical senses.

The Lord Says...

I Am here. I Am there. I Am with you everywhere. Give Me your burdens and your fears. I release you to believe that which I have spoken for your circumstance. Everyone wants a prophetic word of knowledge. Jesus is the greatest prophet of all time. Read and receive His words for your life today.

If you believe it, say, "Oh yeah!"

MAY 31
IF YOU CAN'T SAY ANYTHING NICE...

HAVE YOU EVER STOPPED AND LISTENED TO YOURSELF TALK? DID IT CAUSE A WHIRLWIND OF CHAOS? OR DID IT BRING PEACE TO YOUR STORM? CHOOSE YOUR WORDS CAREFULLY IN ALL CIRCUMSTANCES. HIS WORDS BRING LIFE. WHAT DO YOUR WORDS BRING? THINK ABOUT IT.

LIFE IS VERY GOOD!

God speaks so much about the tongue and our speech. Remember what your mother and grandmother used to say, "If you can't say anything nice, don't say anything at all." Sometimes I think this principle should be practiced. What would happen if not one negative thing was spoken? Proverbs 21:23 says, "Whoever keeps his mouth and his tongue keeps himself out of trouble". Think of the fights, political bashing, negative celebrity publicity, rifts between families and business partners that could be saved if this tongue tying were practiced more often. Here is my challenge to you: Speak the Word, be an encourager and when you have to speak a truth that's not so easy to deliver, do it in love. Remember those bracelets kids use to wear: WWJD - "what would Jesus do?" Maybe when it comes to speech, it's time to start asking that question again. How would Jesus respond? What would He say to that comment? How would He defend His position, His family, His job, etc...? Think about it, for a tongue out of trouble is a good thing.

The Lord Says...

Have you ever heard Me speak anything but life to you? Then why must you speak anything but life to one another? Life is power to the tongue and allows the heart to bloom. My Words over you are blessings and promises that empower you to grow and mature into greater dimensions. Bring peace and love into all situations of your life and into others as you speak what I have proclaimed.

If you believe it, say, "Oh yeah!"

JUNE 1
THE OPPORTUNITY OF TROUBLE

HOW DO YOU VIEW YOUR CRISIS? DO YOU SEE IT AS A DAY OF TROUBLE OR AS AN OPPORTUNITY FOR BLESSING? CRISIS CAUSES YOUR FAITH (OR FEAR) TO SHOW ITS TRUE COLORS. IT'S THE TURNING POINT THAT CAN MAKE YOU STAND STRONG OR RUN AWAY. LET THIS PRESSURE GIVE YOU THE OPPORTUNITY TO GO DEEPER AND SEE GOD'S GREATER WORK THROUGH YOU.

LIFE IS VERY GOOD!

Pressure in the midst of challenging moments in your life can often be like a pressure cooker. A pressure cooker cooks and provides you with tender meat because it uses very high temperatures, mixed with a small amount of liquid to create steam. When the steam penetrates the meat, it cooks and tenderizes the meat. Then, your dinner is done. Just imagine your time of crisis is a pressure cooker. Let God allow the steam (faith) to penetrate you, the temple of God. When the process is complete, you will come out a greater individual; more tender-hearted towards others, compassionate and God will have done a good work in you. A little pressure can be a good thing.

The Lord Says...

I will never give you more than you can handle. Sometimes pressure is the opportunity for you to go beyond what you think you can do and meet Me in what I know you can do. I have more confidence in you than you think. Be willing to stretch and every day will be an adventure, for the same old thing often gets mundane.

If you believe it, say, "Oh yeah!"

JUNE 2
REJOICE IN ALL THINGS

SOMEONE ONCE WROTE, "PAIN IS INEVITABLE BUT SUFFERING IS OPTIONAL." JESUS NEVER PROMISED US A LIFE WITHOUT PROBLEMS, BUT THE BIBLE OFFERS A WAY TO ENDURE THEM. IT SAYS TO CONSIDER TESTS AND CHALLENGES AS A GIFT. WHEN WE REALIZE WE CAN CHOOSE HOW LONG WE SUFFER, OUR WEEPING WILL ONLY ENDURE THE NIGHT. HIS JOY WILL COME IN THE MORNING.

LIFE IS VERY GOOD!

Sometimes people use pain and suffering interchangeably. They are, however, vastly different. The body is equipped to notice and release pain innately. If you cut your finger, the nerves send signals to the brain telling the brain you are injured. You mend the wound and in due time the pain disappears and the wound heals. Pain then becomes an element of change in your life. Suffering is caused by the inability to let a deep pain go. For example, maybe you lost a child, a spouse or a parental figure abandoned you. It is easy to stay in that grief/pain frame of mind and dwell there constantly because you cannot let go of the pain. This is suffering and overwhelming feeling of despair due to pain.

God's will is that you not suffer, but rather rejoice within your sufferings. This changes the whole outlook of suffering. Romans 5:3-5 says, "Not only so, but we also glory in our sufferings, because we know that suffering produces perseverance; perseverance, character; and character, hope. And hope does not put us to shame, because God's love has been poured out into our hearts through the Holy Spirit, who has been given to us". Just a little light, a little sunshine in the world of suffering can turn your mourning into dancing.

The Lord Says...

Don't grieve for what once was, but rejoice for today is a good day. Change comes in the wind as seasons move forward, but you can be comforted by Me, the One who changes not. In all things give thanks and praise. I have made the the new day for you.

If you believe it, say, "Oh yeah!"

JUNE 3
FORGET THE PAST

WHEN THE UNEXPECTED MANIFESTS IN OUR LIVES, GOD WAITS TO SEE HOW WE RESPOND. MANY WANT TO SIT AND DO NOTHING EXCEPT WAIT FOR GOD TO STEP IN, BUT HOW WE REACT DETERMINES WHAT HAPPENS NEXT. THE 4 LEPROUS MEN SAID, "WHY SIT WE HERE AND DIE?" THEY MADE A CHOICE TO SURRENDER THEIR LIVES AND GOD USED THEIR ACTION TO BRING BREAKTHROUGH TO THE REGION. CHOOSE TO DO SOMETHING GREAT TODAY.

LIFE IS VERY GOOD!

If you had no obstacles in your way, what would you do in life? What can you do to change your world and the Kingdom of God? Let me encourage you with this: Nothing is impossible with God. All things are possible, because He has taken every barrier away and you are free to make a choice, to surrender your life to do something great today.

Look at Isaiah 43:16-21, "This is what the Lord says—he who made a way through the sea, a path through the mighty waters, who drew out the chariots and horses, the army and reinforcements together and they lay there, never to rise again, extinguished, snuffed out like a wick: 'Forget the former things; do not dwell on the past. See, I Am doing a new thing! Now it springs up; do you not perceive it? I Am making a way in the wilderness and streams in the wasteland. The wild animals honor me, the jackals and the owls because I provide water in the wilderness and streams in the wasteland, to give drink to my people, my chosen, the people I formed for myself that they may proclaim my praise'".

The first part of this scripture reminds you of God's power and might. Then it goes on to tell you to forget the past, that He's doing a new thing and you just don't see it yet. Even when you don't see it, He is making a way where there seems to be no way, providing for you in the desert season. You, His chosen people that He Himself formed so that you can praise Him. Wow, that is powerful. So do not let obstacles stand in your way. Don't allow any disability to dictate what you could do. What can you do today?

The Lord Says...

All are able because I Am able and with Me all things are possible. You must believe that what I say is true. Then, you must believe that you can accomplish all that I have given you to accomplish on this earth. Together we are a force to be reckoned with and together we can change the world.

If you believe it, say, "Oh yeah!"

JUNE 4
MAKE A DIFFERENCE

THINK ABOUT THIS: THE ACTIONS YOU TAKE IN A MATTER REVEAL THE INTENT OF YOUR HEART. IN LUKE, JESUS TELLS THE STORY OF 2 PRIESTS WHO WALK BY A MAN WHO WAS BEATEN AND HALF DEAD. BUT WHEN THE SAMARITAN SAW HIM, HE WAS MOVED WITH COMPASSION, GAVE THE INJURED MAN OIL AND WINE, TOOK HIM TO AN INN AND PAID FOR HIS CARE. WHAT IS YOUR HEART SAYING? DON'T JUST WALK BY; MAKE A DIFFERENCE IN SOMEONE'S LIFE TODAY.

LIFE IS VERY GOOD!

Do you know why random acts of kindness are so important? It's because kindness is a fruit of the Spirit and, when you are kind, show compassion and mercy upon others, you are revealing the heart of God; His nature inside of you. There is much that can be done in this world and it's not your pastor's job to reach the multitudes alone. What can you do? Here are just some ideas. If you have a college or university near you, why not open your home for Thanksgiving or Christmas dinner? Many young people can't afford to go home for the holidays or are international students that spend the holidays alone. Adopt your block and get to know your neighbors. Be the light. What do they have need of? What are they struggling with? Find ways you and others in your church can help meet those needs. Go out of your way to help a student with college tuition. Imagine if churches started scholarship funds for the high school seniors in their congregation. It's not hard. Ask yourself, where is my heart taking me and what do I love to do?

A friend of mine knew of a lady at their church who had a heart for foster kids. This woman's concern stemmed around the fact that, once a foster child turned 18, the children were considered adults and transitioned out of the foster system. They were basically on their own with no support. This lady started an organization and a home for foster kids who were aging out of the system. One day, someone in the church found out and went hunting. Coming back, they had a lot of meat and asked if she'd like some. To make a long story short, it was so much meat that she had to buy two long freezers to store it all. I tell you this story because, when you begin to walk and make a difference, God always shows up, because He's all about people and we should be too.

The Lord Says...

Give and it shall be given to you, more than you can handle, more than you can store. Get an image of it! Show the people around you My kindness and My love so their lives can be fulfilled in a greater way. Reveal My heart of compassion, reveal My hands of help, reveal My voice of life to those who are crying out and see the difference you can make when you flow with Me.

If you believe it, say, "Oh yeah!"

JUNE 5
PUT ACTION INTO YOUR DREAM

IN ORDER TO PROPEL OURSELVES TO THE NEXT LEVEL, MOMENTUM MUST BE ESTABLISHED. WE MUST MOVE OUT OF THE REALM OF JUST SAYING SOMETHING; WE NEED TO DO SOMETHING FOR THE KINGDOM. A VISION WITHOUT ACTION IS JUST A DREAM. PUT MOTION INTO WHAT YOU'RE DECLARING AND SEE IT COME TO PASS.

LIFE IS VERY GOOD!

Have you ever heard someone say, "Someday, I'm gonna... When I get enough money I'm gonna... If I had the opportunity I would... I wish I could...?" Turn it around. Make your someday today, create your own opportunity, save until you can and stop wishing. Most dreams do not occur because of these lame reasons; dreams do not manifest because they often stay dreams and do not move to the plans stage where you can pursue a goal. Dreams are supposed to be the bench-mark of your pursuits; the pot of gold at the end of your rainbow. Instead of the 'someday' line, I want to hear that today, you are doing x, y and z to pursue that passion. Instead of the 'when I get enough money' line, I want to hear that you are saving like crazy to reach that goal. Instead of the 'if I had the opportunity I would' line, figure out how you can create your opportunity. What can you do? And most of all, stop wishing for dreams to come true. Just do it. Put a plan into action and have goals to get your dream to the next level of reality. Proverbs 21:5 says, "The plans of the diligent lead to profit as surely as haste leads to poverty". Take that scripture and run!

The Lord Says...

Be diligent, be timely, declare the Word, know the seasons, pray without ceasing and love the journey. See the vision for your life and follow after it. The vision is there because I placed it inside of you. When I provide the vision, I also make the provision. Never worry, just declare it to be established for you.

If you believe it, say, "Oh yeah!"

JUNE 6
HIS PEACE WILL CHANGE YOUR CRISIS

WHEN CRISIS MANIFESTS, IT'S EASY TO DEVELOP AN ATTITUDE, POINT FINGERS AND BLAME OTHERS AND EVEN BLAME GOD FOR OUR HARDSHIP. WE MUST REMEMBER, THOUGH, THAT OUR RESPONSE IS A REFLECTION OF WHAT'S IN OUR HEART. IN THE STORY OF RUTH, NAOMI SAID, "DON'T CALL ME NAOMI; CALL ME BITTER. THE STRONG ONE HAS DEALT ME A BITTER BLOW." DON'T LET FRUSTRATION CHANGE YOUR IDENTITY. LET YOUR CRISIS BE CHANGED BY HIS PEACE.

LIFE IS VERY GOOD!

Isaiah 41:10 says, "So do not fear, for I Am with you; do not be dismayed, for I Am your God I will strengthen you and help you; I will uphold you with my righteous right hand". If you will purpose in your heart to declare the Word for every circumstance, your outlook and your circumstances will most surely change. So when you get frustrated, learn and memorize this scripture and let it be spoken from your heart. It says that you don't need to be frustrated or worried because God is with you. Don't be dismayed because He IS your God and He gives you strength and helps you. Powerful. Don't let frustration or crisis change your heart; declare His Word and be a man or woman of peace and trust. For when you are at peace, you tell God that you trust Him completely.

The Lord Says...

Trust me with your whole heart, not a piece of it. I Am your God and I fail not. I never have failed and I never will. The peace that I give passes all understanding, so rest in Me.

If you believe it, say, "Oh yeah!"

JUNE 7
POVERTY IS A MINDSET

POVERTY IS A MINDSET THAT MUST BE CRUSHED. IT'S A SYSTEM THAT DISEMPOWERS YOU BY ROBBING YOU OF THE TRUTH. THE TRUTH IS, WHEN GOD CREATED US, HE GAVE US DOMINION AND DECLARED US FRUITFUL. GOD CREATED US IN AN ATMOSPHERE OF BLESSING. DON'T SETTLE FOR ANYTHING LESS THAN WHAT GOD HAS PROMISED YOU. THIS IS YOUR DOUBLY FRUITFUL YEAR.

LIFE IS VERY GOOD!

Jeremiah 17:10 says, "I the Lord search the heart and examine the mind, to reward each person according to their conduct, according to what their deeds deserve". In other words, God wants you to have dominion, prosperity and abundance, but He's also looking at your heart. The Bible tells us that if we are faithful with the little, then He will give us much. Think about it like this: If you inherited a large sum of money at 18, it might not be as wise as receiving an allotted amount at a variety of ages and stages of life, with the full amount dispersed at around 35. Why? Because your maturity level is different and your wisdom will likely have increased over time and what you do with the money matters. The same can be said about God your father. He is not likely going to thrust you into abundance. When you started the business, He gave you the mind to begin, and He will prosper you over time. But never doubt, just because you don't receive a lump sum of abundance, prosperity or dominion all at once in your life's journey doesn't mean you are settling for anything less than what God promised. It certainly does not mean that you aren't doubly fruitful, abundant, prosperous or have dominion. Be abundant where you are. Be wise and prosperous with what you are presently given and take dominion over every area of your life.

The Lord Says...

Abundance and prosperity are not just references to money. Be abundant in your time, your talent and your money. Make your home an abundant place of love and affirmation. Be prosperous in your giving, but be prosperous with kindness, gentleness and the other fruit of the Spirit. Take dominion over your finances, your relationships, your ideas, your time, your energy, your fun and entertainment. Be as I would be walking on the earth.

If you believe it, say, "Oh yeah!"

JUNE 8
TITHING IS AN OPPORTUNITY FOR INCREASE

CONSIDER THIS: IF YOU GIVE SOMETHING AWAY THAT DOESN'T BELONG TO YOU, YOU HAVE TO KNOW THAT YOU WILL CAUSE DISAPPOINTMENT IN SOMEONE'S LIFE. WHEN WE HOLD ONTO GOD'S TITHE AND GIVE IT AWAY TO SOMETHING ELSE, WE'RE TELLING GOD, "I DON'T NEED YOUR FAVOR, YOUR PROTECTION OR YOUR BLESSING OVER MY LIFE; I CAN HANDLE IT." BUT DOING THIS CAUSES GOD TO BE CHEATED OUT OF AN OPPORTUNITY TO BLESS YOU IN THE WAY HE WANTS. REMEMBER, HIS TITHE IS HOLY. BEING FAITHFUL DESTROYS POVERTY.

LIFE IS VERY GOOD!

In the Jewish culture, Jews are required to give 10% of their income (the tzedakah) to the poor. The highest form of tzedakah is when someone gives to someone in a way that allows them to become self-sufficient. Jews are among the most philanthropic people on record and tzedakah can be given not just to synagogues but to institutions of health and education and anywhere that will help people. The Jewish culture does not, for one moment, cheat God out of an opportunity to bless them. In fact just the opposite; they pay their tzedakah in an effort to thank God for all He has done for them. It is also common for many Jews to give way beyond their 10% tzedkakah. Those raised in the Jewish culture are trained from a very young age to give to the poor. Most homes have a box that coins are dispersed into for the poor. Anytime something good or bad occurs, a coin is inserted. What a concept! A continuous way to worship and give God thanks and praise for the good and the bad. In return, showers of blessing. Don't cheat yourself of all that God has for you. Be good stewards of your time, talent and treasure.

The Lord Says...

Many think that discipline is a bad word but it's not. Discipline trains My saints for reigning. Kings must train their troops to fight in times of war as well as equip them to become lovers of humanity. My way is the best way, for blessing always follows. Where My blessing reigns, there is also My abundance.

If you believe it, say, "Oh yeah!"

JUNE 9
YOU ARE THE KING'S KID

YOU CAN BE GREAT IN MANY AREAS OF YOUR LIFE BUT STILL STRUGGLE WITH AN IDENTITY CRISIS. DAVID WAS A SHEPHERD, A WORSHIPER, A WARRIOR AND ANOINTED TO BE KING, BUT AS A YOUNG MAN, HE VIEWED HIMSELF AS POOR AND PART OF A COMMON FAMILY. HE CALLED HIMSELF A NOBODY WITH NOTHING TO OFFER. 1 SAMUEL 18:23 SAYS, "THE KING'S SERVANTS TOLD ALL THIS TO DAVID, BUT DAVID HELD BACK. 'WHAT ARE YOU THINKING OF? I CAN'T DO THAT. I'M A NOBODY; I HAVE NOTHING TO OFFER'» (MSG). SO DON'T SEE YOURSELF AS OTHERS WOULD, SEE YOURSELF AS GOD WOULD. GOD CALLED DAVID A MAN AFTER "MY OWN HEART." HE'S MADE YOU GREATER THAN YOU EVEN REALIZE.

LIFE IS VERY GOOD!

Sometimes you need to ask yourself this question. If God is a God of love, who loves you unconditionally, forgives you daily, encourages you constantly and has plans to prosper you, then why can't you see yourself through His eyes? It's when you begin to change your image by seeing yourself as God sees you that your self-confidence will soar because you then recognize who you truly are. You are not just a housewife or just an electrician, just a teacher or just a dad. You are special. You are a King's kid.

The Lord Says...

You are fearfully and wonderfully made. There is no one like you and I have a heart after you. When you tell Me you can offer Me nothing or you are nobody, you crush My heart, for you are a part of Me and I am a part of you. I pray you can begin to see what I see in you.

If you believe it, say, "Oh yeah!"

JUNE 10
HONOR PRESERVES LIFE

IT'S POSSIBLE TO KILL A MAN, BUT IMPOSSIBLE TO KILL A MAN THAT HONORS. HONOR IS MORE THAN A LANGUAGE; IT'S AN ATTITUDE OF ONE'S HEART. SAUL COULDN'T KILL DAVID AND, BECAUSE OF HONOR, DAVID WOULDN'T KILL SAUL. EVEN WHEN GIVEN THE OPPORTUNITY, DAVID DIDN'T STRETCH HIS HAND AGAINST THE LORD'S ANOINTED. TRUE HONOR NOT ONLY PRESERVES YOUR LIFE BUT KEEPS YOU FROM MAKING FOOLISH CHOICES. HONOR GOD AND HIS PEOPLE.

LIFE IS VERY GOOD!

The world today is so caught up in the "me, mine and my" syndrome, that many have lost sight of honor because they think too highly of themselves. However, honor is so important to God that He states in Ephesians 6:2-3, "Honor your father and mother"—which is the first commandment with a promise— "so that it may go well with you and that you may enjoy long life on the earth". Give honor where honor is due and live a long life on earth, that's what God says. But what is honor? It means to have the highest respect for someone and to hold them in high regard. When you honor God's people, you honor God. So lift up and show esteem for someone besides yourself, it's the right thing to do and will bring you much joy.

The Lord Says...

Honor...it isn't always easy because the past can be painful. But every second that goes by is a part of yesterday. In your life, choose to honor your mentors, your parents, your family, your leader and one another. For, it is true, to whom much is given, much is required. And as you honor others, I will also bestow honor on you.

If you believe it, say, "Oh yeah!"

JUNE 11
HONOR IS A LIFESTYLE

To honor someone is an action, not just something you say. David honored his father by tending the sheep with his life. When a bear or a lion took one from the flock, he chased it, caught it, killed it and delivered the lamb back to the flock. Honor is more than a word, it's a lifestyle. Let your actions strengthen what your mouth is saying.

Life is very good!

I Peter 2:17 says, "Show proper respect to everyone, love the family of believers, fear God, honor the emperor". When honor exudes from your life, it dwells within you as a piece of your character. It becomes second nature to "show proper respect to everyone." You honor God in all aspects of your life, time, talents and treasure, not because you have to or someone requires you too, but because of the lifestyle of honor you have pursued. So pursue honor, it's the way of God.

The Lord Says...

Honor shows that you care and the fruit of the Spirit are living inside of you. Treat My people and all living things in this world with the highest regard for they are all of My creation and of My design. When you honor one another, you truly honor Me.

If you believe it, say, "Oh yeah!"

JUNE 12
HONOR GOES THE EXTRA MILE

TO BE A MAN OF HONOR IS TO TREAT OTHERS AND THEIR POSSESSIONS AS WELL AS IF THEY WERE YOUR OWN. BEFORE DAVID WAS SENT TO THE BATTLEFIELD TO BRING REPORT OF HIS BROTHERS, HE PLACED THE SHEEP IN THE HANDS OF A KEEPER. THIS CARETAKER HAD TO BE WILLING TO RISK HIS LIFE FOR THE FLOCK IN THE SAME WAY DAVID DID. A MAN OF HONOR IS WILLING TO GO THE EXTRA MILE. WHEN YOU VALUE WHAT GOD HAS GIVEN YOU, OTHERS WILL VALUE IT IN THE SAME MANNER.

LIFE IS VERY GOOD!

The Bible is rich with stories of hospitality that are often glanced over. But in the Jewish culture, hospitality, particularly during the age of antiquity, was mandated by Jewish law. The tone towards hospitality in that culture was out of gratefulness. The Jews understood that their history once took them into a new land and they themselves were strangers. Therefore, they are thankful that God blessed them and, in turn, as not to forget what it was like to be a stranger, they had to themselves welcome strangers. If a stranger came to the door of a Jewish home, that household was obligated to feed and house them and take care of the stranger's needs. Matthew 5:38-48 depicts how Abraham and Lot went the extra mile to show honor through hospitality to strangers. As three men were walking by, Abraham took notice and walked out to greet them. Abraham invited the men into his home. He gave them water, fed them, let them wash up from the journey and provided a place of rest. This seems like a simple enough task because our fridges are full and our water comes from a tap, but think about how much water had to be hauled to wash Abraham's own family plus three other individuals just for one night. Or what it meant for Sarah and Abraham to butcher their best calf for supper in honor of people they had no previous relationship with. It took a lot, but it was second nature because it was not only a part of their culture, but a part of who they were as people of God. Will you go the extra mile no matter how long it takes? The reward is great.

The Lord Says...

When you do all things as done unto Me and with a heart of gratefulness, you will see the world from a different perspective; one where you want everyone to experience My goodness. Be willing to pass it on and go the extra mile.

If you believe it, say, "Oh yeah!"

JUNE 13
STRENGTH IN SERVANTHOOD

WHEN IT COMES TO BUILDING THE KINGDOM, WE MUST HAVE AN ATTITUDE OF SERVANTHOOD. WE ARE TO FOLLOW CHRIST'S EXAMPLE: LAYING OUR LIVES DOWN FOR OTHERS, MAKING PEOPLE FEEL VALUED AND PUTTING OTHERS' NEEDS BEFORE OUR OWN. WHAT YOU DEPOSIT INTO A RELATIONSHIP IS WHAT YOU'LL RECEIVE FROM IT. LET'S BUILD THE KINGDOM TOGETHER.

LIFE IS VERY GOOD!

John 12:26 says, "Whoever serves me must follow me; and where I am, my servant also will be. My Father will honor the one who serves me". When you live a life of service to God and others, it is heart changing. I think you'll find that most people who serve love people. When you can serve and love people, you will have taken on a small piece of God's heart, for all He has ever done has been for people. In turn, when you serve, the scripture says that God Himself will honor you. Relationships are important to God. He is the one who started the family when the world began. So ask yourself these questions: How can I serve and deposit into my relationships? How can I serve my family, my community and my church better?

My friend read a social media post that really touched my heart. There was an elderly man who owned a beautiful but rundown old house in Oregon. One day, some young kids walked by and said that the house should be burned down because it looked so bad. A man who saw this take place later found out the elderly man's house could not be insured because it looked so dilapidated and run-down. After approaching the homeowner about the home, this man had a connection with a local business that donated the paint to re-paint this old house. He then went onto social media and asked how many friends would come out on a Saturday to paint this elderly homeowner's house with him. The response was amazing. People committed to come out and paint, donate water, food and supplies. That is service to others as unto the Lord! It was a beautiful sight. That act of servanthood not only placed a lasting deposit into this homeowner's life and made him smile, but blessed a community as well. Do you have an attitude of servanthood? Get on the servanthood train; it does a world of good for you and benefits others.

The Lord Says...

Giving to and for the benefit of others is an act very dear to My heart, for I myself gave of the greatest sacrifice. When you give to and for others, it blesses Me immensely, encourages you greatly and brings hope and the light of life to the recipient. Give and give some more and watch your life be enriched in so many ways.

If you believe it, say, "Oh yeah!"

JUNE 14
STRENGTH IN WEAKNESS

IT'S BEEN SAID, IN TIMES OF GREAT ADVERSITY THAT ONLY THE STRONG SURVIVE. BUT, LIFE IS NOT ABOUT OUR INDIVIDUAL STRENGTH BECAUSE IT IS IN OUR WEAKNESS THAT HIS STRENGTH IS PERFECTED. HIS MIND IS WHAT TRULY MATTERS. IF YOU HAVE THE MIND OF CHRIST DURING YOUR ADVERSITY, YOU WILL MORE THAN SURVIVE; YOU WILL THRIVE, CONQUER AND DIVIDE. "THEREFORE WILL I DIVIDE HIM A PORTION WITH THE GREAT AND HE SHALL DIVIDE THE SPOIL WITH THE STRONG." LET HIS STRENGTH RISE UP IN YOU.

LIFE IS VERY GOOD!

Here is what I have found: Many people know of the Word, but they do not know the Word. You can know the Word and what it says, but "His mind IS what truly matters." To have the mind of Christ, you must know the Word as it abides in you. Why? Because when adversity comes (and it will), you need to get out that victory scripture and declare it in the face of what your natural circumstances are declaring to you. This is how the strong survive. So, the doctor said you have an illness or disease. Instead, in the face of the doctor's proclamation, you declare I Peter 2:24, "He himself bore our sins" in His body on the cross, so that we might die to sins and live for righteousness; "by his wounds you have been healed". Then declare this and other scriptures every day, take them to memory, get them into your spirit and make it your second nature to speak spirit and not flesh. Make a declaration that "by His wounds I have been healed." Watch and see how His strength rises up within you as adversity becomes an opportunity for God to do a work.

The Lord Says...

The Words I give to you are a lamp unto your feet, a guide to everyday life and your book of secrets to living. I will never fail you. Remember, it is the truth that sets you free.

If you believe it, say, "Oh yeah!"

JUNE 15
LOOK FOR YOUR NOW MOMENT

WHEN DISAPPOINTMENT COMES INTO OUR LIVES, WE OFTEN REFLECT ON THE PAST. WE THEN LOOK TO THE FUTURE IN SEARCH OF HOPE. MARTHA, UPSET OVER HER BROTHER'S DEATH, SAID JESUS COULD'VE HEALED HIM IF HE HAD BEEN THERE. SHE THEN SAID SHE WOULD SEE LAZARUS AT THE RESURRECTION. MARTHA FAILED TO SEE THE NOW MOVE OF GOD AND WHAT CHRIST DECLARED, "I AM THE RESURRECTION." QUIT DWELLING ON THE PAST AND STOP LOOKING SO FAR INTO THE FUTURE THAT YOU MISS WHAT CHRIST IS DOING NOW IN YOUR LIFE. DON'T MISS YOUR MOMENT.

LIFE IS VERY GOOD!

Language is a gift God has given us to convey our thoughts, ideas and expressions. However, many Christians read the Bible and fail to understand its language. For example, Isaiah 53:5 says, "But he was pierced for our transgressions, he was crushed for our iniquities; the punishment that brought us peace was on him and by his wounds we are healed". The scripture says "by his wounds we ARE healed. The word ARE is a verb and the present form of be, meaning it exists in the present right now. So why do you keep asking God to heal you? It's already done. The word 'are' implies that right now healing exists, it has already occurred. You're praying the wrong thing. Stop praying for your healing and remember, He said I AM the resurrection. Start quoting the scripture that says you are healed and start speaking it, knowing that it's done and your spirit will begin to manifest that which you speak. This is your moment, but first you must change your mind.

The Lord Says...

Renew your mind daily, child, for this world is a fight of flesh and spirit. When your flesh is stronger than your spirit, you will declare what the world declares. But, when your spirit is stronger than your flesh, you will declare the Word as your voice and know that it is so. Abide in Me and I will therefore abide in you.

If you believe it, say, "Oh yeah!"

JUNE 16
YOUR NOW SEASON

In life, you'll be surrounded by thieving mindsets that will try and sway you like a game of tug-of-war; one pulling you into your past to make you feel inadequate or the other yanking you one day into the "sweet bye-and-bye". Jesus found Himself in the middle of 2 thieves, one challenging Him of His identity and the other searching for redemption some day in the future. But Jesus' response was, "today (or NOW) you shall be with Me in Paradise." Don't let these mindsets rob you of your Now season.

Life is very good!

Matthew 6:34 says, "So don't worry about tomorrow, for tomorrow will bring its own worries. Today's trouble is enough for today". In other words, whether your life feels like it's being played out like a game of tug-of-war or not, when you have Jesus and you learn not to worry, the past can't dictate your life and the future can't persuade you because you live a life that is worry-free and you trust God completely. Jesus knew enough to know that today is what mattered. So take advantage of your moment. Carpe Diem, seize the day! Let today be blessed, yet plan for tomorrow. Declare this everyday: This is my **NOW** season and I will Nix my life **Of** Worry; **NOW!**

The Lord Says...

Trust is a simple yet complex word. Grab it by the horns and find out how much of yourself you can let go of and how much of Me you can hold onto for your life and circumstances. When you know who I Am and what I do, letting go gets easier and easier because, child, I will never fail you. Not now, not ever.

If you believe it, say, "Oh yeah!"

JUNE 17
CHANCES

THERE ARE TIMES IN OUR LIFE WHEN WE FEEL OUR PAST IS TOO GREAT OF A HINDRANCE FOR GOD TO USE US. BUT WE FORGET HOW GREAT OUR GOD IS. PAUL, IN HIS PAST, WAS THE LAST PERSON ANYONE THOUGHT COULD BE CONVERTED BUT WAS TRANSFORMED BY THE POWER OF GOD TO BECOME THE GREATEST APOSTLE OF THE EARLY CHURCH. WHEN THE SCALES FALL OFF OUR EYES, WE REALIZE GOD IS A GOD OF THE 2ND CHANCE, THE SLIM CHANCE, THE FAT CHANCE AND THE NO CHANCE. HE BELIEVES IN US FAR MORE THAN WE DO OURSELVES. NOTHING IS TOO GREAT FOR A GREAT GOD.

LIFE IS VERY GOOD!

Come on, somebody! When you know that you serve a 2nd Chance, Slim Chance, Fat Chance and No Chance God, you've got it made. God takes a chance on you every time you ask for forgiveness and then He acts like nothing ever happened by throwing it all into the Sea of Forgetfulness. Wow, you don't get a 2nd chance in sports when an injury sidelines you from the game; you're out until you recover. Look at it like this: the world doesn't offer you do-overs but every day is a do-over with God. So pick up your Chance card (like in the game of Monopoly). Your card may read, "Today receive a second chance, courtesy of God's Grace." Where will you spend your 2nd chance today? Or perhaps your card says, "Today you have received a Get Out of Jail Free card." What is holding you captive? Here is your chance to be free. Take a chance and know that when you serve a God of the 2nd Chance, Slim Chance, Fat Chance and No Chance, He will see you through.

The Lord Says...

I got you in My hands. If you will only seek Me, I will be found. When the scales come off your eyes you will recognize who I really am and, more importantly, who you really are. You are My child. Nothing is too great for you, because nothing is too great for Me. I believe in you and you are enough.

If you believe it, say, "Oh yeah!"

JUNE 18
RECEIVE YOUR REWARD

REMEMBER THIS: UNHEALTHY MINDSETS ARE THIEVES THAT ROB YOU OF YOUR REWARD. THEY MAKE YOU THINK YOU'RE UNDESERVING OF RECEIVING ALL GOD HAS PROMISED YOU. WE HAVE TO GET TIRED OF THIS WAY OF THINKING. BE LIKE POPEYE AND BREAK OPEN THE WORD OF GOD (SPINACH), CONSUME IT AND LET IT FILL US UP WITH HIS STRENGTH SO WE CAN OVERCOME THESE OBSTACLES (BRUTUS). IT'S TIME TO PUT THE UNHEALTHY MINDSETS UNDER YOUR FEET SO YOU CAN RECEIVE YOUR REWARD. YOU DESERVE IT.

LIFE IS VERY GOOD!

Colossians 3:2 says, "Set your minds on things above, not on earthly things". When a challenge or obstacle comes your way, what is your first natural instinct? Do you talk about it? Call a family member or friend for prayer? Do you complain about it? Well, if you're not finding spinach for your issue by opening the Word and getting it into you, then you're doing the wrong thing. Spinach provided Popeye with unimaginable strength. When you memorize God's Word and put into your heart, it provides you with more than unimaginable strength; it becomes your remedy for all situations. Without God's Word, you revert to the world's tactics: whining, complaining, and accepting the circumstances with complacency and fear. The Bible tells us that God will give you a sound mind and it is because of the world we live in that renewing our minds daily is a necessary process in our spiritual walk. So, take the plunge and set your things on high (God's mind) and not on things below (earthly mind).

The Lord Says...

The mind is a beautiful place. I know for I created it. But, it is also where the battleground for your heart begins. Renew your mind daily by washing it with the Word; the truth that lives and breathes. Arise with the truth and recline at rest with the truth in your mind. Speaking My truths will become but second nature to you in your everyday life.

If you believe it, say, "Oh yeah!"

JUNE 19
YOUR DREAM MAP

THE SPIRIT OF PROCRASTINATION IS MORE THAN DELAYING OR PUTTING SOMETHING OFF, IT'S A THIEF OF YOUR TIME AND EVEN MORE, IT'S SOMETHING THAT ROBS A MAN OF GOD-GIVEN IDEAS. IT CAUSES ONE TO PUT OFF GOD'S PURPOSE FOR A LATER TIME. REMEMBER, EVERY MOMENT CAN BE USED TO FURTHER ADVANCE THE KINGDOM OF GOD. CARPE DIEM...SEIZE THE DAY!

LIFE IS VERY GOOD!

I see many people dreaming but few who have actually sat down to sketch out a plan to make their dreams a reality. Proverbs 16:3 says, "Commit to the Lord whatever you do and he will establish your plans". If you purposed to be a concert pianist, you must sketch out a plan. It first starts with piano lessons, then practice and recitals. Every year you take lessons, the more you practice, the better you become. You then go to college to fine-tune your craft and become a music major. You graduate and get a job with the local symphony orchestra. You perform your first solo concert. You make connections, record your music and create your brand. Your dream is now a living reality and all because you put a plan in place. When you commit whatever it is you love to do unto the Lord, the Bible says that your gifts make room for you. Colossians tells us that He will establish your plans. So run with Him, not behind Him or in front of Him or without Him. Put your plan in place and trust Him. Watch and see what He will do.

The Lord Says...

I Am a right NOW God for I Am alive. I live and breathe in and through you. NOW is the time. Yesterday was then, it has come and gone. Tomorrow awaits you NOW; today in this moment. Plan to pursue your purpose and watch as I establish your plan with you. It's always all about team work. No man fulfills his/her dreams alone.

If you believe it, say, "Oh yeah!"

JUNE 20
BE STRONG AND COURAGEOUS

LOCATION, LOCATION, LOCATION! ALTHOUGH THIS IS WHAT THE WORLD CONSIDERS IMPORTANT, GOD ALWAYS HAS A SPECIFIC PLACE FOR US TO BE. THOUGH IT MAY NOT LOOK PLEASANT TO THE EYE, IT HAS A PURPOSE. MOSES HAD TO SPEND TIME IN THE BACKSIDE OF A WILDERNESS TO HAVE HIS BURNING BUSH EXPERIENCE. WHEN WE UNDERSTAND GOD HAS ORDAINED OUR STEPS, EVEN THE PLACES THAT LOOK UNAPPEALING CAN LEAD TO A GREATER DESTINY. DON'T LET YOUR PERCEPTION STEAL YOUR VISION.

LIFE IS VERY GOOD!

In Joshua 1:1-6, Moses had died and Joshua received his marching orders. God gave Joshua some instructions and encouragement: He told Joshua to get the people ready to cross the Jordan River because He was going to give the Israelites the land that was promised to Moses; every place their feet landed. He provided the boundaries for him and told him that He was with them, would never leave them nor forsake them and no one could come against them. Then He instructed Joshua to be strong and courageous.

Joshua led the Israelites to the river's edge and, on the other side, they saw their destiny. In between them and their destiny was a barrier: the Jordan River. What's interesting is that the residents of Jericho and the Canaanites worshipped Baal and one thing Baal was best known for was being the god of water. The scripture says that the river was at flood stage. In the natural, the river was Baal's way of keeping the Canaanites and residents of Jericho safe from the Israelites but God was about to come on the scene. He was about to change things up and show that He was, once again, mightier and above all other gods. Though God was with Joshua, He required them to step into the water before HE moved. You have to understand, it wasn't just a gradual "get your feet wet, then your knees wet" sort of immersion. The water was at flood stage. It was an "all in, float down the river" sort of deal. Imagine the unity. Imagine the unwavering, 'no doubt' type of faith. God has ordained your steps just like He did for the Israelites and, more than likely, you'll intersect with a barrier on your way to destiny. Never let it steal what belongs to you, for all things are possible. The impossible will often become your opportunity. Trust and walk forward with your eyes on the prize.

The Lord Says...

What I did for Joshua and My people I will do for you. Barriers are only mental blockades. Trust and believe and keep your eyes on Me and together we will find a way across whatever barrier you face. Speak life.

If you believe it, say, "Oh yeah!"

JUNE 21
GREAT THINGS ARE COMING

WHAT MAKES MOVING FORWARD SO DIFFICULT IN LIFE? LETTING GO OF WHAT WAS, OR WHAT IS, IN PURSUIT OF WHAT'S GOING TO BE. WHEN STEPPING INTO THE FUTURE, REMEMBER THIS: JUST BECAUSE IT SEEMS TO BE UNCERTAIN, DOESN'T MEAN THAT IT IS. GOD GAVE A PROMISE TO TAKE CARE OF US AND NOT TO ABANDON US. HE PLANS TO GIVE US A FUTURE AND A HOPE. STAND ON HIS PROMISE; GREAT THINGS ARE COMING TO YOU.

LIFE IS VERY GOOD!

Isaiah 43:18 says, "Forget the former things; do not dwell on the past". This has been an age-old issue. Abram had to do it. He left his homeland and family and started walking, and <u>then</u> God told him where to go. Joshua and the Israelites had to do it when God required them to get into the water to reach their future. Lot's wife went through it but had no vision of the future God had for her, so she perished along with her future. The scripture says that without a vision people perish. Every minute that goes by becomes your past, so stop dwelling on yesterday. If you know who you are in Christ and what He wants for you, then just sit back and rest, declare His Word to be "yes and amen" and let His timing work out in your life. Our lives are so clock based, but God's time is not like our time. He might come through in the midnight hour, but He always comes through. Stand, lift your hands and thank Him for the journey is sweet.

The Lord Says...

I give you sunshine. Do you see it? I give you cool breezes. Do you feel it? I give you nature. Do you walk through it and see Me? I give you hope. Do you know it? I give you abundance. Do you receive it? I stand by My promises. Do you know it? In the future you see Me, feel Me, walk with Me, recognize Me, believe in Me, know Me and live in the abundance I have created for you, even if it looks like it's a late arrival. Great things are always in store. Keep walking forward. I Am always on time.

If you believe it, say, "Oh yeah!"

JUNE 22
PERFECTION PERSPECTIVE

WHEN YOUR EYES BECOME OPEN TO TRUTH, YOU WILL SEE YOURSELF FROM THE REALM OF COMPLETION. THE FIRST THING ADAM SAW WHEN HE OPENED HIS EYES WAS GOD, A TRUE REFLECTION OF WHO HE WAS. YOU WERE MADE PERFECT AND THIS PERFECTION STILL IS TODAY! CHANGE YOUR PERSPECTIVE, SEE YOURSELF FROM HIS EYES.

LIFE IS VERY GOOD!

Genesis 1:31 says, "God saw all that he had made and it was very good. And there was evening and there was morning—the sixth day". Remember that within those six days of creation, God created man in His image. Therefore, as mommas used to say back in the day, "God don't make any junk." When God made you, He created goodness on this earth. You need to change your perspective and your internal dialogue about yourself. Say this, "I am a child of God. I am fearfully and wonderfully made. There is no one like me. I am unique, gifted, and full of life and I was born with purpose. I am a warrior who is filled with faith, hope and love. I am loved; therefore I love myself and others. I am a King's kid and my daddy God is the same, yesterday, today and forever. Amen." Now go and say that prayer every day if you need to until you believe it.

The Lord Says...

I have given you life, literally. Therefore, you are good and you are destined to live it more abundantly. Find abundance in relationships, in personal growth, in your time, your talent and your treasure. Find abundance in My love and hope in My love for you, the you I made. You're enough for Me as I Am more than enough for you.

If you believe it, say, "Oh yeah!"

JUNE 23
NOW IS YOUR TIME

THE BAD MEMORIES OF DAYS PAST ARE BONDAGE FOR TODAY. THE EFFECT OF THE PAST
PARALYZES YOU FROM YOUR NOW MOMENT. JESUS SAID TO THE MAN, "DO YOU WANT TO BE
MADE WELL?" HIS RESPONSE WAS, "I HAVE NO MAN TO PUT ME IN THE WATER." DON'T LET
WHAT HAPPENED YESTERDAY STOP YOU FROM STEPPING INTO YOUR NOW TIME. THE WATER IS
STIRRING!

LIFE IS VERY GOOD!

John 14:26 says, "But the Advocate, the Holy Spirit, whom the Father will
send in my name, will teach you all things and will remind you of everything I
have said to you". The water is stirring; don't be afraid because it looks different
than it did before. The future can seem overwhelming until you step into it. God
has given you a gift to help see you through: the Holy Spirit. Let the Holy Spirit
be your lawyer and your advocate. Take the hand of the Holy Spirit and get ready
for the ride of your life. If you are not filled with the Holy Spirit, worship, pray and
ask God to fill you and He will fill you to overflowing with the Him. When you
pray in the Spirit you, will be strengthened and empowered like the disciples were
in the upper room. He is all you need.

The Lord Says...

We are three Persons yet one; God the Father, God the Son and God the Holy
Spirit. Jesus came and the Holy Spirit is with you. We are here and We are able to
meet you where you are. Let Our power see you through the pain of yesterday and
walk with you through today, preparing you for all your tomorrows.

If you believe it, say, "Oh yeah!"

JUNE 24
DESTINY IS BONE DEEP

THE IMPOSSIBLE IS POSSIBLE WHEN THERE IS A PROMISE OVER YOUR LIFE. ELISHA HAD THE PROMISE OF THE DOUBLE PORTION BUT HE DIED JUST ONE MIRACLE SHORT OF HIS DOUBLE PORTION. THAT LAST MIRACLE CAME WHEN THE BODY OF A DEAD MAN WAS DROPPED INTO ELISHA'S GRAVE AND CAME BACK TO LIFE WHEN THE BODY HIT ELISHA'S BONES. EVEN WHEN IN THE TOMB, THE WORD OF GOD STILL MANIFESTED. NEVER FORGET YOUR PROMISES FOR THEY ARE BONE DEEP.

LIFE IS VERY GOOD!

Think about that. In the natural it looked like God wasn't true to His Word because Elisha was going to be one miracle short of the double portion. But God... His power is His alone and He is the One who breathed breath into Elisha when he was born. He is the same God who breathed the breath of life into you. This is the same God that created the universe in six days then rested, parted the sea and multiplied fish and bread for the masses. You must understand, your destiny was breathed into you from the day you were conceived...bone deep. That is awesome. It's just like God to show that it was never Elisha's power but God's power all along. By the body coming back to life after hitting Elisha's dead bones, God showed His power, His might and more importantly, that His Word was always good and always right on time. Psalm 68:35 says, "You, God, are awesome in your sanctuary; the God of Israel gives power and strength to his people. Praise be to God!". You see, He never fails to fulfill His promises, to love and care for you, to give you strength and empower you. People are but vessels. As Elisha was a vessel, so are you. It is, however, God's power that changes the lives of people, for He is the giver of power and strength. You are His trumpet; His voice to the nations.

The Lord Says...

To Abraham I made a covenant, a promise to which you were grafted into. Remember, I Am the vine and you are the branches. I will never leave you nor forsake you and My Words were good then and they are good now. Seek Me and My promises for your life. They shall be found and you will be blessed indeed.

If you believe it, say, "Oh yeah!"

JUNE 25
FAITH IS BORN IN DIFFICULT TIMES

PERSPECTIVE. DO YOU SEE YOUR SITUATION AS A CRISIS OR DO YOU SEE IT AS AN OPPORTU-
NITY FOR CHRIST TO BE FORMED IN YOU? REMEMBER THIS, DIFFICULTIES CAUSE FAITH TO BE
BORN WHEN MAN'S ABILITY FAILS. DON'T LET YOUR SITUATION DICTATE TO YOU WHO YOU
ARE. LET HIS FAITH ARISE AND ALL ELSE SCATTER.

LIFE IS VERY GOOD!

2 Corinthians 4:18 says, "So we fix our eyes not on what is seen, but on what is unseen, since what is seen is temporary, but what is unseen is eternal". So when you fix your perspective on the things unseen, it changes your outlook on everything because your senses come into subjection to the Word of God. Maybe you're dealing with rejection. Then, instead of allowing your senses and emotions to dwell on it, declare Ephesians 1:6, "To the praise of the glory of his grace, wherein he hath made us accepted in the beloved" (KJV). Pretty soon your perspective will change because you've trained it to know and care about what God says versus what others say about you. After all, God says that you are the salt of the earth, so be the savor your world needs and allow God to arise within your life.

The Lord Says...

When I arise, all the enemies scatter, for they are no match for the God of Abraham, Isaac and Jacob. I was with My children in the fiery furnace. I turned the water into wine. I build, plant and care take of. I do not destroy and tear down. I Am with you always!

If you believe it, say, "Oh yeah!"

JUNE 26
SAFETY EVEN IN TURBULENCE

THE JOURNEY IN LIFE IS LIKE AN AIRPLANE FLIGHT TRAVELING FROM ONE DESTINATION TO ANOTHER. SOMETIMES IN THAT JOURNEY THERE IS UNEXPECTED TURBULENCE. WHEN YOU EXPERIENCE ROUGH AIR, BEFORE YOU REACT, LISTEN FOR HIS SOOTHING VOICE THAT SAYS TO REMAIN CALM, RETURN TO YOUR SEAT AND BUCKLE UP. HIS VOICE COMFORTS IN THE TIME OF TROUBLE.

LIFE IS VERY GOOD!

John 10:27 says, "My sheep hear my voice and I know them and they follow me". It's pretty simple, really. If you are a child of God and you spend time with Him, you will come to know His voice. Knowing God's voice is imperative in this earthly world because you can either be safe from unexpected turbulence in your life or mistake it for something else. The enemy would love nothing better than to sideline you from your purpose, so keep your eyes on God and your ears ready to hear. Buckle up and get ready for the greatest ride of your life. Never fret, Jesus is with you every step of the way.

The Lord Says...

I Am with you always, even unto the ends of the earth. Where I go, you go. Where you go, I go. I walk with you out the door every morning. I sit in the passenger seat of your car. I Am there in the midst of your conversations with your family members and colleagues. I Am there with you as you contemplate integrity in the business decision you're about to make. I Am there with you during your exams, when you're grocery shopping and wherever you are. I never, never leave you. You have a friend that sticks closer than a brother. A Father who loves you beyond measure. All that you need, I Am. I Am enough!

If you believe it, say, "Oh yeah!"

JUNE 27
LIFE IS NOT A SOLO JOURNEY

SOMETIMES IN LIFE, WE PRAY FOR GOD TO DO THINGS FOR US INSTEAD OF ASKING WHAT HE CAN DO THROUGH US. OUR PURPOSE SHOULD NEVER BE AN "I" THING, BUT A "WE" THING. PETER AND JOHN CAME OUT OF THE UPPER ROOM AND IMMEDIATELY HELPED A MAN IN NEED AT THE GATE BEAUTIFUL. THEY GRABBED HIM BY THE HAND AND POURED OUT WHAT THEY CONTAINED. THIS IS YOUR HOUR TO HELP SOMEONE "RISE UP AND WALK"!

LIFE IS VERY GOOD!

This journey called life was never meant to walked alone. God cared deeply about relationships and people from the beginning of time. He cared that Adam felt lonely, so He created a helper. He cared that Adam take dominion in the world and had order in his life so He created the universe with a sky, water, plants and animals, the sun, the moon and the stars. God cares about people and that's why He made the ultimate sacrifice and sent Jesus. Luke 24:49 says, "I Am going to send you what my Father has promised; but stay in the city until you have been clothed with power from on high". And this is why God sent His Holy Spirit to you. That same power that raised Jesus from the dead and empowered His people in the upper room, is the same power you have access to today. So rise in His power for "you have been clothed with power from on high," is what the scripture says. If it applied then, it applies now. Give to your world all that God has given you and one life at a time will be changed by His goodness. Just think of what He can do through you.

The Lord Says...

I Am the source of light. You are the lamp. I Am the bulb. You are the switch and I Am the power. Light up your life like a lighthouse beacon where all the light points your world into My arms of safety, love, compassion and grace.

If you believe it, say, "Oh yeah!"

JUNE 28
THE FAMILY RESEMBLANCE

UNDER THE OLD COVENANT, MAN HAD TO BRING A LAMB AS A SACRIFICE FOR THE ATONEMENT OF HIS SINS. TODAY, WE KNOW CHRIST WAS THE LAMB SLAIN FOR THE FORGIVENESS OF ALL SIN. WHEN WE REPENT AND RECEIVE HIS FORGIVENESS, IT SETS OUR FEET IN A NEW DIRECTION AND RENEWS OUR MIND, BUT IF WE CONTINUE TO SEE OURSELVES IN OUR OLD NATURE, WE'LL NEVER FEEL WORTHY. IT'S TIME TO CHANGE OUR MINDS FROM SIN CONSCIOUSNESS TO BEING GOD AWARE. HE CAME TO SET US FREE. WALK IN IT.

LIFE IS VERY GOOD!

Freedom comes when you know the truth and the truth renews your mind. Have you noticed that when God talks of His people, He calls them His "children"? Put that into perspective. First, you're His child and when you receive Christ in your heart He makes all things new. What does it mean to be the child of God? It means you are loved unconditionally, forgiven continually, given an abundant life. It means that you have authority over the enemy and can live a Kingdom life. So look in the mirror and see the resemblance between you and your Father. Look into your family history book called the Bible and experience the history and ancestry you were grafted into. Then, you will walk in a freedom that knows no boundaries because you know the truth and it has set you free. You will live with the trust of a child who knows their daddy is always for them, 24/7. So renew your mind daily and begin to see Christ's image when you look in the mirror. Sooner than later your mind will transform and you will walk in freedom.

The Lord Says...

The truth that I have spoken will always set you free. See it. Take it. Experience it. Dwell on it and you shall become all that it says you will be. I have always believed it for your life. It's time that you believe it for yours as well.

If you believe it, say, "Oh yeah!"

JUNE 29
THE POWER OF HIS WORD

WHEN EVERYTHING AROUND YOU SEEMS TO BE SLIPPING AWAY AND YOU'RE DWELLING IN THE LANDS OF UNCERTAINTY, THE PROMISE OF YOUR FUTURE STILL REMAINS. REMEMBER THIS: THE SUFFERINGS OF THIS PRESENT TIME ARE NOT WORTHY TO BE COMPARED WITH THE GLORY WHICH IS TO BE REVEALED. BE CERTAIN OF THIS, HIS WORD OVER YOU WILL NOT RETURN VOID.

LIFE IS VERY GOOD!

Isaiah 55:11 says, "So is my word that goes out from my mouth: It will not return to me empty, but will accomplish what I desire and achieve the purpose for which I sent it". Sometimes it's easy for people to take this scripture to mean a word of knowledge that comes from a prophetic voice. However, the Bible is God's inspired Word and Jesus, the greatest prophet of all time. Therefore, we can conclude that the book of Isaiah is also talking about God's very Words in the Bible, because they were spoken by God and the scripture says 'My words...from My mouth'. Whose words? God's Words. Come on, somebody! It's time to shout. All of God's Words are yes and amen; they will not come back to you empty. Claim your victory now. It's on the way.

The Lord Says...

I Am a keeper of My Word through all generations and every Word has purpose for your life. Find the Word for your life and claim it as victory today.

If you believe it, say, "Oh yeah!"

JUNE 30
THE BEST IS YET TO COME

To possess the promise, one must start moving forward. Dwelling on thoughts of the past can reopen wounds that you're not fully healed from, or cause you to become frustrated in the present moment. Paul says, forgetting those things which are behind and reaching forward to those things which are ahead. It's time to forget what was and reach for what is! His promises today are greater than the pains of yesterday.

Life is very good!

Isaiah 43:18-19 says, "Forget the former things; do not dwell on the past. See, I Am doing a new thing! Now it springs up; do you not perceive it? I Am making a way in the wilderness and streams in the wasteland". If you keep looking behind you instead of looking forward, you will miss out on the new thing God has in store. Forget about the past! Wouldn't you rather have the new things God has for you instead of the 'same old same old'? Learn to discern the times and the seasons and watch as, even in your wilderness experience, He makes a way where there seems to be no way.

The Lord Says...

I Am the well of living water in your life. My mercies are new every morning and every day is a day to move forward instead of back. To live, be strong and dwell along the water's edge with Me in the cool of the day. Let's walk together and reach for what is and is to come.

If you believe it, say, "Oh yeah!"

JULY 1
JESUS IS YOUR ONE TRUE FRIEND

IT'S BEEN SAID THAT THE HARDEST THING TO FIND IN LIFE IS A TRUE FRIEND; A PERSON WHO UNDERSTANDS YOUR PAST, BELIEVES IN YOUR FUTURE AND ACCEPTS YOU JUST THE WAY YOU ARE WITH NO STRINGS ATTACHED. JESUS IS A FRIEND THAT STICKS CLOSER THAN A BROTHER. HE NEVER LEAVES NOR FORSAKES. HE NEVER JUDGES YOU UNFAIRLY. HE'S THERE TO ANSWER YOUR CALL. HE'S A SHOULDER TO LEAN ON. HE'S ALWAYS HAPPY TO SPEND TIME WITH YOU. HE LOVES YOU IN SPITE OF YOURSELF. DON'T MAKE HIM JUST AN ACQUAINTANCE; HE'S HERE TO BE EVERYTHING TO YOU.

LIFE IS VERY GOOD!

Proverbs 27:17 says, "As iron sharpens iron, so one person sharpens another". What better way to sharpen your iron than with a friend and mentor like Jesus. You spend quality time with your best friend, right? You go to the movies, a ball game, shopping, to lunch, talk on the phone and they are a joy to hang out with. Jesus wants to be that best friend in your life; more than an acquaintance. He may fulfill the need of comforter, counselor, teacher, father and even friend. He is all that you need and more; HE is your one TRUE friend.

The Lord Says...

I Am all that I Am in your life. I Am enough for any situation and I will be your forever friend. Walk with Me. Talk with Me. Seek Me and find Me.

If you believe it, say, "Oh yeah!"

JULY 2
PROMISE-FILLED OPPOSITION

When we're in a land of opposition, we always think God has us in the wrong place. But we need to realize God gave us the Promised Land and commanded us to drive out the giants. It may not look good and it may not feel good, but facing opposition doesn't change the fact that God's promise is in it. Hold on to what God has declared over your life. You'll see the reward in the end.

Life is very good!

Opposition is a part of life's journey. Abraham faced a barren womb. David faced a giant. Gideon faced an army. Mary faced social injustices. Paul and Silas faced prison. Jonah faced the belly of a giant fish and Moses faced a pharaoh. These warriors all have two things in common; they faced opposition and God delivered them. God opened Sarah's womb for Abraham, gave David wisdom on how to kill the giant, fought the army on Gideon's behalf, protected Mary from Herod, freed Paul and Silas from prison, released Jonah from the belly of the giant fish and delivered Moses along with the Israelites. He will do the same for you. Your victory is closer than you think. In fact, Deuteronomy 20:4 says, "For the Lord your God is the one who goes with you to fight for you against your enemies to give you victory". It doesn't always come when and how you think it will, but it's always right on time...Victory!

The Lord Says...

Do you believe you have the victory today? It has been written. It has already been done, conquered, settled and delivered because I have taken care of it all. Believe it with all your heart, receiving nothing less. I Am no respecter of persons, for I Am able to do above what you could ever think or imagine, but you must believe without wavering.

If you believe it, say, "Oh yeah!"

JULY 3
THE LIVING INHERITANCE

WHEN A NOW MOMENT IS EXPERIENCED, THERE IS A TRANSITION FROM WHAT WAS (THE PAST) OR WHAT MIGHT BE (THE FUTURE) INTO WHAT IS (TODAY). CALEB WAS A MAN TIRED OF THE MEMORY OF SPYING OUT THE PROMISED LAND AND TIRED OF WAITING FOR A SOMEDAY PROMISE TO COME. SO CALEB ROSE UP AND SAID, "NOW, GIVE ME MY MOUNTAIN. I'M READY TODAY FOR MY INHERITANCE." STEP INTO WHAT GOD HAS TODAY! HIS NOW MOMENT FOR YOU IS HERE.

LIFE IS VERY GOOD!

Have you ever wondered why people wait until they die to hand over an inheritance to their children? I love to see the smile on a giver's face when they hand out portions of an inheritance to their loved ones while they are alive. It's beautiful. They take such joy and pride in providing such wealth and amazing gifts. I mean, why not? Why not enjoy the fruits of your labor into the next generation right now? The same is true for God. Take a look at Ephesians 1:11-14, which says, "In him we were also chosen, having been predestined according to the plan of him who works out everything in conformity with the purpose of his will, in order that we, who were the first to put our hope in Christ, might be for the praise of his glory. And you also were included in Christ when you heard the message of truth, the gospel of your salvation. When you believed, you were marked in him with a seal, the promised Holy Spirit, who is a deposit guaranteeing our inheritance until the redemption of those who are God's possession—to the praise of his glory".

So tell that mountain to be removed and pick up your inheritance today. He never said it was for tomorrow. He gave you the Holy Spirit, who guarantees your inheritance. Get a hold of it and don't let go.

The Lord Says...

My kingdom and all I have is available to you. You see, satan wanted more than all I had. I was never enough. Therefore his heart could not reside in heaven. I was enough for the man next to Me on the cross that day and I was enough for you when the stone rolled away. Life is all about giving and receiving. Your inheritance is great indeed.

If you believe it, say, "Oh yeah!"

JULY 4
IMAGINE AWAY LIMITATIONS

In life, your imagination can be greater than knowledge. Knowledge is limited to the things you've learned or know whereas imagination is endless. Don't let what you've learned be a limitation to what God can do. Imagine the impossible and believe for the inconceivable. If He can do it for Jacob with the spotted, speckled and streaked, He can do it for you. He's the God of all possibilities.

LIFE IS VERY GOOD!

Imagine it, as a type of shepherd, Jacob knew about epigenetics and recessive genes even then. It seems impossible, but somehow Jacob learned how the bark could change the chemical compound in his herd and therefore could cause them to be born spotted, speckled and streaked (Gen. 30:29-40). God did the impossible for Jacob, what more can He do for you? Be like Ezekiel and tell the dead bones in your life to live. When you speak the Word to the deadness in your life, those dead bones cannot help but begin to shake, rattle and restore themselves to their rightful place because God's Word is restorative and resurrects. So let the Creator of imagination tap into your imagination and take the limits off what He can do.

The Lord Says...

I create. How do I create? By seeing and speaking. I saw the universe as it should be and spoke it into existence. I see wholeness and speak healing. I see a need and speak resources into existence. What more can be done when you and My Word agree on anything in this earth?

If you believe it, say, "Oh, yeah!"

JULY 5
GOD DOESN'T MAKE MISTAKES

UNDERSTAND YOUR ORIGINATION BECAUSE THEN YOU CAN FULLY WALK IN YOUR IDENTITY.
YOU DIDN'T COME FROM THE SEED OF YOUR FATHER OR THE WOMB OF YOUR MOTHER, YOU
JUST CAME THROUGH THEM. THE FACT IS THAT YOU CAME OUT OF THE BOSOM OF YOUR HEAV-
ENLY FATHER AND HE PLACED YOU AS A SEED INTO THIS WORLD. DON'T LET PAST ISSUES OF
YOUR EARTHLY FAMILY STOP YOU FROM YOUR HEAVENLY DESTINY.

LIFE IS VERY GOOD!

Psalm 139:13 says, "For you created my inmost being; you knit me together in my mother's womb". Never forget, God had His hand in your arrival here on this earth. You are His child, ambassador of heaven, given to a set of parents here on earth that you might thrive and come alive within your purpose to fulfill His calling. You are the seed of Abraham. To God, you are family. Destiny awaits you, no matter how dysfunctional your earthly family may seem. God is the God of 2nd chances, the God of hope and a future. Keep your eyes on Him and you will not fail.

The Lord Says...

When you keep your eyes on Me, I can lead you, guide you and talk to you that you might gain wisdom and understanding in a world of chaos and crisis. Together we will be great navigators in this life. I placed you in a particular family for a purpose. What will you contribute and what will you learn as you serve there?

If you believe it, say, "Oh yeah!"

JULY 6
BE THE CHANGE THE WORLD NEEDS

WHEN YOU UNDERSTAND THE POWER THAT LIVES IN YOU, YOU BECOME A GIFT TO THOSE
AROUND YOU. RELEASE HIS PRESENCE TO THOSE IN NEED AND WATCH HIS MIRACLE POWER
BECOME THEIR HOPE. IT'S TIME TO CHANGE LIVES BY THE POWER OF DEMONSTRATION! RE-
LEASE HIM TO THOSE IN NEED.

LIFE IS VERY GOOD!

I've heard people ask what someone would do if Jesus showed up at their house. Ever have a neighbor come to the door for sugar? Ever see a need somewhere? John 13:34-35 says, "A new command I give you: Love one another. As

I have loved you, so you must love one another. By this everyone will know that you are my disciples, if you love one another"00. Want to see Jesus on the earth? Obey His commandments and look in the mirror. The scripture says that you were created in His image and when you love one another, others will know you are the disciple of Christ. It all goes back to giving. Give of your time. Give of your talent (or learn a new one) and give of your treasure. Someone needs gas today, a hug, a smile, their groceries or coffee paid for. Someone needs a night out or free babysitting. Maybe a woman you know needs to feel beautiful or a man needs to feel needed. We are the change the world needs. It's not the government's job to support the widows and the orphans; that job belongs to you and me.

The Lord Says...

Be the gift that keeps on giving because I have placed much inside of you that is meant to be given away; love, joy and peace; this is what the world needs.

If you believe it, say, "Oh yeah!"

JULY 7
BREAK THROUGH THE BARRIERS

THE POWER OF LIFE VESTED IN US IS NOT MEANT TO BE CONTAINED, BUT REVEALED. REMOVE THE LIMITATIONS OF WHERE AND WHEN YOU CAN RELEASE HIS PRESENCE AND JUST DO IT. SHARE HIM WITH THOSE IN NEED AND WATCH THEIR LIVES BE CHANGED AND SO WILL YOURS. MIRACLES ARE NEEDED IN THE STREETS AS WELL AS THE CHURCH AND YOU ARE A CARRIER OF HIS GLORY. TOUCH HEARTS AND CHANGE LIVES EVERYWHERE YOU GO!

LIFE IS VERY GOOD!

People, especially church people, need to get outside the four walls. Jesus was a marketplace kind of guy but, for some reason, the church has tried to get the marketplace to their congregation. What would happen if church closed down for four weeks and all the churches took church to the marketplace, the street, the beach, the parks and the neighborhoods? Mark 16:15-16 says, "He said to them, "Go into all the world and preach the gospel to all creation. Whoever believes and is baptized will be saved, but whoever does not believe will be condemned". And the Lord says in Acts 1:8, "But you will receive power when the Holy Spirit comes on you; and you will be my witnesses in Jerusalem and in all Judea and Samaria and to the ends of the earth". In other words, it's not up to your pastor to do all the touching and changing of lives in your community. His job is to disciple and shepherd the flock; to lead and guide. It's our job to take the gospel to the marketplace and be Jesus in the city, at work and at play; by land, by air and by sea. Wherever you go, be the light. Be the encourager. Be the comforter, helper, friend...Be like Jesus here on earth.

The Lord Says...

I have given you the tools, provided you with favor in the marketplace and prayer so that you might talk to Me about the needs of your world. Take My Word and let it breathe life into all that you set out to do and say because you are the My light in this world. Just be the light. I Am right beside you. You cannot fail. Be bold and watch what I do.

If you believe it, say, "Oh yeah!"

JULY 8
TIME + WISDOM = VICTORY

SOMETIMES IN LIFE YOU HAVE TO TAKE A STEP BACK IN ORDER TO MOVE FORWARD. WHEN YOU'RE FACING A DIFFICULT MOMENT, IT'S BETTER TO GIVE YOURSELF A LITTLE SPACE TO THINK A MATTER THROUGH BEFORE EMOTIONS CAUSE YOU TO MAKE A FOOLISH CHOICE. A FRUSTRATED EMOTION CAN LEAD TO FAILURE, BUT A LITTLE TIME AND WISDOM WILL LEAD YOU INTO HIS VICTORY. MATURITY IS THE KEY.

LIFE IS VERY GOOD!

James 1:19 says, "My dear brothers and sisters, take note of this: Everyone should be quick to listen, slow to speak and slow to become angry." The tongue has so much power. God himself spoke the universe into existence. There is an art to listening. In times of frustration, most people are only listening to what they want to hear and are only partially listening. Focus and do more than hear. Listen for what is really being said. Take down the walls and be willing to put the other person first. Choose wisdom in that moment, which means to hold your tongue. Let God arise in that moment and ask yourself, "What would Jesus do?" Practice listening and not just hearing. How? By holding your tongue. Taking down walls and adjusting your priorities will lead to your own maturity. Jesus is always the answer. Through Him, hope is alive.

The Lord Says...

Let worry fall far from you and be not dismayed. Through love, don't just hear but listen. As you practice you will hear Me when I call and listen when I speak. My sheep know My voice.

If you believe it, say, "Oh yeah!"

JULY 9
TODAY IS YOUR DAY!

WHY IS IT EASIER TO BELIEVE GOD FOR EVERYONE ELSE'S MIRACLE, BUT SO DIFFICULT TO BELIEVE HIM FOR OUR OWN? TODAY, TRANSFORM THE WAY YOU THINK. THE WORD SAYS, "PERCEIVE THAT GOD IS NOT A RESPECTER OF PERSONS". KNOW THAT WHAT HE DID FOR ONE, HE CAN DO FOR ALL. TODAY IS YOUR DAY! BELIEVE THAT WHAT YOU HAVE NEED OF HAS BEEN SET IN MOTION.

LIFE IS VERY GOOD!

The ways of God consist of miracles and, if the scripture says in Malachi 3:6 that He changes not, the same miracles that were available in antiquities time are available today. We often think of miracles when Jesus turned water into wine, multiplied loaves and fishes for the masses, healed the sick, the lame and the blind, or provided oil for the widow continuously, or when He rose from the dead. Yes, there were miracles of transformation (the wine), miracles of multiplication (the oil, the bread and fish), miracles of healing (the lame, the blind...) and miracles of resurrection (raising of the dead) and the miracle of birth/new life. One of the greatest miracles was that, through the sacrifice of a man, we might be saved, forgiven of our sins and our lives transformed. Think about salvation as a miracle and you will feel more than just blessed, you will know you are redeemed; that you yourself have received the miracle of resurrection and new birth and all other miracles are available to you. In fact, we were created to worship the Lord and win souls. Matthew 28:19-20 says, "Therefore go and make disciples of all nations, baptizing them in the name of the Father and of the Son and of the Holy Spirit and teaching them to obey everything I have commanded you. And surely I Am with you always, to the very end of the age." Here is another miracle; God says if you do as He asks, make disciples, baptize them, teach them and to love and obey His commandments, if you do that, He is with you ALWAYS. You can't fail on a deal like that. If He is with you always then all the miracles your life might need are available because you are a friend of God. That's good stuff. Do you believe it?

The Lord Says...

Believe - without wavering, without doubt for I Am able to do above and beyond what you could think or imagine. Ask and you shall receive. Seek and you shall find. Knock, for I have office hours 24/7 and, when you input, I will provide the output.

If you believe it, say, "Oh yeah!"

JULY 10
JUMPSTART YOUR LEADERS

ARE YOU FEELING RESTLESS IN YOUR SPIRIT OR DO YOU FIND YOURSELF IDLING IN NEUTRAL, GOING NOWHERE FAST? IF SO, CHECK WHO YOU'RE FOLLOWING. WHEN LEADERS LOSE VISION OR FIND THEMSELVES PARKED IN COMFORT, THEY ARE NOT LEADING AND THOSE FOLLOWING THEM CAN BECOME RESTLESS AND FRUSTRATED. IF YOUR LEADER IS NOT MOVING FORWARD, YOU MIGHT FIND YOURSELF STUCK. LEADERS MUST ADVANCE, SO THOSE FOLLOWING HAVE SOMEWHERE TO GO! RECOGNIZE THAT GOD HAS CALLED YOU TO LEAD SOMEONE. SHIFT GEARS TODAY.

LIFE IS VERY GOOD!

Imagine that you're Samuel. You're approximately 12 years old. You serve the Lord but you have never really heard God speak before because the Word of the Lord was a rare thing in your environment, though you knew of it. Now imagine you heard someone say your name two times. You would think you're either crazy or your parents called you. You go into your parents' room and they tell you no, it wasn't them, you're dreaming so go back to bed. You go back to bed and it happens again so you repeat the routine. This would prove to be frustrating in the middle of the night when you want to sleep. By the third time, your parents are now fully awake and beginning to discern that something's going on. They begin to recognize that, when your name is called once, no big deal but when it's called two and three times, it means something. If your mom has to call you two and three times to take out the trash, you know you're already in trouble, right? So, the parent finally recognizes the significance of being called three times and tells you (like Eli) that if it happens again, it's the Lord, so answer Him. You see, it may seem like all that time was wasted for God to call Samuel four times before Samuel answered. Someone had to know the gravity and importance it meant to God. If God says something more than once, He's trying to establish something. Sometimes your frustration is in listening to others before you listen to God. When you listen to God, His plan and His ways will always lead you down the narrow path. Doesn't His Word say, "all things work together for the good of those who love the Lord and are called according to His purpose?" That's you. Talk to Jesus and you'll find that your frustration will come down to a minimum.

The Lord Says...

If you'll just talk to Me, you'll find that I Am the peace that passes all understanding. I Am the way to wisdom and the door to answers. You think you need to talk to your best friend, your mother, your pastor or your spouse because they are great listeners, but sometimes you just need to talk to Me. I Am here and I wait for you.

If you believe it, say, "Oh yeah!"

JULY 11
MAD ABOUT YOU

TODAY MANY PEOPLE THINK THAT GOD IS MAD OR EVEN DISAPPOINTED IN THEM BECAUSE OF SIN. THE TRUTH IS, THE ONLY MAD GOD IS, IS MADLY IN LOVE WITH YOU. HE DEALT WITH SIN AT THE CROSS SO DON'T LET CONDEMNATION ROB YOU OF YOUR FREEDOM. WHOM THE SON SETS FREE IS FREE INDEED! WALK IN HIS LIBERTY.

LIFE IS VERY GOOD!

What an amazing gift...freedom and unconditional love. Our world is starving for unconditional love. I have hugged grown men who have never been hugged or who have never had a father figure in their lives and they are starving for someone to love on them. Can we not love on one another? Grown men need to love on one another and break the chains. Women are good at loving one another, but they too, could use a dose of "unconditionalness" in their love. Love your husband for who God sees him to be. Love your kids, your neighbors and your co-workers all for who God sees in them. We may not like the choices or behaviors of people, but that's okay, even Jesus was kind to the lepers when no one else considered such love. It was love that healed and broke their chains, for they could see themselves as Jesus saw them; clean, whole and redeemed. The battle always begins in the mind. Never let the enemy allow you to think you are not free. Condemnation is a trick of the mind. Refuse to receive it for you are the child of the King above ALL Kings!

The Lord Says...

If you ask who I Am, I would tell you that I Am LOVE. You receive it freely, now give it freely. The world needs more love...more of Me and less of you.

If you believe it, say, "Oh yeah!"

JULY 12
ANGER CAN MAKE EVEN THE BEST FRUIT ROTTEN

ANGER AND LOVE BOTH PRODUCE RESULTS, BUT WHAT THEY REPRODUCE IS COMPLETELY DIFFERENT. ANGER GIVES BIRTH TO BITTERNESS, REBELLION, FRUSTRATION OR EVEN HATRED. LOVE GIVES BIRTH TO CONFIDENCE, SELF-WORTH, AND SUCCESS. IT'S TRUE; LOVE NEVER FAILS. BE A VOICE OF AFFIRMATION AND DEMONSTRATE LOVE TO THOSE AROUND YOU. IT WILL MAKE A DIFFERENCE IN SOMEONE'S LIFE.

LIFE IS VERY GOOD!

I Thessalonians 5:11 says, "Therefore encourage one another and build each other up, just as in fact you are doing." Anger is an emotion and you'll find throughout life that you will encounter it, but don't let it rule you. The Word says to encourage one another and build one another up. The fruit of anger is rotten. It looks terrible, smells terrible and eats you from the inside out. Love, however, is a seed that keeps on growing great fruit. Next time you start to get frustrated and angry, stop and think for a moment before you react. What will anger and frustration do to you and the receiver? Then, what will love do? It's not easy sometimes to not be right, put other people first, or love those that hurt you, but God requires it of us. Be the difference maker. If you were created in His image then the fruit of love must reside in you. So let it exude from you like the juice of a Georgia peach. Let it drip from your life in every capacity. He is in you.

The Lord Says...

Love always covers the multitude of sins. It restores, repairs and rescues and I Am the great rescuer. Help Me restore and repair the hearts of this world with a little affirmation. You are not just a good man, woman or child; you are a GREAT man, woman or child. I have made you GREAT!

Declare it every day: God made me great and this is a very good day!

If you believe it, say, "Oh yeah!"

JULY 13
DEMONSTRATE LOVE

LOVE IS MORE THAN A WORD OR TOUCH OF AFFECTION, LOVE IS A DEMONSTRATION AND A MOVEMENT OF COMPASSION. IT'S EASY TO LOVE AND HELP SOMEONE YOU KNOW, BUT IT TAKES HIS LOVE TO SHOW KINDNESS TO A STRANGER AND TREAT HIM LIKE A FRIEND. WE DON'T HAVE TIME TO WALK BY A PERSON IN NEED. BE LIKE THE GOOD SAMARITAN AND LEND A HELPING HAND.

LIFE IS VERY GOOD!

I love the random acts of kindness that I see occur as I travel the world: people buying Starbucks for the car behind them…You don't know what they've been through and perhaps they haven't even been to work yet. Random acts of kindness such as paying for the next person's gas or a mother's groceries at the supermarket, taking the elderly, new visitors and their pastors to lunch, buying clothes and finding the needs of acquaintances, friends and colleagues. Have you ever seen the show, Undercover Boss? It's great that an employer gets to know three or four people, where they are in life and acknowledges their efforts, their dreams and their needs. What if a company employer took the next two to five years to find out similar things about every single employee and could bless them with gifts, words of affirmation and make changes in their company and the lives of people? What if you could do that in your home, or in your church? Imagine the domino effect it would have on our world. Imagine getting debt free and then for a period of time using that money to help someone else become debt free. What a gift. Be the light, be the love. On Undercover Boss, most people are touched because they can't believe someone could care so much for them to do something that amazing to change and affect their life and affirm them. That's love demonstrated. Like Luke 6:38 says, "Give and it will be given to you. A good measure, pressed down, shaken together and running over, will be poured into your lap. For with the measure you use, it will be measured to you." Plus, giving is so much fun. It's a joy to see the wide smiles on people's faces and be a part of a life changing event. How can you demonstrate His love today?

The Lord Says...

Love really does make the world go round. It's your pastor's job to shepherd, it's your job to reach the masses and be My love, affirmation, goodness, kindness and a displayer of the fruit of the Spirit to this world. Are you ALL in?

If you believe it, say, "Oh yeah!"

JULY 14
EXACTLY WHERE YOU ARE

THE AWESOME PLACE OF GOD IS SOMETIMES LOCATED IN THE PLACE OF DIFFICULTY. REMEMBER THIS: EVEN IN DIFFICULT PLACES, GOD WILL MAKE HIS PRESENCE KNOWN TO YOU AT AN APPOINTED TIME, JUST AS HE DID WITH JACOB. IT'S UP TO YOU TO UNDERSTAND THAT THIS PLACE IS REALLY A GATEWAY TO HEAVEN. PRAYER WILL CHANGE YOUR PERSPECTIVE AND REVEAL TO YOU THE LORD IS STANDING OVER YOUR SITUATION AND WILL SEE YOU THROUGH.

LIFE IS VERY GOOD!

Think about Jacob for a minute. I love the story of Jacob. Jacob's story is one of transformation. Jacob goes from having a price on his head for stealing his brother's birthright to meeting God at Bethel at a stairway to heaven. He came to Bethel as a result of his past, but God gave him a hope and a future, available to all according to Jeremiah 29:11. Then later his relationship is restored with his brother and at the same place (Bethel) God changes his name from Jacob to Israel, signifying that he had come full circle in his transformation. No longer did his past keep him running, but he had been redeemed and transformed into a new man. No matter what you are going through, God will meet you exactly where you are. His truths are revealed to you in His Word and it will speak to your situation. Expect Him there and you will find Him standing there all along. You may come out with a reminder of your encounter as Jacob did, but that's okay. Let it be a moment in time you will never forget, one that changes your perspective forever.

The Lord Says...

I Am the way, the truth and the life. I will meet you wherever you are and I Am able in all situations. You can count on Me. I Am the great deliverer.

If you believe it, say, "Oh yeah!"

JULY 15
LET YOUR JOY BE CONTAGIOUS

A SMILE IS AN OUTWARD EXPRESSION OF AN INWARD FEELING OF PLEASURE. LET OTHERS KNOW THAT THE JOY YOU HAVE IS NOT AN EMOTION, BUT A PERSON LIVING INSIDE OF YOU. REMEMBER, A SIMPLE FLASH OF JOY CAN BRIGHTEN SOMEONE'S DAY AND CHANGE HOW THEY FEEL. LET HIS EXPRESSION THROUGH YOU BE CONTAGIOUS.

LIFE IS VERY GOOD!

I believe laughter is contagious. Have you ever been in a room where someone breaks out in that belly laughter? You don't even know what they are laughing about, but just the fact that they are belly laughing becomes funny. Proverbs 17:22 says, "A cheerful heart is good medicine, but a crushed spirit dries up the bones." In fact you can go onto the Mayo Clinic website and learn a lot about how laughter helps the body heal itself; even science is in on God's Words. Oftentimes people get it all wrong. You see, happiness is temporal. You're happy because your best friend is moving to the same city, or you got a promotion, your child got into their first choice college or you got what you always wanted for your birthday. But, you cannot live on happiness though you can live being happy. It's joy...joy is everlasting. Joy is there when someone breaks into your car and yet you can still praise him. Joy is there when you had to declare bankruptcy and you still had optimism for the future. Joy is there when wake up every morning and say, "Today I am going to love my spouse." Joy allows you to have hope knowing that tomorrow is always a do-over, so be grateful and joyful today. It says that Jesus is the reason that you smile, not material goods or things that provide it. Joy, it's found in the mourning/morning (Psalm 30:5), in others and in your gratitude for the littlest of things. Get joy, because people like to be around people of joy.

The Lord Says...

Joy makes people walk in My image, for love is much easier to receive coming from a life filled with joy. Many homes struggle because the individuals work so hard, but they have no joy. They try instead to just be happy. Don't settle for happiness, find Joy in Me, and it will lead you to all the happiness you need.

If you believe it, say, "Oh yeah!"

JULY 16
MOUNTAINTOP PERSPECTIVE

THERE IS A SOMEONE WHO DID SOMETHING TO CHANGE ALL. JESUS IS THE SOMEONE WHO GAVE HIS LIFE, SO THAT ALL WHO BELIEVE IN HIM COULD BE CHANGED AND A MAN OF SIN COULD BE TRANSFORMED INTO A NEW CREATION. LET THIS SOMEONE LIVE THROUGH YOU SO YOU CAN DO SOMETHING GREAT IN THIS WORLD TO CHANGE AND TRANSFORM LIVES. YOU ARE HIS EXPRESSED IMAGE.

LIFE IS VERY GOOD!

I hear a lot of people say things like, "It's transformation Tuesday." And, 'throwback Thursday' is a kudos to the transformation that has taken place via visual image of then until now. I would challenge you that, if Tuesday is 'transformation Tuesday', then ask yourself, how are you transforming your world? Is the transformation you have received through Christ something you want others to be transformed by? If so, then have you shared your transformation story? Transformation...the transfer of transformed information. We are transformed that others might be transformed. If you've lost a ton of weight then help someone else who needs to do the same. You see, once you climb the mountain, the goal isn't to stay there. The goal is to go back down the mountain and get someone else who's never been to the top and help them see with the same new perspective that you have gained. When you're at the top of the mountain, you see the same thing as those in the valley or those climbing the mountain, but the perspective is different, more spectacular, significant and appreciated from a higher place. So get in His high place and transform your world one step at a time, Sunday to Sunday.

The Lord Says...

Be transformed by the renewing of your mind, for if I Am with you, who can be against you? No one. It's pretty simple actually. I've helped you climb the mountain so you can take others along with you the next time. I Am the Someone who has changed your life and I will change the lives of those you minister to.

If you believe it, say, "Oh yeah!"

JULY 17
CHAOS TO THE ENEMY

THE ROAD TO VICTORY STARTS WITH THE WAY A PERSON THINKS. WHEN YOU STEW OVER PAST MISTAKES AND FAILURES, IT FILLS YOUR MIND WITH REGRET AND GRIEF AS IT CASTS A SHADOW OVER YOUR POTENTIAL. STOP LISTENING TO VOICES OF DESPAIR AND LISTEN TO HIS VOICE. HIS VOICE WILL ILLUMINATE YOUR PATH AND MAXIMIZE YOUR POTENTIAL AS IT LEADS YOU TO VICTORY.

LIFE IS VERY GOOD!

In Numbers 13, Moses sent out the twelve spies. Imagine if when the twelve came back Moses refused to listen to the two (Joshua and Caleb) who sided with possibility instead of failure. Imagine if Moses got so caught up in all their failures that he couldn't trust the words of any of them. They never would have went in and conquered. There will always be dissenters, even in your own camp. This is why it is so important to know God's voice and be able to hear His voice amidst the whirlwind, amidst the noise of gossipers, talkers and dissenters. He will never lead you astray. The victory is already yours and if He has to, He'll bring chaos to the enemy so you can walk on through with your head held high.

The Lord Says...

I Am the God of breakthrough. I did it for Israel when the enemy fought itself, when I sent manna from heaven, or chartered the course of a single stone into a giant's head. I Am the God of breakthrough like I was for Daniel in the den of lions or for Shadrach, Meshach and Abednego when they were thrown into the fiery furnace and they lived. I Am the God of breakthrough as praise released the chains from Paul and Silas, gave power to Gideon's army and courage to Esther on her approach to the King. I was the God of breakthrough then and I Am the God of the breakthrough now, for I change not.

If you believe it, say, "Oh yeah!"

JULY 18
ARE YOU SELFISH OR SELFLESS?

WHAT DO YOU VALUE IN LIFE? THERE ARE PEOPLE WHO VALUE THEIR POSSESSIONS AND WHAT THEY OWN, WHILE CHRIST VALUES THE TREASURES IN EARTHLY VESSELS. THERE ARE A PEOPLE WHO ARE CONCERNED WITH THE TIME THEY HAVE TO SACRIFICE, WHILE CHRIST WAS CONCERNED WITH SETTING PEOPLE FREE THROUGH HIS SACRIFICE. WHAT YOU VALUE IN LIFE CAN EITHER MAKE YOU SELFISH OR SELFLESS. BE LIKE CHRIST, PLACING OTHERS BEFORE YOURSELF AND WATCH HIS GLORY MANIFEST.

LIFE IS VERY GOOD!

Matthew 6:33 says, "But seek first his kingdom and his righteousness and all these things will be given to you as well." In other words, the purpose of His kingdom is that the heart and soul of others is really what HE is after. If you seek Him and His kingdom purposes first, He says that all **these** things will be given to you. These things He is talking about are in the previous verses when He talks about not worrying about the food you will eat and the clothes you will wear. He will add all of the things you need unto you upon your commitment to seek Him and His kingdom business. To God it's a simple thing; people before things. People, He's all about people. Are you? You carry a hope that the people need. It's Jesus!

The Lord Says...

I Am the living hope of this world. Will you go with Me into the homes, the city, the state and your nation? Will you pray until change occurs? Will you worship until I move? Will you sow the seed, spend the time and disciple the people? I Am with you always. You can do all things. Speak in the hearts from every cardinal direction and I will bring them like the wind that blows.

If you believe it, say, "Oh yeah!"

JULY 19
CHANGE IS A GOD THING

CHANGE IS NOT A BAD THING, IT'S A GOD THING. WHEN YOU TAKE A PICTURE, A MOMENT IN TIME IS CAPTURED THAT WILL NEVER CHANGE. BUT THE TRUTH IS THAT THE PEOPLE IN THE PICTURE ALWAYS DO. WHEN YOU SEE THE SAME IMAGE DAILY, CHANGE CAN BE VERY SUBTLE, BUT WHEN YOU REFLECT ON THESE IMAGES OVER TIME, IT CAN BE REMARKABLE. EMBRACE THE VARIATIONS. IT'S ALL PART OF GOD'S PLAN TO MAKE LIFE MORE ENJOYABLE.

LIFE IS VERY GOOD!

Imagine your life as a Christian that never changed. Change implies growth. Babies grow and change until they become adults and even then people change until it's their time to leave this earth. Hearts change, physical features change, temperaments and attitudes change. If you never changed, then as a Christian, the revelation you learn today would not be relevant tomorrow. Embrace the change like the seasons in time. God's plan is for you to live an abundant life but He also wants His people to experience His goodness here on earth, to grow, mature and stretch at every corner possible. Change produces hope, for if you can see the change in your head and in your heart, you can become the change you seek.

The Lord Says...

Seek me, Child. I Am in the wind, at the door, on the water and in your image. I Am where you are. Be the change the world needs. Be the change that you need and let hope arise.

If you believe it, say, "Oh yeah!"

JULY 20
WE ARE STRONGER TOGETHER

THE KINGDOM OF GOD IS ONE THAT ADDS AND MULTIPLIES, WHERE SATAN'S KINGDOM SUB-TRACTS AND DIVIDES. GOD'S KINGDOM DRAWS PEOPLE TOGETHER, WHERE SATAN'S STRATEGY IS TO ISOLATE AND SEPARATE. DON'T BE FOOLED BY THESE DEVICES, BUT LET GOD'S LOVE BRING AND KEEP US TOGETHER. WE ARE STRONGER AND BETTER TOGETHER.

LIFE IS VERY GOOD!

1 Corinthians 1:10 says, "I appeal to you, brothers and sisters, in the name of our Lord Jesus Christ, that all of you agree with one another in what you say and that there be no divisions among you, but that you be perfectly united in mind and thought." Unity in love is important because it's God's love that binds us together

and it is with and through love that all things are possible. When you are united in your mind with the word, you are united with Christ and you are stronger than you think. When you are united in one accord with your brothers and sisters in Christ, count it all as good. Be a multiplier. Add to your life and the lives of others. Watch and see what God will do.

The Lord Says...

Love gives, never takes away and I Am love. Therefore, when you abide in Me and I abide in you, My love fills you to overflowing and My love comes out of you. United you stand. Divided you fall. Never divide yourself from my Spirit but stay connected and you will see your life flourish.

If you believe it, say, "Oh yeah!"

JUNE 21
A GOD CHALLENGE IS A GOOD CHALLENGE

WHEN YOU FACE A SITUATION THAT SEEMS IMPOSSIBLE TO CHANGE, WHAT DO YOU DO? DO YOU BECOME FRUSTRATED OR ANGRY WITH GOD, OR DO YOU JUST GIVE UP? NO. SOMETIMES IT'S BETTER TO GIVE IN AND CHALLENGE OURSELVES TO CHANGE, BECAUSE THE SITUATION PROBABLY WON'T. TRUST IN CHRIST TO DO THE WORK WITHIN YOU AND EVERYTHING AROUND YOU WILL AUTOMATICALLY FALL INTO PLACE.

LIFE IS VERY GOOD!

As Christians it seems almost automatic that we give the enemy more credit than he deserves. Challenges are blamed on him but often times it's God, stretching and changing you from the inside out; replacing an old wineskin with the new. Trusting in God can sometimes seem like just talk, "Oh yeah, I trust God." But do you really, or only when your back is up against the wall? Let it be a lifestyle. Don't let challenges keep you from the goodness change has to offer. No one wants to stay stagnant and in the same place for too long. Revelation 21:7 says, "Those who are victorious will inherit all this and I will be their God and they will be my children." So, never let a challenge of the impossible limit God and steal your victory.

The Lord Says...

I live and move and have My being in you and within Me is every victory you need. Change will propel you to greater heights, for the valley is very different from the climb up the mountain. Never give up in the middle of the process because I Am doing a far greater work in you than you can imagine. In the end, you will see My glory shine through you.

If you believe it, say, "Oh yeah!"

JULY 22
KINGDOM INVESTMENTS

THERE IS POWER IN INVESTMENT: JESUS INVESTED HIMSELF INTO 12 MEN THAT CHANGED THE WORLD. HE DEFINED HIS MINISTRY AND LEADERSHIP BY POURING HIMSELF INTO OTHERS AND TRANSFORMING THEM INTO HISTORY MAKERS. LET'S CONTINUE TO EXPAND THE KINGDOM, BY DEPOSITING HIS TRUTH INTO OTHERS.

LIFE IS VERY GOOD!

One of the greatest principals of God is that life is all about relationships. You can never get anywhere in this world by going at it alone, it's just not how God designed life. He made Adam who spent time with God and then He made Eve for Adam. Even today, we have one another and we have a relationship with our Heavenly Father. Your purpose and destiny were meant to be shared with others so they, too, can become successful like you and know the revelation of Christ. Imagine if each one reaches just one, the world would be a much richer place. John 13:34-35 says, "A new command I give you: Love one another. As I have loved you, so you must love one another. By this everyone will know that you are my disciples, if you love one another." So spread the love and pour into others. It's transformative.

The Lord Says...

It's true what they say, that love makes the world go round. I love you so much that I gave My Son for your life...now that's relationship. I believed in you that I invested everything of Myself into My greatest creation. Invest in others and show them how My love can change their lives.

If you believe it, say, "Oh yeah!"

JULY 23
INVEST IN THE FUTURE

WHEN A FATHER BLESSES HIS CHILDREN AND POURS WISDOM AND KNOWLEDGE INTO THEM, THIS IS SOMETHING THAT CAN'T BE LOST OR SPENT. THIS IS EVEN GREATER THAN INHERITANCE; THEY WILL BECOME THE LEGACY OF WHO YOU WERE FOR FUTURE GENERATIONS TO KNOW. IT'S TIME TO INVEST AND IMPART FOR THE FUTURE.

LIFE IS VERY GOOD!

Genesis 49:26 says, "Your father's blessings are greater than the blessings of the ancient mountains, than the bounty of the age-old hills. Let all these rest on the head of Joseph, on the brow of the prince among his brothers." The blessing of the Father is shown throughout scripture and is still a powerful tool in raising up the next generation today. Many don't know the value of the blessing but it is a declaration over the life of future generations. It opens up potential and solidifies and affirms worth. Words and love in action are worth more than any monetary inheritance any day. Become the multiplier.

The Lord Says...

When you become a giver with your words, your time and your affirmations, the seeds will be planted for the next generation to do the same. Become the one to bless your future generations with not only your words, but your actions as well. I blessed My Son at the Jordan River and I blessed you through Him. And just as I blessed Abraham, Isaac and Jacob, I will bless all the generations that follow you because you have chosen to obey My voice.

If you believe it, say, "Oh yeah!"

JULY 24
EMPOWERING ENCOURAGEMENT

HAVE YOU EVER LAUGHED OR ARGUED WITH GOD ABOUT WHAT HE WANTED OR ASKED YOU TO DO? IF SO, REMEMBER THIS: SO DID ABRAHAM, MOSES AND GIDEON. EVERY ONE OF THESE GREAT MEN DOUBTED THEY COULD ACCOMPLISH WHAT GOD SET BEFORE THEM. BUT IN THE END, GOD'S WORD PREVAILED! HE DID IT FOR THEM; HE WILL DO IT FOR YOU!

LIFE IS VERY GOOD!

I'm a firm believer that God has a sense of humor. But as children, life's challenges or the things God asks you to do are not always funny; they might make you angry or frustrated. Have you ever asked your kids to do something and it was a challenge for them? It was so cute you couldn't help but laugh or cover your mouth as you smiled and started to laugh. The child however is frustrated because they just can't get it. Maybe they start to stomp their feet or even cry. But you are right there with empowering encouragement. That's the same way it is with God and you. You may not always understand His rhetoric or His ways but know this, His ways are greater. Then, lean on Proverbs 3:5-6, "Trust in the Lord with all your heart and lean not on your own understanding; in all your ways submit to him and he will make your paths straight." No one said it would be easy, but, if you'll train yourself to trust that your daddy God knows what He's doing in and for your life and submit to Him with even a mustard's seed of faith, you'll find that you'll come out the other side better for having made that decision. His Word always prevails.

The Lord Says...

Let us break bread together you and I. Let us laugh and cry, rejoice and mourn, run and dance together. It is when you stay in step with Me that you will begin to understand the greater picture in your life, for when you walk ahead of Me, you lose My illumination. I want to always be in harmony with you.

If you believe it, say, "Oh yeah!"

JULY 25
GOD IS ALWAYS WITH YOU

DIFFICULTIES ARE NOT A BAD PLACE TO BE IN; THEY CREATE A PLACE THAT LEADS TO FAVOR
AND PROMOTION. EVERY TIME JOSEPH FACED A HARDSHIP OR ACCUSATION, THE SITUATION
CAUSED HIM TO BE FAVORED BY MAN AND PROMOTED BY GOD. NO PIT OR PRISON WILL KEEP
YOU FROM THE PALACE GOD CALLED YOU TO. THE KING HAS CALLED YOUR NAME BECAUSE
YOU HAVE BEEN REMEMBERED. WALK IN HIS FAVOR TODAY.

LIFE IS VERY GOOD!

Re-read the story of Joseph in Genesis 37:1-44:9. I can only imagine the thoughts running through Joseph's heart and mind when at the age of 17 his brothers put him in a pit to die. Then being pulled out by the Midianites, only to be sold to a caravan of Ishmaelite's for 20 pieces of silver (equal to approximately $400 USD today). Upon arrival in Egypt, Joseph was sold again (to Potiphar) and later he was wrongfully imprisoned. Yet according to Genesis 39, God was with Joseph all the time. Sometimes it just doesn't seem like God is with you when you're in a pit, being sold or wrongfully accused and serving time. But in the end, we see how God was with Joseph all along. He took a man of promise and allowed him to be bought by the people of blessing, who all along were a part of God's greater picture in Joseph's life. Don't discount if God is with you or not in your times of trial. He is always there and He will uncover the greater picture for you too, for you are highly favored by the King of all Kings.

The Lord Says...

Joseph didn't understand it, but I did. He was just a kid, but I raised him up to strengthen and restore a people and bring prosperity to a nation. Don't worry or fret, for I see the big picture in your life, too. Just keep believing, for believing is seeing instead of seeing to believe.

If you believe it, say, "Oh yeah!"

JULY 26
LET HOPE ARISE!

HAVE YOU EVER BEEN IN A PLACE WHERE IT'S DIFFICULT TO BELIEVE FOR YOUR BREAK-
THROUGH OR MIRACLE? IF SO, LET HOPE ARISE! HOPE IS PUTTING FAITH INTO ACTION WHEN
THE SITUATION SEEMS IMPOSSIBLE. WHEN THE AXE-HEAD SANK TO THE BOTTOM OF THE
JORDAN, THE SON CALLED ON THE PROPHET FOR HELP. WHEN YOUR FAITH DOESN'T MOVE A
MOUNTAIN, THOSE YOU ARE CONNECTED TO CAN HELP TURN YOUR SITUATION AROUND. CAN
YOU SEE HOPE CHANGING YOUR SITUATION TODAY?

LIFE IS VERY GOOD!

The reason people of the world sometimes react to crisis in tragic ways is because they have no HOPE. Believers have hope. The hope of glory is Jesus. This
is what "Life is Very Good," is all about. Bringing hope to a dying world, encouragement to the broken and downtrodden, and a smile to the sad and hurting. Do
you realize you are a carrier of HOPE to the world? Without hope people lose their
reason for living, and become covered in the thick clay of failure and condemnation. But God can turn this around. Romans 8:31 says, "What, then, shall we say
in response to these things? If God is for us, who can be against us?" So who are
you gonna call on? J.E.S.U.S; His name is Jesus, the hope of all. If Jesus gave you
hope, a reason to sing, to shout and dance then give Him a big praise wherever you
are right now and thank Him for HE is GOOD.

The Lord Says...

Environment is key to your growth. Without hope, faith cannot exist. Without
water, living things will die. Water your friends, your family, your colleagues, you
clients, your students, everyone you know with encouragement, affirmation and
the word, for you know not what hope they have need of. I Am the hope of glory.

If you believe it, say, "Oh yeah!"

JULY 27
SAVED TO BE PROMOTED

SEASONS OF DARKNESS AREN'T BAD SEASONS, THEY ARE GOD-APPOINTED TIMES THAT PRO-
DUCE CHANGE IN US AND MAKE US STRONGER. DANIEL WAS JUDGED BECAUSE HE REFUSED TO
LET A NEW DECREE CHANGE THE REALITY OF WHO HE WAS: A MAN OF PRAYER. HIS ACTIONS
CAUSED HIM TO BE THROWN IN THE LION'S DEN. GOD NOT ONLY CLOSED THE MOUTHS OF THE
LIONS AND SAVED HIM, BUT ALSO PROMOTED HIM. THE SEASON OF TROUBLE BECAME DANIEL'S
TIME OF GREATEST ADVANCEMENT. YOUR DARK SEASON JUST MOVED YOU FORWARD.

LIFE IS VERY GOOD!

We take this story for granted so much. Imagine the terror you would feel as someone put you into a den of lions. The thought of being eaten alive is horrifying. Now imagine trusting God to the point that your life depended on it. This is how much Daniel trusted God. He knew he was called to pray and it didn't matter the circumstances. In your season of trouble, trust HIM like your life depended on it. Then sit back and watch. You'll find that it only seems darkest just before the dawn, for God's favor is already stamped upon you.

The Lord Says...

The fragrance of trust is like perfumed incense that finds its way to Me. Have I not spoken that I will never leave you nor forsake you? Breath in the air of goodness. Walk with Me at the river's edge and come to understand that your season of trouble shall become your opportunity tomorrow.

If you believe it, say, "Oh yeah!"

JULY 28
SOMETHING BIG FROM SOMETHING LITTLE

HAVE YOU EVER WONDERED IF THE LITTLE THINGS YOU DO MAKE A DIFFERENCE? THE ANSWER
IS YES. A LITTLE SMILE CAN BRING JOY TO A HURTING HEART. A LITTLE ENCOURAGEMENT CAN
GIVE A PERSON STRENGTH TO GO ON. A LITTLE LOVE CAN COVER A MULTITUDE OF SIN. WHEN
WE DEMONSTRATE CHRIST, LIVES ARE CHANGED. THE LITTLE THINGS YOU DO MAKE THE
BIGGEST DIFFERENCE.

LIFE IS VERY GOOD!

Luke 16:10 says, "Whoever can be trusted with very little can also be trusted
with much and whoever is dishonest with very little will also be dishonest with
much." When you begin to understand that all He has given you belongs to Him
to begin with and what you do with what He has given you actually matters, then
your perspective will change. For it doesn't take much to make an impact in the
world. There is power in multiplicity. Imagine if it were true that each one reached
one; especially with love, hope and encouragement. What would happen to our
world? I can tell you. The world would transform. You can transform your world;
your family, your community, your state and so on with very little; one person at
a time.

The Lord Says...

Jesus reached the masses but He never did it alone. He reached one and
then another and another and another. Before you know it, Jesus has 12 disciples
spreading the message of hope and love. Be the demonstration of My goodness
on the earth.

If you believe it, say, "Oh yeah!"

JULY 29
FRET NOT...GOD IS IN CONTROL

WHEN THINGS CHANGE BEYOND OUR CONTROL, IT'S NOT WORTH BEING FRUSTRATED OR ANGRY ABOUT IT. TRY TO REMAIN FLEXIBLE AND UNDERSTANDING. SOMETIMES THINGS HAPPEN AND WE WANT A PERFECT EXPLANATION, BUT WE DON'T GET IT. REMEMBER, LIFE HAPPENS. IT'S BETTER TO BEND A LITTLE, AND THEN HAVE TO FIX SOMETHING COMPLETELY BROKEN BECAUSE OF OUR FRUSTRATION. HOLD YOUR PEACE, THE SITUATION WILL CHANGE AGAIN. HE'S IN CONTROL.

LIFE IS VERY GOOD!

Fret not. Ecclesiastes 3:1 says, "There is a time for everything and a season for every activity under the heavens." And, Daniel 2:21 says, "He changes times and seasons; he deposes kings and raises up others. He gives wisdom to the wise and knowledge to the discerning." In other words, things in life change, so be willing to bend with the wind sometimes. There is a reality show on MSNBC called "The Profit," in which an investor upon request of business owners helps turn small businesses around by investing as an owner into the existing business. No matter what percentage of the company the investor is asking for, he always does one thing the same. He only makes the deal once and they understand that no matter the percentage of ownership he retains, he is 100% in charge. It doesn't go over well with people who want control of their business. But smart people who see the bigger picture and want their business to grow beyond what they could ever think or imagine, they take it and run with it. The same is true with God. Let Him have control and flourish. You keep control of your life and you'll limit yourself and Him. Keep the peace, the baton was God's all along. He just likes running relays so He passes it to you now and again to see how far you'll take His vision for your life. He is good and He's got you.

The Lord Says...

Trust means that you let go of your control and understand that things really are beyond your control. There is a reason for that. The control of your life belongs to Me and, when you fully trust Me, you give over control to Me, know that I won't do you wrong - ever.

If you believe it, say, "Oh yeah!"

JULY 30
BENEFICIAL FORGETFULNESS

YOUR FUTURE IS MORE POWERFUL THAN YOUR PAST! WHAT HE DID AT THE CROSS IS GREATER THAN THE LAST SIN YOU COMMITTED. IN CHRIST, EVERYTHING IN YOUR PAST IS FORGIVEN AND PLACED IN A SEA CALLED "I CAN'T REMEMBER." IF HE CAN'T REMEMBER IT, WHY SHOULD YOU? LET GO OF WHAT WAS, AND CAPTURE AN IMAGE OF WHAT IS IN CHRIST. YOU ARE DESTINED FOR GREATER THINGS.

LIFE IS VERY GOOD!

The one thing that keeps people back in life is their mind. Think about it. When Joshua was at the Jordan river looking across the raging waters, directly at their destiny, what would have happened if he would have said, "No way, we camp here, we can't make it. We have women, children, old people and animals; we'll never make it across. I guess we are destined to stay here." It would never happen you know why? Because Joshua had trained himself to think the "Life is Very Good" way. Remember when the 12 spies were sent in? He was one that said, "There may be grasshoppers but we can make it. We can do this." How and why could he say that? He knew without a shadow of a doubt that God was with them. He was raised during the wilderness wanderings. He saw the miracles of manna from heaven and water in the desert. It was the same message as David, just a different delivery. Every generation looks that way - same message different delivery. He captured the image of Christ and a greater destiny in his mind. He knew he and God's people had to get to it. He trusted God. If God said that which He gave to Moses was with him then he knew it was. If God said to step into the river at flood stage and it was knee deep, he knew he was about to move. He expected the unexpected and radical things of God to happen in his life. Change your mind and you will change your life.

The Lord Says...

When you transform your mind daily you make null and void anything the enemy tries to fill into your mind that is not of me. Take the word and like a drive-through car wash, wash your mind with it daily until the word abides in and from every part of your being. Let it fill you and overflow into all that you do. Leave the past behind for tomorrow you are alive and it is a new day in Me.

If you believe it, say, "Oh yeah!"

JULY 31
ALWAYS ONE STEP AHEAD

REMEMBER THIS: BEFORE THERE WAS SICKNESS THERE WAS HEALING, BEFORE THERE WAS PROBLEM THERE WAS AN ANSWER, BEFORE SIN CAME INTO THE WORLD THERE WAS A LAMB SLAIN. NO MATTER HOW BAD OR DIFFICULT THINGS APPEAR TO BE, GOD IS AND WAS A STEP AHEAD OF IT AND HAS ALREADY PROVIDED YOUR VICTORY! OVERCOME YOUR FRUSTRATION AND HARDSHIP BY THE SACRIFICE GIVEN AND REJOICE IN HIS VICTORY.

LIFE IS VERY GOOD!

This makes me think of children. God never calls us men or women; He calls us His children and tells us to be like children. Matthew 18:3 says, "And he said: 'Truly I tell you, unless you change and become like little children, you will never enter the kingdom of heaven'". What does that mean to be like children? Could it be that it refers to a father/child relationship. A child believes their parents because they know they have their best interests at heart. So He's saying to be like kids, to just believe Him when He tells you something. If His Word says X then it means X, not Y. God's done this relationship thing before. Before you were many, many generations of people and, before all them was Adam and then Eve. Guaranteed no matter what you have been through, there's a story for that in the Bible; there is a lesson for that in the Bible. You download all types of apps to make your life more efficient and easier, but God wants you to download His Words and have a conversation. You're not relevant without ApplePay on your phone right? Well, you're not relevant without downloading the Word either...it does you no good to be a Sunday/Wednesday Christian in this life. There has to be more. It's not about religion, it's about relationship.

The Lord Says...

Though We walk together, I Am still one step ahead. I Am big picture minded and I care about your journey and the destination. The thoughts I have for you are of a future and a hope. I see the best for you and have placed the best of Myself, My Son, within you so you can succeed.

If you believe it, say, "Oh yeah!"

AUGUST 1
THE SAVIOR THAT NEEDED TO SAVE

THE WORLD DID NOT NEED A SAVIOR, THE SAVIOR NEEDED THE WORLD. JESUS WAS THE LAMB SLAIN BEFORE THE FOUNDATION OF THE WORLD. GOD MADE AND CREATED AN ANSWER FOR THE WORLD BEFORE ADAM FELL AND HE HAD A SOLUTION BEFORE THERE EVER WAS A PROBLEM. NO MATTER WHAT YOU ARE FACING, THERE IS ALREADY AN ANSWER FOR IT. RISE UP AND LIVE IN HIS VICTORY.

LIFE IS VERY GOOD!

In order to be considered a Savior, He (Jesus) needed something to save; the world. This would allow the world to see Him as the Savior whenever they had a problem. In order to be a Savior, you must have something worth saving. Remember this, Jesus is the answer. He came, died and rose again so you could have the answers; so you would never be alone. Jesus came, died and rose again so you could have victory; so you could live in abundance. Now say it loud...HE IS VERY GOOD!

The Lord Says...

I Am the answer for the world: yesterday, today and for all forthcoming tomorrows. I Am the hope that guides faith, the love that heals pain and sorrow, joy that buries sadness and peace that passes all natural understanding. I Am your God. Rise up, you are victorious.

If you believe it, say, "Oh yeah!"

AUGUST 2
EXPONENTIAL BLESSING

THE POWER OF INCREASE TOOK PLACE WHEN JESUS TOOK THE 2 FISH AND 5 LOAVES AND BLESSED THEM. THE MULTIPLICATION TOOK PLACE WHEN THE DISCIPLES TOOK WHAT HE BLESSED AND FED THE MULTITUDES. JESUS STARTED THE MIRACLE PROCESS BUT THE DISCIPLES FINISHED IT! HE HAS NEED OF YOU TO CARRY OUT WHAT HE HAS BLESSED! LET HIS MIRACLES WORK THROUGH YOUR HANDS.

LIFE IS VERY GOOD!

Think about this: Jesus is the greatest network marketer of all time. In the book of Genesis, He blessed you and said you are good. In His Word, He gives you the tools to reach nations for Him. And since time began, the gospel message has been passed down through spoken stories and messages and then, with the invention of printing, the written word was added. It's over 2,000 years later and Jesus has still blessed us and we, His disciples, are still multiplying to show the miracle power and image of Christ on the earth. Will you be the carrier? John 13:15 says, "I have set you an example that you should do as I have done for you." So be HIS disciple and multiply all He has given you, that you and your world might know His abundance.

The Lord Says...

All you have I have given you and all you have need of I contain. Give and it shall be given. It's a pretty simple strategy; use it for My glory.

If you believe it, say, "Oh yeah!"

AUGUST 3
WAITING PATIENTLY

SOMETIMES WHAT APPEARS TO BE A BAD THING IS REALLY GOD SETTING YOU UP FOR SOME-
THING GREATER. EVERY SITUATION YOU FACE, GOD HAS A PLAN FOR IT! IF JOSEPH HADN'T
BEEN SOLD INTO SLAVERY, HE WOULD NEVER HAVE HAD AN ACCUSATION COME AGAINST HIM.
THAT ACCUSATION CAUSED HIM TO BE IMPRISONED WHERE HE INTERPRETED THE BUTLER'S
DREAM AND, AT THE APPOINTED TIME, THE BUTLER REMEMBERED JOSEPH, BROUGHT JOSEPH TO
PHARAOH AND ALLOWED HIM TO LIVE OUT THE SNAPSHOT OF HIS LIFE! LET GOD WORK OUT
HIS PLAN THROUGH YOUR SITUATION AND LET IT WORK IN YOUR FAVOR!

LIFE IS VERY GOOD!

One of the most difficult things for our human nature to do is to sit and be still, especially when faced with life challenges. We naturally want to step in and try to fix things that are out of sync or out of order. But Psalm 37:7 says, "Be still before the Lord and wait patiently for him; do not fret when people succeed in their ways, when they carry out their wicked schemes." There is hope in knowing that God knows and understands the greater picture in a moment when you possibly can't see any further than your two feet. Do you think in that moment that Joseph could see any further than how to get out of the pit so he didn't die there? Not likely but that's okay because God saw fit to be with him no matter what he went through and Joseph saw God in the little things for sure. Let God hold the camera of your life. You're just in the picture.

The Lord Says...

I have need of you for My plan. My ways are the best ways. You may not understand all that you go through but I Am the photographer of your life. I see the picture in a focus you sometimes cannot see. Trust Me. I know the plans I have for you.

If you believe it, say, "Oh yeah!"

AUGUST 4
HOPE ON THE HORIZON

THE MENTALITIES OF FEAR WILL ROB A MAN FROM TRANSITIONING INTO SOMETHING GREATER. THESE MINDSETS STUNT YOUR GROWTH AND STEAL YOUR ABILITY TO PROGRESS, LEAVING YOU ABANDONED IN THE LAND OF UNCERTAINTIES. DON'T CAMP IN THIS PLACE. OVERCOME YOUR FEAR WITH HIS LOVE AND LET HIM EMPOWER YOU AND BRING STABILITY TO YOUR MIND. MOVE INTO HIS SEASON OF BLESSING FOR YOUR LIFE.

LIFE IS VERY GOOD!

Let's imagine what would have happened if Moses had stayed completely struck by fear when God called him to go back and face Pharaoh to deliver His people. We are talking about a man who, before he had an encounter with God, killed a man and ran for his life from Pharaoh. Where would the people of Israel be if Moses would have said, "Sorry, God. Find someone else, I can't go back to Egypt"? I'm sure he had some sort of anxiety about it, but who wouldn't? The key is that Moses trusted God more than all else; more than he trusted himself or Pharaoh and all his armies. When Moses had the burning bush encounter, he knew in that moment that, if God could make Himself known in a bush, consume it with fire and keep it contained and then tell him that he was standing on holy ground, then what more would God do in Egypt by backing up His Word? Moses knew that he was moving into a season of blessing because God was about to go before him in all that he accomplished. When you come to the understanding that God is with you, there is nothing you cannot do. In fact, Matthew 19:26 says, "Jesus looked at them and said, 'With man this is impossible, but with God all things are possible.'" Believe it, you can do all things. Take off the limits. Hope stands on the horizon.

The Lord Says...

I Am the hope of the world. A hope that breeds a faith that says all things are possible, but you first must believe - no doubting. With Me, you can do anything you set your hand to do. Stand on My Word and believe, then take that step of faith. Don't worry, I'm always by your side.

If you believe it, say, "Oh yeah!"

AUGUST 5
LET GOD COME THROUGH

SOMETIMES IN LIFE, INSECURITIES CREEP INTO OUR MINDS AND HINDER OUR PROGRESS. INSE-
CURITY BREEDS FEAR; FEAR OF THE FUTURE, FEAR OF FAILING, FEAR OF THE UNKNOWN. WE
CAN'T ALLOW FEAR TO HOLD US BACK FROM MOVING INTO WHAT GOD HAS FOR US. ESTHER
WOULD HAVE NEVER SAVED HER PEOPLE IF SHE HAD GIVEN INTO HER FEARS. INSTEAD SHE
STOOD AND SAID, "IF I PERISH, I PERISH." HER FAITH IN GOD SURPASSED HER FEAR OF DEATH.
DON'T LET INSECURITY GRAB A HOLD OF YOU. STAND ON HIS WORD AND ALLOW YOUR FAITH
TO MOVE YOU FORWARD.

LIFE IS VERY GOOD!

Esther had that confidence in the Lord that we all strive to obtain. I think I understand why God tells us to be like children. They have a confidence in their authority figures that is unmatched. They trust them without question until given reason not to. What would happen in your life if you trusted God with such confidence, you paid your tithe, sowed your seeds, loved your family and community and when a need arose just said, "Okay God, here's the thing, this is the need"? Then, walked away and let Him come through. One of the hardest things in life is to let go and let God because there are natural circumstances that arise such as the rent or the light and heat bills getting paid. But God says in Psalm 37:25, "I was young and now I am old, yet I have never seen the righteous forsaken or their children begging bread." Scripture also tells us that God knows the very hairs on your head. If He cares that much for you, He is not going to let you fall by the wayside into despair. He is your hope of Glory. Have confidence in ALL that God is and seek His Kingdom that all else might be added unto you.

The Lord Says...

I Am not someone who intimidates for I love and do not condemn. I Am a light throughout the darkest of times. I Am a beacon to help the lost find their way home. I Am faith, hope and love. Take Me with you wherever you go that others might see My light.

If you believe it, say, "Oh yeah!"

AUGUST 6
CHANGE YOUR MIND TO CHANGE YOUR WORLD

TO BE VICTORIOUS, WE HAVE TO CHANGE OUR MINDSETS. REMEMBER, YOUR THOUGHTS OF SUCCEEDING SHOULD BE GREATER THAN THE FEAR OF FAILING. TO MOVE FORWARD, APPREHEND YOUR DREAM. OUR PASSION SHOULD BE SO STRONG THAT WE DECLARE WHAT WE SEE, BECAUSE OUR DREAM IS THAT REAL. DON'T QUIT ON THE JOURNEY. I WOULD RATHER FAIL TRYING THAN FAIL BECAUSE I NEVER TRIED AT ALL. PURSUE THE PROMISE.

LIFE IS VERY GOOD!

Philippians 3:14 says, "I press on toward the goal to win the prize for which God has called me heavenward in Christ Jesus." So train your spiritual man to be stronger than your flesh. Then your faith will become stronger than your fear and you will answer to challenges as David did with the realization that if God can be there with him to kill a lion and a bear, then with God he can do anything. The same applies to you, so press forward; you are an ambassador of heaven.

The Lord Says...

Never quit. I have never quit on you and I have given you the spirit of love and a sound mind in place of the spirit of fear. Find joy. Walk in love. Ask for wisdom and understanding and you will see your world change.

If you believe it, say, "Oh yeah!"

AUGUST 7
BE THE VOICE OF HOPE

THE MOST DIFFICULT TEST YOU MAY FACE IS WHEN GOD REQUIRES YOU TO BLESS SOMEONE ELSE WHILE YOU ARE GOING THROUGH YOUR OWN STORM. JOSEPH NOT ONLY SERVED THE BUTLER, HE BLESSED THE BUTLER WITH THE UNDERSTANDING OF HIS DREAMS, THOUGH JOSEPH'S OWN DREAMS SEEMED OUT OF REACH. THOUGH JOSEPH WAS DWELLING IN A DIFFICULT PLACE (PRISON), HE ALLOWED GOD TO USE HIM TO BE A VOICE OF HOPE. NO MATTER WHAT YOU MAY BE FACING, LET YOUR LIGHT SHINE IN ALL SEASONS.

LIFE IS VERY GOOD!

God is the greatest giver in the universe. He is the author and finisher of your faith, the One who started it all. He gave Adam a helper, the beautiful gardens he loved so much and allowed him to name every living thing. He gave His Son that you might have life and live it abundantly. He gave you your family, your blessings, your job and all that you have. So you want to know one of the keys to your way out of trials? Giving. Give even if it hurts. I Am not just talking about finances. I Am talking about time, talent and treasure. How can you give to your wife's need for conversation? How can you give to your husband's need for relaxation? How can you give to the need of your children, family and community? What skills can you offer a business or church board, mentoring or community group? How can you give to the needy?

God has gifted you. He has given you special insights into a variety of things and He has given you treasure. What will you do with it when you are in the difficult place? Approaching the man at the Gate Beautiful in Acts 3:6, Peter said to the man that he didn't have any silver or gold, but what Peter did have was the anointing and message of the cross. The man received it. He received the Good News and healing. So, my friend, how will you bring hope to your world, your community? During the summer of 2015, the worst fire in Washington state history raged and raged. At some point there were over 50 fires in the state. Firefighters from Australia and New Zealand brought their knowledge and skills and took time away from their own families to come halfway around the world to help put out the fires. Local residents did what they could to cook food for the firefighters. Allow God to use you as a vehicle of hope and let your light shine in all seasons.

The Lord Says...

Blessing others can be difficult when you are going through a trial yourself. But know that when you do, the greatest blessings for your own life come from it. I honor those who honor others. Let your actions show My love and My grace. You may not understand the difficulties you're going through, but I understand all things and I have the best in mind for you, My children.

If you believe it, say, "Oh yeah!"

AUGUST 8
LET GOD BE YOUR BRIDGE

WHEN LIFE HAS YOU IN TROUBLED WATERS, IT'S NOT A BAD THING, UNLESS YOU ARE STAND-
ING IN THEM WITH THE WRONG MENTALITY. TROUBLED WATERS ARE NOT A PLACE OF DESTRUC-
TION; THEY ARE REALLY THE PLACE OF HEALING. CHANGE YOUR POINT OF VIEW. DON'T SEE
FROM WHAT SOMETHING SEEMS TO BE BUT SEE FROM THE PLACE OF "WHAT IS." KNOW YOU
ARE POSITIONED IN THE EXACT PLACE GOD WANTS YOU!

LIFE IS VERY GOOD!

1 John 5:4-5 says, "For everyone born of God overcomes the world. This is
the victory that has overcome the world, even our faith. Who is it that overcomes
the world? Only the one who believes that Jesus is the Son of God." On their fifth
album, the 70s music duo known as Simon and Garfunkel recorded a song titled
"Bridge Over Troubled Waters." This song was not only the last on the album, but
went on to win Paul Simon and Art Garfunkel five Grammy awards and the pres-
tige of becoming probably their greatest hit world-wide. The message of "Bridge
Over Troubled Waters" resonated with a large community world-wide. The lyrics
said that, when you need comfort, you'll lay yourself down for a friend. You see,
that's the message of Jesus. The bridge over your troubled water is faith. When
you are born of God, you have a hope and a comfort like none other; one that overcomes the world. It is the fuel to your faith and, when you can look beyond where
you are and glimpse the view above or beyond you, you'll realize that HE's had
you in the palm of His hand all along. He has positioned you for a greater today.

The Lord Says...

I Am a friend who sticks closer than a brother and I have sent you My Spirit
to comfort and keep you. You are never alone of this journey called life. When
you encounter troubled waters, I Am the bridge that will bring you safely across.
Believe when I tell you how much I love you and want to see you prosper.

If you believe it, say, "Oh yeah!"

AUGUST 9
A VICTORIOUS POINT OF VIEW

WHEN YOU ARE IN A VALLEY, EVERYTHING AROUND YOU LOOKS BIG. IT'S A PLACE WHERE EVERYTHING SURROUNDING YOU SEEMS TO BE COMING AGAINST YOU. THIS IS WHEN YOU ADJUST YOUR PERSPECTIVE AND KNOW THAT THINGS ARE NOT AS THEY SEEM. WHEN THE SERVANT'S EYES WERE OPENED, THE PLACE THAT APPEARED TO BE DIFFICULT BECAME A LAND SURROUNDED BY GOD'S PRESENCE. REMEMBER ALWAYS, THERE ARE MORE FOR YOU THAN THOSE AGAINST YOU.

LIFE IS VERY GOOD!

There are more than a handful of valleys you can learn lessons from in scripture, but I love the message that comes from the Valley of Achor. In Hosea 2, Israel is not only punished in the Valley of Achor, but they are restored. After God gives them a verbal spanking, all of a sudden life takes a turn. Hosea 2:15 says, "There (the wilderness) I will give her back her vineyards and will make the Valley of Achor a door of hope. There she will respond as in the days of her youth, as in the day she came up out of Egypt." The people of Israel went from punishment to hope and abundance. The valley is the place where God sets you up to set you in. He makes a way where there seems to be no way and, let's remember that, no matter what challenges you face or sin you've been caught in, He will never leave you nor forsake you. If it seems like He's against you and the valley has taken all your strength, stand up one more time and change your point of view. Turn around and see His goodness. Look up! He's got you.

The Lord Says...

Look up, your redemption is near. I may teach and discipline you like a parent disciplines a child, but My heart is for you to live in great abundance. So look up, just when you think you can't make it, I will walk through the door, for I Am your hope.

If you believe it, say, "Oh yeah!"

AUGUST 10
HOLD YOUR GROUND

HARDSHIP MAY BE A PLACE OF DIFFICULTY BUT NOT A PLACE OF QUITTING OR SURRENDERING. IN THE MIDST OF OPPOSITION, WE MUST HOLD OUR GROUND AND KEEP OUR PEACE, KNOWING THE LORD IS WITH US. REMEMBER, STAND STRONG LIKE SHAMMAH, DEFEND WHAT THE LORD HAS GIVEN YOU AND WATCH THE SWORD (PROMISE) STICK TO YOUR HAND. NO RETREAT, NO SURRENDER. THIS IS YOUR LAND.

LIFE IS VERY GOOD!

David was on his death bed and his mighty men surrounded him. One of the listed mighty men was Shammah. We only hear about him here in 2 Samuel 23:11-12, "Next to him was Shammah son of Agee the Hararite. When the Philistines banded together at a place where there was a field full of lentils, Israel's troops fled from them. But Shammah took his stand in the middle of the field. He defended it and struck the Philistines down and the Lord brought about a great victory." Shammah's father, Agee, was considered to be a direct relative of David's best friend, Jonathan. The bond here is great. Shammah knew what God could do for he'd seen it all his life. As a mighty warrior, Shammah had had enough of the Philistines stealing their lentil crop. When the Israelites banded together to fight for what was theirs, they were moved by what they saw: giants in the land. But Shammah was not moved. He felt the lentils were worth fighting for and purposed to take the land. Never surrender. What giant are you facing today? Is your marriage worth fighting for? Is terminal illness worth fighting a battle to win? If you are fighting a battle of infertility, poverty, depression, lack, delay, infidelity, whatever it may be, God is bigger and stronger than any giant presenting itself to you. The giant must surrender to God alone.

The Lord Says...

There are no GIANTS in the land greater than what you give them credit for. Stand and speak victory and together we shall overcome the world. I Am in you and am for you. With Me, everything is possible if you only believe.

If you believe it, say, "Oh yeah!"

AUGUST 11
DREAM A BIG DREAM

TO SEE, YOUR EYES HAVE TO BE OPENED TO TRUTH BECAUSE HIS TRUTH IS ALWAYS GREATER THAN WHAT IS BEFORE YOU. GOD SAID TO JOSHUA, "SEE, I HAVE GIVEN JERICHO THE WALLED CITY INTO YOUR HAND, ITS KING AND ITS MEN OF VALOR." THOUGH HE COULD NOT SEE WHAT WAS INSIDE OF IT, GOD'S WORD PAINTED THE IMAGE OF VICTORY TO JOSHUA. YOU DON'T NEED TO SEE WHAT'S ON THE OTHER SIDE OF YOUR SITUATION. JUST REMEMBER WHAT HE SAID: I HAVE GIVEN YOU THE LAND. THE PROMISE IS YOURS FOR THE TAKING.

LIFE IS VERY GOOD!

If you could just grasp this concept fully and pack it into your spirit, when hopelessness creeps in and when your season of favor seems to have disappeared, you will continue to declare your promises; the scriptures that breathe life in to your body, mind and spirit. God said you'd live an abundant life. It's up to you to proclaim it and live it as such. He is the door and you must walk through. He has given you the land. It's your job to take it.

The Lord Says...

It is for this reason, I tell you, that a people without a vision perish. They perish body, mind and spirit because they cannot see what I see. If you need healing, can you see it, envision it? I Am bigger than any situation, so you must begin to think, dream and imagine bigger than before.

If you believe it, say, "Oh yeah!"

AUGUST 12
A 21 DAY FAST FROM NEGATIVITY

WORDS OF DECEIT IMPRISON A PERSON'S MIND WHILE WORDS OF TRUTH SET MINDS AT LIBERTY. REMEMBER, THERE IS POWER IN YOUR TONGUE; YOUR MOUTH HAS THE ABILITY TO SPEAK DEATH OR LIFE. USE YOUR VOICE TO EDIFY AND BUILD, RATHER THAN TEARING DOWN AND DESTROYING. BECOME A LIVING WORD OF HOPE TODAY, SPEAKING LIFE TO THOSE AROUND YOU.

LIFE IS VERY GOOD!

You remember the days when your mother would say, "If you can't say anything nice, don't say anything at all." It truly is better that way, you know, to train yourself to hold your tongue. The tongue tends to speak out of response. Proverbs 18:21 tells us that our tongues yield either life or death. I challenge you, for 21 days to refrain from criticism and negativity and only speak life to people. It will change you. It makes you feel empowered, affirmed, capable, appreciated and just plain good. Plus, they say it takes 21 days to break a habit and form a new one. Be a habitual giver of life and hope to your community.

The Lord Says...

Have you ever heard Me speak a negative thing about you or to you? No. Discipline helps you grow but a negative tongue tears down the hearts and minds of men. It creates stress and it makes people sick. I Am the God of hope and in Me there is life, abundant life. Decree and declare My Word over and above all.

If you believe it, say, "Oh yeah!"

AUGUST 13
FROM IMPOSSIBLE TO ENDLESS POSSIBILITIES

LIFE'S JOURNEY CAN BE LOOKED AT AS A COLLAGE, OR A COLLECTION OF IMAGES, THAT MAKES UP A BEAUTIFUL PORTRAIT OF A PERSON'S LIFE. BUT SOMETIMES, THE IMAGE OF OUR FUTURE CAN BECOME MARRED BECAUSE OF OUR PAST EXPERIENCES AND WHAT IS HAPPENING IN OUR PRESENT. WHEN WE CAN'T VISUALIZE THE END AND WHAT IT LOOKS LIKE, WE OFTEN GIVE UP. SO REMEMBER, GOD HAS DECLARED THE END FROM THE BEGINNING AND HAD A SOLUTION BEFORE THERE WAS A PROBLEM. KEEP YOUR EYES ON HIS IMAGE AND LET IT LEAD YOU FROM THE IMPOSSIBLE INTO ALL POSSIBILITIES!

LIFE IS VERY GOOD!

Revelation 1:8 says, "'I Am the Alpha and the Omega,' says the Lord God, 'who is and who was and who is to come, the Almighty.'" Do you understand what's being said here? The word alpha is the first letter of the Greek alphabet, while omega is the last letter. Scholars believe that, when this scripture was translated, it was translated incorrectly because the first letter of the Hebrew alphabet is aleph and the last letter is tau. In the Hebrew alphabet, letters often have meanings that, in themselves, stand alone. This is the case here. Aleph means unity, while tau means Perfection. So read it like this: I Am the unity and the perfection, says the Lord God, who is and who was and who is to come, the Almighty. Now that is powerful! He longs to bring you into one accord with His mind and His vision for your life. Catch it. Then, His perfection has made all things possible to them who believe. Get an image of it. When you are in unity with Christ, walking with Him instead of in front or behind Him, then He will lead you into His perfection today and tomorrow, while also covering your past. Now that's something to shout about.

The Lord Says...

I once asked Peter, "Who do you say that I Am?" Now I ask you, "Who do you say that I Am?" I Am that I Am, all Whom you need Me to be. Do you need healing? I Am the healer. Do you need deliverance? I Am the deliverer. Do you need comfort, support, finances or joy? I Am more than enough for I purpose for you to live the abundant life. So I ask you, "Who do you say that I Am?"

If you believe it, say, "Oh yeah!"

AUGUST 14
PRAISE TURNS THE CRISIS AROUND

WHEN DESPERATION SETTLES IN A MAN, IT CAN LEAVE HIM WITH LITTLE TO NO HOPE. THIS FEELING CAN LEAD TO ANXIETY AND FRUSTRATION IN THE HEART DURING A TIME OF CRISIS. TURN IT AROUND BY LETTING PRAISE BE THE MOMENTUM THAT CAUSES CHANGE. USE THE DIFFICULT SITUATION AS FUEL TO LIGHT YOUR FIRE. DON'T WORRY; YOUR SEASON WILL NOT END IN DARKNESS.

LIFE IS VERY GOOD!

Jeremiah 20:12-13 says, "Lord Almighty, you who examine the righteous and probe the heart and mind, let me see your vengeance on them, for to you I have committed my cause. Sing to the Lord! Give praise to the Lord! He rescues the life of the needy from the hands of the wicked." In Jeremiah 20, Jeremiah was frustrated, scared and felt isolated and alone. People thought he was a false prophet. He had faced evil and was in a time of crisis. He thought God had left him to die and he was lamenting in these verses of poetry. But wait...there's more...as much as he tried to get away from God due to his frustration, he couldn't. The Hope of Glory was deep in his bones and, when he got to his bottom, he made a turn towards hope. Look what happened in verses 12-13. Jeremiah finally began to get his fire back. Even through the crisis, he began to Praise the Lord with singing. So sing His praises and send the incense of worship up to the Lord. No matter the season, He shall prevail.

The Lord Says...

I hear your complaints, just as I heard Jeremiah's. This world is not without its challenges. Without challenges you would not stretch or grow. When you can find your praise and your place of worship in the midst of crisis, it will bring you that peace that passes all understanding. And behold, nothing will seem as bad as it looks for when you look in the mirror and see Me, you see you: a mighty warrior.

If you believe it, say, "Oh yeah!"

AUGUST 15
THE BARRIER OF MONOTONY

IT'S BEEN SAID THAT, OVER A PERIOD OF TIME, THINGS CHANGE. CHANGE CAN HAPPEN GRADU-
ALLY BUT, THE GREATER TRUTH IS, FOR CHANGE TO HAPPEN, IT STARTS WITH YOU. DON'T LIVE
IN THE REPETITIVE CYCLE OF WAITING FOR 'ONE DAY' OR 'SOME DAY', BUT CHOOSE TO LIVE IN
THE NOW OF GOD. LIVING IN HIS PERFECT DAY IS WHERE THE FULLNESS OF JOY IS. BREAK THE
BARRIER OF MONOTONY AND REACH FOR HIS PROMISE.

LIFE IS VERY GOOD!

A friend of mine applied to a university for admissions and had to write the infamous college essay. This essay was interesting because it wasn't your usual "tell me about your life" essay. The prompt was: what would you do with your one wild and crazy life? So, I ask you, "what would you do with your one wild and crazy life?" And I would encourage you not to be in the same place this year that you were last year. When you break the barrier of monotony, you grow, you stretch your faith, you step into your destiny, you reach your dreams or at least get one inch closer. John 10:10 says, "The thief comes only to steal and kill and destroy; I have come that they may have life and have it to the full." In other words, if you're going through repetitive cycles in life and nothing is changing, you are allowing the enemy to steal your time and delay your destiny. Time is something you cannot get back. Once it's used, it's gone. And delay is just a time waster. Both of these things (stolen time and delay) steal from your purpose. So, come on! Break the barrier! Choose to change your mind. Joshua had to do it. When they came to the Jordan River, they could see their destiny across the flooded river and upon the soil of the river bank opposite them. They made a decision; they were done with monotony and whatever it took, they would reach their destiny. Jesus breaks every chain. Will you allow Him to break the chain in your life?

The Lord Says...

When you assess your life, ask yourself, "How do I live the abundant life?" Do I have joy? Am I embarking on my destiny? Do I feel fulfilled? Am I helping others in my family, church and community, leaving my mark on the world? Does life come from my tongue? Am I patient?" When you abide with Me and seek My face, all these things will be added unto you. You can live an abundant life. You can have joy and feel fulfilled. When you begin the change in your life first, everything and everyone around you will notice the difference and be curious. Then all you have to do is allow My light to shine through you.

If you believe it, say, "Oh yeah!"

AUGUST 16
STRAIGHTEN THAT CROOKED PATH!

WHEN THE UNEXPECTED TWISTS AND TURNS TAKE PLACE IN YOUR LIFE, IT CAN PLACE YOU IN THE LAND OF HARDSHIP OR FRUSTRATION. REMEMBER THIS: IT'S NOT ONLY WHAT YOU SAY THAT CAUSES THIS CROOKED PATH TO BE MADE STRAIGHT, IT'S ALSO WHAT YOU DO. TAKING ACTION IS GREATER THAN EMOTIONALLY REACTING. GRAB HOLD OF HIS PRESENCE AND LET HIM LEAD YOU ALL THE WAY THROUGH. HE HAS GIVEN YOU LOVE, POWER AND A SOUND MIND TO OVERCOME EVERY STRUGGLE YOU FACE! LIVE IN FAITH, NOT FEAR.

LIFE IS VERY GOOD!

The reference to "crooked places made straight" is found in Isaiah 45:2 where God calls Cyrus. What it actually means is to make level, as if paving a gravel road. A level road is less difficult because you are not gaining much elevation or walking up then down. However, no matter how straight, narrow, crooked or level the pathway is, whether you choose to follow Christ and His ways is up to you. The pathway is of no use when it is not used. So, if you're on a crooked path and God said to be on the straight, narrow and level pathway, then make a decision today that, no matter how difficult the obstacle is you're facing, it's never too much for God. He is able to meet your needs wherever you are and in His presence there is fullness of JOY!

The Lord Says...

When you walk the level road, you find joy in nature, joy in company and joy in simple conversations because you don't have to work so hard to climb uphill. It is a refreshing walk, a stroll, an unwinding. Breathe in and breathe out as you walk with Me and the power of a sound mind overcomes you and every struggle is handed to Me.

If you believe it, say, "Oh yeah!"

AUGUST 17
THE POWER IN CONTRARINESS

GOD HAS AN ABILITY OF CALLING THINGS THAT DON'T EXIST INTO EXISTENCE, OR SPEAKING A WORD CONTRARY TO WHAT A SITUATION MAY BE. HE TOLD ABRAM TO NUMBER THE STARS OF HEAVEN AND SO WOULD HIS DESCENDANTS BE, THOUGH AT THE TIME ABRAM HAD NO SON. HE CALLED GIDEON A MIGHTY MAN OF VALOR AND A DELIVERER, EVEN WHILE ISRAEL WAS BEING OPPRESSED BY THE ENEMY. IF GOD HAS SPOKEN IT, IT'S BECAUSE HE'S ALREADY SEEN IT. SEE IT THROUGH HIS EYES, BELIEVE WHAT HE HAS SAID AND LET HIM BRING IT TO PASS! HIS WORD NEVER FAILS.

LIFE IS VERY GOOD!

One of my hopes is that you will begin to see yourself as God sees you, not as man or other people see you. God says that you are, according to John 15:15, HIS friend. In Psalm 139:14, you are fearfully and wonderfully made. In Ephesians 1:3, you are blessed. In Ephesians 2:10, you are His workmanship. When you look in the mirror and see HIS image, there is so much you should see. Call yourself a "Friend of God" for a week or two and see how you feel inside. It'll make you feel very good to have Jesus for your BFF (Best Friend Forever). He will never fail you.

The Lord Says...

The thing about a best friend is that they are with you come rain or shine; downpours, snow, hail, sleet and scorching temperatures. They bring out the best in you, offer constructive criticism for growth, laugh together and share their deepest secrets. Will you be My best friend, hang out with Me and have coffee with Me in the morning? I will be forever there for you.

If you believe it, say, "Oh yeah!"

AUGUST 18
WHEREVER YOU ARE, HE IS

Many times we want to get to the mountaintop because we think it's better than dwelling in the valley. But it's all a matter of perspective. We need to realize that, wherever we are, God is present with us. David knew that from the highest heavens to the darkest depths, God was there. When we recognize He is where we are, our mindset can change because our perspective changed. Don't allow the outside circumstances to affect you, see through His eyes and know He has it all under control.

Life is very good!

There are many important places in the Bible, but one place that interests me the most is the Valley of Achor. Let's back up a bit. God's people had just experienced sweet victory at Jericho and Ai was the next place to conquer. However, God required that Ai had a ban on it, meaning God wanted all the spoils such as gold and silver to be dedicated to Him and not touched for personal use. Because Achan sinned by coveting and stealing objects God said not to, Israel was defeated in battle and received a verbal rebuke from God. Achan and his whole family were killed as a result of their actions in the Valley of Achor (Joshua 7). Then God did something amazing. He didn't just punish His children and leave them to learn a lesson. He did like any good father; He redeemed them and blessed the Valley of Achor. Hosea 2:15 says, "There **I will give her back her vineyards** and **will make the Valley of Achor a door of hope.** There she will respond as in the days of her youth, as in the day she came up out of Egypt." So, here you see that God now is turning something terrible into something good. Now the Valley is to become a door of hope and it will again have vineyards. The goodness for today is that this is a type and shadow of what Christ is and does for us. John 10:9 says, "I Am the door: by me if any man enter in, he shall be saved and shall go in and out and find pasture." So let go of your Achan experiences in life; we've all failed and sinned at some point. God is the door. Walk through for He is the abundant vineyard planted in your life and you will be fruitful. The Bible says that He makes all things new. He trades beauty for ashes, mourning for dancing and He is, above all, GOOD!

The Lord Says...

Live from lessons learned and always keep hope, like a pistol in your holster waiting and ready to be activated. In Me is faith, hope and love. You are My beloved. Though you may have fallen short, My grace still reaches out to you and forgives you. I will make you fruitful as long as you remain planted in Me.

If you believe it, say, "Oh yeah!"

AUGUST 19
LET GOD ARISE

WHEN A MAN FEARS CHANGE, IT LEAVES HIM DWELLING IN A STATE OF FRUSTRATION. THIS DISAPPOINTMENT CAUSES A MAN'S HEART TO BE FILLED WITH ANGER. DON'T LET FEAR DICTATE HOW YOU FEEL. LET GOD ARISE AND ALLOW HIS PEACE TO SURROUND YOU. IF HE IS FOR YOU, NOTHING CAN STAND AGAINST YOU. THIS TOO SHALL PASS.

LIFE IS VERY GOOD!

Romans 8:31 says, "What, then, shall we say in response to these things? If God is for us, who can be against us?" It really is that simple. It's our human nature to control our lives and everything in it. Have you ever been around an individual who is in the midst of losing their independence? It is difficult to rely on and trust others to know and understand how you think, how you like things done, your routine and that they can be there like you would be for yourself. Your relationship with God is much like that. What would you do if you had to daily trust Him completely like Israel did to receive manna? God will always arise in your life; He's your Father God. Don't let frustration get the best of you, for truly He tells you that He is for you and not against you, so believe it with all your heart. Get a vision of God supplying your every need according to His riches and glory. He is able.

The Lord Says...

I Am more than enough. Give Me a chance to shine in your life, to spoil you with My goodness. I have many children and I love them all, especially you. You are the apple of My eye. As long as I am in your life, fear doesn't have to have a hold on you. I will surround and protect you with My love.

If you believe it, say, "Oh yeah!"

AUGUST 20
PURSUE YOUR PROMISE

FEAR PARALYZES WHILE FAITH MOBILIZES. DON'T LET FEAR KEEP YOU FROM PURSUING THE PROMISE BY STOPPING YOU DEAD IN YOUR TRACKS. TEN SPIES HAD A MINDSET THAT SAID, "WE ARE LIKE GRASSHOPPERS IN OUR OWN SIGHT AND IN THEIRS." CALEB SAID, "WE ARE WELL ABLE TO OVERCOME IT, LET US GO UP AT ONCE AND POSSESS IT." LET HIS FAITH ARISE AND MOVE YOU BEYOND YOUR FEAR.

LIFE IS VERY GOOD!

Have you ever been in a fearful situation and just stood there? It's that moment when you're at an amusement park, and you're getting in line for a ride but can't even move because you are paralyzed in that moment. You tell yourself, "No, I am not going on that!" Fear of failure in math kept someone I know from attending college in their younger years. But, when you look at the victory on the other side, the journey is greater and, though fear doesn't dissipate, the thought of victory becomes stronger and it becomes more manageable to walk it through. So take the first step to conquer your fears by gaining a vision of victory. My friend did. She may have graduated from college with a Bachelor's Degree at age 45, but she did it. She looked at the victory and walked through the defeat like the overcomer she is and conquered. Possess your land.

The Lord Says...

I Am LOVE and perfect love casts out all fear. Trust Me and conquer your fears. I will never leave you alone. Whatever you set your hand to, I will prosper it so there is no need for you to fear. Your promise is set before you; go after it.

If you believe it, say, "Oh yeah!"

AUGUST 21
FEAR IS AN OPTICAL ILLUSION

WHEN FEAR ENGULFS YOUR EMOTION, IT CAUSES YOU TO BE OVERWHELMED. REMEMBER, WHEN YOU FIRST LOOK AT A SITUATION, IT CAN BE DECEIVING. YOUR MIND CAN PLAY TRICKS ON YOU AND CAUSE YOU TO MISINTERPRET YOUR SITUATION. IT'S LIKE AN OPTICAL ILLUSION. LET HIS CLARITY COME AND MOVE YOU PAST THE FEAR AND HELP YOU TAKE YOUR FIRST STEP INTO OVERCOMING THE TRIAL. THE TROUBLE YOU FACE IS ALWAYS SMALLER THAN THE GOD YOU SERVE!

LIFE IS VERY GOOD!

Fear can often be like an optical illusion. An optical illusion is deceptive to the eyes until your eyes figure out its patterns. You've likely seen the pattern of two long lines drawn over a star of lines (when the lines are drawn up, down and in between). The two long lines look bent and the question is which one is straight? The answer is that they are both actually straight lines but they look bent due to the nature of the lines underneath it. Philippians 2:13 says, "For it is God who works in you to will and to act in order to fulfill his good purpose." In other words, when you abide in Christ and He abides in you, the optical illusion of fear begins to fade as you embrace Him, for it is He who works in you. The victory is always greater, but there is something to be said about enduring and overcoming the potholes of your journey along the way. Let HIS purpose be fulfilled in you and keep clarity of mind. When thoughts of negativity or despair come your way, think on Jesus.

The Lord Says...

Whatever is good, whatever is lovely and whatever things are a good report, think on these things for I have overcome the world and every obstacle you face. Don't give fear a place in your heart. Believe in faith and watch My hand work on your behalf.

If you believe it, say, "Oh yeah!"

AUGUST 22
YOU CAN DETERMINE THE OUTCOME

IT DOESN'T MATTER THE TIME OF YEAR; SUMMER, FALL, WINTER OR SPRING, THERE WILL ALWAYS BE GOOD DAYS AND BAD, SUNNY DAYS AND STORMY ONES, CALM ONES AND WINDY ONES. BUT THE WAY YOU FACE THE DAY DETERMINES YOUR OUTCOME. REMEMBER, WEATHER DOESN'T DETERMINE IF YOU ARE STABLE OR UNSTEADY. JUST BECAUSE THE WEATHER CHANGES DOESN'T MEAN YOU HAVE TO. YOU'RE NOT A BAROMETER GOING UP AND DOWN AS THE PRESSURE CHANGES; YOUR LIFE IS BUILT ON A ROCK THAT CAN'T BE MOVED!

LIFE IS VERY GOOD!

The Bible is full of individuals who had good and bad days, victories and defeats and it provides a good representation of everyday life. I'm sure you've heard the phrase that we are "in the world but not of the world", right? Well, it's been said so many times that many people think it's a biblical verse. It is actually a phrase birthed from John 17:16 which says, "They are not of the world, even as I Am not of it." In other words, you live in this world but it doesn't and shouldn't determine your stability. Your life is built on the chief cornerstone, the rock of ages, who Himself is not of this world. You were born of heaven. Your home is heaven. You are on loan in this earth to do His work and fulfill His destiny in your life. Let Christ be your barometer of change in your life, the solid rock.

The Lord Says...

I Am the Rock and I will always lead you through any weather, any season and any challenge. Like I told Peter, keep your eyes on Me and you cannot fail. Trust in your own power and it will only last you for a moment. Together we achieve greatness for two are greater than one, especially when it's you and I.

If you believe it, say, "Oh yeah!"

AUGUST 23
PRAISE TO WIN THE BATTLE

WHEN WE THINK OF THE MANY CHALLENGES WE FACE IN LIFE, IT'S EASY FOR THE MIND TO
THINK FROM A NEGATIVE STANDPOINT. INSTEAD, LOOK AT IT AS A CALL TO BATTLE; A SUM-
MONING OF THE INNER WARRIOR, THE "CHRIST" IN YOU, TO RISE UP! THESE CHALLENGES,
ONCE OVERCOME, BECOME A TESTIMONY OF GOD'S SIGNIFICANT VICTORY IN YOUR LIFE.
WEEPING ENDURES THROUGH THE NIGHT, BUT HIS JOY COMES IN THE MORNING! LIVE AS AN
OVERCOMER.

LIFE IS VERY GOOD!

Why reinvent the wheel? Instead shouldn't we replicate what has already been
done? Judah represents the banner of praise, a representation that God goes before
you in battle. In 2 Chronicles 20, Jehoshaphat cried out to God for direction and
intervention as three kings formed an alliance and were coming after their people,
whom were no match for an army of such numbers. God spoke through the priest
Jahaziel, giving direction. He said: 1) Don't be afraid or dismayed, 2) The battle is
not yours, it's God's, 3) You will not fight, 4) Position yourself and stand still, and
5) See the salvation of the Lord, who's with you. In response, Jehoshaphat began
to thank the Lord for the victory in advance. He told the people to: 1) Believe, 2)
Have faith in the prophets, 3) Send the worshippers before the battle, and 4) They
were instructed to praise the Lord and give thanks for His mercies that endure forever. This was a statement that they believed solely in God for delivering them to
victory. Miraculously the men of the three enemy armies fought among and killed
themselves. This became a testimony of their faith to the overcoming power and
victory of God's mighty power and how He stands by His Word, for indeed they
did not fight, they just praised and thanked their way through.

So what challenges are you facing? Give them over to God and stop declaring
negativity. Look at your challenge the way Jehoshaphat did. If God can do it for
him, He can do it for you. Become a warrior of praise, worship and thanksgiving
and your weeping will turn from pain to victory. This is the overcomer's life.

The Lord Says...

I have given you the power of the sword. Use it. Wield it with your tongue to
overcome every circumstance that befalls you. With My Words I created the world
and with My Words you can change your life.

If you believe it, say, "Oh yeah!"

AUGUST 24
WHO HE IS IS WHO YOU ARE

WHEN YOU IDENTIFY WHO HE IS, YOU WILL DISCOVER WHO YOU ARE. THIS DISCOVERY REVEALS THE TRUTH ABOUT YOUR GREATNESS. GOD SEES YOU GREATER THAN YOU SEE YOURSELF. DON'T LIMIT WHO YOU ARE AND WHAT YOU CAN ACCOMPLISH IN LIFE.

LIFE IS VERY GOOD!

The Bible is filled with pieces of who God is. He is above all, love (1 John 4:8). He is a God of mercy and justice and a God of peace and wisdom. He is holy and righteous. He is filled with grace and creativity. He is a rock, a refuge or fortress in times of trouble. He is the truth and the light in a darkened world. He is King, father, friend, comforter and teacher. If you need a mentor, then look closely; Jesus has His hand raised and He's saying, "Pick me, pick me!" When you can identify who He is, you can look in the mirror and find the traits He's blessed you with to accomplish all He's set out for you to do. Nothing is too great for Him. You may think you're the shyest person on the planet but God's put you through some situations so you can change the hearts of people who need victory from the same place. When you see that He is father, friend, teacher, refuge and merciful, you will begin to understand that He is perfect in all His ways and He's holding your hand all the way through the journey. You can make it and you can do anything when God is by your side. Rise up and get excited for He is with you.

The Lord Says...

Take off the limits in your mind, your will and your emotions, for greater things can I do than you can even presently imagine. Dream bigger than before for with Me all things are possible.

If you believe it, say, "Oh yeah!"

AUGUST 25
THE BEAUTY OF THE PROPHETIC WORD

THE PROPHETIC WORD IS LIKE A PAINTER WHO SEES AN IMAGE AND PAINTS IT SO EVERYONE CAN SEE WHAT HE SAW. A PROPHETIC WORD IS A PORTRAIT WITH WORDS INSTEAD OF A BRUSH. THIS WORD HAS THE POWER TO CAPTURE BEAUTY HIDDEN INSIDE OF EARTHLY VESSELS AND SPEAKS THEM INTO EXISTENCE SO EVERYONE ELSE CAN SEE IT. YOU ARE GOD'S ARTWORK AND HIS SPOKEN WORD MANIFESTING ON THE EARTH.

LIFE IS VERY GOOD!

What a gift to have a life painted by the greatest master painter of all time, the creator of the universe - God. An artist doesn't always get it right the first time around, but God does. And when you think you have to step in and give the artist some pointers, take over the brush and make the masterpiece all about you, you miss out on the manifestation of His creative force in your life. So, let go and let God. Let Him finish the work He started in you. Philippians 1:6 says, "Being confident of this, that he who began a good work in you will carry it on to completion until the day of Christ Jesus." Anything He can do is greater than what you can do, so don't be afraid of a little creative force in your life. He will mold you, shape you and create you in and with HIS best in mind, for you are His creation.

The Lord Says...

You are My creation and My creative force does live inside of you, but let Me paint the masterpiece or your life. Let Me sculpt you to become that in which I know your full potential lies. Let Me color you with beauty and transform your life. Walk the good walk. Talk the good talk. See with My eyes and hear with your ears that which I speak. I have the best in mind for you.

If you believe it, say, "Oh yeah!"

AUGUST 26
THE POWER OF THE PROPHETIC WORD

A PROPHETIC WORD CAN CALL A THING INTO EXISTENCE WHAT IS SEEN FROM A SPIRITUAL PERSPECTIVE BUT MAY NOT BE VISIBLE TO THE NATURAL EYE. IT HAS THE POWER AT THE SAME TIME TO RELEASE HOPE TO A PERSON, WHILE CAUSING THE INVISIBLE REALM TO BE MADE KNOWN. WHEN A MYSTERY IS REVEALED, IT BECOMES AN UNEXPECTED BLESSING. PROCLAIM WORDS OF EDIFICATION, EXHORTATION AND COMFORT.

LIFE IS VERY GOOD!

I Corinthians 14:3 says, "But the one who prophesies speaks to people for their strengthening, encouraging and comfort." Some of you are only one word of encouragement away from your victory. So, what is a person to do when the prophet is not in your town? I'll tell you. Jesus was the greatest prophet of all time. Not only does He sit in the office of the prophet, but He is your priest and King. Look no further than the Good Book, your Bible. It's filled with encouragement. It exhorts you to make it through, renew your mind, live an abundant life, to love and do good to all people. It speaks of comfort and tells you that God has sent His Holy Spirit to comfort you and keep you. He tells you in scripture that He is your rock and that, if you cast your burdens on Him, He will take them. Honestly, a prophet on the earth is just a conduit of what God wants to say to you anyway, so dive into the Good Book and see what HE has to say for and about you.

The Lord Says...

Whatever you have need of, I Am. When you seek Me, I will be found and all you need will be given unto you. Many ask but few take time to seek. Don't just stand at the door. Knock and I will be opened to you, for I Am the doorway to your blessing.

If you believe it, say, "Oh yeah!"

AUGUST 27
ONE WORD CAN SAVE A LIFE

A WORD OF ENCOURAGEMENT IS THE ABILITY TO SEE AND SPEAK CLEARLY FROM GOD'S PERSPECTIVE AND EDIFY A PERSON'S SPIRIT. THIS TYPE OF WORD OFTEN COMES TO HELP CHANGE A PERSON'S POINT OF VIEW ON A MATTER AND LET THEM KNOW HE CARES. THE LORD WILL SEE YOU THROUGH!

LIFE IS VERY GOOD!

Do you remember the first time God read your mail through a word of knowledge, or spoke into a situation in your life that maybe no one knew about but you and a handful of others? Perhaps you've watched Christian TV programming and a word came through and it was as if it was spoken directly to your situation. It may have seemed creepy at first but, for some reason, you knew it was God. Or perhaps someone just gave you a word of encouragement and affirmation that broke the chains and made you feel important again. God wants you to know that He's always there with you and He brings a timely word of encouragement to give you hope so faith can be renewed and your mind can set itself up for victory.

Hebrews 4:12 says, "For the word of God is alive and active. Sharper than any double-edged sword, it penetrates even to dividing soul and spirit, joints and marrow; it judges the thoughts and attitudes of the heart." Look at how powerful the Word of God is. What would happen if you began to speak the Word into the lives of those around you just as a means of encouragement every day? Not only would their point of view change, but so would yours because when you see through the eyes of Jesus, you can't help but see differently. It may only take one word of encouragement to save a life, to launch a career, or send someone on the road to their destiny. What will you say? Be His hope in the world.

The Lord Says...

It is because I love you that I love language. Language communicates thoughts and ideas. It changes circumstances and lives. It sends creative miracles into action. It allows you to know Me and Me to know you. Language is a beautiful thing. Use it for the benefit of others. What will you say to your world? How will you pray and seek Me? What will you say as you pray for your neighbors and nation? Remember, My WORD is sharper than a double-edged sword. It is active and alive and it penetrates the atmosphere when it is spoken. Language creates. How will you use your language today? Use it to lift someone up.

If you believe it, say, "Oh yeah!"

AUGUST 28
REFRESHING RAIN

WHEN TIMES OF TROUBLE VISIT IN YOUR LIFE, LIKEN IT TO A STORM PASSING THROUGH. IT MAY RAIN HARD FOR A TIME BUT EVENTUALLY THE RAIN CEASES AND THE SON WILL SHINE OVER IT. AFTER IT PASSES, STEP OUT, SMELL THE REFRESHING SCENT AND ALLOW IT TO RENEW YOUR STRENGTH. DON'T WORRY, BRIGHTER DAYS ARE AHEAD.

LIFE IS VERY GOOD!

Often times when it rains in Hawaii and it's not the rainy season, the locals can always tell who the tourists are. You see, the rain is usually a warm and quick rain and the locals usually continue in the water as opposed to the tourists who take cover out of the water. God wants you to be a local; a Kingdom local. Let His rain fall on you and hold His hand through the storm, for it shall pass. People who love the Pacific Northwest of the United States have an affection for the rain; it gathers them to drink more coffee and tea together, experience early evenings under a blanket with an excuse to have hot cocoa (not always bad, right?) or take in the refreshing smell in the air after a good downpour. Sometimes the refreshing rain is a nice break in the heat of summer, or a visual blessing to see the flowers bloom. Other times it can be destructive, washing away bridges and roads, creating sink holes and causing damage beyond the imagination.

No matter if the weather in your life is refreshing or damaging, God is with you. He is the hand the holds you, the rock that keeps you, the shoulder that takes on your burdens. John 4:24 says, "God is spirit and those who worship him must worship in spirit and truth." So, do like Job did in the midst of his storm; worship Him. Do like Paul and Silas did in their storm; worship and praise Him. Do like David did in his storm as he faced a lion and a bear; call on His name and He will be there. Call on His name and worship Him. The storm will surely pass. The lessons learned will renew your strength.

The Lord Says...

Rain or shine, sleet or snow, I Am with you wherever you go. Just call My name and I'll be there, for I walk with you everywhere. Lift your head and raise your voice for it is all a matter of choice. When Peter took his eyes off Me, it was then that he could not see. When you keep your eyes on Me through any storm, you will walk in places you never have before. I Am with you rain or shine. I Am with you ALL the time.

If you believe it, say, "Oh yeah!"

AUGUST 29
YOUR LIFE IS NOT JUST "ALL ABOUT YOU"

THE CHOICES A PERSON MAKES IN LIFE AFFECT MORE THAN THEMSELVES. GOD CHOSE TO RE-DEEM HUMANITY WITH HIS SON; HIS SON CHOSE TO WALK IT THROUGH TO THE CROSS. THEIR DECISION IS STILL CHANGING THE WORLD. WHAT HAVE YOUR CHOICES DONE? REMEMBER, IT'S NOT JUST ABOUT YOU. CHOOSE WISELY, CHOOSE HIS LIFE.

LIFE IS VERY GOOD!

Have you ever been in a situation when you just wanted to react because your flesh hurt so, so badly? I'm sure you've been there. I know I have. Our human nature wants to protect every part of our heart and make others pay for doing us wrong. But whatever decision you make in that moment can have life changing consequences. Someone once said to me, "I just want the world to know what they did and I want them to know the pain they've put me through." But Jesus says in Ephesians 4:29, "Do not let any unwholesome talk come out of your mouths, but only what is helpful for building others up according to their needs, that it may benefit those who listen." Wow, now that is a piercing to the flawed Adamic nature that wants to react to hurt and pain. But what does the scripture say? 1). Let no unwholesome talk out of your mouth, and 2). Only speak what builds others up. Before you react, step away and get alone with God. Don't react in anger and say things you will regret a moment later. Choose your words wisely. Make good choices with your words in your family, your marriage, at work, at play, amongst your colleagues or peers, everywhere. You never know who is watching and how a decision to react could change your world.

The Lord Says...

What have your choices done in your world? Have they been for good in your neighborhood, in your family, your church and amongst your friends? Do you choose to speak life and not death with the tongue you've been given? Take account of your decisions in your world. Your tongue has power; use it for the edification and comfort of others. Your words don't only affect you, but others around you. Let My love and grace flow through all that you say and do.

If you believe it, say, "Oh yeah!"

AUGUST 30
THE STRENGTH IN SACRIFICE

WHEN YOU NEED SOMETHING TO CHANGE DRASTICALLY IN YOUR LIFE, REMEMBER THE PRIN-
CIPLE OF TRUE SACRIFICE. A SACRIFICE IS MORE THAN GIVING SOMETHING UP, IT'S A WILLING-
NESS TO LAY SOMETHING DOWN FOR THE BETTER OF OTHERS. JESUS SACRIFICED BY LAYING
HIS LIFE DOWN AND CHANGED THE WORLD FOREVER. WHEN YOU LAY SOMETHING DOWN IN
SACRIFICE, IT NOT ONLY CHANGES YOUR LIFE, BUT OTHERS' LIVES AS WELL.

LIFE IS VERY GOOD!

God required Abraham to do it. He put Isaac upon a bed of sticks to become
the sacrificial lamb offering. God just wanted to see if Abraham would lay down
the most important thing in his life for God alone. Would you? Is it the television
that has you hooked to movies and video games? Is it your cell phone that is attached to your hip? Is it alcohol or pornography? Perhaps it's sugar or junk food.
Maybe you're a workaholic and your possessions like your home, your car, your
computer, your Rolex watches, your dapper suits or Coach purses are what you
hold on to. God wants to know that you could lay them down and still serve Him.
John 12:25 says, "Anyone who loves their life will lose it, while anyone who
hates their life in this world will keep it for eternal life." Remember, when you
lay something down, it is often only for a season. God's ways are higher than our
ways. Allow Him to guide and mold your life; yet ask yourself, does He precede
all that is important to me in this life?

The Lord Says...

Many say they know Me, yet there is but one God; the God of Abraham, Isaac
and Jacob, that's who I Am. I have kept you and shaped you, breathed life into
your bones. I Am father, friend and teacher, the first and the last, always faithful,
always true. I Am your Jehovah Jireh, the author and finisher of your faith.

If you believe it, say, "Oh yeah!"

AUGUST 31
CELEBRATE LIFE!

REMEMBER THIS: IN LIFE THERE ARE THOSE WHO WILL CELEBRATE YOU AND OTHERS WHO WON'T. THOSE THAT WON'T WILL TRY TO SOUR WHO YOU ARE, BUT DON'T LET THEIR WORDS OR ACTIONS RUIN IT FOR OTHERS. KEEP WALKING AS THE PERFECT GIFT GOD MADE YOU TO BE, SHINING ABOVE THE NEGATIVE OPINIONS OF MAN.

LIFE IS VERY GOOD!

Romans 12:14 says, "Bless those who persecute you; bless and do not curse." This is in no way an easy task, for you are human and your flesh naturally leans towards reaction when others hurt you. But God yearns for your spiritual nature to reign over your fleshly nature and become a man or woman of exceedingly great love no matter what opinion comes towards you; arrows or no arrows. Try it, you'll like who you become.

The Lord Says...

Love by its nature is forgiving, tender-hearted, merciful and generous. Be the love you seek, as I Am the love for you. Don't worry about what others think or say about you, because all that matters is what I have already declared over you. You are My child, the work of My hands, the gift I have sent to the earth to make a difference.

If you believe it, say, "Oh yeah!"

SEPTEMBER 1
MAKE YOUR CHOICE AND LIFT YOUR VOICE

STAND STRONG FOR WHAT YOU DESIRE. REFUSE TO LET OTHERS CLASSIFY WHAT YOU CAN DO OR BECOME IN LIFE. BREAK THE MINDSETS OF LIMITATION AND CRY OUT FOR WHAT YOU WANT! BARTIMAEUS CRIED OUT ALL THE MORE WHEN A SYSTEM TOLD HIM TO BE QUIET. LIFT YOUR VOICE LOUD ENOUGH TO BE HEARD BECAUSE GOD ANSWERS THE CRIES OF HIS CHILDREN. YOUR VOICE IS SIGNIFICANT.

LIFE IS VERY GOOD!

Jesus knew what it was like to be rejected. Some believed in Him and some still do, while others did and do not. It's just part of life. If you lived your life based on the limitations and opinions of man, you'd get nowhere in life, for every man owns his own set of limitations and opinions. Be true to yourself and true to the vision Christ put within you. God gave Joseph a vision of who he was and even his own family didn't agree with it. Don't take it personally, just seek God. Matthew 6:33 says that when you "seek His Kingdom first, all those things will be added to you." So lift your voice like Bartimaeus and call out His name. Seek Him until He answers you.

The Lord Says...

I hear your voice and your cries in the midnight hour when no one is watching and you're on your knees. I do not take your tears for granted. Do you hear My voice? My sheep know My voice as I know theirs. Listen for Me in the stillness, in the wind, in the grieving and the mourning, in the laugher and joy, in times of indecision and contemplation. I Am always here. Listen and hear.

If you believe it, say, "Oh yeah!"

SEPTEMBER 2
LIFE ABOVE REPROACH

IT COULD BE SAID THAT YESTERDAY'S MISTAKES BECOME THE FOUNDATION OF STRENGTH YOU WALK ON TODAY. WHO YOU WERE IS NOT WHO YOU ARE! DON'T LET OTHERS HOLD YOUR PAST AGAINST YOU TODAY. GOD DOESN'T. REMEMBER, YOUR SIN HAS BEEN FORGIVEN. LIVE ABOVE REPROACH.

LIFE IS VERY GOOD!

Philippians 3:13-14 says, "Brothers, I do not consider that I have made it my own. But one thing I do: forgetting what lies behind and straining forward to what lies ahead. I press on toward the goal for the prize of the upward call of God in Christ Jesus." In other words, every minute of the past is the past. Though it is a part of who you've become, it does not determine who you are. God didn't let it stop David, who committed adultery and had a hand in a man's murder. It didn't stop Abraham, who slept with another woman, thinking he'd help God with his plan for a son. It didn't stop the disciples, who were persecuted for His Name's sake. Don't let the opinions of others regarding your past determine your altitude in life.

The Lord Says...

Move forward, press on, for there is much work to be done. Nations need to find Me and cities and people in dark places need to find Me. You are above and not beneath, the head and not the tail in all things. Don't allow your past to hold you back anymore. I see you through My blood and that's the way it will always be.

If you believe it, say, "Oh yeah!"

SEPTEMBER 3
BRING LIFE INTO FOCUS

IF WE ARE NOT MINDFUL OF ALL THE LITTLE THINGS IN OUR LIVES, THEY WILL CAUSE THE GREATEST FRUSTRATIONS OR BECOME THE BIGGEST DISTRACTIONS. TODAY, STOP AND LOOK AT THE BIGGER PICTURE, UPROOT WHAT IS INSIGNIFICANT AND FOCUS ON WHAT'S TRULY IMPORTANT. REMEMBER, IT'S THE LITTLE FOXES THAT DESTROY THE VINE. FOCUS ON HIS PURPOSE FOR YOUR LIFE.

LIFE IS VERY GOOD!

God's pretty simple. Scripture says in Psalm 119:15, "I meditate on your precepts and consider your ways." When you do that - fix your eyes, your ears, your mouth, your feet and your hands to and towards Jesus - it's much easier to bring life into focus and rid yourself of the distractions keeping you from your purpose and destiny. If the enemy can delay you, he can potentially keep you from ever achieving your mission. So purpose in your heart to meditate on Him day and night and keep those foxes in check.

The Lord Says...

So many people never take the time to stop, look and listen. And when they do, often times they think they are listening, but they do not hear at all; they only hear what they want to hear. Wisdom is not in the listening only, but in the hearing. You have My mind and you have My word. Use it wisely and always hear for My voice and listen to what I say to you.

If you believe it, say, "Oh yeah!"

SEPTEMBER 4
AVOID THE POTHOLES OF NEGATIVITY

REMEMBER, JUST BECAUSE SOMETHING WENT WRONG IN YOUR LIFE DOESN'T MEAN ALL THINGS ARE WRONG IN YOUR LIFE. DON'T GIVE POWER TO A NEGATIVE THING AND ALLOW IT TO MAKE ALL THINGS WORSE THAN THEY REALLY ARE. IT'S TIME TO STOP THE EMOTIONAL ROLLER-COASTER AND BE THANKFUL, REMEMBERING THE MERCIES OF THE LORD ARE NEW EVERY MORNING. THIS TOO SHALL PASS.

LIFE IS VERY GOOD!

Sometimes those draining life experiences can be like a spring pothole. From the onset it just looks like a pothole filled with water until you step in it. Then you quickly find out the pothole is much deeper than you originally had thought. You're going to have times like that in life, potholes filled with water that get your feet wet. But here's the good news. You don't have to stand in it to enjoy the spring rain. Likewise, don't give so much place to negativity. When you do it's like the pothole, it seems bigger than it normally would have. Ephesians 4:27 says, "And do not give the devil a foothold." In other words, don't give him any place to stand in your life. Lean on His mercies and thank the Lord that every day is a do-over.

The Lord Says...

Moments change as time is no respecter of persons. What you dwell on will become, so dwell on Me and My kingdom purpose, leaving all the negative behind. Situations, both positive and negative, will come in your life but I Am with you in all of it. Trials will come and go, they won't stay forever. A new day in Me will arise.

If you believe it, say, "Oh yeah!"

SEPTEMBER 5
CHARACTER SHINES BRIGHTEST
DURING TROUBLED TIMES

IN LIFE, SOME PEOPLE WILL TALK ABOUT YOU, OTHERS WILL COMPARE YOU UNJUSTLY AGAINST OTHERS AND SOME WILL JUST SHAKE THEIR HEADS WITH DISGUST AT YOU. WHATEVER THEY DO, DON'T LET THEIR ACTION BREAK YOU. STAND STRONG AND LET THE ACTION REFINE YOU! YOUR CHARACTER IN TIMES OF TROUBLE DEFINES THE TRUTH OF WHO YOU ARE.

LIFE IS VERY GOOD!

When you know who you are in Christ, it changes everything: the way you walk, the way you talk, the way you carry yourself, your actions and your character. I Peter 2:9 says, "But you are a chosen people, a royal priesthood, a holy nation, God's special possession, that you may declare the praises of him who called you out of darkness into his wonderful light." This is who you are: chosen or hand-picked, royalty in the priesthood, a nation that's holy and God's possession. Wow, that's worth striving for some good character, wouldn't you agree? Let God be God during the troubled times of your life and let His character in you speak for itself.

The Lord Says...

I Am light and in Me there is no darkness. If you are My image then you also are light. You see the light, you crave the light and you want more of the light in your life. May your character reflect My ways of Galatians 5:22 and, in troubled times, the world will know your God.

If you believe it, say, "Oh yeah!"

SEPTEMBER 6
PURPOSE AND DESTINY ARE POWERFUL TOOLS

THE HARDEST THING TO STOP IS A MAN THAT IS MOTIVATED TO FULFILL A PURPOSE IN LIFE. YOU CAN'T STAND IN HIS WAY BECAUSE HE WILL NOT STOP UNTIL HE FINDS A WAY AROUND, OVER, UNDER OR THROUGH. AND WHEN THAT DOESN'T WORK, HE ALLOWS GOD TO LIFT HIM OVER TO ACCOMPLISH HIS PURPOSE. NO OBSTACLE IS BIG ENOUGH TO STOP YOU.

LIFE IS VERY GOOD!

Purpose and destiny are powerful tools. Anyone will fight to get to their destiny or operate in it. Something happens to you when you walk in those things that God called you to do. Atmosphere is everything. Hebrews 11:3 says, "By faith we understand that the universe was formed at God's command, so that what is seen was not made out of what was visible." So never stop. God spoke the universe into existence. You were made in His image, so keep speaking and don't let anyone keep you from the promise God intended for you to fulfill. He spoke, now you keep speaking too and then watch and see what He will do. There is life in His Words that you speak.

The Lord Says...

Speak life and keep on moving forward towards destiny. There will be battles, for no one wants to be in the desert but everyone wants to be in the promised land. Stay the course and fight the good fight of faith. I Am and will always be on your side.

If you believe it, say, "Oh yeah!"

SEPTEMBER 7
YOUR PURPOSE IS WORTH FIGHTING FOR

THIS ABOUT THIS: HAVING A GOAL OR A VISION GIVES LIFE. WITHOUT VISION, THE PEOPLE PERISH, SO THE OPPOSITE HAS TO BE TRUE AS WELL. WHEN YOU HAVE SOMETHING TO RUN AFTER, YOU HAVE THE MOTIVATION TO CONTINUE YOUR JOURNEY NO MATTER HOW DIFFICULT THE ROAD MAY GET. FOLLOW THE PATH TO WHAT GOD HAS PLACED IN YOUR HEART FOR HE IS THE LIFE WITHIN YOU.

LIFE IS VERY GOOD!

Do you ever feel like an underachiever? Many underachievers are highly gifted individuals who are missing just one aspect of the purpose-filled life: they lack goals. Underachievers may have big dreams and grand visions but, without goals and a plan to achieve those dreams and that vision, they spin their wheels in the same way, in the same place and at the same time day after day. Turn that spinning into forward motion by setting aside time to develop steps and goals to make those dreams and that vision become reality in your life.

Goals are like the steps to your purpose. It's one thing to have a vision of God's destiny and purpose for your life but that, in itself, isn't enough. Where the people perish is by not having a full vision. Instead, many have a partial vision or dream. In order to make that dream a reality, you must take steps of preparation. Those steps require goals. Ask yourself this question: What is it going to take in order to accomplish that dream? If you are called to teach children and be a voice for God in the schools, then it takes effort. Your goals might be to save money, earn a bachelor's degree, get a teaching credential or get a job - purpose fulfilled! Don't let obstacles detour or delay you from that which you CAN accomplish. It's never easy but anything worth having is worth fighting for. Proverbs 24:27 says, "Put your outdoor work in order and get your fields ready; after that, build your house." God explains it quite simplistically; get your life in order, including getting ready for your occupation, then build your house. Get goals and get a good thing, for they will lead you to your promised land.

The Lord Says...

I know the plans I have for you and they are great; line upon line, precept upon precept, you can do all you set out to accomplish and then more. Don't let obstacles like detours and delays side track your progress for preparation is the key in a dream fulfilled. I believe in you and I know you can accomplish all you set your heart and mind to do.

If you believe it, say, "Oh yeah!"

SEPTEMBER 8
LOVE OTHERS LIKE GOD LOVES YOU

GOD KNOWS OUR POTENTIAL AND OUR TRUE DESTINY AND LOOKS BEYOND OUR FAILURES AND SHORTCOMINGS. HE CALLED DAVID A MAN AFTER HIS OWN HEART, THOUGH DAVID AT ONE TIME WAS AN ADULTERER AND A MURDERER. BE LIKE CHRIST AND SEE THE GREATER IN PEOPLE, EVEN WHEN THEY MAKE FOOLISH CHOICES. VIEW OTHERS THROUGH HIS EYES.

LIFE IS VERY GOOD!

There is a time and a place for criticism, particularly constructive criticism. Jesus himself was critical of people but His truth was always watered with love as was the case with the Pharisees in Matthew 23. Ephesians 4:15 says, "Instead, speaking the truth in love, we will grow to become in every respect the mature body of him who is the head, that is, Christ." So remember, before you criticize or chastise someone, that God sees greater in them, so be like Christ and see them through His eyes. Ask yourself if you are part of the problem or a part of the process. If you are part of the problem, change it. Instead, be His mouthpiece. What would Jesus say?

The Lord Says...

Be slow to speak and well at hearing and you will earn the respect of others. You may not know where they have been or what they've been through, but it doesn't matter because I love them just the same as I love you. Would you love like Me, in deed and with your mouth? If you do, you can change the world around you.

If you believe it, say, "Oh yeah!"

SEPTEMBER 9
GOD'S GREATEST CREATION IS YOU

HUMMINGBIRDS HOVER, CATERPILLARS TRANSFORM AND BUMBLEBEES FLY. THESE ARE ALL WONDERFUL CREATIONS BUT HOW MUCH MORE MAGNIFICENT IS YOUR CREATION? THERE IS NOTHING GREATER ON THE EARTH THAN YOU. YOU ARE THE MOST GLORIOUS OF ALL HIS CREATIONS. BELIEVE IT!

LIFE IS VERY GOOD!

Honestly, you can't help but get outside and not see God in His creation. When you see wonders like the Grand Canyon, Niagara Falls, the Hawaiian volcanoes, the majesty of snow-topped mountain peaks and beautiful animals across the globe, the foliage and His people, you can't help but see God. Yet, on this earth, you are His greatest creation. There are many types of cats: lions, tigers, cheetahs, panthers and house cats, just to name a few. But guess what? There is only one YOU. There is no one like you. Even if you're a twin, there is something unique, special and different about YOU! Genesis 2:7 says, "Then the Lord God formed a man from the dust of the ground and breathed into his nostrils the breath of life and the man became a living being." He created you from the very depths of HIS creation. Adam came from the richest part of the earth; the ground. You are His gift to the world.

The Lord Says...

The world smiled when you came to this earth and it still smiles today because you are part of it. I paint sunsets for you, flowers that bloom, rivers that run. I made lakes that glisten, food for you to harvest and hunt, friends to spend time with and WORDS to live by. All that I have accomplished has been for you. You are the apple of My eye, My beloved.

If you believe it, say, "Oh yeah!"

SEPTEMBER 10
LET GO TO MOVE ON

THE POWER OF CHANGE CAN BE EXPLAINED AS A WILLINGNESS TO RELEASE CONTROL OF A SITUATION. THOUGH LETTING GO MAY NOT BE EASY, IT'S NECESSARY SO YOUR LIFE CAN PROGRESS. LETTING GO IS MORE THAN OPENING YOUR HAND, IT'S MOVING IN THE RIGHT DIRECTION. CONQUER YOUR FEARS AND MOVE INTO HIS PEACE.

LIFE IS VERY GOOD!

This is the reason that change is so difficult. People are comfortable in their little town, with their good steady jobs, their modest mortgage and so God can't get you to step out of the boat. Why? Because you have such a death grip on the control of your life that you wouldn't hear Him if He shouted at you to move. Let go. Release your plans by opening your hand and taking the hand of Jesus. Give it all to Him and He will direct your path if you will only trust Him. It's never easy to do, but when God is in, it's worth it.

The Lord Says...

It's never easy to give control of something you have a personal investment in to someone else. But I Am not just anyone else. I care about all that concerns you and the things which you cannot see today but will find need of tomorrow. Don't let fear move you, step into faith and move with Me.

If you believe it, say, "Oh yeah!"

SEPTEMBER 11
YOU CAN CHOOSE WHAT DEFINES YOU

YOUR LIFE IS NOT DEFINED BY A PAST MOMENT OF UNCERTAINTY, FEAR OR STRUGGLE. YOU ARE FAR GREATER THAN WHAT YOUR PAST ISSUES HAVE MADE YOU BELIEVE. THOMAS WAS CALLED 'DOUBTING THOMAS' BECAUSE OF HIS MOMENT OF UNBELIEF, BUT JESUS CALLED HIM DIDYMUS OR 'TWIN'. BREAK THE MOLD AND REMEMBER THAT YOU LOOK MORE LIKE CHRIST THAN YOU REALIZE. YOU, LIKE THOMAS, ARE MADE IN HIS PERFECT IMAGE.

LIFE IS VERY GOOD!

September 11th is a day that will forever be etched and imprinted in minds of every American and is known now as Patriot's Day. It was a day in the past where fear, uncertainty and grief struck our land. And, though we remember this day annually and memorialize the heroes and those who lost their lives that day, the act of terrorism did not define us as Americans. Instead, it drew a nation together and we became one nation under God once again. On that day, the good will of people began to put their brother and sister, their neighbors and friends, before themselves; now that's looking like Christ. Galatians 6:2 says, "Carry each other's burdens and in this way you will fulfill the law of Christ." You want to know how to make it through your own struggle of uncertainty? Put on the image of Christ and do something for others.

The Lord Says...

Sometimes seeing isn't believing, but believing is seeing. Begin to see the shift. Begin to see the change. Begin to see the abundance, the prosperity, the goodness, the harmony and walk forward helping someone else come out of the same valley you've just come through. When Thomas saw My wounds, it changed him. Who will you touch and allow My image to change?

If you believe it, say, "Oh yeah!"

SEPTEMBER 12
LET SUCCESS BE YOUR PROTOTYPE

DON'T LIMIT YOURSELF BECAUSE OF PAST MISTAKES. MISTAKES CAN BE USED AS STEPPING STONES INTO A GREATER DIMENSION. PETER CUT OFF THE EAR OF THE HIGH PRIEST'S SERVANT AND ALSO DENIED CHRIST 3 TIMES. BUT, ON THE OTHER HAND, HE WALKED ON THE WATER AND WAS USED TO HEAL THE MAN AT THE GATE BEAUTIFUL. YOU SERVE A GOD OF MANY CHANCES, SO GET UP AND KEEP GOING!

LIFE IS VERY GOOD!

So much can be said about failure. It is the opportunity that propels one to greatness. Many celebrities failed before they made their mark on the world. I'm sure you've heard of the Dyson vacuum cleaner. But, did you know that James Dyson made over 5,000 prototypes of his first vacuum and no one would help him bring it to market and manufacture it? So instead, he manufactured it himself. Look at him now. Don't let the past stop you and refuse to be a prototype of your dream. Keep going and march forward.

The Lord Says...

The only limitations that limit you are the ones you allow. For with Me, you cannot fail and all things work together for the good of those that I love and are called according to My purpose. My word is true today, yesterday and forever.

If you believe it, say, "Oh yeah!"

SEPTEMBER 13
YOU ARE CAPTIVE NO MORE!

THE SEASON OF TRIALS ENDS WHILE IT'S STILL DARK OUTSIDE. THE STONE BEFORE CHRIST'S TOMB WAS ROLLED AWAY WHILE THE SKY WAS STILL DARK. REMEMBER, WHAT WAS HOLDING YOU CAPTIVE HAS ALREADY BEEN REMOVED. LET NOTHING KEEP YOU FROM ACHIEVING YOUR DREAMS. THE PRICE HAS ALREADY BEEN PAID IN FULL AND THE SON IS SHINING.

LIFE IS VERY GOOD!

Maybe you've heard the saying, it's darkest before the dawn. Or perhaps you've heard the analogy that life is sometimes like remodeling; it always looks worse (especially in the middle of demolition) before it gets better. Well, it's true. The word 'trial' stands for something: **T**each **R**eal **I**ndividuals **A**ll **L**essons. In other words, the stuff you go through, it wasn't just a journey meant for you alone. The lessons from that journey were meant to help someone else in their journey; lessons of hope, lessons of faith, lessons of love, comfort, care and kindness. Acts 20:35 says, "In everything I did, I showed you that by this kind of hard work we must help the weak, remembering the words the Lord Jesus himself said: 'It is more blessed to give than to receive.'" So remember, you're never alone, so don't be afraid of the dark. God is with you wherever you go and today, because He paid the price, YOU can stand in victory from wherever you are.

The Lord Says...

Be victorious, in speech and in deed, for the steps of the righteous are ordered by God. And today you are more than a conqueror. I have declared it as such over your life. Believe it for it was spoken from My heart.

If you believe it, say, "Oh yeah!"

SEPTEMBER 14
BE A GREAT LEADER

GOOD LEADERS CAPTIVATE YOU; GREAT LEADERS MOTIVATE YOU AND TEACH YOU TO WALK IN VICTORY. GOOD LEADERS ENCOURAGE YOU IN YOUR TIME OF HARDSHIP, BUT GREAT LEADERS LOVE YOU THROUGH YOUR HARDSHIP AND HELP YOU UNDERSTAND YOU'VE ALREADY OVERCOME. SO DON'T JUST BE A GOOD LEADER, BE A GREAT LEADER AND HELP SOMEONE ELEVATE.

LIFE IS VERY GOOD!

Remember, you are more than a conqueror (Romans 8:37). But, don't just say that scripture lightly. If we take a look at the language, what does it really mean to be more than a conqueror? What is a conqueror? Someone who conquers, defeats a foe. What does 'more than' mean? 'More than' refers to a mass amount, above and beyond the regular. If you give your child a half-cup of chocolate milk at dinner and your child says they want more than that, then they are asking for above the quantity they usually receive. God is saying that you are more fierce than the regular conqueror because you are more than just a simple conqueror when you are in Christ Jesus. You're like those in the upper room; filled with power from on high. That's something to get excited about. So captivate those whom you lead by speaking into them who they are; that they are more than conquerors and they can make it through. Then love on them so they know you really are with them and you're not just preaching words. Great fathers take the time and spend it with their children. Great leaders must also do the same. When your offspring are raised this way, they will multiply the mentality and you can say, "Job well done."

The Lord Says...

Blessed are the pure in heart, for they will surely see Me and I shall know them by their fruit. Be the fruit the world needs and the salt they so longingly look for in this life. I have place in you all the potential and ability you need to become not just a good leader, but a great one, for My Spirit lives within you. Stand up and take your place in leading others into My kingdom blessing.

If you believe it, say, "Oh yeah!"

SEPTEMBER 15
AIN'T NO MOUNTAIN HIGH ENOUGH

THE SITUATION YOU ARE FACING IS NOT A MOUNTAIN OF TROUBLE, BUT A CALL OF GOD TO A HIGH PLACE. ACCEPT THE CHALLENGE AND KNOW THE MOUNTAIN IS ONLY THERE TO BE CONQUERED! THERE IS NO MOUNTAIN HIGH ENOUGH THAT THE CHRIST IN YOU CAN'T OVERTAKE! YOU ARE BUILT TO SUCCEED.

LIFE IS VERY GOOD!

The high place is a place of worship. It is in worship that healing occurs. It is in worship that lives are transformed. If you have ever watched healing services conducted by Benny Hinn? What is the common denominator of all those services? Worship. When the power and presence of God is ushered in through the praise and worship of God's people, the people manifest God's presence in healing. When you worship, there is no mountain high enough for God to take. Mark 11:23 says, "Truly I tell you, if anyone says to this mountain, 'Go, throw yourself into the sea,' and does not doubt in their heart but believes that what they say will happen, it will be done for them." Wow, what is the key here? Do not doubt in your heart, but believe and you will succeed. Let worship open the door and know the mountain has already been conquered.

The Lord Says...

Come unto Me and I will give you rest and, as you run the race of life, peace will be unto you. Don't be afraid of the mountain that is before you. I gave My life for you on a mountaintop and as I overcame death, hell, and the grave, so you have already overcome also. There is no trial that you and I cannot handle together.

If you believe it, say, "Oh yeah!"

SEPTEMBER 16
FOCUS ON GOD'S GOODNESS

REMEMBER THIS: STAY FOCUSED ON CHRIST IN TIMES OF DIFFICULTY BECAUSE IT WILL LEAD YOU AND OTHERS INTO VICTORY. BECAUSE THE YOUNG GIRL KEPT HER HEART IN ORDER IN THE MIDST OF BEING TAKEN CAPTIVE AND BECOMING A SERVANT IN NAAMAN'S HOUSE, SHE BECAME THE WORD OF THE LORD THAT LED NAAMAN TO HIS DELIVERANCE AND HEALING. FOCUS ON HIS GOODNESS AND BECOME GOD'S SPOKEN WORD!

LIFE IS VERY GOOD!

Ephesians 2:10 says, "For we are God's handiwork, created in Christ Jesus to do good works, which God prepared in advance for us to do." If you can remember this scripture, you'll begin to see your challenges differently. Your focus is on God's work that He prepared you for. So don't give up. Stay the course and keep your mind on Christ. Then sit back, trust God and see what He can do. Speak the word, it works!

The Lord Says...

My Words created the universe and My Words change circumstances even today. Remember, your victory is never far from you; declare and receive My goodness.

If you believe it, say, "Oh yeah!"

SEPTEMBER 17
THE RIGHT PERSPECTIVE BUILDS FAITH

THE RIGHT PERSPECTIVE IN A DIFFICULT MATTER HELPS POSITION YOUR HEART AND MIND TO OVERCOME YOUR CIRCUMSTANCE. WHILE YOUR PERSPECTIVE CAUSES FEAR, WORRY AND DOUBT, HIS PERSPECTIVE BUILDS FAITH. STAY FOCUSED, KNOWING WHAT YOU PAY ATTENTION TO WILL MANIFEST. SO MANIFEST HIS GLORY OVER YOUR TROUBLE!

LIFE IS VERY GOOD!

Genesis 13:14-17 says, "The Lord said to Abram after Lot had parted from him, 'Look around from where you are, to the north and south, to the east and west. All the land that you see I will give to you and your offspring forever. I will make your offspring like the dust of the earth, so that if anyone could count the dust, then your offspring could be counted. Go, walk through the length and breadth of the land, for I am giving it to you.'" This is God's perspective towards His covenant people. You have been grafted into the vine, therefore this promise is yours. So when challenges come your way and, believe me, they will, set your heart on the perspective of promise. Look around where you are. God has given you the same dominion in all that you do. So set your mind on His goodness, the dreams, purpose and passions He has put inside your heart and do like Abram did, go, walk through the land, for He is giving it to you. Thank Him in advance and stand in your place of victory.

The Lord Says...

I Am no respecter of persons. Obedience may be the only difference between Abram and yourself. When I asked Abram to go, he went. Would you do the same? Is your perspective and focus centered on Me? If it is, then you can walk on water in any circumstance and walk in any direction. I Am with you always, even unto the ends of the earth.

If you believe it, say, "Oh yeah!"

SEPTEMBER 18
RELEASE YOUR BREAKTHROUGH

THERE ARE TIMES IN LIFE WHERE IT SEEMS LIKE GOD'S VOICE IS SILENT OR PEOPLE CAN NO LONGER HEAR HIM. REMEMBER: JUST BECAUSE PEOPLE CAN'T HEAR HIS VOICE, DOESN'T MEAN THAT HE CAN'T HEAR YOURS! LIFT UP YOUR VOICE LIKE A TRUMPET SO THE HEAVENS HEAR YOUR SHOUT AND RELEASE YOUR BREAKTHROUGH. IT'S TIME TO BREAK YOUR SILENCE!

LIFE IS VERY GOOD!

A friend of mine had been a Christian her whole life. One day she felt like God was telling her to have a conversation with Him and to write these conversations in her journal. She didn't really get what they looked like so she just began talking to God in her journal as she would if He was sitting next to her. She thought to herself, what is the point of a one-sided conversation? That is, until God spoke back. She had heard God speak through the prophetic voice and word of knowledge, and she herself saw God showing her words of encouragement for others. But, she had been a Christian her whole life and had never known that God could speak back to her in conversation. One Sunday morning, God told her to pray because someone was going to die that day in the morning church service. She wrote it down and began to pray. Sure enough what God said, happened. John 10:27 tells us that God's sheep know His voice. So don't be surprised if you feel like God's voice is silent. Sometimes, He might be waiting on you to sit down and chat. He loves to have conversations with His children. Isaiah 64:24 tells us that HE Will Answer and HE Will Hear. So lift up your voice, Jesus is a friend forever and your breakthrough is already here.

The Lord Says...

My conversations with My children did not end with the disciples in Bible times. I have sent Myself to you, My Holy Spirit and, though I know what you have need of, I also have need of you. For in My presence is fullness of joy. In My presence are the answers. And conversations happen in the presence of another. Seek Me and I will be found, I promise. Take My hand and let us walk and talk together. It is well.

If you believe it, say, "Oh yeah!"

SEPTEMBER 19
FOCUS ON THE GREATNESS OF GOD

WHATEVER YOU SPEND TIME FOCUSING ON IS WHAT YOU WILL SEE TAKE PLACE IN YOUR LIFE. SO STOP WASTING TIME DWELLING ON THE BAD THINGS OF THE PAST, SO IT DOESN'T HINDER YOUR PRESENT. YOU CAN'T CHANGE YESTERDAY BUT YOU CAN CHANGE TODAY. RENEW THE WAY YOU THINK, START MANIFESTING CHANGE AND LIVE IN THE NOW.

LIFE IS VERY GOOD!

2 Kings 6:15 says, "When the servant of the man of God got up and went out early the next morning, an army with horses and chariots had surrounded the city. 'Oh no, my lord! What shall we do?' the servant asked." So imagine it. You go outside and an army is surrounding your house. The servant just that but he focused his thoughts and attention on death and became fearful. In the verses that follow this scripture, however, the Prophet Elisha refused to focus on the army surrounding him. Instead, he focused on the greatness of what God had given them. He knew that God had called them to be (like you) more than a conqueror and, therefore, their company of people was greater for the King of all Kings was their rear guard. He didn't just stop there though. He asked God to open the eyes of the servant, prayed for a blindness to overcome the army and God made a way where there seemed to be no way. It's time to rejuvenate your thinking. Are you faced with a challenge? What does the word say? Find out and declare it as your focus. You are after all, more than a conqueror.

The Lord Says...

I have made you more than a conqueror. My very blood runs through your veins. No child of a King is without strategy and yours is found in the Good Book of My Word. It is life to your bones and a light unto your path. Partake of it and you will become the light and salt to the world.

If you believe it, say, "Oh yeah!"

SEPTEMBER 20
LIVE YOUR LIFE IN REAL TIME

REGRET IS A THIEF OF YOUR PRESENT MOMENT. DON'T LET YOUR MIND GET STUCK ON PAUSE WHERE IT'S UNABLE TO MOVE, OR STUCK IN FAST-FORWARD WHERE THERE'S NO CLARITY. GET BEYOND YESTERDAY AND LOOK AT TODAY AS A DAY FILLED WITH NEW POSSIBILITIES. THE GREATER TIME IS IN THE NOW.

LIFE IS VERY GOOD!

Philippians 3:13-15 says, "Brothers and sisters, I do not consider myself yet to have taken hold of it. But one thing I do: Forgetting what is behind and straining toward what is ahead, I press on toward the goal to win the prize for which God has called me heavenward in Christ Jesus. All of us, then, who are mature should take such a view of things. And if on some point you think differently, that too God will make clear to you." Regret is the stealing of your joy in a circumstance. If you know the enemy comes to steal, kill and destroy (John 10:10), then don't allow him to have your joy. Choose to live your life with no regrets and when life throws you a curve ball, just count it all joy. Philippians says this is the mature thing to do. Why? Because it allows you to move on so you can forget what is behind you and press forward into that greater time...the NOW in your life. NOW ALL things are possible. He is with you NOW and forever. Today is your do-over, so soar like an eagle.

The Lord Says...

If everyone in life regurgitated their yesterdays, where would one find joy in tomorrow? Yesterday brings people wisdom, while Today and Tomorrow are filled with My promise. Let Me bring you wisdom in learning from your Yesterdays and I will guide you into your Tomorrows, for what I have for you is great. Walk with me and your life can be filled with much joy.

If you believe it, say, "Oh yeah!"

SEPTEMBER 21
THE POWER OF BOLD PRAYER

PRAYERS OF FAITH MOVE GOD. MOSES PRAYED AND GOD PARTED THE SEA. ELIJAH PRAYED AND RAIN CAME TO END A 3 1/2 YEAR DROUGHT. PAUL AND SILAS PRAYED AND SANG, AND CAUSED THE EARTH TO SHAKE AND PRISON DOORS TO OPEN. YOU ARE A PRAYER AWAY FROM SEEING YOUR GREATEST BREAKTHROUGH! BOLD PRAYERS HONOR GOD AND GOD HONORS BOLD PRAYERS.

LIFE IS VERY GOOD!

Bold prayers change the atmosphere and circumstances. Just look at what can happen to nations when they pray. 2 Chronicles 7:14 says, "If my people, who are called by my name, will humble themselves and pray and seek my face and turn from their wicked ways, then I will hear from heaven and I will forgive their sin and will heal their land." If the people will do the following: humble themselves, pray, seek God's face and turn from their wicked ways, then God will hear from heaven, forgive and heal the land. You can have confidence in your prayers because 1 John 5:14-15 says, "This is the confidence we have in approaching God: that if we ask anything according to His will, He hears us. And if we know that he hears us—whatever we ask—we know that we have what we asked of him." If you ask anything according to His will, He hears you and because you know He hears you, you can expect whatever you ask. Powerful. Your breakthrough just might be caught up in a bold prayer. Now give Him thanks in advance and worship His Holy Name.

The Lord Says...

Come boldly before My throne, sending your prayers to the high place. I Am One of honor and I honor your prayers. Shake the doors of your prison open with prayer and a shout of praise. Faith will move My hand as it stretches you further out onto the water, but don't fear for I Am always with you.

If you believe it, say, "Oh yeah!"

SEPTEMBER 22
PRAY TO IMPACT THE ATMOSPHERE

ALTHOUGH WE PRAY AND DON'T ALWAYS SEE WHAT WE ARE CRYING OUT FOR, DON'T QUIT PRAYING; REMAIN PERSISTENT. ELIJAH BOWED WITH HIS FACE BETWEEN HIS KNEES AND TOLD HIS SERVANT TO "GO NOW AND LOOK TOWARDS THE SEA." HIS SERVANT SAID THERE WAS NOTHING THERE. BUT ELIJAH DECLARED TO GO AGAIN AND AGAIN. AFTER 7 TIMES, THERE WAS A CLOUD RISING! YOUR CONSISTENT PRAYER OF FAITH CAUSES THE SEASON TO CHANGE. I HEAR THE SOUND OF THE ABUNDANCE OF RAIN!

LIFE IS VERY GOOD!

Have you ever noticed how dry ice seems to migrate towards the floor? That's because cold air is dense and things that are dense tend to sink. Hot air, on the other hand, is less dense, therefore it floats and rises. Your prayers are like hot air rising. They ascend and ascend and ascend until, like Elijah, they impact the atmosphere. What happens when the clouds get full of the hot air? It begins to cool, and as they expand in the atmosphere they become water vapor. Then the water droplets come down because they are cooler than the atmosphere. We call it rain. Your prayer is just like hot air that rises. Eventually it turns into the cloud just like Elijah saw in the heavens, then God rains down His blessing of abundance upon you. The seasons and principles of nature do not change; it's your prayers that impact the atmosphere. It's your prayers that change nations and circumstances. It is your prayers. Isaiah 45:8 says, "You heavens above, rain down my righteousness; let the clouds shower it down. Let the earth open wide, let salvation spring up, let righteousness flourish with it; I, the Lord, have created it." So be a man and woman of prayer and listen for the sound of the abundance of rain.

The Lord Says...

I come that you might have life and though you may tarry in prayer for a considerable time, just remember, the cloud of glory is lifted and in the heavens the rain will surely fall upon you and your prayers shall find their answers.

If you believe it, say, "Oh yeah!"

SEPTEMBER 23
A PRAYER NEVER PRAYED WILL NEVER SEE AN ANSWER

REMEMBER THIS: THE ONLY PRAYER GOD DOESN'T ANSWER IS THE ONE THAT WAS NEVER PRAYED. THERE IS NOTHING THAT'S TOO SMALL OR TOO BIG TO ASK GOD FOR HELP, GUIDANCE OR DELIVERANCE FROM. IF IT'S IMPORTANT ENOUGH FOR YOU TO PRAY ABOUT, IT'S IMPORTANT TO HIM TO ANSWER. THE PRAYERS OF THE RIGHTEOUS MAN AVAILS MUCH! DON'T GIVE UP, HIS ANSWER'S ON THE WAY.

LIFE IS VERY GOOD!

James 4:2 tells us that we have not because we ask not. Even though God knows what you have need of, He desires relationship with you. It would be easy for a father to pay his child's bills when he knows they are struggling to make ends meet. But to just throw out money without that relationship does nothing for the giver or the receiver. So don't give up; ask in prayer, believing that He more than hears or answers you, but that He cares for your heart and wants to know you more. Christ is the key. Prayer can often seem mundane but it's not the quantity, it's the quality of your prayers that matter.

The Lord Says...

Never, never give up. You may be one prayer short of your answer, so never stop. I Am with you always, even unto the ends of the earth. I hear you and I listen. And I will give you an answer to your prayers.

If you believe it, say, "Oh yeah!"

SEPTEMBER 24
YOUR PRAYERS HAVE BEEN ANSWERED

PRAYER IS ASKING GOD TO DO SOMETHING IN THE FUTURE, WHILE YOUR PRAISE AND THANKS-
GIVING IS KNOWING THAT GOD HAS ALREADY DONE IT IN THE NOW. REJOICE WITH A SHOUT
AND KNOW YOUR PRAYER HAS BEEN ANSWERED AND GOD HAD OPENED THE DOOR TO GREATER
PROMISES!

LIFE IS VERY GOOD!

Psalm 103:1-4 says, "Praise the Lord, my soul; all my inmost being, praise his holy name. Praise the Lord, my soul and forget not all his benefits—who forgives all your sins and heals all your diseases, who redeems your life from the pit and crowns you with love and compassion." When you praise and when you worship, you cannot help but remember what the benefits of being an heir to the King means. So give Him the thanks He's due. Your physical body may not feel healed, but He said, "It's done." You may feel forgotten, but He is still with you even in the pit. Have the attitude of a child; God said it, that settles it, so believe it. He is the door; your answer has come.

The Lord Says...

I Am the answer for the world. Every ailment, every attitude, every trace of sorrow and pain, when laid at My feet will make your burdens lighter. Walk through the door and lay your burdens down at the altar. Then, as you leave, leave the burden there because it is now Mine to carry. The burden you have is easy for I Am carrying them for you.

If you believe it, say, "Oh yeah!"

SEPTEMBER 25
THE POWER OF PERSEVERANCE

TO PERSEVERE IS THE ABILITY, WHILE UNDER PRESSURE, TO WAIT CALMLY AND STAND COURAGEOUSLY IN THE MIDST OF OPPOSITION. SO DON'T LET YOUR SITUATION PUSH YOU AROUND. STAND STRONG, HOLD YOUR GROUND AND OVERCOME YOUR CONFLICT BY THE POWER OF HIS FAITH INSIDE OF YOU. BE A SHAMGAR OF YOUR DAY, REFUSE TO TAKE THE BYWAYS AND SEE THE HIGHWAY THE LORD HAS OPENED FOR YOU.

LIFE IS VERY GOOD!

Shamgar happened to be another in the line of Israel's deliverers. Judges 3:31 says he used a simple ox-goad to kill 600 Philistines. An ox-goad is a weapon similar to a lance but it's made of wood, approximately 7-8 feet long and has a spear like feature on the end of it. Its proper use was meant to prod the oxen to move in a desired direction. So in looking at Shamgar, he was not afraid to stand up and he didn't let his situation determine his outcome. Mind you, he had no shield to protect himself against any army. But the Bible says, when you are weak, the God of Abraham, Isaac and Jacob who lives inside of you, is strong. And if that is true and then this is also: no weapon formed against him (and you) can prosper, for greater is He that is in you, than he that is in the world. So take that to the battle field. He is with you. He opens and closes the doors and His YES is amen.

The Lord Says...

I Am your sword, your shield, your refuge and your high tower. Lean on Me and I will see you through. I stand before you in battle and fight on your behalf. You don't have to worry because the battle is mine, and I Am victorious. In Me, you are already victorious too.

If you believe it, say, "Oh yeah!"

SEPTEMBER 26
BELIEVE BIG AND PRAY BIG

PRAYERS OF FAITH MANIFEST WHEN YOU KNOW AND BELIEVE THAT GOD IS FOR YOU! IT'S TIME TO PRAY BIG AND BELIEVE BIG. IF GOD BE FOR YOU, WHO CAN STAND AGAINST YOU? MUSTARD SEED FAITH IS IN YOUR HOUSE! LET YOUR FAITH IN HIM CHANGE EVERYTHING.

LIFE IS VERY GOOD!

Have you ever actually seen a mustard seed? It's a tiny seed no larger than the tip of a ball point pen. You see, God doesn't require much. He requires your 10% and He leaves you with 90%. He makes things possible with mustard seed faith, not watermelon sized faith. He requires you to love, live by His commandments and apply His Words to all your circumstances. So take Romans 8:31 to heart: "What, then, shall we say in response to these things? If God is for us, who can be against us?" You got it (faith) and you got the King of Kings on your side, so don't be afraid, believe that His Words are YES and AMEN!

The Lord Says...

I Am for you so anyone who comes against you, comes against Me. It only takes a little faith to see mountains move. Uncover your faith today and believe all things are possible.

If you believe it, say, "Oh yeah!"

SEPTEMBER 27
THE MESSAGE WITHIN THE MESS

WE'VE BEEN TOLD TO "NEVER JUDGE A BOOK BY ITS COVER", SIMPLY BECAUSE LOOKS CAN BE DECEIVING. WHAT'S DEEP INSIDE CAN BE COMPLETELY DIFFERENT THAN WHAT YOU EXPECT. SAUL WAS A PERSECUTOR OF THE CHURCH AND A MURDERER, BUT WAS TRANSFORMED AND BECAME A LIVING EPISTLE OF GOD'S WORD. POTENTIAL IS HIDDEN IN DARK PLACES. BE THE GIFT THAT PULLS OUT THE REAL STORY.

LIFE IS VERY GOOD!

What would happen if Jesus took a look at you and said, "Oh wow, they have a past. How can I rub shoulders with them? How can I bless someone like that?" The world would be in a sorry state because we are all imperfect, we make mistakes and we do have a past. Thankfully, God is our redeemer and we are saved by grace. Jesus is a lover of mess. He takes our mess and finds potential within it. Psalm 139:13-16 says, "For you created my inmost being; you knit me together in my mother's womb. I praise you because I Am fearfully and wonderfully made; your works are wonderful, I know that full well. My frame was not hidden from you when I was made in the secret place, when I was woven together in the depths of the earth. Your eyes saw my unformed body; all the days ordained for me were written in your book before one of them came to be." No matter what you look like, or where your past has taken you, it doesn't change how He feels about you. Regardless of your history, He says you were fearfully and wonderfully made. His works are wonderful, that's what the scripture declares. You are one of His works. When the days of darkness come and cloud your path like a fog, lean on HIM, on Jesus, the author and finisher of your faith.

The Lord Says...

I knew you before you were born and formed you into the person you are today. We are on a journey together and I, your Father in Heaven, have given you My attributes and the blessings that come with being My heir. Walk in your kingly identity; be strong and courageous.

If you believe it, say, "Oh yeah!"

SEPTEMBER 28
LET YOUR JOY SHINE BRIGHT

THE POWER OF PERCEPTION/IMAGINATION IS THE ABILITY TO SEE WHAT OTHER CAN'T SEE. MICHELANGELO SAID, "THERE IS AN ANGEL IN THE STONE", AS HE LOOKED AT A FLAWED PIECE OF MARBLE. FOR TWO YEARS HE CHISELED AND CHIPPED AWAY AT THE MARBLE AND THE IMAGE OF DAVID EMERGED. BEAUTY CAN BE HIDDEN IN STRANGE PLACES, BUT WITH A LITTLE WORK YOU CAN HELP PULL IT OUT.

LIFE IS VERY GOOD!

When you look at yourself in the mirror you tend to see all your flaws. Yet when God looks in the mirror to view your reflection, He is like Michelangelo; He sees your beauty and not your flaws. Song of Solomon 4:7 says, "You are altogether beautiful, my darling; there is no flaw in you." So know this, in the Lord's sight, you are flawless. Learn to look past what your earthly eyes see and see yourself how God sees you. Let your beauty in Christ come forth so others will see the light that makes you glow with joy and happiness.

The Lord Says...

I Am the light of the world and I see goodness, for all that I have created IS Good - flawless! I have hidden My treasure in you, My earthen vessel, to show that

My power is within you. Walk in the fullness of who I have created you to be: My beautiful child upon this earth.

If you believe it, say, "Oh yeah!"

SEPTEMBER 29
FIND THE HIDDEN TREASURES

WITH EYES OF DISCERNMENT YOU CAN SEE TRUTH IN THE MIDST OF A LIE. WITH THE EYES OF PERCEPTION YOU CAN SEE TREASURES OUT OF DARKNESS AND, WITH THE EYES OF FAITH, YOU CAN SEE MOUNTAINS REMOVED. THROUGH HIS EYES, YOU CAN SEE MORE THAN MEETS THE EYE. SEE THE UNSEEN.

LIFE IS VERY GOOD!

2 Corinthians 4:18 says, "So we fix our eyes not on what is seen, but on what is unseen, since what is seen is temporary, but what is unseen is eternal." Before the universe was spoken into existence, God saw it as it should be. If you only fix your eyes on what is seen you will have no hope for the future because you will allow the present to dictate your future. But, when you can see your future through God's eyes, then you see the eternal hope He has provided. If you need to see it before you can believe it, set the principals of Christ in your head and watch your purpose be fulfilled. Doesn't the Word say He has plans for you to prosper and plans to keep you? If you aren't prospering in your finances, health or relationships, then begin to see those areas (and others) prosper in your life. What would it look like? God wants you to create a blueprint in your mind of your prosperity. Declare it so and thank Him in advance. He is able.

The Lord Says...

I AM able, to do above and beyond what you can ever think or imagine. I will meet your needs according to My riches in glory. I Am all you will ever need, today and in days to come.

If you believe it, say, "Oh yeah!"

SEPTEMBER 30
STEP UPON YOUR LOW PLACES

IN LIFE THERE ARE HIGHS AND LOWS. THERE ARE GOOD DAYS AND BAD ONES, TOO. THE KEY
TO LIFE IS REMEMBERING THAT THIS STORM, TOO, SHALL PASS AND EVERY SITUATION YOU FACE
IS A TEACHER OF GREAT THINGS. LET YOUR LOW PLACE BECOME YOUR STEPPING STONE IN HIS
GREAT DIMENSIONS.

LIFE IS VERY GOOD!

Isaiah 40:4 says, "Every valley shall be raised up, every mountain and hill
made low; the rough ground shall become level, the rugged places a plain." In other words, all things will work together for the good of those that love God and are
called according to His purpose (Romans 8:28). No matter if you are in the valley
or up on the mountain, on rough or level ground, God is with you and He is going
to take you to the next level. Each part of the journey is a stepping stone to a greater dimension. Learn from where you are and take that wisdom to where God is
leading you next. Let each step you take bring you to a higher dimension in Him.

The Lord Says...

Don't get discouraged when the journey isn't what you thought it would be.
Keep speaking My promises. Keep believing in My word. Keep seeing My hand
do the impossible. No matter where you are, it's just a stepping stone; a moment
in a storm that is passing by. Though it may seem that storms linger around you,
just know that the seasons always change. Let the change become that in which it
is and seek Me for your new season.

If you believe it, say, "Oh yeah!"

OCTOBER 1
THE SON SHINES BRIGHTLY

WHEN TROUBLES HIT YOUR HOUSE AND THE FORECAST IS DARK AND GLOOMY, REMEMBER TO PRAY FOR RAIN. NOT ONLY WILL THE STORM PASS, THE WATER WILL DRY UP, AND THE SON WILL SHINE AGAIN. AND FINALLY, THERE IS ALWAYS A FRAGRANCE. THIS TOO SHALL PASS.

LIFE IS VERY GOOD!

Psalm 34:17-20 says, "The righteous cry out and the Lord hears them; he delivers them from all their troubles. The Lord is close to the brokenhearted and saves those who are crushed in spirit. The righteous person may have many troubles, but the Lord delivers him from them all; he protects all his bones, not one of them will be broken." That verse should make you shout! It doesn't matter if your day is dark and gloomy, the Lord hears your cry. He is a friend to the brokenhearted and He wills for your life to be filled with abundant joy. The scripture says that He delivers you from ALL your troubles. You can't ask for more sunshine than that. HE is indeed good.

The Lord Says...

Though darkness may loom in your world, My Son is always shining over you. Uncover the light with the Light of the word and see clearly that which is already before you.

If you believe it, say, "Oh yeah!"

OCTOBER 2
CHOICES CAN LEAD TO GREATER REWARD

REMEMBER: WHERE A MAN WALKS, STANDS, OR SITS IN LIFE DETERMINES WHAT HE RECEIVES. THE WORD SAYS, "BLESSED IS THE MAN WHO WALKS NOT IN THE COUNSEL OF THE UNGODLY, NOR STANDS IN THE PATH OF SINNERS, OR SITS IN THE SEAT OF THE SCORNFUL." (PSALM 1:1). TODAY, BE WISE WHERE AND WITH WHOM YOU WALK, STAND OR SIT WITH. THIS CHOICE CAN LEAD YOU TO A GREATER REWARD. IT'S TIME TO MAXIMIZE GOD'S PROMISED BLESSING IN YOUR LIFE.

LIFE IS VERY GOOD!

I Corinthians 15:33 says, "Do not be misled: 'Bad company corrupts good character.'" In other words, have a watchful eye on the character of those you choose to dedicate your time to. I know many grandmothers who have said this phrase over the years: 'show me your friends and I'll show you who you are', or 'your friends will make you or break you'. Remember, scripture tells us that wisdom is the principle thing. Maximize the potential of your connections, for it is said that two are greater than one.

The Lord Says...

Choice is a powerful tool connected to the will of man. When not yielded with wisdom, it can change the path of an individual in an instant. Seek Me and I will answer you. I Am the light unto your path. I will show the path in which to go and with whom to connect. My ways are higher than yours. Follow My voice because I will not lead you astray.

If you believe it, say, "Oh yeah!"

OCTOBER 3
YOU ARE ALWAYS ON HIS RADAR

THERE ARE TIMES IN LIFE WHEN PEOPLE DILIGENTLY SEARCH FOR GOD IN ALL THE RELIGIOUS PLACES AND CAN'T FIND HIM. THEN THERE ARE TIMES WHEN YOU ARE NOT LOOKING FOR HIM AT ALL AND HE FINDS YOU. GOD'S SPIRIT IS LIKE THE WIND THAT BLOWS WHERE HE PLEASES. NO MATTER WHERE YOU ARE IN LIFE, GOD HAS YOU LOCATED. HOLD ON... HIS BREATH IS COMING TO REFRESH YOU.

LIFE IS VERY GOOD!

Proverbs 15:3 says, "The eyes of the Lord are everywhere, keeping watch on the wicked and the good." He is omnipresent. No matter where you are in life, God knows where you are. He knows, sees and understands the season you are in. He is there in the pit of darkness and when the sun is shining. He is not found in the church pew or in objects of religious tradition. He is found in your worship and in your prayers. He is in the hearts of man. He is found in the marketplace, when love, extended by you, reaches another. He is found in the mercy you extend to family, friends and colleagues when they make mistakes that hurt you; after all, HE has extended the same grace to you. He is found in the beauty of nature and all living things. Truly, no matter where you are in life, His fresh breath is waiting for you.

The Lord Says...

Through My breath all living things came into existence. Through My breath, you are refreshed. And through the breath of My Words you shall prevail. Fresh breath awaits you.

If you believe it, say, "Oh yeah!"

OCTOBER 4
BE A POWERHOUSE OF HOPE

HOPE GIVES LIFE TO THE DARKEST OF TIMES. IT'S A STRENGTH THAT NEVER GIVES UP AND NEVER GIVES IN. IT'S A POWER THAT OVERCOMES FEAR AGAIN AND AGAIN. LET YOUR HOPE ARISE AND SCATTER YOUR PAIN AS IT GIVES YOU THE PASSION TO DREAM AGAIN. KEEP BELIEVING, KEEP TRUSTING IN HIM AND SEE HIS VICTORY RISE AGAIN. REMEMBER, HOPE GIVES YOU THE POWER TO SURVIVE. DON'T EVER LET YOUR HOPE DIE.

LIFE IS VERY GOOD!

Hope is a necessary ingredient to faith. Therefore hope is important to your spiritual walk. The Bible says in Hebrews 11:1, "Now faith is the substance of things hoped for, the evidence of things not seen" (KJV). Faith is grounded in hope. This is why the world needs Jesus because, without Him, hopelessness can rear its head at the first sign of dark times in life. If you let your hope die, then faith dies too. So let hope arise and strengthen your faith.

The Lord Says...

Let hope arise and your enemies will be scattered, for hope gives birth to faith. And faith, coupled with love, will see you through the darkest of times. Your faith will be My light shining through you, and it will bring you strength and joy.

If you believe it, say, "Oh yeah!"

OCTOBER 5
THE POWER OF YOUR CHOICES

THERE IS POWER IN YOUR CHOICES. WHEN YOU CHOOSE WHAT'S RIGHT IN GOD'S EYES, THERE IS OFTEN VERY LITTLE TO NO SUPPORT. DON'T BE DISCOURAGED. NO MATTER HOW YOU CHOOSE TO MOVE FORWARD, DON'T RESENT THOSE WHO DON'T SEE LIFE CHOICES THE SAME WAY THE GOD IN YOU DOES. PURSUE HIS JOY FOR YOUR LIFE. IN ALL THINGS...

LIFE IS VERY GOOD!

When you walk in your gifts and talents, it isn't always easy. When we first set out into ministry, there weren't a whole host of people out there supporting us. It seemed like it was easier for people to see us fail than to succeed. But God says that His sheep know His voice. So when you hear God calling you, you're operating in your God-given gifts and talents and you are bearing fruit, don't be discouraged. Many people will have something to say, but God's opinion is the one that matters. He didn't say you needed people's permission to go into all the world and preach the gospel. He said simply, GO. So use the power of your choices to pursue all things in Christ. He has given you great authority in this earth. You are HIS child.

The Lord Says...

When people reject you, they reject Me. Do not worry; go because I have told you to go, not because man says that you can. For it is I whom has equipped you. Be My disciple and cast your nets.

If you believe it, say, "Oh yeah!"

OCTOBER 6
LET WISDOM BE YOUR GPS

REMEMBER, LIFE IS FULL OF CHOICES. WHAT YOU CHOOSE MAKES A DIFFERENCE IN YOUR LIFE AS WELL AS OTHERS. IF YOU CHOOSE WICKEDNESS, IT BRINGS FORTH INIQUITY, CONCEIVES TROUBLE, BRINGS FORTH FALSEHOODS AND DESTROYS LIVES. BUT IF YOU CHOOSE RIGHTEOUSNESS, IT DELIVERS YOU FROM THE PIT DUG FOR YOUR CAPTIVITY, ALLOWS GOD TO BE YOUR JUDGE ACCORDING TO YOUR INTEGRITY AND ALSO ALLOWS GOD TO BE YOUR DEFENSE. HE IS THE ONE WHO SAVES THE UPRIGHT.

LIFE IS VERY GOOD!

The ability to choose is one of the greatest gifts God has bestowed upon you: your will. He instructs His children how to choose on the narrow path. Proverbs 4:5-9 says, "Get wisdom, get understanding; do not forget my words or turn away from them. Do not forsake wisdom and she will protect you; love her and she will watch over you. The beginning of wisdom is this: Get wisdom. Though it cost all you have, get understanding. Cherish her and she will exalt you; embrace her and she will honor you. She will give you a garland to grace your head and present you with a glorious crown." So get wisdom and understanding and treasure it like the most precious gift you have ever been given. Wisdom and understanding will take you far in the choices you make. You will be able to avoid making decisions which will take you in the wrong direction. You can protect yourself and others by using God's wisdom. And in it, God will be your defense.

The Lord Says...

Wisdom is indeed the principal thing. Get wisdom and the potholes along the path of life's journey will become easier to navigate. Following My path will help you in your life and believe Me when I say, I want to give you all My best for your today and tomorrow.

If you believe it, say, "Oh yeah!"

OCTOBER 7
CUSTOM MADE FOR YOU

IN THE SEASON OF DARKNESS OR TROUBLE REMEMBER, GOD IS THE ONLY ONE WHO CAN COMFORT YOU. HE IS AND ALWAYS WILL BE YOUR STRONG TOWER AND PLACE OF REFUGE. PUT YOUR TRUST IN HIM AND SEE HIS LOVE DELIVER YOU. BETTER TIMES ARE COMING!

LIFE IS VERY GOOD!

Proverbs 18:10 says, "The name of the Lord is a fortified tower; the righteous run to it and are safe." When you run towards the Lord, you're running towards your daddy, maker of the heavens and the earth, ruler of the universe, comforter, friend and victorious King of Kings and Lord of Lords. He's more than just a band-aid to your ailments and your circumstances. He is indeed your refuge and, when you find Him, He hides you in the shadow of His wings and within Him, you will find rest.

The Lord Says...

The shadow of My wings were made for you. Come to Me all who are weary and there you will find rest. I Am with you in the midst of your greatest victories but also when you feel defeated. I Am your comfort and your place of peace.

If you believe it, say, "Oh yeah!"

OCTOBER 8
TROUBLE IS ONLY A SHADOW

NO MATTER THE STRUGGLES WE MAY FACE IN LIFE, REMEMBER, GOD HAS IT UNDER CONTROL. THE SITUATIONS MAY SEEM IMPOSSIBLE WITH NO SIGNS OF HOPE BUT HOLD FAST KNOWING HE WILL TURN THE SITUATION IN YOUR FAVOR. REJOICE! HE WILL SEE YOU THROUGH.

LIFE IS VERY GOOD!

Psalm 23:4 of the King James says this: "Yea though I walk through the valley of the shadow of death, I will fear no evil: for though art with me; thy rod and thy staff they comfort me..." It may seem like the darkest of times in your life but remember, it is the valley of the shadow. No shadow ever took a man out. A shadow is only the magnification of something. It is the unknown that causes fear and anxiety. So remember, it may seem impossible, but when you're in the valley, you can often be surrounded by an enemy. But, God is the shepherd of His sheep and you should take comfort in knowing that His rod and staff will guide and protect you no matter what you are going through. He is the HOPE you need, so look up towards the mountaintop and rejoice for HE is walking you through in the Now time.

The Lord Says...

Be still and know that I Am God - in every dark place, every low and every high place. I Am with you always, the light unto your path. You don't have to fear for I will light up your paths.

If you believe it, say, "Oh yeah!"

OCTOBER 9
EXCHANGE YOUR CARES FOR HIS CARE

REMEMBER, GOD'S COMPASSION FOR YOU IS GREATER THAN YOU BELIEVE. HE NOT ONLY CARES ABOUT THE BIG PROBLEMS THAT OVERWHELM YOU, BUT ALSO THE SMALL BURDENS THAT WEIGH YOU DOWN. REMEMBER THIS: THE KEY TO OVERCOMING IS CASTING ALL YOUR CARES AND BURDENS ON HIM, KNOWING HE CARES FOR YOU. HIS LOVE WILL NEVER FAIL.

LIFE IS VERY GOOD!

Psalm 55:22 says, "Cast your cares on the Lord and he will sustain you; he will never let the righteous be shaken." The Word tells you to cast your cares on the Lord. What will He do in return? He will sustain you. In other words, all you have need of, He will supply. He in no way wants you to get to the place of anxiety. So if all it takes to be free from anxiety is to cast your burdens upon the Lord, then that's a prescription worth putting into play, don't you think? Here's a challenge. Take all your anxiety and cast it upon the Lord today. It's worth it.

The Lord Says...

Is your heart heavy? Does worry get the best of you? Do your problems in this life overwhelm you? Fear not, for I Am with you. I Am the way, the truth and the life. Send your burdens to Me and be free once and for all.

If you believe it, say, "Oh yeah!"

OCTOBER 10
THE MOTIVATION OF CRISIS

REMEMBER THIS: DON'T CURSE THE CRISIS YOU'RE FACING. THIS DIFFICULTY SET BEFORE YOU SERVES A GREATER PURPOSE. IT HELPS RELOCATE YOU FROM ONE PLACE TO ANOTHER BECAUSE THE LAND YOU WERE IN HAS DRIED UP AND THE PLACE YOU ARE GOING IS FILLED WITH SUPERNATURAL PROVISION FOR YOU AS WELL AS FOR OTHERS. PRESS ON AND INTO YOUR NEXT SEASON.

LIFE IS VERY GOOD!

From the east coast to west coast, I travel the U.S.A extensively. Experiencing many landscapes, I have often pondered the wonder of where we came from as a nation then until now. Think about it. Before the U.S.A became the diverse nation it is today, it was once coast and forests. The settlers back in the day didn't just get in a car and drive from Maine to California. They had to clear lands with simple tools. With every generation that came, they made travel a bit easier, until finally one could cross the United States by horse and wagon, then by train and car. The difficulty in building roads, dams, rails and bridges was for a greater purpose. It was so the next generation could live in abundance and have choices. One season's work on a vision of access in the United States became the provision for you to travel this beautiful country in style. So know that whatever you go through today is really to set you up for a greater tomorrow. There's a purpose in everything. Your trials are strengthening you, stretching you and causing you to trust the Lord like never before, while your victories are keeping your focus on the finish line. Psalm 42:8 says, "By day the Lord commands his steadfast love and at night his song is with me, a prayer to the God of my life." You can't get much better than that. Know His love and sing His praise. Today is a new day.

The Lord Says...

Now is the time. The time to trust and cling to the cleft of the rock. The time for peace and rest. The crisis you face is not greater than you, because I dwell within you and I Am the Great and Mighty One; the One who loves you and will see you through. Everything you go through in this life - the good and bad, the laughing and weeping, the joys and sorrows - serve a purpose. Press through and grab a hold of the harvest I have set before you.

If you believe it, say, "Oh yeah!"

OCTOBER 11
WORSHIP OPENS POSSIBILITIES

There are times in life we feel struck with blindness and can't see. The way out is by letting His hand lift you up and lead you out in order to restore you. Jesus did more than touch the blind man. He led him out of this city, spit on his eyes and prayed to restore his sight! If He did it for him, He will do it for you!

LIFE IS VERY GOOD!

---

2 Samuel 22:1 says, "And David spoke to the Lord the words of this song on the day when the Lord delivered him from the hand of all his enemies and from the hand of Saul." What did David do? He penetrated the heavens with praise and worship, changing the atmosphere and setting himself up for God to move on his behalf. If you cannot see even your feet in front of you or the batteries for your life's flashlight have gone dim, do like David did. Praise and worship the King of all Kings; this is your ticket to sight. This is your ticket to restoration. Surely God is all about His children; and that means you.

The Lord Says...

As a father, your worship moves Me. Let it be made known on the earth that you declare your love for Me and your trust is in My ability to do as My Word says I will do.

If you believe it, say, "Oh yeah!"

OCTOBER 12
A NEW FOCUS CAN CHANGE YOUR CONDITION

There are times in life when we lose focus on WHO we love and get bound to WHAT we love. When a crisis like this happens, we can allow God to step in. He will cause a new focus and help change the condition of our heart. It's time to let a sanctification begin, to strip us of WHAT is, so we can come back to WHO is. Hear God's voice calling you today to Himself.

LIFE IS VERY GOOD!

Proverbs 4:25 says, "Let your eyes look straight ahead; fix your gaze directly before you." Remember, when you keep your eyes fixed straight ahead and your gaze is upon Jesus, you will never lose sight of WHO He is in your life. He is all you need. So don't let the things (WHAT) of this world detract you or detour you from hearing God's voice and remembering WHO He is in your life. He is able.

The Lord Says...

Never let the circumstances of WHAT IS to determine the direction of your life, but direct your prayers towards the GREAT I AM, your journey's light. What you focus on, you will pursue. Love Me as I love you and pursue Me as I pursue you. Come back to Me as I call your name. I have My best for you.

If you believe it, say, "Oh yeah!"

OCTOBER 13
THE POWER IN LETTING GO

JACOB CAME TO A PLACE WHERE HE WAS ALL ALONE. IN THAT PLACE HE HAD AN ENCOUNTER AND WRESTLED WITH A MAN. TO WRESTLE MEANS TO SWAY ONE'S MIND. WHAT YOU HOLD ONTO IN THIS SEASON DETERMINES WHERE YOU GO NEXT IN LIFE. LET YOUR MIND SHIFT AND MAKE SURE YOU HOLD ONTO THE RIGHT THINGS. GOD'S LOVE WILL NOT FAIL YOU!

LIFE IS VERY GOOD!

It takes a lot for grapes to not only grow but become grape juice or wine. In order for grapevines to produce a successful harvest, there are two things they need prior to their planting. First, a treillage type system must be built so the grapes can grow upward and the grapevines must to be soaked in water for several hours. Then when you're ready to plant them, make sure to plant them in very deep soil with access to direct sunlight. This is an amazing foreshadowing of our spiritual life. First, you must build and develop a pattern of worship in order to take your life upward. Then, soak yourself in his presence and in His Word. Then plant your life deeply in the Son and develop a relationship with the King of Kings. When you begin here, your mind will be trained to come into order under Christ no matter the season. When you walk with Christ, you will come to understand that the journey isn't easy but neither is the life of a grape. Yet when the grape produces a harvest, it is great. What will your harvest look like when you finally come to understand that you cannot fail because He will never fail you?

The Lord Says...

I Am the vine, you are the branches. When you are planted in Me properly, your fruit will show it when harvest time comes. Keep going in your journey in My Kingdom.

If you believe it, say, "Oh yeah!"

OCTOBER 14
PRESS THROUGH FOR CHANGE

IF YOU CAN TOUCH HIS PRESENCE, YOUR ISSUE CAN CHANGE. THE WOMAN WITH THE ISSUE OF BLOOD REACHED OUT TO TOUCH HIS GARMENT BY COMING TO THE FOOT OF HIS PRESENCE AND HER CIRCUMSTANCE WAS SWALLOWED UP BY VIRTUE. VIRTUE MEANS WHEN THE IMPOSSIBLE BECOMES POSSIBLE. YOUR SEASON CHANGES IN HIS PRESENCE. IT'S TIME TO PRESS THROUGH!

LIFE IS VERY GOOD!

In one of several places in the gospels, Mark 5:26-33 tells the story of the woman with the issue of blood. This woman, for 12 years, was afflicted with an illness. She traveled 30 miles to be changed by Jesus. Her actions were taboo in her culture because anything she touched would have been considered unclean. Her faith, however, was not sick. Her faith gave her a vision for change in her life that allowed her to believe for the impossible. She had to literally push through the crowds and likely faced social rejection and bullying. But she wasn't going to let anyone steal her blessing. So be like the woman with the issue of blood. Press through toward His presence and watch your season change.

The Lord Says...

Seasons come and go but I Am with you always. Change is constant, for with it you will grow. Press through and linger in My presence. Desire transformation for your life and I will bring it. Your faith will make you whole.

If you believe it, say, "Oh yeah!"

OCTOBER 15
FOCUS ON TODAY

IN THE MIDST OF ADVERSITY, THERE ARE MOMENTS TO REFLECT AND TO PONDER. THE DIFFERENCE IS THIS: TO REFLECT IS TO LOOK BACK WHILE TO PONDER IS TO DWELL ON WHAT COULD BE. THE KEY TO OVERCOME IS TO FOCUS ON THE DAY YOU ARE IN. THIS IS THE DAY THE LORD HAS MADE. SO REJOICE AND BE GLAD!

LIFE IS VERY GOOD!

Psalm 119:15 says, "I meditate on your precepts and consider your ways." When you ponder on the things of Christ and His ways, it will become easier to overcome in the day you are in because He is your guide. Make every day a day in which you lean on the Lord, for truly it is a day the Lord has made. Rejoice for all is well even when it may not look as though it is. He has made each day for you to be victorious.

The Lord Says...

Don't look back for today and tomorrow are more powerful than yesterday. Seek Me now and I will be found Now. The door is open. Walk through it. I have made every path straight for you on the other side.

If you believe it, say, "Oh yeah!"

OCTOBER 16
LET GOD MEET YOUR EVERY NEED

LIFE IS NOT ABOUT DESIRES AS MUCH AS IT IS ABOUT NEEDS. DESIRES ARE THINGS WE SEARCH FOR WHILE NEEDS ARE THE BASIC PRINCIPLES THAT FULFILL YOUR LIFE WITH LOVE. WHEN YOUR DESIRES ARE NOT HIS, THE THINGS YOU FIND WILL LEAVE YOU EMPTY. BUT WHEN HE MEETS YOUR NEEDS, YOU ARE FULLY SATISFIED WITH HIS LOVE AS WELL AS OTHERS. LET HIS LOVE MEET EVERY NEED IN YOUR LIFE.

LIVE IS VERY GOOD!

Matthew 5:6 says, "Blessed are those who hunger and thirst for righteousness, for they will be filled." When you hunger for more of God and He fully satisfies you, your desires begin to change; you'll begin to desire more of God and His will to be done in your life instead of your will being done. When the two become of one mind and in one accord, you can shake the heavens. The atmosphere of your circumstances changes because it's in His presence that you will find His love and enter His rest.

The Lord Says...

My promises are yes and amen. I Am the living water, the bread of life and the light of the world. When you hunger and thirst for Me, I Am quick to meet your needs. All things are possible.

If you believe it, say, "Oh yeah!"

OCTOBER 17
REGRETS LIVE IN THE PAST

REGRET IS A DESTRUCTIVE LOOK AT YOUR PAST BUT HIS PROMISE IS A BRIDGE TO A BRIGHTER FUTURE. IT'S TIME TO TAKE CAPTIVE THE THOUGHTS OF YESTERDAY AND PULL DOWN STRONG-HOLDS BY LETTING GO AND EMBRACING HIS PROMISE OF TODAY.

LIFE IS VERY GOOD!

When you have regret, you are saying that you have a sense of loss or disappointment regarding something that has already occurred. The Bible is pretty clear on having regret. Isaiah 43:18-19 says, "Forget the former things; do not dwell on the past. See, I Am doing a new thing! Now it springs up; do you not perceive it? I Am making a way in the wilderness and streams in the wasteland." Stop dwelling on the past because that is the place that regrets come from. When you pull down the strongholds from yesterday today, you are able to live the abundant life now; a life without regrets. You can do it. Live your life with no regrets today.

The Lord Says...

Yesterday is gone. Today is precious and tomorrow will be a fresh perspective. Live in My Word NOW for it is a right now Word for all seasons. Lot's wife looked back and could never move into what God wanted for her and her family. Don't be like Lot's wife. My plans for you are of a hope and a future. Look forward to that.

If you believe it, say, "Oh yeah!"

OCTOBER 18
THE PAST SHOULD BE LEFT BEHIND

IN THE JOURNEY OF LIFE, HOW DOES ONE GET OVER THE PAST? THE TRUTH IS THAT YOU DON'T HAVE TO GET OVER THE PAST. THE PAST IS OVER! QUIT LOOKING BACK AT WHAT WAS AND LOOK AHEAD TOWARDS THE FUTURE OF WHAT CAN BE. YESTERDAY IS GONE, TODAY IS AT HAND AND TOMORROW IS FULL OF ENDLESS POSSIBILITIES. LET YOUR ACTIONS OF TODAY SHAPE WHAT TOMORROW LOOKS LIKE.

LIFE IS VERY GOOD!

2 Corinthians 5:17 says, "Therefore, if anyone is in Christ, the new creation has come: The old has gone, the new is here!" Here's the thing: if the enemy can keep your mind focused on your mistakes and on your past, then He can keep you from your now victories and create delay in your life's purpose. Yesterday is

gone. Its lessons can be used as wisdom's guide, but they cannot keep you from your victories. Say good-bye to yesterday and turn over a new leaf. The season has changed. Remember, when it's autumn, change is in the air, but beauty still lingers.

The Lord Says...

Yesterday I was with you. Today I Am with you and tomorrow I will be with you. Rejoice for when you knock, I always answer. When you seek Me, I Am found in your today and your tomorrow. Rejoice, for I Am near.

If you believe it, say, "Oh yeah!"

OCTOBER 19
THERE IS POWER IN THE BLOOD

No matter what your need is, remember this: His blood is full of power. Not only does it heal your past, deliver your present and redeem your future, it also eradicates sin. His blood - there is nothing like it. One drop will make you free.

Life is very good!

Hebrews 13:12 says, "And so Jesus also suffered outside the city gate to make the people holy through his own blood." Robert Lowry wrote it well when he penned the song Nothing But the Blood. "What can wash away my sin? Nothing but the blood of Jesus; What can make me whole again? Nothing but the blood of Jesus." Jesus is your redeemer. His blood covers your past, your present and your future. Just one drop of the sacrifice will make you free indeed.

The Lord Says...

I love you so much that I sent My only Son. If you believe in Me, you can be set free from the bondages holding you down and the limitations holding you back. The blood shed on Calvary is powerful enough to break any stronghold. That is My desire, to see you in the fulness of your freedom and walking in your destiny.

If you believe it, say, "Oh yeah!"

OCTOBER 20
BE EXTRAORDINARY

IF YOUR RELATIONSHIP IN LIFE IS AT A STALEMATE, IT WILL TAKE ONE OF YOU TO INITIATE CHANGE. REMEMBER THIS: NEVER TREAT SOMEONE THE WAY THEY TREAT YOU. GO THE EXTRA MILE AND LOVE THEM THE WAY CHRIST LOVES YOU. DON'T BE MEDIOCRE IN ANYTHING YOU DO. BE EXTRAORDINARY.

LIFE IS VERY GOOD!

Matthew 5:44 says, "But I tell you, love your enemies and pray for those who persecute you." It is certainly not easy. It is against your human nature to not defend yourself. But God is asking you to bring yourself into subjection to Him by going the extra mile by doing the extraordinary; loving the unlovable. Sure, the person on the other side may deserve a few choice words from you, but honestly, God knows. Don't allow the enemy to gain a stronghold in your life by always putting you on the defensive. Step above and let the image of Christ in you come forth so that others might see His light.

The Lord Says...

I Am love. If I Am love and you were created in My image, then you must display the light of love to your neighbor as well. Be the light in the midst of the darkness and shine My love to those around you.

If you believe it, say, "Oh yeah!"

OCTOBER 21
THE WHOLE WORD IS IN HIS HAND

YOU MAY NOT LIKE WHAT LIFE HAS BECOME, OR WHAT IT LOOKS LIKE AT THE PRESENT MOMENT, BUT REMEMBER THIS: IT DOES NOT NEGATE THAT GOD IS STILL IN CONTROL. HE HAS EVERYTHING IN THE PALM OF HIS HAND AND HE WILL NOT LET YOU FALL OUT. HIS LOVE IS GREATER THAN YOU THINK. HE WILL CARRY YOU THROUGH.

LIFE IS VERY GOOD!

2 Corinthians 12:9 says, "But he said to me, 'My grace is sufficient for you, for my power is made perfect in weakness.' Therefore I will boast all the more gladly about my weaknesses, so that Christ's power may rest on me." Today, just thank Him for His grace. Have you ever noticed that sometimes, in the midst of struggles, God just requires you to rest? When we are weak, He is strong, but you can't be strong all the time without recharging. He will carry you and, during those

times, just learn to rest in Him as He fills you up so that His power may rest on you.

The Lord Says...

I hold the universe in My hand and the enemy is under My feet. My grace is My gift to you. Take it and lay your burdens down that I might bring you rest, for rest in Me will provide you with much peace.

If you believe it, say, "Oh yeah!"

OCTOBER 22
LET THE WIND OF HIS SPIRIT CARRY YOU

IN LIFE, THERE ARE TIMES TO FLY BUT THEN THERE ARE SEASONS TO SOAR. THE DIFFERENCE IS THIS: FLYING TAKES EFFORT, WHILE SOARING DOESN'T. WHEN AN EAGLE SOARS, IT'S BECAUSE THE WIND CURRENT PUSHES HIM UPWARD TO A NEW HEIGHT. ALWAYS REMEMBER, THE STORM YOU FACE IS REALLY A GOD-GIVEN OPPORTUNITY TO PUSH YOU TO A HIGHER HEIGHT AND GREATER GLORY. DON'T FLY IN YOUR STRENGTH, SOAR IN HIS.

LIFE IS VERY GOOD!

Isaiah 40:31 says, "But those who hope in the Lord will renew their strength. They will soar on wings like eagles; they will run and not grow weary, they will walk and not be faint." Have you ever heard someone say, "I wish I could fly like an eagle?" What they are really picturing is the eagle soaring. There seems to be a freedom in such an experience. In our Adamic nature, we can only fly so far. After that we must soar with God, for in Him we trust. Let the wind of His Spirit carry you to places you have never been. Let the wind of His Spirit give you rest as you experience His goodness. It is His strength in the wind and His voice that will carry you through; no matter the season, He is ABLE.

The Lord Says...

I will do above what you can think or imagine. Things may not always manifest in the way you planned or thought they would, but I Am still in your midst. So rest under the shadow of My wings as I take you to places you have never been. Trust in Me and I will deliver.

If you believe it, say, "Oh yeah!"

OCTOBER 23
FORGET ABOUT GETTING EVEN

THE WAY TO MOVE FORWARD AND OUT OF TROUBLE IN RELATIONSHIPS IS BY REMEMBERING PRINCIPLES OF TRUTH. SO THINK ON THIS: YOU NEVER GET AHEAD OF SOMEONE WHEN YOU TRY TO GET EVEN WITH THEM. FORGIVE, FORGET, PUT THE PAST BEHIND YOU AND MOVE FORWARD TOGETHER IN HIM.

LIFE IS VERY GOOD!

Hebrews 12:15 says, "See to it that no one falls short of the grace of God and that no bitter root grows up to cause trouble and defile many." When you work to control what God wants you to release unto Him, it often challenges your emotions and bitterness can often set it. There is HOPE in God's grace. Maybe you can forgive but are challenged to forget. As challenging as it may be, learn to activate this scripture by speaking words of blessing over the other party. Pray something like this: "Lord, I don't want to be bitter because of how I was wronged. I pray for the heart of this individual. Bless them Lord because You love them." Try to see them as God sees them. Hand it over to God and He will release you so you can move forward.

The Lord Says...

Look forward. Never look back. Lot's wife never made it because she had no vision for a better tomorrow. She was not willing to put the past behind her, felt wronged and could not dream of her tomorrows becoming better than her yesterdays. She died in her own mediocrity. Dream for the best in tomorrow and leave yesterday behind. Forgive, forget and be a forward thinker.

If you believe it, say, "Oh yeah!"

OCTOBER 24
BREAK FREE FROM BITTERNESS

ANGER OR BITTERNESS CAN PUT YOU IN AN EMOTIONAL PRISON WHERE THERE SEEMS TO
BE NO ESCAPE. BUT REMEMBER: ONLY HIS LOVE CAN BUST YOU OUT. REFUSE TO STAY
LOCKED UP OR BOUND IN MENTAL OPPRESSION AND FIND FREEDOM IN HIS PRESENCE. IN IT,
THERE IS FULLNESS OF JOY.

LIFE IS VERY GOOD!

You want to know how to unlock the prison doors in your life. First, let go and second, worship the Lord. John 4:24 says, "God is a Spirit: and they that worship him must worship him in spirit and in truth." It wasn't fancy talk to the prison guards or securing the key for their release that God did to get Paul and Silas out of prison. It was their worship that moved the hand of God to release them. Something happens when you worship; your body, soul and spirit are transformed and they are renewed within the Mind of Christ. Therefore it is inevitable; when you trust God with your whole heart by letting go, worship Him and you will be set free.

The Lord Says...

The truth will set you free and I Am the living truth. In Me is a love that will unlock the doors to your freedom. Let your worship fill My throne room and allow it to free your mind and spirit. In My presence, you will find all you have need of.

If you believe it, say, "Oh yeah!"

OCTOBER 25
GOD ADVENTURES ALWAYS END WITH SUCCESS

LIFE IS NOT A DESTINATION; LIFE IS A JOURNEY. NO MATTER THE DIFFICULTIES YOU FACE, SEE
IT AS A GOD ADVENTURE AND YOUR LIFE WILL END WITH HIS SUCCESS. GOD'S PROMISE OVER
YOU DOESN'T CHANGE. NO MATTER WHERE LIFE'S TRIALS TAKE YOU, THERE HE WILL BE ALSO.

LIFE IS VERY GOOD!

Hosea 10:1 says, "Israel was a spreading vine; he brought forth fruit for himself. As his fruit increased, he built more altars; as his land prospered, he adorned his sacred stones." Too often people want the fruit and success the destination offers, but they want to skip the journey because of the aches and pains that come alongside the joy of reaching their destination. But if you look at the grape, you'd see that it goes through so much before it ever has a harvest. It is pruned and pruned and pruned. In fact, the more it is pruned, the more vines it will grow and the better the harvest will become. So the grape is harvested...finally success; unless, of course, your purpose in life as a grape is to become grape juice or wine. Then the grapes are pulverized by crushing. Their juice is separated from the bits and pieces until they arrive at their destination. So you may go through a pruning and you may go through a crushing, but no matter what trials come your way, just know that you will bear fruit for God is in this adventure with you just as He was with Israel.

The Lord Says...

When you go through pruning and crushing, it is never meant to harm you, but to stretch you so that you may grow in maturity and become the fulfillment of My purpose for you in this life. I walk with you on your journey; you are never alone.

If you believe it, say, "Oh yeah!"

OCTOBER 26
BE DILIGENT IN YOUR DEVOTIONS

MANY TIMES IN LIFE, THE JOURNEY STARTS OFF WELL. THEN COMPLACENCY CREEPS IN AND SLOWLY ONE DRIFTS OFF THE MARK AND GETS STUCK IN CHAOS. BE DILIGENT IN YOUR DEVOTIONS AND AVOID THE UNNECESSARY TURBULENCE, SO WHEN STORMS DO COME, KNOW YOU WILL OVERCOME. HIS LOVE WILL KEEP YOU ON THE RIGHT PATH.

LIFE IS VERY GOOD!

Revelation 3:15-16 says, "I know your deeds, that you are neither cold nor hot. I wish you were either one or the other! So, because you are lukewarm—neither hot nor cold—I Am about to spit you out of my mouth." To be complacent means to be satisfied with how things are in your present. Refuse to get stuck in complacency. Once you become complacent you stop growing. You were never meant to stay in the valley. Everyone is supposed to trek up the mountain at some point in life and reach their destiny. Stay close to God by being in hot pursuit of Him. He will be your guide.

The Lord Says...

I Am your field guide; we spend some time in the country, by the river, in the valley, on the mountain and we do it all together. I Am in pursuit of you. Will you pursue Me?

If you believe it, say, "Oh yeah!"

OCTOBER 27
MOVE OUT OF THE OLD SYSTEM

IF YOU WANT TO PROGRESSIVELY WALK FORWARD IN CHRIST, YOU HAVE TO CONTINUALLY MOVE OUT OF AN "OLD SYSTEM" MENTALITY AND LIFESTYLE. MOVE INTO HIS KINGDOM OF RULE AND REIGN BY PUTTING ON THE MIND OF CHRIST. IT'S TIME TO LIVE AND BE TRANS-FORMED INTO HIS IMAGE.

LIFE IS VERY GOOD!

You want to know how to move out of an old system of mentality and life-style? Renew your mind in the word daily and stop complaining. Train your brain, your heart and soul to seek the Word for every circumstance in your life. Until you know all the scriptures pertaining to that circumstance and can, from your own spirit, assist in training others to renew their minds daily by a washing of the Word as well. Romans 12:2 says, "Do not conform to the pattern of this world, but be transformed by the renewing of your mind. Then you will be able to test and approve what God's will is—his good, pleasing and perfect will." This is how you move from the old mentality to a Kingdom mindset. If God says it, then believe it, because that should settle it.

The Lord Says...

When you renew your mind, you uncover My image daily and begin to know and understand My will and My ways. You will trust Me because My word is your absolute truth to your situation. I Am all that you need and more, so trust Me with your whole heart, mind, soul and strength.

If you believe it, say, "Oh yeah!"

OCTOBER 28
CHANGE YOUR MIND AND YOUR HEART WILL FOLLOW

REMEMBER THIS: IF YOU DON'T ALLOW THE TRANSFORMATION OF YOUR MIND TO CONTINUE TO TAKE PLACE, YOUR HEART WILL NOT CHANGE. THIS MINDSET COULD LEAVE YOU BITTER AND CAUSE YOU TO RETURN TO AN OLD NATURE AND LIFESTYLE. DON'T BE LIKE ORPAH WHO RETURNED TO WHAT WAS; BE LIKE RUTH AND HOLD ON TO WHAT IS. HIS COVENANT IS EVER-LASTING.

LIFE IS VERY GOOD!

Ruth had a vision of the future that presented herself within a NOW moment. All things considered, she was a poor widow without children who, in her own country, was considered desolate without a husband. She, however, chose to follow a wise woman and went from being an immigrant in a foreign land to the most well-known grandmother of ancient history: King David's great-grandmother. How did this happen? She clung to Naomi, a foreshadow of the wisdom of God. And Ruth was not afraid to step out and change her life. When you're at the bottom, things can only get better. So cling to God's promises and the wisdom He provides and don't be like Orpah, the one who kisses it all good-bye.

The Lord Says...

Change can often look intimidating. Do not be afraid, walk the straight and narrow road, seeking wisdom along the journey. The promises I have for you are yes and amen in Me. Change your mindset, which will change your attitude and in the end, your life. My will is that your life changes and transforms into what I see for you. And what I see is the very best.

If you believe it, say, "Oh yeah!"

OCTOBER 29
THE PAST IS NOT IN THE PRESENT

THE POWER OF FORGIVENESS ALLOWS US TO RECOVER FROM SOMETHING THAT NO LONGER EXISTS (SIN). HIS LOVE COVERS SIN AND THEN HIS BLOOD REMOVES IT FROM EXISTENCE WHILE GIVING YOU THE POWER TO HEAL AND OVERCOME WHAT HE REMOVED. LEAVE THE PAST BEHIND YOU AND LET HIS FORGIVENESS MOVE YOU ONWARD AND UPWARD TO GREATER THINGS.

LIFE IS VERY GOOD!

You hear many people talk about forgiveness in the context of forgiving others. However, you don't often hear people talk about forgiving themselves. Many of you are too hard on yourselves. Forgive yourself for your hand in a failing relationship, your financial immaturity, your lack of time with God and family or any other mistake you've walked through. 1 John 1:9 says, "If we confess our sins, he is faithful and just to forgive us our sins and to cleanse us from all unrighteousness." Remember, the memory of something forgiven is meant to be a lesson learned, not a noose around your neck. Forgive yourself and be free.

The Lord Says...

Freedom truly comes when you hand over your past baggage to Me. I will sort it out and put it in its place, in the sea of forgetfulness. I Am the carrier of your burdens and My truth will set you free. Whom I set free is free indeed. Be filled with joy in My presence.

If you believe it, say, "Oh yeah!"

OCTOBER 30
NOTHING CAN STOP YOU

IF YOU'RE NOT WILLING TO LEARN, NO ONE CAN HELP YOU. ON THE OTHER HAND, IF YOU ARE DETERMINED TO LEARN, NOTHING IN THIS WORLD CAN STOP YOU. DON'T BE SO HARD ON YOURSELF. HEAR WHAT GOD DECLARES OVER YOU. YOU'RE THE HEAD AND NOT THE TAIL, LIVE FROM ABOVE AND NOT FROM BENEATH. YOU ARE ON TOP AND RISING.

LIFE IS VERY GOOD!

We all sometimes get to a place in our learning where we plateau and need to move forward. That may mean we begin to learn something new or acquire a new teacher. But we can't allow the plateau to stunt our learning; we need to continue. That's how growth takes place. Moses didn't think he was able to lead the children of Israel out of Egypt but God told him He would teach him. When Moses was still hesitant, God suggested for Aaron, Moses' brother, to go as his spokesman. God meant for Moses to stand against Pharaoh himself, knowing that God would be his backing, but Moses was too afraid. He only thought of his limitations and frailties, but God saw him as a leader. Don't stop yourself in the same way Moses did, don't see yourself as less because God sees you as more. God declared you to be a king and a priest, which means you have dominion and authority through your worship and intimacy. The two work hand in hand. Stop looking at what you feel you can't do and start declaring what you can do through Christ. With God before you, nothing can stand against you.

The Lord Says...

I have placed endless potential within you to do and accomplish all that is in your heart. Let My joy be your strength and do not allow the enemy to let you think you aren't able, for you are. My Word says greater things will you do on this earth. You are blessed for I have declared it so. Stand in the authority I have placed on you as a king and priest and continue to rise to greater levels in Me.

If you believe it, say, "Oh yeah!"

OCTOBER 31
THE POWER OF SIMPLICITY

IN JOURNEY OF LIFE, THERE WILL BE TROUBLES YOU FACE THAT YOU HAVE NO LOGICAL ANSWER FOR AND THE ART OF REASONING BECOMES IRRATIONAL. WHEN YOU FACE THESE KINDS OF TROUBLES, THE ONLY THING YOU CAN DO IS PUT THE SITUATION INTO GOD HANDS. BY LAYING IT DOWN, YOU SURRENDER THE PROBLEM TO BE RESOLVED. REMEMBER, GOD USES THE SIMPLE THINGS TO CONFOUND THE WISE. THE WAY OUT OF YOUR TROUBLE IS SIMPLE. THE MORE TIME SPENT THINKING ABOUT THE PROBLEM, THE WORSE IT GETS. STEP AWAY AND STEP INTO WORSHIP. LET HIM SEND THE ANSWER.

LIFE IS VERY GOOD!

So many people come to the altar for the same thing over and over again. Why? Because they never fully surrender by laying down their issues. I am reminded of the classic hymn, "I Surrender All". The lyrics begin with: All to Jesus I surrender; All to him I freely give; I will ever love and trust him, in his presence daily live. So, surrender all to Jesus and worship and praise His holy name for He is good, really good.

The Lord Says...

To surrender your will to Me, your wants, your desires and your plans in exchange for My peace, My plans and My purpose will be the best exchange you'll ever make. Trust Me for I Am good and all things work together for the good of those who love Me and are called according to their purpose.

If you believe it, say, "Oh yeah!"

NOVEMBER 1
GET UP AND DUST YOURSELF OFF

LIFE CAN KNOCK YOU DOWN MANY WAYS DIFFERENT WAYS, BUT A RIGHTEOUS MAN FINDS A WAY TO GET UP AND KEEP GOING 7 TIMES. LIFE MAY HAVE YOU DOWN BUT YOU ARE NOT OUT! GET UP IN HIS RIGHTEOUSNESS AND SEE HIS VICTORY! PERSEVERE AND OVERCOME.

LIFE IS VERY GOOD!

2 Corinthians 4:9 says that you may be "persecuted, but not abandoned; struck down, but not destroyed." In other words, if you still have breath, you can praise the Lord in any circumstance. So get up, you're still alive and that means you still have a shot at victory. See his victory and walk from a place of victory before it ever comes. When victory comes, it will be like you've already been there before. The battles in your life are first won in the crevices of your mind.

The Lord Says...

Be grateful and give thanks for the smallest of victories in your journey. It is the smallest of victories that bring you to the greater victory. Be therefore grateful and shout for victory in your praise now and always. I Am with you. I overcame and so have you.

If you believe it, say, "Oh yeah!"

NOVEMBER 2
DON'T QUIT NOW

IN LIFE, EACH INDIVIDUAL'S JOURNEY TO THE MOUNTAIN PEAK IS DIFFERENT. WE WILL ALL FACE TROUBLES AND TRIALS ON THE JOURNEY BUT THE DIFFERENCE IS ONE'S WILLINGNESS TO OVERCOME. SOME PEOPLE MAY CLIMB HILLS WHILE OTHERS WILL CLIMB MOUNTAINS TO ACHIEVE THEIR GOALS. HOW HIGH ARE YOU WILLING TO CLIMB? DON'T QUIT NOW; GO ALL THE WAY!

LIFE IS VERY GOOD!

You will only get as far in life as you are willing to go. If you tell your mind that you can do it then you will do anything to make the climb happen, no matter how long it takes. If you tell your mind, "It's too high, I can't keep walking, I'm too tired, my muscles hurt", your focus becomes all that you are struggling with in order to reach your goal instead of the goal itself. If this is where you are, no, you will not make it until you shift your mind from your own strength to God's strength and tell yourself that YOU CAN. Luke 11:28 says, "But he said, "Blessed rather are those who hear the word of God and keep it!" So take this scripture for what it is and apply it. Philippians 4:13 says, "I can do all this through him who gives me strength." In other words, you're blessed if you hear God's Word and keep it and Philippians says that you can do all things through Him. Tell yourself every day if you need to, "I can make it." Change that inner dialogue. You can because God said you can.

The Lord Says...

All things are possible to those who believe. If your faith is lacking, strengthen it every day by changing your speech. I believe in you and you CAN!

If you believe it, say, "Oh yeah!"

NOVEMBER 3
TRIALS PRODUCE BEAUTY

THERE'S AN OLD SAYING THAT SAYS, "THE GEM CANNOT BE POLISHED WITHOUT FRICTION; NOR MAN PERFECTED WITHOUT TRIALS." YOUR TRIALS DON'T DETERMINE WHO YOU ARE, THEY DEFINE WHO YOU BECOME. LET YOUR HARDSHIP BECOME HIS WORKMANSHIP AND POLISH THE GEM THAT YOU ARE! YOUR TRIAL WILL PRODUCE HIS BEAUTY.

LIFE IS VERY GOOD!

Romans 5:3-5 says, "Not only so, but we also glory in our sufferings, because we know that suffering produces perseverance; perseverance, character; and character, hope. And hope does not put us to shame, because God's love has been poured out into our hearts through the Holy Spirit, who has been given to us." Look at what transpires when you persevere. It creates a domino effect of goodness in your life. The Bible tells us that in the beginning "God created". He created you and the universe and said that it was GOOD. That should give you comfort in knowing that all God's workmanships are good to begin with and only get better.

The Lord Says...

You are precious in My sight. I see you; you are a diamond in the rough, My brilliant gem! Allow Me to sand off the rough edges and polish you into the shiny gem I see in you. Overcoming your trials will only cause you to shine brighter. Be the diamond I have called you to be.

If you believe it, say, "Oh yeah!"

NOVEMBER 4
VICTORY COMES ONE STEP AT A TIME

To overcome in life, your determination must be greater than your discouragement. Life is too short to give up. So rise up and persevere. Trust Him and know He will see you through. Remember, the journey is one step at a time and before you know it, you will be at the top. March into His total victory.

LIFE IS VERY GOOD!

When a child learns to walk, they encounter their first experience with discouragement, but they continue to get up and try over and over again until they master the task. John 16:33 says, "I have told you these things, so that in me you may have peace. In this world you will have trouble. But take heart! I have overcome the world." So hold on for the ride and strive for His peace in your life because this world has its trouble but you can take heart in knowing that indeed He has overcome the world. This isn't just good news, this is great news.

The Lord Says...

Trouble will always be around you, but you live in the world yet are not of the world. When you walk with Me, you walk in victory. Choose to believe that My victory is greater than the dread of your circumstances. I can change it all in just one moment.

If you believe it, say, "Oh yeah!"

NOVEMBER 5
SEE THE BEAUTY ALONG YOUR JOURNEY

REMEMBER THIS: YOU DON'T HAVE TO LIVE IN THE PAINFUL MEMORIES YOU HAVE EXPERI-ENCED. ALL YOU NEED TO DO IS WALK THROUGH THEM BY PLACING YOUR TRUST IN HIM. YOU CAN OVERCOME WHEN YOU PERSEVERE. KNOW HIS LOVE NEVER FAILS AND HE'LL LEAD YOU THROUGH.

LIFE IS VERY GOOD!

Have you ever seen an arbor that vines grow over? Imagine an arbor with vines and cascading flowers positioned one after the other to create a tunnel. It is beautiful, right? But, before it could be beautiful, the plants had to be watered, nurtured and trained to grow in the right direction. Walking through a well grown arbor is what God wants your journey to look like: peaceful, beautiful, thriving, purposeful, abundant and exceptional. However, too many people are walking through dark tunnels as digital frames of condemnation flash all around them trying to engrain those memories into the DNA of who they are. But God says NO, He has come that you might have life and there is beauty along the journey. There is peace, life, abundance, laughter and joy which must not be forgotten. Trade your sorrows for the joy of Jesus and watch your tunnel become the purposeful arbor it was destined to become. Psalm 30:11 says, "You turned my wailing into dancing; you removed my sackcloth and clothed me with joy." Persevere; it only takes one more step than where you are right now. He never fails!

The Lord Says...

Make a decision to keep walking forward on the straight and narrow no matter what you run into or what detour may come your way. Enjoy the journey as you walk it through and trust Me, I Am the best guide one could obtain. I will never lead you astray.

If you believe it, say, "Oh yeah!"

NOVEMBER 6
ENJOY THE JOURNEY

IN LIFE, PEOPLE HAVE LEARNED TO BE IN A HURRY TO ARRIVE AT A DESTINATION, BUT HAVE NEVER BEEN TAUGHT TO APPRECIATE THE JOURNEY. REMEMBER, THERE ARE NO SHORT CUTS IN LIFE. LET EVERY STEP YOU TAKE COUNT AND BECOME A STEPPING-STONE TO YOUR DESTINY, BECAUSE EVERY STEP CAN TEACH YOU SOMETHING NEW IN HIM.

LIFE IS VERY GOOD!

Numbers 33:1-2 says, "Here are the stages in the journey of the Israelites when they came out of Egypt by divisions under the leadership of Moses and Aaron. At the Lord's command Moses recorded the stages in their journey. This is their journey by stages." The journey was so important to God that it became a part of Israel's recorded history and is in the Bible. Don't take the journey lightly. God never said it would be easy. He said seek Him, listen to Him, obey Him and walk with Him. Refuse to complain, live in complacency, familiarity, look back or take a short cut. Live in the NOW He has given you, with the NOW word He has provided. It is filled with resurrection power. It is better than the Fairy Godmother's wand. It is better than any magic potion. It is better than what money can buy. It is alive and filled with power from on high. It gives you hope. Step into that.

The Lord Says...

Hope is NOW. Hope is ALIVE. Hope is FREEING and it births FAITH. Hold on to My Hope, for it is for you, TODAY and NOW! I Am walking with you every step of the way.

If you believe it, say, "Oh yeah!"

NOVEMBER 7
BE PATIENT THROUGHOUT THE JOURNEY

FAILURE IS NOT AN OPTION BUT MAY BE A REALITY WE FACE. AT TIMES, WE MAY COME UP SHORT BUT WE MUST LEARN TO PICK OURSELVES UP AND CONTINUE THE JOURNEY UNTIL WE BECOME SUCCESSFUL. DON'T QUIT NOW, YOU'RE ON THE VERGE OF BREAKTHROUGH. GOD WON'T LET YOU LIVE IN FAILURE.

LIFE IS VERY GOOD!

Romans 12:12 says, "Be joyful in hope, patient in affliction, faithful in prayer." Things don't always work out as YOU have planned, but it doesn't mean that God isn't with you. Take your example from God. He is faithful, so you be faithful too. Be faithful to pray, patient through the journey, living in joy and hope. Nothing is impossible with Him. It's when you walk without Him that you lose hope.

The Lord Says...

Hope deferred makes the heart grow sick. Keep hope alive at every turn, through every pothole and as you ascend in elevation up to the mountaintop. I Am with you always. Though you may sometimes face failures, it doesn't mean you are a failure. I have called you more than a conqueror in Me. Stand on that.

If you believe it, say, "Oh yeah!"

NOVEMBER 8
LEAVE THE PAST BEHIND

THINK ABOUT THIS: WHEN THE PAST QUARRELS WITH THE PRESENT, THERE CAN BE NO FUTURE. QUIT FIGHTING WITH WHAT IS BEHIND YOU, MAKE PEACE WITH YOUR PRESENT AND SEE YOUR FUTURE UNFOLD. HE HOLDS YOUR LIFE IN HIS HANDS. CALL EVERYTHING INTO HIS EXISTENCE.

LIFE IS VERY GOOD!

Ecclesiastes 7:10 says, "Do not say, 'Why were the old days better than these?' For it is not wise to ask such questions." The Word says there is no wisdom in comparing the good ol' days with your present and constantly looking back to what was. Why? Because when you're constantly looking back, you cannot walk into your tomorrows; tomorrow is never good enough and your eyes become blind to the blessings you have right now. So hold on, no one said it wouldn't be a bumpy ride. Call on His name and HE will be there. Call all that He has promised into existence, for His Word is Yes and Amen.

The Lord Says...

Wisdom is the principle thing and it always moves forward not back. It is the lens of your life's camera. Focus it to your advantage. Keep your eyes on Me, the One who holds your future.

If you believe it, say, "Oh yeah!"

NOVEMBER 9
A FLOOD OF LOVE

REMEMBER THIS: IT'S NEVER YOUR DUTY TO JUDGE A PERSON'S SIN, BUT YOUR RESPONSI-
BILITY IS TO LOVE THEM THROUGH IT, UNDERSTANDING SIN JUDGES ITSELF. THE WORD SAYS,
"FOR THE WAGES OF SIN IS DEATH, BUT THE GIFT OF GOD IS ETERNAL LIFE." DEMONSTRATE
HIS LOVE AND BECOME A VESSEL OF HEALING.

LIFE IS VERY GOOD!

Loving through the sin is one of the most challenging things you may ever try to accomplish in this life. It is the moment where your flesh and your spirit meet. Your spirit is supposed to conquer in this area, but often times the flesh wins because it convinces the spirit that judging based on right vs. wrong is the right thing to do. What God wants to know is if you can love through the process. Can you see Jesus in people regardless? Can you see what He sees? Can you flood them with love and encouragement and live by example? Years ago these beaded WWJD ("What Would Jesus Do?) bracelets were really popular. It was a constant reminder to ask oneself that question in every circumstance. I challenge you to do that today. Demonstrate His love and in all the circumstances you face, and ask yourself: WWJD?

The Lord Says...

When you seek Me and find out what I would do, you will find Me along with the answers you look for. But, above all, the greatest of My commandments is to love one another for I Am love. Surround others with the love I have for them and watch their lives transform.

If you believe it, say, "Oh yeah!"

NOVEMBER 10
LET THE WORD BE YOUR GUIDEBOOK

REMEMBER: SUCCESS IS FAILURE TURNED INSIDE OUT! SO, LET YOUR DOWNS BECOME UPS AND MAKE YOUR WRONGS INTO RIGHTS, SO WHAT WAS CAN BECOME WHAT IS, KNOWING THE PAST SHORTCOMINGS CAN'T STOP YOUR DESIRE TO ACHIEVE HIS PROMISE. YOUR TRUE SUCCESS IS WRITTEN IN THE BOOK OF LIFE.

LIFE IS VERY GOOD!

Nowadays you can find a guidebook online for just about anything. In fact, on one of the most popular video websites you can type in 'how to' anything and likely find a video providing that information. The Word is your guidebook and Jesus is your life coach, i.e., tour guide for life. Psalm 119:105 says, "Your word is a lamp for my feet, a light on my path." The Bible also tells us that HE is the Word and the Word is with God. So plant each of your failures on the stairs; the stairs to success. Just look at them as a stepping stone and a bridge you must cross. You can do this. He tells you that you CAN!

The Lord Says...

You CAN do all things through Me because I give you the strength you need for every step you take. Believe and receive. Failure should never stop you from achieving your dreams. I Am on your side and you were created to succeed.

If you believe it, say, "Oh yeah!"

NOVEMBER 11
THE GREATEST STORY OF ALL TIME

AS STORYTELLERS OF GOOD NEWS, WE HAVE THE ABILITY TO RESTORE HOPE TO THE BROKEN-HEARTED BY WRITING A NEW ENDING. A STORYTELLER'S GIFT MAY NOT BE TO PHYSICALLY CHANGE THE PAST, BUT TO HEAL IT BY WRITING A GREATER SCRIPT FOR THE FUTURE. HIS STORY WILL LEAD YOU OUT OF DARKNESS AND INTO AN ABUNDANT LIFE.

LIFE IS VERY GOOD!

Think of it...let it soak in a bit...Jesus is all about re-writing history...the history of people. The Good News IS the Gospel. It is Jesus that gives people a hope and a future. Sometimes that is all a person needs. A little bit of hope, a little bit of Jesus. Let His story become your story and when you tell that story, hearts will be set free. It only takes a storytellers gift. Be the conduit of the Good News.

The Lord Says...

If you are looking for some of the greatest stories of all time, look no further than the Good Book; filled with history, romance, war, intrigue, architecture, agriculture, proverbs, language, culture, but most importantly: redemption. I filled it. I gave it to you. It is truth that sets the captives free. It is bread that feeds the soul. It is alive and filled with resurrection power. Immerse yourself in its wisdom and live the abundant life.

If you believe it, say, "Oh yeah!"

NOVEMBER 12
PUT YOUR TRUST IN GOD

THINK ABOUT THIS: HAVE YOU BEEN HURT AND FIND IT DIFFICULT TO TRUST? THE WORD OF GOD NEVER SAID TO PUT YOUR TRUST IN PEOPLE SUCH AS YOUR HUSBAND, WIFE, FRIENDS OR FAMILY. THE WORD SAYS TO PUT YOUR TRUST IN HIM. WHEN YOU TRUST HIM, YOU WILL AGAIN GAIN FAITH AND LEARN TO TRUST OTHERS. LEAN NOT ON YOUR OWN UNDERSTANDING.

LIFE IS VERY GOOD!

Proverbs 3:5-6 says, "Trust in the Lord with all your heart and lean not on your own understanding; in all your ways submit to him and he will make your paths straight." Remember, you can't just give Him a single piece of your heart for He wants all your heart. As you begin to trust Him, your trust in others will grow. Trust yourself enough to lean on His understanding instead of your own. His ways are greater indeed.

The Lord Says...

I Am after your heart, dear child. There I will provide you with peace, faith, hope, love and trust. You are My goodness. Trust Me as your Father to lead you in the ways you should go and you'll never go anywhere alone.

If you believe it, say, "Oh yeah!"

NOVEMBER 13
YOU CAN DO IT!

FROM TIME TO TIME, THE JOURNEY OF LIFE WILL CAUSE YOU TO FACE SOME CONTRARY OR EVEN BOISTEROUS WINDS. REMEMBER THIS: WHEN YOU FEEL LIKE YOU'RE SINKING, BE LIKE PETER AND CRY OUT, "LORD, SAVE ME!" JESUS STRETCHED OUT HIS HAND, CAUGHT HIM AND RETURNED HIM INTO THE BOAT. IN THIS SEASON, DON'T DOUBT OR BE A MAN WITH LITTLE FAITH. ALLOW YOUR FAITH TO ENDURE AND BEFORE YOU KNOW IT, YOU WILL BE ON THE OTHER SIDE.

LIFE IS VERY GOOD!

Let's take a look at endurance. To have endurance means that you have trained yourself to go the distance through all hardships that come your way and through the stress that comes along with it. It means you can be optimistic in a pessimistic world. It means you have the strength to keep on pushing through until you make it to your destination. Hebrews 10:36 says, "You need to persevere so that when you have done the will of God, you will receive what he has promised."

It is God's will that you have endurance and persevere. Just one more step, just one more time, breathe in, breathe out, close your eyes and cry out...He will meet you wherever you are. He is Able.

The Lord Says...

Life will push you and pull you. It will bring many trials and victories your way. Before molten glass can become something beautiful, it first must go through the firing and shaping process. Likewise, your trials by fire will shape you and mold you with a strong faith and endurance to keep running the race. You can do it.

If you believe it, say, "Oh yeah!"

NOVEMBER 14
THE POWER IN FAITHFULNESS

IT DOESN'T MATTER IF YOU HAVE MONEY, EDUCATION, OR INTELLIGENCE; TO BE BLESSED BY GOD REQUIRES FAITHFULNESS. BLESSED IS THE MAN WHO IS FAITHFUL WITH THE LEAST, FOR HE WILL BE FAITHFUL WITH MUCH. YOUR FAITHFULNESS WILL CAUSE HIM TO REWARD YOU, NOT BECAUSE OF WHAT YOU POSSESS, BUT HOW YOU TAKE CARE OF WHAT HE'S GIVEN YOU.

LIFE IS VERY GOOD!

Remember, you are but caretakers on this earth. Your true position in life is being an ambassador of heaven. When you are an ambassador, you represent a nation that you are faithful to serve. Ask yourself this question: how do you represent heaven? Are you faithful to the cause of the Good News? Does your life and character represent that of a faithful ambassador? 2 Corinthians 5:20 says, "We are therefore Christ's ambassadors, as though God were making his appeal through us. We implore you on Christ's behalf: Be reconciled to God." He has given you the world and all that is in it. Take care of yourself, your family and your world. Be faithful to uphold the principles of heaven every day, for He is good and watches how you care for His garden called life.

The Lord Says...

The circle of life is My garden and everything that has breath still praises Me. Be the image you were made to be, the ambassador of heaven, the giver of My love and the fruit of My Spirit.

If you believe it, say, "Oh yeah!"

NOVEMBER 15
DESTINED FOR GREATNESS

HAVE YOU EVER FELT LIKE YOUR LIFE IS GOING IN CIRCLES? IF SO, REMEMBER THIS: GOD HAS A WAY OF FUNNELING YOU THROUGH DIFFICULTIES TO PRODUCE DESTINY! EVERY STORM YOU FACE AWAKENS THE GREATER CALL IN YOU. YOU WERE PURPOSED FROM THE WOMB... KNOW IT! YOU ARE DESTINED FOR GREATNESS.

LIFE IS VERY GOOD!

Think about it...it was with great difficulty for Mary to endure such a culturally crazy notion that she could be impregnated by the Holy Spirit instead of a man. Even in today's world, people would think you were crazy. Then when Jesus did come, they had to try and keep Him alive as people like Herod tried to kill Him.

But God had a destiny for Jesus that came to be known over time, and no matter what challenges came his way, Jesus had a destiny. Though He was a man, He was the Son of God, who was destined to die and rise again so that you might have eternal life. The only one who can keep you from your destiny is you. Stand strong and through every storm God will make a way where there seems to be no way.

The Lord Says...

I Am the God who gave My people manna and water in the desert places. I Am the God who told them to dig ditches and uncover the wells of their fathers. I Am the God who multiplied bread and fish, turned water into wine, healed the lepers, the dead, the blind, the crippled, the demon-possessed and the same resurrection power that lives in Me, now lives inside of you.

If you believe it, say, "Oh yeah!"

NOVEMBER 16
THE BEST IS YET TO COME

REMEMBER, THERE IS POWER TO RESTORE YOUR HOPE THROUGH IMAGINATION. WHEN EVERY-THING SEEMS TO BE AT A LOSS, DON'T GIVE UP, PRESS IN. JACOB WAS IN A DIFFICULT PLACE UNTIL HE HAD A DREAM THAT GOD WAS STANDING HIGH ABOVE HIS SITUATION. KNOW HE IS WITH YOU AND WILL KEEP YOU WHEREVER YOU GO. THE BEST IS YET TO COME.

LIFE IS VERY GOOD!

God has the greatest imagination ever discovered. He saw the universe as He wanted it and spoke it into existence and called it good. I remember growing up in the 80s with the movie, "Back to the Future". Back then, the future seemed so far away; the 21st century seemed like an eternity away and now we're here. Most brand name things you see and purchase were once ideas imagined that came to be. Many, like Disneyland, never would have been had Walt Disney given up instead of pressed on through the difficult times. The Bible says to write the vision and make it plain. Seek His wisdom and let God be the architect of your dreams.

The Lord Says...

I stand high above you and your situation just as I did for Jacob. Believe and receive My wisdom, My counsel and My love. The best is here so walk in it now.

If you believe it, say, "Oh yeah!"

NOVEMBER 17
STICK TO THE JOURNEY

IF LIFE HAS POSITIONED YOU IN A DIFFICULT PLACE, REMEMBER THIS: THERE IS NO GROWTH WITHOUT CHANGE. THERE IS NO CHANGE WITHOUT LOSS. AND THERE IS NO LOSS WITHOUT PAIN. CHANGE, LOSS AND PAIN ARE PREREQUISITES IN LIFE THAT PRODUCE THE GREATER YOU. DON'T GIVE UP ON THE JOURNEY.

LIFE IS VERY GOOD!

Loss is difficult. We try to avoid it because pain is uncomfortable and it takes people from their happy place. Psalm 34:18 says, "The Lord is close to the brokenhearted and saves those who are crushed in spirit." You can take comfort in knowing that as you stretch and grow through the process of hurt and pain, God is still with you. He gives you hope for a brighter tomorrow, the endurance to know you can survive and the heart does heal. Too many people give up before their journey is over. Stay the course and your faith will become stronger than before.

The Lord Says...

My hope is that you will always put hope in tomorrow. The sun never stops shining even though you may not see it at every given moment. Likewise, the seasons always know when to change. Hope renews itself every day and My mercies are new every morning.

If you believe it, say, "Oh yeah!"

NOVEMBER 18
GOD ALWAYS HAS A PLAN

IN LIFE, THERE ARE STORMS WE FACE THAT COME TO DESTROY US. THE STORM MAY HAVE LEFT YOU FEELING LIKE YOUR LIFE IS IN RUINS. BUT, COULD IT BE THAT THE BROKEN PARTS OF YOUR LIFE HAVE BECOME A LIFE RAFT FOR OTHERS? CHANGE YOUR PERSPECTIVE AND UNDERSTANDING TO KNOW GOD CAN AND WILL USE ALL THINGS FOR HIS GLORY.

LIFE IS VERY GOOD!

Sometimes storms can be terrifying, leaving you broken, wounded, stranded or just plain devastated. But God always has a plan. Romans 8:31 says, "What, then, shall we say in response to these things? If God is for us, who can be against us?" Your journey was never meant for you alone. When hope sees you through another day, help pick someone else up from their similar despair and give your hope, the hope of Jesus, away. He is meant to be shared.

The Lord Says...

In the brokenness lives are transformed, stretched, shaped and changed, for I will pick up the pieces and mend the fragile heart. Lean on Me for I have given you the victory. Throughout your history you have and will continue to overcome.

If you believe it, say, "Oh yeah!"

NOVEMBER 19
CHOOSE YOUR WORDS WISELY

A PERSON FILLED WITH COMPLAINTS IS POWERLESS TO CHANGE THEIR SITUATION. REMEMBER, YOUR ATTITUDE DETERMINES YOUR ALTITUDE. A NEGATIVE EMOTION WILL LEAVE YOU MENTALLY GROUNDED AND PHYSICALLY OVERWHELMED, WHILE AN OPTIMISTIC OUTLOOK LEADS TO A SILVER LINING. LET HIS PRAISE FILL YOUR MOUTH. IT WILL EMPOWER YOU AND CAUSE YOU TO SOAR OVER YOUR SITUATION. TODAY, SOAR HIGH ABOVE.

LIFE IS VERY GOOD!

A pilot must go through a routine ground check before take-off. I think Christians should have a daily ground check protocol before we take off into our day - our meetings, our interpersonal relationships and our commitments. Maybe your ground check might look like this: prayer and seeking God in the morning...check. Attitude evaluation...check. Heart condition...check. Filled with joy...check. Fruit of the Spirit operational and in order...check. Time with the family...check. Imagine if we had a ground check system for our lives on a daily basis and kept His praise on our lips. I Corinthians 14:3 says that prophecy is for the edification, exhortation and comfort of the hearts of man. So let the words of knowledge God has given you in the Bible speak to your situation. Let the WORD, which is the lamp unto your feet and the light to your path, let it empower you to greater heights.

The Lord Says...

Be encouraged, for darkness is only the absence of light. If your world seems dark right now, it's okay, be optimistic and remember, this too shall pass. I Am the Light of the world, and I will shine in the midst of any situation. When you praise Me in the midst of your trials, My presence will fill you with strength and joy. Let your praises fill the temple and My glorious light will shine about you.

If you believe it, say, "Oh yeah!"

NOVEMBER 20
BE INSPIRED

WHEN YOU ARE FEELING UNINSPIRED IN LIFE, ALIGN YOURSELF WITH SOMEONE THAT'S AC-
COMPLISHING GREAT THINGS. HIS JOY, THROUGH THEM, CAN INSPIRE YOU TO PRESS FORWARD.
LET HIS GREATNESS BE THE LIFESTYLE THAT FLOWS THROUGH YOU.

LIFE IS VERY GOOD!

Mentorship is very important in the Bible. Jesus studied the trade of carpentry under his earthly father, Joseph's, tutelage. In turn, Jesus mentored the twelve disciples in the message of the Good News, signs and wonders. For every great leader, there are countless others behind the scenes that help make the vision a reality. God is family orientated, a team player. If you don't have a spiritual or occupational mentor, find one. They will be the greatest gift you could ever have. Proverbs 27:17 says, "Iron sharpens iron and one man sharpens another." In other words, you have something to give and someone has something to deposit into you. When we sharpen on another's iron we become mighty men and women of God.

The Lord Says...

You are inspiring, but that in itself is not enough. When you've gained endurance and hope, which is My gift you carry in your pocket on a daily basis, then faith has made you stronger than you think. Get up and run to the person who needs My hope in their pocket to keep on going.

If you believe it, say, "Oh yeah!"

NOVEMBER 21
GOD'S ABILITY OVERCOMES YOUR INABILITY

WHEN YOUR MINDSET SHIFTS TO A KINGDOM PERSPECTIVE, YOU DON'T GROW OLD, YOU GROW
MORE ABLE. CALEB WAS ABLE TO ACCOMPLISH AT 85 YEARS OLD WHAT HE HAD INITIALLY SET
OUT TO DO AT 40. IT'S TIME TO TAKE YOUR MOUNTAIN, NO MATTER YOUR AGE. WITH GOD ON
YOUR SIDE, YOU ARE ABLE TO DO ANYTHING.

LIFE IS VERY GOOD!

Understanding kingdom perspective is essential in taking your mountain in life. Why? Because the WORD of God has the final say in your life and the words it keeps must become the life to which you speak instead of the world's language. So when you're in a crisis, what does the Word say? It says that all things are possible to them that believe (Matthew 19:26). In the world's economy, you're about to go bankrupt, so what does the Word say? Trust in the Lord with all your heart and lean not on your own understanding, but to acknowledge God and He will direct your paths (Proverbs 3:5-6). Do you believe it? Take His Word at face value. Take His Word as the truth that it is and begin declaring it; that it is kingdom. This is how you grow more able. It's not about age, it's about being doers of the word and not hearers only.

The Lord Says...

Change your language and it will change your life. It will change your outlook, your vision, and your hope. Kingdom language is life changing. And with Me on your side, anything you set your mind to do, you can accomplish. Don't worry about how young or mature you are, stand and believe that all will be fulfilled in your life.

If you believe it, say, "Oh yeah!"

NOVEMBER 22
GOD'S PROMISES WILL CHANGE YOUR LIFE

IF LIFE HAS LEFT YOU WITH UNCERTAINTY AND YOUR VIEW OF TOMORROW LOOKS WORSE THAN TODAY, REMEMBER THIS: GOD SAID TO ABRAHAM, "GO OUTSIDE AND LOOK UP." GOD GAVE A PROMISE TO A MAN WITH A BARREN WIFE THAT HIS SEED WOULD BE AS MANY AS THE STARS IN THE HEAVENS. HOLD ON TO GOD'S PROMISE; IT WILL CHANGE YOUR OUTLOOK ON LIFE.

LIFE IS VERY GOOD!

Have you ever received a word of knowledge that you held onto with everything you had? It became a part of you and your identity because it spoke to the very image of who you are or about to become. The Bible is filled with words like that; words that declare His promises to and for you. Hold onto the word. Hide it in your heart. Speak it daily. Then, watch as it changes you from the inside out. You will be barren in your life no more. II Corinthians 1:20 says, "For no matter how many promises God has made, they are 'Yes' in Christ. And so through him the 'Amen' is spoken by us to the glory of God." That deserves an AMEN indeed. His promises will change your life.

The Lord Says...

Look up! Send your worship toward the heavens and come to know My promises, for they are Yes and amen! My promises have been spoken over you and they will not return to Me void. They will accomplish all they have been sent to do.

If you believe it, say, "Oh yeah!"

NOVEMBER 23
NO MORE NONSENSE

THE WAY TO DISTANCE YOURSELF FROM COMPLAINERS IS TO KEEP MOVING FORWARD. YOUR CONTINUAL PROGRESSION THROUGH A DIFFICULT TIME WILL LEAVE COMPLAINERS CONTAINED BY THEIR OWN ATTITUDE. LEAVE THE NONSENSE BEHIND AND ALLOW YOUR POSITIVE MINDSET TO ELEVATE YOU TO A NEW PLACE.

LIFE IS VERY GOOD!

Philippians 2:14 says, "Do everything without grumbling or arguing." It can't get any simpler than God advising us to leave the grumbling and arguing behind. I challenge you to keep moving forward along the straight and narrow path and when the opportunity for grumbling comes along, check your tongue and say something positive; something that edifies. For it is this attitude that births the hope of glory for all men.

The Lord Says...

Grumbling, complaining and arguing - they are all symptoms of a heart that is not fulfilled or satisfied in its present state. Change the language to My words, change the company to My people and you will change your circumstance to a positive one. Complaining will keep you stuck but keeping praise upon your lips will move you forward into what I have for you.

If you believe it, say, "Oh yeah!"

NOVEMBER 24
SCARS OF FREEDOM

SCARS, MENTALLY OR PHYSICALLY, LEAVE BEHIND A MARK. WHEN YOU SEE YOUR SCARS, WHAT DO YOU THINK OF? ARE THEY REMINDERS OF PAST PAIN OR ARE THEY MEMORIES OF GOD'S VICTORIES? WHAT COULD HAVE DESTROYED YOU ONLY LEFT A MARK AS A TESTIMONY. THE VERY PLACE THAT WAS FILLED WITH PAIN HAS HEALED OVER AND IS STRONGER NOW. THERE IS POWER IN HEALING.

LIFE IS VERY GOOD!

We all have scars - heart scars or flesh scars - but when I think of scars I think of Jesus. Jesus' scars only represent pain to the individual that lacks a personal relationship with Him. For those who know Christ, His scars became His victory - your victory. John 3:16 says, "For God so loved the world that he gave his one and only son, that whoever believes in him shall not perish but have eternal life."

Don't let your scars dictate your life; turn them into your victories and your healing will flow from God's hand to your heart. Scars can be sources of strength. Let the healing begin.

The Lord Says...

Scars can only determine your altitude if you let them affect your attitude. Refuse the pessimism of this world and continue to be a people of hope, change and healing. Take your scars and give them to Me. I will bear your burdens and you will be free.

If you believe it, say, "Oh yeah!"

NOVEMBER 25
GET WISDOM AND UNDERSTANDING

A REVELATION WITHOUT UNDERSTANDING IS ONLY INFORMATION. REFUSE TO BE LIKE THE 50 SONS OF THE PROPHETS THAT WERE ABLE TO HEAR BUT NOT UNDERSTAND THE POWER OF WHAT WAS SPOKEN TO THEM. LACK OF UNDERSTANDING WILL LEAVE YOU ON THE WRONG SIDE OF WHAT YOU'RE ABLE TO RECEIVE. IT'S TIME TO CROSS THE JORDAN AND RECEIVE YOUR FULL PORTION.

LIFE IS VERY GOOD!

When Joshua and the children of Israel came to the Jordan River they had two perspectives to choose from. They could have viewed the land as just another place to pitch their tents, but instead they saw it as destiny - their full measure. They had to see God's promise as a reality for their lives and not just words. Revelation can become that - merely words - when we don't have the full understanding of what the revelation means to us. Be sure to dive into God's word to receive the fullness of what He has spoken over you. Understand it so you can walk in the revelation and live it out. Do as Proverbs 16:3 suggests: "Commit to the Lord whatever you do and he will establish your plans." And as always do not only get wisdom, but wisdom and understanding.

The Lord Says...

Hear the Word that I have spoken over you for it is sharper than a two-edged sword. It provides wisdom to the seeker and understanding to those who study its principles. Hide My Word in your heart and commit to do your best work always. I Am with you and I will open up your spirit to understand the revelation I have given to you.

If you believe it, say, "Oh yeah!"

NOVEMBER 26
FOCUS ON TODAY

THINK ABOUT THIS: SOME PEOPLE SPEND MORE TIME WORRYING ABOUT THE UNKNOWN FUTURE RATHER THAN FOCUSING ON THE NOW AND PRESENT. TOMORROW HAS A WAY OF WORKING IT-SELF OUT, SO USE YOUR TIME WISELY AND FOCUS ON CHANGES THAT CAN BE MADE TO BETTER YOUR TOMORROW TODAY. REMEMBER, PREPARATION IS THE ROADWAY TO ACCOMPLISHMENT.

LIFE IS VERY GOOD!

II Timothy 2:15 says, "Do your best to present yourself to God as one ap-proved, a worker who does not need to be ashamed and who correctly handles the word of truth." In other words, look at preparation as part of the process in life. Focus on it now and you can have peace about tomorrow. God has your future in His hand therefore it's all under control. There is no reason to worry. Prepare yourself for the road God has you on and God will take care of the rest. At the Sermon on the Mount, Jesus taught about many different things, one being not to worry about tomorrow. "Can any one of you be worrying add a single hour to you life?… But seek first his kingdom and his righteousness, and all these things will be given to you as well. Therefore do not worry about tomorrow" (Matthew 6:27, 33-34). Focus on God and He will take care of focusing on you.

The Lord Says...

Don't fret about tomorrow when you have today. If you worry about tomor-row, you will miss the peace and fulfillment I want to give you in this new day. Stay the course. Never give up. I Am with you, always.

If you believe it, say, "Oh yeah!"

NOVEMBER 27
LET GOD BE YOUR TEACHER

REMEMBER THIS: WHEN YOU DON'T THINK YOU CAN, POSITION YOURSELF NEXT TO SOMEONE WHO IS. SUDDENLY, WHAT YOU COULD NOT DO BECOMES DOABLE. WHAT WE CARRY IS TRANSFERABLE SO WHEN YOU'RE IN NEED, LET OTHERS INSPIRE AND PROPEL YOU TO NEW HEIGHTS. GO TO THE NEXT LEVEL!

LIFE IS VERY GOOD!

II Timothy 3:17 says, "Do your best to present yourself to God as one approved, a worker who does not need to be ashamed and who correctly handles the word of truth." One way to accomplish this goal is to learn and rub shoulders with someone who has already scaled the mountain you are attempting to climb. They will share their victories and their defeats, transferring their wealth of knowledge to you. This WILL take you to the next level. And, the climb won't seem nearly as bad. Before you know it, you'll be on your way.

The Lord Says...

Teachers and mentors are an essential tool for your life because they provide knowledge for your journey and insight you may never have thought of before. Let Me be your teacher in all areas and in all things. I Am the answer to the questions you may have.

If you believe it, say, "Oh yeah!"

NOVEMBER 28
TURN BITTERNESS INTO BETTERMENT

CHOOSING NOT TO FORGIVE IS CHOOSING NOT TO HEAL. REMEMBER, YOU CAN CHOOSE TO BE ANGRY OR YOU CAN CHOOSE TO BE HEALED; BE BITTER OR FORGIVE. SO IN ALL YOUR CHOOSING, CHOOSE WISELY. YOUR WISE CHOICE CAN LEAD YOU TO HIS VICTORY.

LIFE IS VERY GOOD!

If unforgiveness could be played out in a drama between two people, it may look something like this: two people walk into communication and/or action like any other day; happy, joyful, courteous and conversational. An event occurs between them; someone or both are hurt and/or offended. They leave the company of one another in anger with a large set of chains around their wrists. Each chain on the wrist is attached to a concrete block; this is unforgiveness. Every move they make becomes difficult and a constant reminder of the unforgiveness that they carry daily. Now, ask yourself, why in the world would anyone in their right mind want to willingly carry around such a heavy load? But, this is what you are doing when you are holding onto unforgiveness in your life. You carry around a heavy load that chains you up and keeps you from fully moving into your potential. You can't run too fast when you're carrying a concrete block.

So choose wisely. Matthew 11:28-30 says, "Come to me, all you who are weary and burdened and I will give you rest. Take my yoke upon you and learn from me, for I Am gentle and humble in heart and you will find rest for your souls. For my yoke is easy and my burden is light." Hand your concrete over to Jesus and bring your life into order.

The Lord Says...

Freedom comes in giving, so give Me your burdens and be free; it's the way to live an abundant life. I want for you to want in the fullness of My healing. Give to Me your anger, your bitterness, your pain and your suffering. Don't hold onto it anymore. Be free from the chains of bondage by giving Me all that is holding you down. Choose to be healed and to walk in all I have for you.

If you believe it, say, "Oh yeah!"

NOVEMBER 29
LIFE ABOVE FRUSTRATIONS

FOOD FOR YOUR SPIRIT: NEGATIVE THOUGHTS BECOME NEGATIVE WORDS, WHICH IS A GATEWAY OF WRONGFUL ACTIONS. BE CAREFUL, BECAUSE YOUR ACTIONS SPEAK LOUDER THAN WORDS. SO LIVE ABOVE YOUR FRUSTRATIONS, KNOWING GOD HAS MADE YOU THE HEAD AND NOT THE TAIL. LET YOUR MIND THINK AND RESPOND IN A HEAVENLY WAY, SO YOU CAN LIVE IN HIS PEACE.

LIFE IS VERY GOOD!

It only takes one moment for breakthrough to occur. You may have been through a drought and you may have been through the fire, but keep your head up and your words speaking truth because after the drought and fire, God sends the rain. Shift your mind towards God's ways and keep on smiling. Negative words can easily gain momentum and snowball into something huge. To get out of it, not only your words have to change, but your attitude as well because it can affect your actions. Turn it all around by believing and declaring the word of God over your life. Remember, God is in control.

The Lord Says...

The world may tell you to be frustrated, but I tell you the opposite; rejoice for abundance is yours. Here the Words of the Lord, know them and secure them to your heart. They will give you the life you need and the light to brighten the darkness. Drown out the negative by speaking My life!

If you believe it, say, "Oh yeah!"

NOVEMBER 30
LIVE KINGDOM MINDED

MAKE NO ROOM FOR FRUSTRATION. WHEN NEGATIVE THOUGHTS ENTER YOUR MIND, MOVE THEM OUT WITH TRUTH. DON'T LET NEGATIVITY LIVE IN YOUR MIND AS AN UNFRUITFUL TENANT. EVICT THOSE THOUGHTS AND ALLOW GOD'S WORD TO TAKE UP RIGHTFUL RESIDENCE.

LIFE IS VERY GOOD!

God wants you to shake up your mind. You are in Him and He is in you. Therefore His thoughts are your thoughts and speaking negativity is not speaking His thoughts. Be kingdom-minded and it will shift your life into a new direction. Ephesians 4:29 says, "Do not let any unwholesome talk come out of your mouths, but only what is helpful for building others up according to their needs, that it may benefit those who listen." Sometimes, the other is also YOU. You tell the tongue what you will say. Declare good things at all times.

The Lord Says...

I have great purpose for your life; things you cannot even imagine. There is nothing you cannot accomplish. Declare it as so. Build up one another with hope and faith, then watch and see what I will do. There is no room for frustration or resentment, only Me.

If you believe it, say, "Oh yeah!"

DECEMBER 1
WHEN HIGHER IS REALLY LOWER

WHEN WE THINK OF GOING TO THE NEXT LEVEL, WE THINK OF GOING TO A HIGHER PLACE
IN CHRIST. COULD IT BE THAT A HIGHER DIMENSION IS ACTUALLY LOWER? AS WE HUMBLE
OURSELVES TO THIS PLACE, IT ALLOWS THE GOD WE SERVE TO BECOME GREATER. JOHN SAID,
"I MUST DECREASE THAT HE MIGHT INCREASE." LESS OF US AND MORE OF HIM PRODUCES
GLORY.

LIFE IS VERY GOOD!

Ask yourself this question: Who was at the foot of the cross when Jesus died? His family. They stood and sat at the low place, literally at His feet just to be in His presence. Shed your plans and your ambition for a place with Him. Just one moment with Jesus changes everything.

The Lord Says...

I walk in the coolness of the day and I long for just one moment with you. Will you talk with Me and walk with Me, putting away your childish things to come down and meet Me? I Am available, are you? Humble yourself so I can be exalted in your life and others will see My glory shining through you.

If you believe it, say, "Oh yeah!"

DECEMBER 2
LOVE AS GOD LOVES

WHEN WE THINK OF A COMFORT ZONE, WE THINK OF COMPLACENCY AND A PLACE WHERE
A PERSON BECOMES SO COZY, THEY REFUSE TO LEAVE. WE OFTEN SEE A COMFORT ZONE
THROUGH A NEGATIVE PERSPECTIVE BUT REALLY IT'S A PLACE OF REFUGE AND A RELIEF FROM
AFFLICTION. IT'S TIME TO SEE THE OTHER SIDE OF THE COIN AND BE A HELPING, LOVING HAND
OF RELIEF. LOVE AS CHRIST LOVES.

LIFE IS VERY GOOD!

Do you remember your parents quoting to you the golden rule? Do unto others as you want them to do to you (Matthew 7:12)? This verse requires interpretation from the reverse. In other words, if you want someone to be a helping, loving hand of relief in your life, then first be what you desire to others. It is all about the law of sowing and reaping. So put in some time that affords comfort to someone else, for you never know what someone is going through or what a smile, or afternoon lunch, can do to just even change their day.

The Lord Says...

I Am in you and you are in Me, therefore love as I love; unconditionally without reservation for I Am love. I Am your comforter and the lifter of your head. Don't get comfortable where you are for I Am wanting to take you into the deeper levels of My Spirit.

If you believe it, say, "Oh yeah!"

DECEMBER 3
HAVE A PLAN...A BIG PLAN!

HAVE YOU HEARD THE SAYING, "REACH FOR THE STARS"? IT MEANS TO SET BIG GOALS OR HAVE HIGH STANDARDS FOR YOUR LIFE. REMEMBER, IF YOU DON'T REACH FOR SOMETHING, YOU WILL NOT ACHIEVE THE GOALS YOU SET. SO REACH FOR SOMETHING GREAT. HE WAS VICTORIOUS AND SO ARE YOU.

LIFE IS VERY GOOD!

Proverbs 21:5 says, "The plans of the diligent lead to profit as surely as haste leads to poverty." In other words, it can only profit you to reach for the stars. Sure, you may have some construction along the way, some stops, re-evaluations and even some detours, but when you are focused on the plan, you're way better off than if you didn't have a plan at all. So many people in life reach for nothing; they just live day to day. Nothing + nothing = yep, that's right, nothing. God wants you to live the abundant life. Set goals and make them realistic ones and when you reach one goal, enjoy the ride and then set another. If I give you $100 and you have something in mind that you need or want, then your money has purpose. In the same way, your goals need purpose. You can do this. Nothing is impossible with Jesus and He only requires a mustard seed amount of faith.

The Lord Says...

Refuse to live life only to live. Set a goal and accomplish it. It will make you feel amazing. I set out to save the people of this world and every time a name is written in the Lamb's Book of Life, I rejoice - My mission is being accomplished. I will continue to work with you so you can enjoy success in this life.

If you believe it, say, "Oh yeah!"

DECEMBER 4
TO LIVE AND DIE BY THE SWORD

THE SAME GOD THAT CREATED THE HEAVENS AND THE EARTH BY SPEAKING THEM INTO
EXISTENCE LIVES IN YOU. TODAY, SAY SOMETHING AND LET HIM DEMONSTRATE HIS CREATIVE
POWER THROUGH YOU AND PRODUCE CHANGE IN THE EARTH. HE WAS A WORD SENT FROM
HEAVEN AND NOW WE ARE A LIFE CONTAINING IT!

LIFE IS VERY GOOD!

Romans 8:11 says, "And if the Spirit of him who raised Jesus from the dead is living in you, he who raised Christ from the dead will also give life to your mortal bodies because of his Spirit who lives in you." We live, work and communicate on this earth so sometimes it's challenging to remember that we are spirit beings too, and our spirit should rule our flesh; this is kingdom living. Kingdom living says that you live and die by the sword; the sword of the Spirit, which is the word of God. God said it. I believe it so that settles it. When you live the kingdom life, you know the power that lives inside of you and you speak to your circumstances with that authority. You change the atmosphere with worship. You speak truth into your life's journey and tap into the creative power God has given you to decree and declare His Word in your life. Speak it and God will move!

The Lord Says...

It is easy to be double minded in your ways. It's a place between flesh and spirit; one reality and another. The world will ask you who you believe when you receive a terminal diagnosis. And I ask you, who will you believe; the living creator of all things who gave you the Bread of Life, or doctor who means well but is not all-knowing? I Am the great I Am in all your circumstances. I move mountains, part waters, send the rains, multiply for the needs of others, heal, deliver and consume enemies...can I not still do the same? Who do you say that I Am? Am I the hope that keeps your faith alive? Am I your all in all? Declare who I Am in your life and speak My promises for you into existence.

If you believe it, say, "Oh yeah!"

DECEMBER 5
JESUS IS OUR ALL-IN-ALL

DEFEAT IS A STATE OF MIND. VICTORY, ON THE OTHER HAND, IS THE UNDERSTANDING THAT JESUS OVERCAME DEATH, HELL AND THE GRAVE AND TOOK THE KEYS OF THE KINGDOM BEFORE ASCENDING INTO THE HEAVENS. THROUGH THE FINISHED WORK OF THE CROSS, HE GAVE US THE KEYS TO LIVE VICTORIOUSLY. IN HIM, THERE IS NOTHING WE CANNOT CONQUER.

LIFE IS VERY GOOD!

Hebrews 13:8 says, "Jesus Christ is the same yesterday and today and forever." This may be a difficult concept for some of you to understand because as individuals on this earth, we tend to change over time. We go through some stuff. We solidify our belief systems and the goal is to grow stronger and wiser because we all are saved by grace. Jesus, on the other hand, is the same today as He was yesterday; all powerful, all knowing, a healer, deliverer, comforter, father, priest, king, prophet, teacher and friend. And, with Jesus, you are bound for victory after victory. With Jesus, all things are possible.

The Lord Says...

I Am the same yesterday, today and forever; it's true. So if you are wondering where I Am, just remember this; I have been here all along. It's you who changes. Seek Me no matter where you are and I will always be found. I stand at the door, just open it up to find Me.

If you believe it, say, "Oh yeah!"

DECEMBER 6
CHANGE YOUR THOUGHTS TO CHANGE YOUR LIFE

IT'S DIFFICULT TO CHANGE YOUR ACTIONS WITHOUT FIRST CHANGING YOUR THOUGHT PATTERNS. AS A MAN THINKS IN HIS HEART, SO HE IS. REMEMBER, YOUR FRUSTRATIONS ARE NOT LOCATED IN YOUR MIND, BUT THEY ARE UNRESOLVED IN YOUR HEART. LET NOT YOUR HEART BE TROUBLED. CHOOSE HIS JOY TODAY.

LIFE IS VERY GOOD!

Here's how you begin to change your thought patterns: Philippians 4:8 says, "Finally, brothers and sisters, whatever is true, whatever is noble, whatever is right, whatever is pure, whatever is lovely, whatever is admirable—if anything is excellent or praiseworthy—think about such things." Change the way you think first...think on all the good things. Don't complain, hold bitterness or anger towards another. When you think on these things, according to Philippians 4:8, your heart cannot help but be joyful. Your heart will be happy to see such greatness and give God such high praise. So I challenge you: no matter what is going on in your life, whether you're in the pit of darkness and cannot see the light, begin to speak life to your situation. Give God praise anyhow. This is what a kingdom person does; they recognize that there is something in life that is very good, even in the midst of the darkest of times. Start thanking God for the little things. If you love sports, start thanking God for the athletes that entertain you. If you love conveniences in your home, start thanking God that you have a microwave. If you love what you do, start thanking God that you have a job you love and enjoy. Maybe you picked up a penny from the ground; it's not so insignificant, give Him praise... even a little counts. Start today and watch your vocabulary begin to change. Become kingdom minded and let the frustration go.

The Lord Says...

If you can change your language and the vocabulary that come from your tongue, you can change your world. Begin with thanking Me for the little and it will grow from there. See your atmosphere begin to transform when your words change. My joy will fill you up.

If you believe it, say, "Oh yeah!"

DECEMBER 7
THE POWER IN DISCIPLINE

IN LIFE, THERE IS A WAY TO EXTINGUISH A PROBLEM OR TO ADD FUEL TO IT. REMEMBER, YOUR WORDS AND RESPONSE TO A SITUATION DETERMINES WHAT HAPPENS NEXT. REMEMBER, A SOFT ANSWER TURNS AWAY WRATH, BUT A HARSH WORD STIRS UP ANGER. IN THE MIDST OF CONFLICT, LET YOUR ANSWER BE HIS AND SEE THE FIERY FRUSTRATIONS GET BLOWN OUT. THINK BEFORE YOU SPEAK.

LIFE IS VERY GOOD!

It certainly isn't always easy to think before you speak. Like anything else, it takes practice and discipline. Next time you have the opportunity to respond to something do the following: Stop. Then challenge yourself to hold your tongue, even if you want to say something very badly. Really think for a moment about what you wanted to say and whether those words would provide any edification, exhortation or comfort to the circumstances. Sometimes it truly is better to become a good listener. Who holds more value: your words and opinions, or others? Bring others hope, not death by your tongue.

The Lord Says...

Abundant living requires discipline: a disciplined tongue, disciplined time, disciplined priorities and among other things, disciplined finances. So purpose in your heart to be disciplined. Think before you speak. Let your words echo My love and grace and not anger. Have them lift up, not tear down.

If you believe it, say, "Oh yeah!"

DECEMBER 8
THE ART OF STILLNESS

IT'S BEEN SAID, 'TIME HEALS ALL WOUNDS'. BUT IN REALITY, TIME ITSELF ISN'T WHAT HEALS; GOD IS HE WHO HEALS. SPEND TIME IN HIS PRESENCE, SO YOUR FULL HEALING CAN MANIFEST. IN HIS PRESENCE, ALL THINGS ARE MADE WHOLE.

LIFE IS VERY GOOD!

Exodus 33:14 says, "The Lord replied, 'My Presence will go with you and I will give you rest'." Rest comes in two forms: physical rest and an inner peace. When you spend time in His presence, He delivers, restores and refreshes you; body, mind and spirit. Sometimes, as Christians, we need to learn the art of being still. Get into the deep waters of worship and let the cascading waterfall of God's presence overtake you. Life is busy and it's easy to just sleep, eat, work and do it all over again. When will you just stand and let Him wash you with the water? It is there you will find that all things truly are possible.

The Lord Says...

I Am the living water. Take a load off from the chaos of life and let Me refresh you with My presence. Soak in My word and you will never be the same again.

If you believe it, say, "Oh yeah!"

DECEMBER 9
EMBRACE YOUR VICTORY

REMEMBER THIS: ONCE YOU'VE BEEN SET FREE, THE CHAINS THAT ONCE HELD YOU IN BOND-AGE BECOME AN INSTRUMENT FOR HIS PRAISE. GOD CAN USE ALL THINGS TO MAKE A SOUND OF WORSHIP. REJOICE IN HIS FREEDOM.

LIFE IS VERY GOOD!

Whatever sin kept you from your purpose is now the victory lap on your journey. Have you ever seen someone get free and get Jesus? They dance. They shout. They sing. They give testimony of where they were and what they've come out of. They give God the highest praise. Why? Because the chains that bound them can no longer keep them. God uses praise to get you out of bondage and your victory of praise to get others out as well. Remember, your victory isn't just for you. It is a demonstration of the freedom someone else needs who seeks it.

The Lord Says...

Let freedom ring for every human soul. And those who were in bondage will shout for glory singing it is well. I have come to set every person free from every thing that held them bound. I love My children and I wish for every one to have life more abundantly. Praise for the salvation I have given you and allow that to shower on others around you, so they can praise also.

If you believe it, say, "Oh yeah!"

DECEMBER 10
TO HAVE AND TO HOLD

IN THE MIDST OF A CRISIS, THE HARDEST THING TO DO IS TO HAVE OR HOLD ONTO YOUR FAITH. KNOW THIS, FAITH WAS NEVER MEANT TO GET YOU OUT OF PROBLEMS; FAITH IS WHAT GETS YOU THROUGH THEM. HOLD ON AND KEEP BELIEVING. HE IS FAITHFUL TO SEE YOU THROUGH.

LIFE IS VERY GOOD!

Romans 10:17 says, "Consequently, faith comes from hearing the message and the message is heard through the word about Christ." In other words, if your life is in crisis mode and you're not reading the Word and hearing its revelation, then your faith will become stagnant. Faith is like a hang glider; it must be operated to be effective - it requires action. The Word says that 'faith without works is dead' (James 2:20). So, if you need your faith to get you through, put it into action today. The hope of Jesus will become the fuel your faith needs and will bring you to the next level.

The Lord Says...

Do not let your faith rest in the power of men, but rather in the power of My mighty hand. As your faith arises, so will My hand arise in the midst of your situation. I will work on your behalf and will be with you, whatever the crisis. My hand will hold you and see you through, because of your faith.

If you believe it, say, "Oh yeah!"

DECEMBER 11
START SMALL TO FINISH BIG

REMEMBER, IF YOU NEVER FACE THE HILLS, YOU'LL NEVER SCALE THE MOUNTAINS. LIFE'S JOURNEY BEGINS WHEN YOU'RE WILLING TO FACE WHAT'S BEFORE YOU. OVERCOME SMALL THINGS AND THE BIG THINGS BECOME EASIER. KNOW YOU WERE BORN TO CONQUER.

LIFE IS VERY GOOD!

Luke 16:10 says, "Whoever can be trusted with very little can also be trusted with much and whoever is dishonest with very little will also be dishonest with much." You don't start out climbing Half Dome on your first climb. You start small and work your way up towards your goal. Then, before you know it, you've conquered your mountain. Be willing to move forward one step at a time. As I am sure you've heard it said before: Rome wasn't built in a day. Build your faith line upon line, precept upon precept.

The Lord Says...

Practice is preparation in action and, to climb any mountain in life, preparation is required. Don't get frustrated with your preparation for it's part of the process. Allow Me to work in you and through you to help you in climbing your mountain. In due time, you shall conquer because I Am on your side.

If you believe it, say, "Oh yeah!"

DECEMBER 12
DON'T DESPISE THE SMALL THINGS

SMALL THINGS MAKE BIG DIFFERENCES. REMEMBER, BEFORE YOU WALKED, YOU CRAWLED AND BEFORE YOU CRAWLED, YOU ROLLED. SMALL ACCOMPLISHMENTS WILL PROPEL YOU TO DO GREATER THINGS. REJOICE IN THE LITTLE AND, BEFORE LONG, YOU WILL REJOICE WITH MUCH.

LIFE IS VERY GOOD!

Are you familiar with the story of the Little Hen? When she is about to make bread, she asks everyone on the farm to assist but no one wants to. However, when she finishes baking the bread, everyone wants to eat it. Don't be like the farm animals that wouldn't assist with the bread. Small things garner great rewards. If the farm animals would have helped, they would have been partakers in the fruits of their labor. Ecclesiastes 4:9-12 says, "Two are better than one, because they have a good return for their labor: If either of them falls down, one can help the other up. But pity anyone who falls and has no one to help them up. Also, if two lie down together, they will keep warm. But how can one keep warm alone? Though one may be overpowered, two can defend themselves. A cord of three strands is not quickly broken." God is a team player and you were never meant to accomplish your purpose on your own. If Jesus needed 12 disciples to spread the message of the kingdom, how much more do we need others? Don't be fearful of starting out small, for those smalls accomplishments will cause great rejoicing and propel you into bigger and better things.

The Lord Says...

Gideon started small in numbers but his army accomplished mighty acts. Don't be afraid of the small steps and remember, two is always better than one. I created Eve to be a helpmate to Adam because I didn't want him to be alone. I Am with you always so you are never alone. When we gather together, more can be accomplished for My kingdom.

If you believe it, say, "Oh yeah!"

DECEMBER 13
FREEDOM'S SONG

JESUS WAS A SACRIFICIAL LAMB THAT ALLOWED HIS LIFE TO BE PLAYED AS AN INSTRUMENT OF WORSHIP TO BRING GLORY TO HIS FATHER AND REDEMPTION TO MANKIND. THE SOUND OF HIS SUFFERING WAS A BEAUTIFUL SONG TO THE HEAVENS THAT FREED US ALL. LIVE IN HIS FREEDOM TODAY.

LIFE IS VERY GOOD!

When I think of freedom, I think of singing. On July 4th, Americans in the United States celebrate our nation's birth with symphonies, bands of music and singing of patriotic songs: "America the Beautiful", the "Star Spangled Banner", "The Grand Ole Flag", "This Land is Your Land" and "America (My Country Tis of Thee)", just to name a few. Victory is marked with singing because of its sacrifice. Psalm 96:1 says, "I sing to the Lord a new song; sing to the Lord, all the earth." So, remember His sacrifice. You may be in the midst of the fire but just know this: when clay is fired it becomes something beautiful. It's never over until it's over, so sing to Him a new song from the depths of your thankful soul. He IS very good!

The Lord Says...

Sometimes you just need to know that it is well, even when it doesn't look like it. Trust Me, I will never leave you nor forsake you. I Am here with the voice of freedom. Your chains are broken. Rejoice in Me.

If you believe it, say, "Oh yeah!"

DECEMBER 14
THERE'S POWER IN THE PAUSE

WE OFTEN THINK TO STOP OR PAUSE IS A BAD THING. BUT IF YOU'RE SICK, A DAY IN BED AL-
LOWS YOU TO RECOVER; IF YOU HAVE A SURGERY, IT REQUIRES TIME TO HEAL. IT'S THE SAME
PRINCIPLE WHEN DEALING WITH SPIRITUAL, EMOTIONAL OR NATURAL TROUBLES. A PAUSE IS
THE TIME NEEDED TO BE WHOLE. STAYING STILL IS NOT A BAD THING FOR A SEASON.

LIFE IS VERY GOOD!

In our digital, fast paced age, we constantly find ourselves moving from one thing to another; appointment to appointment. Some of your households look like this. You work all day, pick the kids up from school or meet them at home, make them a snack, head off to extra-curricular activities/sports, come home, make dinner, have the neighbor over to play for an hour, head off to church, come home and you're exhausted. Some pastors are so busy doing ministry that Sundays are never a day of rest for them or their families, let alone the rest of the week with traveling ministry, hospital visits, prayer for the sick or the city. Before you know it, your family is all grown up and duplicating the same thing with the next generation. God said "rest" for a reason. You must not only recharge your body, but reconnect with your family, re-evaluate your priorities and assess your quality time with God. Sometimes you're so busy you don't even hear Him speak. Psalm 46:10 says, "Be still and know that I Am God", and Exodus 14:14 says, "The Lord will fight for you; you need only to be still." Being still is wise and needed.

The Lord Says...

In the stillness, there are many virtues: hearing, and not just listening. Peace, rest, focus, reflection and emptying the mind of all of life's stuff. Be good to yourself and the world around you; stop and be still. Know that I Am God in your life and in the life of your family. Rest and hear My voice speaking to you.

If you believe it, say, "Oh yeah!"

DECEMBER 15
SPEAK LIFE!

IN A WORLD FILLED WITH NEGATIVITY, MORE PEOPLE TALK ABOUT WHAT WE CAN'T ACHIEVE INSTEAD OF WHAT WE CAN. LIFE IS NOT BASED ON WHAT WE CAN'T DO BUT IS A MATTER OF BELIEVING THE OPPOSITE. SPEAK LIFE AND BE A VESSEL OF HOPE IN ALL YOU DO AND SAY.

LIFE IS VERY GOOD!

If you were constantly told you can do nothing, then you would indeed accomplish nothing because no one ever trained you to accomplish anything. If however, you are told you can accomplish all that you set your mind to, you will eventually do it because that is what your mind and your heart are trained to do. Be consistent. Even when life throws you a lemon, don't let the sourness rule and reign in your life. Instead, you rule and reign over the lemon; this is how lemons are made into lemonade. Proverbs 16:24 says, "Gracious words are a honeycomb, sweet to the soul and healing to the bones." If that's the case, speak life and keep on speaking it over and over and over again. You may be the only voice of hope someone receives today.

The Lord Says...

Be the light as I Am also the light. A light brings hope to darkness, for darkness itself is only space absent of light. My Words will bring illumination to the hearts and souls of all men.

If you believe it, say, "Oh yeah!"

DECEMBER 16
THE JOY OF LIVING FOR TODAY

THE MINDSET THAT'S STUCK IN THE PAST CAN NEVER CELEBRATE WHAT'S TAKING PLACE IN THE PRESENT. WHEN WE LOOK BACK WITH A NEGATIVE MINDSET, WE ONLY SEE OUR FAULTS AND FAILURES THAT KEEP US FROM PRESSING ONWARD. TODAY, HOLD ONTO THE PROMISE OF GOD'S WORD AND REFUSE TO LET GO.

LIFE IS VERY GOOD!

I've heard it said that it takes more muscles to frown than it does to smile. So smile through. Train yourself the kingdom way. When and if you look back, only look at the things that made you smile unless you're sharing where you were and how God brought you through. Our past must become the place of lessons learned.

And lessons learned only make our journey's more adventurous and our faith that much stronger. Keep walking in His promises by never, ever letting go.

The Lord Says...

Life is an adventure. You have ups and downs but above all, you experience the joy in life. Joy was the key to Job's successes. He triumphed with victory because he did not allow his past to dictate his future. His joy made his life full and I restored unto him all things. Will you count it all for joy? Don't turn back and look at your past, but if you do, only look to the cross where I gave you victory.

If you believe it, say, "Oh yeah!"

DECEMBER 17
LIVE A LARGE LIFE

LIVE LIFE LARGE AND BREAK THE BOX OF ALL LIMITATIONS. THROW OUT SMALL THINKING AND NEGATIVE THOUGHTS THAT SAY, 'I DON'T DESERVE HIS BEST'. KNOW GOD'S BEST IS YOUR PORTION AND YOU DESERVE ALL HE HAS PROMISED YOU. REMEMBER, YOU'RE BLESSED WITH ALL SPIRITUAL BLESSINGS.

LIFE IS VERY GOOD!

Lamentations 3:24 says, "I say to myself, 'The Lord is my portion; therefore I will wait for him'." Would a king keep the best for himself and not provide the same for his heirs? No, he would not. If you are the King's kid, your mistakes are not a prerequisite to your future. It is because you are His child that you deserve the best. His blood runs through your veins. God's best portion was and is Jesus. He is your portion. So wait on the Lord and renew your strength for all blessings flow from above from the King to his heirs.

The Lord Says...

Remember to not let life's limitations dictate your successes. Blessings are My gift to you. It's up to you to walk them out and pursue their fullness. Don't worry about how you'll find victory, just dig the ditches and I will fill them. If I brought you through yesterday, I will do it for you today and forever.

If you believe it, say, "Oh yeah!"

DECEMBER 18
RESIST NEGATIVITY

The prophetic word of the Lord is not spooky, scary or weird. It's a word of life that speaks edification, exhortation, or comfort to someone in need. So when you open your mouth, bless someone with hope.

Life is very good!

I don't know about you, but I certainly heard my mom say, "If you can't say anything nice, don't say anything at all", several times throughout my life. I often wonder what would happen if we actually put that phrase into practice on a daily basis. Try it. Refuse to say something negative about anyone and instead speak life into them as you exhort them, edify them and comfort them with God's Word and the language you speak. Colossians 4:6 says, "Let your conversation be always full of grace, seasoned with salt, so that you may know how to answer everyone." In other words, be wise with your words because you are the carrier of hope for someone.

The Lord Says...

My Words bring life to the defeated, broken and lonely hearted by restoring their hope, their confidence and lending a heart of love. If you truly are My disciple, then speak as I would speak and walk as I would walk, touching with My goodness, all those in need.

If you believe it, say, "Oh yeah!"

DECEMBER 19
THE POWER-FILLED TRIAL

REMEMBER, IN THE PLACE WHERE YOU FEEL CONFINED, ALONE OR ABANDONED, GOD CAN USE THIS SEASON OF DARKNESS TO BE THE GREATEST PLACE OF HIS REVELATION. JUST AS PAUL WROTE MOST OF HIS WRITINGS FROM A PRISON CELL, YOUR CONFINED PLACE CAN BE TRANSFORMED TO A QUIET PLACE TO PEN OUT GOD'S MYSTERIES. YOUR TRIAL CAN BE A TEACHER, NOT ONLY FOR YOU BUT FOR OTHERS IF YOU CHOOSE TO LEARN FROM IT. TURN YOUR DARK SEASON AROUND FOR HIS GLORY.

LIFE IS VERY GOOD!

I remember a time when I was a young believer. I was rejected by the church because the leadership did not believe in the prophetic that I was called to. Disappointment had settled in and left me feeling alone and confused. I realized, however, that the rejection of man was not God's rejection. Instead, it was God's promotion awakening me to the greater gift that I was. I was awakened that I had a prophetic gift and was a greater person in His kingdom than I thought; even through adversity He was with me and teaching me. Sometimes in life we experience unexpected rejection and just need to find our tribe. I experienced my greatest growth in the time when I felt the most alone. Take your quiet times and allow God's maturing to take place in your life. You will see your greatest growth in the midst of it. God will be glorified through you. Just allow Him.

The Lord Says...

If you look back on your trials in life, there will undoubtedly be something you have learned. Some say experience is the best teacher. It's not necessarily the experience, it's the trials you came through, the lessons they provided and the wisdom you received. And remember, I will never leave you nor forsake you. Place your life in My hands - with the trials and tribulations - and watch Me do great and mighty things through you.

If you believe it, say, "Oh yeah!"

DECEMBER 20
BE THANKFUL FOR THE CLOSING DOOR

WHEN LIFE IS IN TRANSITION, WE TEND TO FOCUS ON THE DOOR THAT'S CLOSING INSTEAD OF PAYING ATTENTION TO THE NEW DOOR GOD IS OPENING. WHEN THE DOOR CLOSES, IT'S AN EXITING FROM THE OLD AND ENTERING INTO THE NEW THAT GOD HAS. REMEMBER, CHRIST IS THE DOOR AND THE WAY TO GREATER BLESSINGS IN LIFE.

LIFE IS VERY GOOD!

Sometimes I think we give the closing door more attention because it often makes the most sound, while doors that open are less noisy and more welcoming. Revelation 3:20 says, "Here I Am! I stand at the door and knock. If anyone hears my voice and opens the door, I will come in and eat with that person and they with me." If you will focus on entering in to the door, which is Christ, your life will be transformed. Let what is supposed to go out the door go and you come on in.

The Lord Says...

My child, I Am the door. Do not just open the door, but invite Me in. Together let us dine, let us converse and you will learn that together, we are greater in this life than apart. I stand at the door and I bring hope alive to and for your life.

If you believe it, say, "Oh yeah!"

DECEMBER 21
LEAVING "THE FIXING" TO GOD

SOMETIMES IN LIFE, WE SEEM TO THINK WE CAN FIX EVERYONE. BUT, AS MESSENGERS OF THE KINGDOM, OUR DUTY IS NOT TO FIX PEOPLE, BUT TO LOVE THEM. GOD WILL TAKE CARE OF THE REST. BE STILL AND KNOW HE IS GOD AND HAS EVERYTHING AND EVERYONE, IN HIS HANDS.

LIFE IS VERY GOOD!

I think sometimes we love with limits, but God wants us to take down the walls, see through what's right in front of you and see His view of the human heart. He loves, period. He doesn't look at the drugs you're taking or the promiscuity you're involved in or the cheating the system when you file your taxes or lying to your boss. He sees you as a man or woman in need of Him and HE loves you through every moment. Why? Because it's His love that transforms the drug addict into a Jesus Junkie. It is God's love that transforms the promiscuous and heals and restores them with His true love. It is the love of God that makes you long to have integrity in all circumstances. Love. I Corinthians 16:14 says, "Do everything in love." Today, I challenge you to love beyond your limits. Take down the walls and see who and what God sees in his creation. His will is that all would come to know Him and LOVE is the drawing force. Do everything in love and God will show up in the midst.

The Lord Says...

It really is simple. Love is free of condemnation. So love others while remembering that I Am the only judge needed in this life. If you abide in Me and I abide in you, then love, it is the greatest of My commandments, for I have first loved YOU.

If you believe it, say, "Oh yeah!"

DECEMBER 22
ARE YOU PRODUCTIVE OR JUST BUSY?

WE OFTEN ASK PEOPLE, HOW ARE YOU DOING? THEIR RESPONSE IS OFTEN, "I'M SO BUSY." IN-STEAD OF BEING BUSY, FIND YOURSELF BEING PRODUCTIVE. DON'T JUST RUN AROUND TIRING YOURSELF OUT, GET THINGS DONE FOR THE KINGDOM SO WHEN SOMEONE ASKS YOU, HOW ARE YOU DOING, YOU'LL FEEL GOOD ABOUT YOUR ANSWER.

LIFE IS VERY GOOD!

Life these days is just plain busy, it's true. Anyone can be busy with the busyness of doing anything, but busyness does not accomplish goals. Busyness is a detractor that wastes your time. Instead, 'carpe diem' or seize the day! If you tracked every 15 minutes of your day, you would be surprised how much time you waste. Purpose in your heart to be productive. These days, there are numerous ways to be productive. Some people make lists of their daily tasks to accomplish, whether on paper or in an app. Some people use regular calendars or schedules, while many are moving to smartphone, tablet and computer versions that are mobile. Psalm 111:7-8 says, "The works of his hands are faithful and just; all his precepts are trustworthy. They are established for ever and ever, enacted in faithfulness and uprightness." Let it be so and let the works of your hands be as faithful and just to accomplish all you have set out to do and God will be your guide.

The Lord Says...

Running around in circles accomplishes nothing, it only wastes time. It causes delay, and is an unnecessary detour. Don't be like the children of Israel, who walked in circles for years. Walk the straight and narrow, for there with Me, you will accomplish much.

If you believe it, say, "Oh yeah!"

DECEMBER 23
SLAY THOSE GIANTS!

WHEN A PERSON REALIZES THEY'RE NOT OF THIS WORLD BUT OF A "DIFFERENT SPIRIT", THEY BECOME AN UNSTOPPABLE PRESENCE. THEY GAIN A GOD-GIVEN REVELATION TO SLAY THE GIANTS BEFORE THEM AND POSSESS THE ABILITY TO OVERLOOK WHAT OTHERS SEE AS SHORTCOMINGS, TO CONTINUE IN WHAT GOD HAS PROMISED THEM. GOD HAS SOMETHING GREAT FOR YOU, BECAUSE YOU ARE HIS CHILD.

LIFE IS VERY GOOD!

I have often pondered this question: If God said you, His people, can do something, then why do you question whether you actually can? A kingdom thinker not only knows and understands that they are not of this world but only in it, and God gave them the same power that overcame death, hell and the grave to conquer any giants in the land. He gave you the ability to praise like Judah before any battle you may enter, and to serve like Mary and Martha, to multiply what He has given. Your shortcomings don't matter. The question is, are you a negative thinker or are you reformed to kingdom thinking? Giants are first slain in the mind, then in the gut. You got this. God has something great for you indeed; it's called His promises. Philippians 4:13 says, "I can do all things through him who gives me strength." Now is the time to take His Word for what it says and just DO IT!

The Lord Says...

The adventure of life begins when you say I Can because, until you say it with confidence, you will accomplish very little. Through and with Me, all things are possible. I have lifted the limits from you and given you a hope and a future. Today is a glorious day.

If you believe it, say, "Oh yeah!"

DECEMBER 24
THE STRAIGHT AND NARROW IS YOUR DIRECT PATH

DARKNESS IS NOT A SEASON; IT'S A PLACE ABSENT OF TRUTH! LET HIS WORD SHINE AND ELIMINATE ALL FEAR BY ILLUMINATING THE PLACES OF IGNORANCE. HIS TRUTH WILL LIGHT UP YOUR PATH AND MAKES YOU FREE.

LIFE IS VERY GOOD!

Interestingly, light travels in a straight direction (unless bent) and at very fast speeds. The Bible tells us to walk the straight and narrow path. Could it be that God is telling us to walk the straight and narrow because that is where He is? Light is an illumination of darkness, for darkness itself is but space without light. May His truth, the Light of Glory, light the way for you and lead others to your pathway of light during their time of darkness.

The Lord Says...

I Am the light and you will find Me illuminating the dark places on earth, the secret places in the hearts of man that bleed with pain and anguish. Take the Gospel and go be the light to this world. I need you and your shoes on the ground. A pathway is meant for foot soldiers and you are My carrier.

If you believe it, say, "Oh yeah!"

DECEMBER 25
NEVER, NEVER GIVE UP

WHEN A PERSON OVERCOMES A DIFFICULT SITUATION WITH GOD, IT'S AMAZING. BUT THEN, TO RENEW THEIR MIND AND BE ABLE TO CONQUER OTHER HURDLES, IT IS EXTRAORDINARY. NO MATTER WHAT YOU FACE IN LIFE, NEVER GIVE UP, BECAUSE WITH GOD, ALL THINGS ARE POSSIBLE!

LIFE IS VERY GOOD!

Galatians 6:9 says, "Let us not become weary in doing good, for at the proper time we will reap a harvest if we do not give up." In other words, it doesn't matter how bad the situation is. As long as you do not let yourself become weary, you will reap the harvest in your life. I see too many people quit before they were meant to and they miss out on the blessings because they just couldn't hold on. You are stronger than you think. Remember, in your weakness, He is strong.

The Lord Says...

Rise up child. Rise up with wings like eagles and soar to new heights. Never give up but turn your sorrow into joy as you worship and praise My name and take shelter in My wings.

If you believe it, say, "Oh yeah!"

DECEMBER 26
MORE OF HIM

REMEMBER THIS: YOU DON'T NEED BIG FAITH IN A DIFFICULT TIME; YOU NEED A BIG GOD. KNOW A SMALL MEASURE OF FAITH CAN CHANGE ANY DIFFICULT CIRCUMSTANCE. SO SPEAK TO YOUR MOUNTAIN WITH MUSTARD SEED FAITH AND SEE THE MOUNTAIN BE REMOVED.

LIFE IS VERY GOOD!

Have you ever noticed that God leaves most of the work to Himself? He requires only a mustard seed size of faith for you and He'll do the rest. He only requires 10% of your income and then He'll work with your 90%. What if all you had to do was speak the Word to your mountain combined with mustard seed faith? That is all you have to do! Find a scripture for your circumstance and hide that Word in your heart. Decree and declare it. Then believe it is so. Watch as God removes the obstacles standing in your way. You may still climb a mountain but that's okay, the climb will be just a little bit easier with Jesus; more of Him and less of me, that's the way that it should be. Speak and believe!

The Lord Says...

When you put a plant in the ground and the rains come, do you expect it to die? Will not the seeds of My Word, sown in the soil of your life, then not sprout to become that in which they were intended? Have faith that the garden you plant with the seeds of My Word will grow into much fruit for you. All things work together for the good of those who love Me and are called according to My purpose.

If you believe it, say, "Oh yeah!"

DECEMBER 27
WHEN THE MOUNTAIN BECOMES A TESTIMONY

DIFFICULTIES CAN BE SEEN LIKE MOUNTAINS; THEY ARE THERE TO BE CONQUERED. ONCE THIS MOUNTAIN IS SCALED, IT BECOMES A TESTIMONY THAT ENCOURAGES OTHERS TO DO THE SAME. YOUR JOURNEY HAS A PURPOSE SO DON'T QUIT. SOMEONE NEEDS TO HEAR THE WORDS OF AN OVERCOMER!

LIFE IS VERY GOOD!

To see this concept in action, all you have to do is walk into a local bookstore and catch a glimpse of all the self-help books; those "I made my millions, here's how you do it", "I was successful, here's how you do it", "I overcame addiction, here's how you do it" books. Those are stories of individuals taking their mountains and sharing it with the world. Luke 8:39 says, "Return home and tell how much God has done for you." So the man went away and told all over town how much Jesus had done for him." Your testimony was meant for the service of others for, through Christ and the Word of your testimony, the world will be reached; one by one.

The Lord Says...

The ability to tell your story is one of the greatest tools of evangelism in your tool belt. Keep it handy. It will change lives because someone needs to overcome just like you did. The testimony of how My hand transformed your life will give others the hope they need to continue their journey.

If you believe it, say, "Oh yeah!"

DECEMBER 28
PRACTICE TO HIT THE MARK

HAVE YOU EVER FELT THIS WAY IN LIFE...YOU TAKE "ONE STEP FORWARD AND TWO STEPS BACK"? IF SO, REMEMBER THIS: IT'S NOTHING MORE THAN GOD STRINGING UP THE BOW OF THE MIGHTY ARCHER. THE STEP FORWARD IS GOD LOADING YOU UP WHILE THE FEELING OF STUMBLING BACK IS HIM PULLING ON YOU TO CREATE TENSION AND LAUNCH YOU INTO PURPOSE AND DESTINY. WITH HIM, YOU WILL ALWAYS HIT THE MARK.

LIFE IS VERY GOOD!

When you think of your life as an archer, it sets you up to think of yourself in a whole new light. You are a warrior with a sharp focus that is aimed at destiny. You don't always get the bullseye, but you do your best and, with practice, you hit the mark more times than not. So just remember, when you feel like you've taken two steps back, focus in a little harder and aim a little better. Let go and let God do a work in you. He hits the mark. Every time. He is very good that way.

The Lord Says...

Never mistake tension for misplaced purpose. Sometimes tension is a good thing. It proves the necessary change, the focus and aim required for the next leg of a journey. Do not be afraid for I Am your perfect peace and you shall rest in Me. I will see you through.

If you believe it, say, "Oh yeah!"

DECEMBER 29
SHAKE OFF THOSE LIMITS!

WHEN WE ALLOW THE POWER OF CHRIST THAT LIVES WITHIN US TO FLOW THROUGH US, THERE IS NOTHING WE CAN'T DO, NOTHING WE CAN'T OVERCOME AND NOTHING WE CAN'T POSSESS. KNOW THAT HIS LOVE CANNOT FAIL AND HIS MERCY WILL NOT LET YOU FALL. IN HIM, WE ARE VICTORIOUS!

LIFE IS VERY GOOD!

Hebrews 4:16 says, "Let us then approach God's throne of grace with confidence, so that we may receive mercy and find grace to help us in our time of need." Aren't you thankful for His mercy and His grace? Where would you be had the Lord not been on your side? Remember that all your victories, whether large or small, are from Jesus. So give Him all the praise.

The Lord Says...

It's not about how fast you finish the race, but that you endure until the end. Victory is only as sweet as your endurance is strong. Any test will ask you, "How bad do you want it?" Be strong and of good courage for I have made you great. You are My child and in you I Am pleased.

If you believe it, say, "Oh yeah!"

DECEMBER 30
GOD WILL ILLUMINATE YOUR PATH

IGNORANCE IS NOT A GOOD ENOUGH EXCUSE TO STAY IN DARKNESS; IT'S TIME TO RISE UP OUT OF IMMATURITY AND LET TRUTH REIGN IN YOUR LIFE. REMEMBER, HIS WORD IS A LIGHT THAT DESTROYS CHAOS AND DARKNESS. KNOW THE TRUTH AND BE SET FREE.

LIFE IS VERY GOOD!

Ephesians 4:18 says, "They are darkened in their understanding and separated from the life of God because of the ignorance that is in them due to the hardening of their hearts." Because God IS the light, when you walk in ignorance, you walk without the light. So purpose in your heart to let hope shine in the darkest place. It is like a headlamp to a miner, finding their way towards the light. Keep frustration far from you by the Son's illumination of your heart. Hallelujah, He is very good. He came that you might have life and live it more abundantly.

The Lord Says...

Listen, My sons and daughters. I Am the lamp that keeps on burning, the guide that keeps on leading and the wisdom that delivers the answers you are looking for. Search Me out and I will illuminate your life in all areas. It is a good day to be alive.

If you believe it, say, "Oh yeah!"

DECEMBER 31
TIMES OF STRETCHING

THE CIRCLE OF LIFE IS CONSTANT; ONE THING ENDS SO SOMETHING NEW MAY BEGIN. AS THE YEAR COMES TO AN END AND, THOUGH YOU MAY LOOK BACK AND SEE ALL THE TROUBLES AND REMEMBER DIFFERENT PAINS, DON'T DWELL UPON IT AS A TIME OF DIFFICULTY. SEE IT AS A TIME OF STRETCHING WHICH HAS PREPARED YOU FOR THE GREATER INCREASE. FINISH STRONG BECAUSE IN THIS NEW YEAR, YOU ARE MARKED FOR GREATNESS.

LIFE IS VERY GOOD!

Sometimes I am so thankful that every day is a do over, but every year that goes by stretches me, as my daughters get older and time passes that I cannot get back. So make every day count. Don't let your ambition for the things of ministry, or your career, get in the way of what is standing right in front of you. If you don't finish the year strong with your family or relationships, then your life of ambition will leave you empty. Be diligent, love beyond limits. If and when you look back on yesterday, remember the joy for it is here that hope is found. Romans 15:13 says, "May the God of hope fill you with all joy and peace as you trust in him, so that you may overflow with hope by the power of the Holy Spirit." Be empowered for tomorrow is a new day.

The Lord Says...

Whether sunshine, wind, snow or rain, I Am the same. My love, My grace and mercy allows you to get up every time you fall and start again. Let every journey be marked with greatness. This year has come to an end. Look forward to what I have for you in this next season.

If you believe it, say, "Oh yeah!"

RESOURCES

January 21: "My Girl" by The Temptations. Recorded at Hitsville USA (studio A) September 25, November 10 and November 17, 1964 on the Gordy label. Written and Produced by Smokey Robinson and Ronald White for the album The Temptations Sing Smokey.

February 5: Isaac Watts, pub.1707. ref. by Ralph E. Hudson, 1885. At the Cross (Hudson). Copyright: Public Domain

February 10: reference to the Orthodox Jewish Bible Orthodox Jewish Bible (OJB). Copyright © 2002, 2003, 2008, 2010, 2011 by Artists for Israel International

March 15: Weisberg, Chana. "Nitzevet, Mother of David: The Bold Voice of Silence." thejewishwoman.org. 15 My 2015. Web.

September 12: Helm, Burt. inc.com. February 28, 2012.

October 13: almanac.com. "The Old Farmer's Almanac." Grapes. 1 Oct. 2015. Web.

October 19: Lowry, Robert. Nothing But the Blood. "library.timelesstruths.com. Public Domain. 1876. Web. 1 October 2015.

October 31: Van De Venter, Judson W and Weedon, Winfield S. I Surrender All. (public domain, 1896).

To find more resources by Prophet Rob Sanchez Ministries
Visit: www.prophetrobsanchez.com

Get more of Prophets Rob's #LIVG quotes daily by following on
Facebook (facebook.com/ProphetRobSanchez)
& Twitter (@prophetrobpfi)

If you have a book and would like to publish
with Firstfruits Publishing, contact us at:
firstfruitspublishing@prophetrobsanchez.com